Additional Praise for

OUTPOST:

"A great introduction to the difficult game of diplomacy. Rather than a turgid tome, Hill's book is lively, entertaining—even at times laugh-out-loud funny. He spends just enough time to let readers understand the gist of a complicated diplomatic problem, without getting too bogged down in the weeds."

—*The Washington Post*

"Christopher Hill was one of our best diplomats, taking on our biggest challenges from Kosovo to North Korea to Iraq in a thirty-year career. In *Outpost*, Hill gives us unique insight into these assignments. In addition, he describes the remarkable dedication of his fellow Foreign Service officers. They represent the United States every day, under conditions that are rarely glamorous, and often cold, dusty, exhausting, and downright dangerous. They deserve a book this good, written by a man who loves his country, and his work. A good read."

—**Madeleine Albright, former Secretary of State**

"This is how diplomacy really works. It involves danger, hard choices, and colorful personalities playing high-stakes games. Christopher Hill is a master at both negotiations and storytelling. His book is an indispensable guide for a complex world and a fascinating behind-the-scenes adventure tale."

—**Walter Isaacson, author of *Steve Jobs***

"A wry, wise glimpse into the engrossing, exasperating, whipsawed, but sometimes triumphant, even ennobling life of an American diplomat in these messy times."

—**Fred Kaplan, author of *The Insurgents***

"Hill is one of our most accomplished diplomats. In *Outpost*, he grippingly renders a candid and insightful insider's account of the most significant U.S. diplomatic and political-military efforts of the past two decades."

—**General George Casey, former Army Chief of Staff**

"Hill's career covers a lot of territory, both geographically and in terms of our diplomatic history. . . . A must for anyone contemplating a Foreign Service career and for general readers looking for insight into diplomacy conducted at the highest levels."

—*Kirkus Reviews* (**starred review**)

"A diplomatic career spent under fire—sometimes literally—is recounted with energy and humor in this lively memoir. . . . Written in graceful, witty prose and studded with insights into many international crises, Hill's narrative critiques American diplomacy even as he defends its importance."

—*Publishers Weekly* (**starred review**)

"Engaging. . . . An enlightening look at the hard work of diplomacy through the lens of one man's career."

—*Booklist*

"A personal story, filled with the intricacies of living abroad, coping with the bureaucracy of the huge U.S. foreign-policy establishment and trying to persuade some very difficult people that America really does want to help them."

—*The Providence Journal*

"A candid, behind-the-scenes look at how the diplomatic sausage is made."

—*Dallas Morning News*

OUTPOST

A Diplomat at Work

Christopher R. Hill

SIMON & SCHUSTER PAPERBACKS

New York   London   Toronto   Sydney   New Delhi

Simon & Schuster Paperbacks
An Imprint of Simon & Schuster, Inc.
1230 Avenue of the Americas
New York, NY 10020

First Simon & Schuster trade paperback edition October 2015

SIMON & SCHUSTER PAPERBACKS and colophon are
registered trademarks of Simon & Schuster, Inc.

All photos courtesy of the author, except for images 5, 17, and 19, which are official
White House photos, and image 28, which is a U.S. State Department photo.

For information about special discounts for bulk purchases,
please contact Simon & Schuster Special Sales at
1-866-506-1949 or business@simonandschuster.com.

The Simon & Schuster Speakers Bureau can bring authors to your live event.
For more information or to book an event, contact the
Simon & Schuster Speakers Bureau at 1-866-248-3049 or
visit our website at www.simonspeakers.com.

Interior design by Ruth Lee-Mui

Manufactured in the United States of America

10 9 8 7 6 5 4 3 2 1

Library of Congress Cataloging-in-Publication Data is available.

ISBN 978-1-4516-8591-6
ISBN 978-1-4516-8593-0 (pbk)
ISBN 978-1-4516-8595-4 (ebook)

Dedication

To the memory of my parents and all they taught me about the world,

and

*To all the men and women of the foreign service and their families
who accepted difficult assignments in outposts far from home,*

and

*To my children Nat, Amy, and Clara
who did their share of time in far-flung outposts,*

and

To my loving wife, Julie.

Contents

Contents

OUTPOST

OUTPOST

PROLOGUE

It was July 2009 and I had never been to the capital of Dhi Qar Province before. Nasiriya lies in south-central Iraq about 185 dusty miles southeast of Baghdad. It looked like other impoverished southern Iraqi towns I had seen in my first few months in Iraq, neglected for decades by Saddam Hussein, left out in the desert sun and sandstorms to fend for themselves. The motorcade trip up from Tallil Air Base, where I had arrived in a small military prop aircraft earlier in the morning, took about an hour and a half but seemed much longer as we passed endless two-story buildings, dilapidated fences, and dry riverbeds and canals. Men wrapped their heads in traditional keffiyeh and moved slowly along the side of the road, as if to conserve energy in the July heat, not appearing to notice the added dust caused by our six black armored Chevy Suburbans as we made our way to a meeting with the Provincial Council. Signs and posters bearing Muqtada al-Sadr's dyspeptic glare didn't seem to add to or detract from the décor of the otherwise drab surroundings. His image, too, was cloaked in dust. I stared out the window from my seat in the back of the vehicle, my mind wandering at times to the broader project of Iraq, what it had done to us, what it had done to the Iraqis, and thinking perhaps not so literally: when are we going to get there?

I had come from Baghdad to Dhi Qar Province to do what U.S. ambassadors do all over the world: meet with local officials and get a sense of what is on people's minds outside the confines of the capital city. U.S. forces had liberated Nasiriya in their triumphant march to Baghdad in 2003. The province was almost entirely Shia, the majority sect in Iraq that included some of the most trod-upon victims of the Saddam Hussein regime. Our forces expected jubilant crowds to greet them with rose petals, as our vice president at the time had predicted on national television with his confident tone of matter-of-fact certainty that fooled some and infuriated the rest. Instead, when our marines burst through Nasiriya in spring 2003, scattering Saddam's forces, they saw pretty much what I saw: no joy in dustville, just ordinary people who, all things being equal, would probably have liked us to leave as soon as possible.

We arrived at the city hall and slowly piled out of our vehicles. I had taken my flak jacket (required attire on these trips) off in the car, not wanting to be seen by the staring Iraqis as if I expected one of them to shoot at me. It seemed so lacking in trust. I glanced around at the five-story apartment buildings surrounding us, wondering how the security advance team could possibly manage to deal with the kinds of random threats that could come from behind any one of those numerous windows. I looked around at the shops and the people on the streets, whose languid pace was in sharp contrast to the frenetic movement of the taxis and pickup trucks that seemed to be in a perpetual drag race. I walked up the half-dozen steps and met the Iraqi protocol official, who greeted me warmly (as Iraqis do so well) and escorted me and a few others into the building, while the rest of the security team waited in front of the building inside the SUVs, their motors still running to ensure a fast getaway, and, perhaps more practically, to keep the air conditioners going.

The head of the provincial assembly was not in town that day, so I was greeted as I emerged from the coffin-sized elevator with the leader of my security detail by the deputy head of the provincial council, Abdul Hadi Abdullah Mohan. The elevator had grunted and groaned the three-floor distance as if it had been asked to do something utterly beyond its capabilities. Mohan, perhaps out of shyness or something else, didn't appear any more enthusiastic about greeting me than the elevator had been in conveying me, so I set to work to try to put him at ease, and say how pleased I was to be in Dhi Qar Province for the first time.

We sat down in his small office and were soon joined by several members of the provincial assembly, who together with the embassy and provincial reconstruction team staff made the office seem even smaller. Iraqi staffers dragged extra chairs through the door, their wooden legs screeching on the hard marble floor as if, like the elevator, they were being taken to a place they didn't want to go.

After initial pleasantries, a ritual I knew all too well from my years living in the Balkans (the western part of the same Ottoman Empire that Nasiriya had spent so many centuries under), I opened with a point I would often make in such settings: the United States desires a long-term relationship with the people of Iraq, provided that the people of Iraq want the same. Our troops would be drawing down, but our interest in the well-being of the Iraqi people is enduring. I told him that while it is true the United States is very far away, Iraq would always be very close to our hearts. The war was a very difficult time for all. I described the agreements we had put in place with Iraq, the first governing the presence of our troops, and the second setting out our civilian relationship with Iraq. Thin gruel, to be sure, but nonetheless the documents could show the Iraqis that somebody had at least taken the time to put down on paper the accoutrements of what a normal relationship could eventually look like.

I always thought that our "Strategic Framework Agreement," as it was called (or SFA, as it was inevitably abbreviated—in U.S.-military-occupied Iraq, everything under the sun seemed to be known by its abbreviation or acronym), looked very much like a 1950s-style Soviet "friendship" agreement with an Eastern European satellite. I had served in Poland during the early 1980s and could recall the government exhortations—often expressed in banners unfurled over streets and roads and on large billboards—to "implement" the friendship agreement, whatever that really meant. For the communist authorities it was an agreement to remind the public that the Soviet Union was their friend and would protect them. For the Soviets, it was an effort to legitimize their subjugation of Poland, but not a particularly successful one. As a Pole once explained to me, it is very bad manners to draw up a treaty with a country you have just invaded.

The U.S.-Iraqi SFA was, of course, none of the above, but it did represent an attempt to show there was a future in this odd relationship. But for each side it represented something very specific—and different. For the Americans, it was a document that took the relationship beyond one based only on military ties. Those were to be addressed in an instrument called the Security Agreement (SA), whose purpose was to serve as a Status of Forces Agreement (SOFA), much like the ones many countries have with the United States to provide the legal basis for troops on their soil. Needless to say, not all SOFAs are equal. Having worked in Japan on my previous assignment, I knew very well the complexity of the security agreement there, and the obvious fact that the U.S.-Japan SOFA, for example, does not permit U.S. forces to set up roadblocks and checkpoints in downtown Tokyo, or anywhere else in Japan for that matter. The U.S. military in Iraq welcomed the framework agreement, the SFA, as an agreement whose ultimate purpose would serve as a follow-on agreement that would put the U.S.-Iraqi relationship on a "normal" basis, even if there were to be further SOFA agreements to govern the future basing of U.S. troops.

Diplomatic agreements work best when both countries have a similar level of experience dealing with them. The SFA didn't pass that test. For Iraqis, at least those who were aware of the existence of something called a Strategic Framework Agreement, the SFA actually represented much more than it did for the Americans. The document laid out the relationship for years to come, and most important, in the minds of some Iraqis, it required the United States to provide assistance in all forms—especially money—to them for the rest of history.

Of course, this was not how State Department lawyers saw the agreement. Prior to my departure for Iraq, I met with two of the lawyers from the legal department, who proudly went through each section of the agreement to point out how they had written it in a way that did not compel the United States to do much of anything. The pièce de résistance was that the agreement did not have to go to the U.S. Senate for its approval as a treaty.

Meanwhile, back in Nasiriya, I gave a message of tough love, cautioning the Iraqis that we could no longer be solving Iraqis' problems for them. But more optimistically I also pointed out that the embassy was busy setting up relationships with Iraqi universities and that just that morning I had met with law professors and students from Dhi Qar University to discuss their needs. I told them I would arrange for a team of lawyers from the embassy to come down in the next few weeks to talk in greater depth about enhancing our educational cooperation.

The Iraqis gave me that studied look of indifference, one that I suspect they have perfected over the centuries, reserved for pitiable foreigners who do not quite understand that what they really want are things and money, not forms of cooperation.

Deputy Council Chairman Mohan was gradually warming up, evidently energized by his heavily sugared glass of black tea. Within ten minutes he clarified what he really wanted by marching through the list of goodies he was looking for us to provide for him. He explained the tough fiscal environment he was facing, the fact that he had had to cancel 74 projects due to Baghdad's budget issues, and had suspended work on another 113 already started. We need schools, he told me, and a hospital. too. "We could name it for President Obama," he generously offered, hoping that could clinch the deal. He said they needed libraries and businesses and agricultural investments also. And finally—Mohan was on a roll—we need an international airport, he told me, saving the best for last as other members nodded their approval of Mohan's request for the creation of Nasiriya International Airport. Those others chimed in with their own requests, explaining the drought conditions that had particularly affected the marsh areas, and how the United States could solve this problem, too. During my time in the Peace Corps decades before, I had visited some of the poorest villages in the world, and yet I had never heard such a list. All problems were laid at our doorstep, and the United States was responsible for addressing all of the province's challenges— and, going forward, for fulfilling the hopes and dreams of its inhabitants. I kept trying to steer back to providing some expertise in small business development, sanitation, health, and education. And Mohan kept returning to the subject of an international airport.

It was clear that the deputy chairman had come to regard Americans as visitors bearing gifts, and who could blame him. The U.S. military, having rediscovered the fact that money can be a weapon of war, to paraphrase from the redrafted field manual of counterinsurgency (COIN), had spent billions of dollars in the Commander's Emergency Response Program (CERP), itself a euphemism for a program whose purpose was as old as the history of warfare: provide money to local chieftains so that they will forbid their people to shoot at your soldiers the next time. This time honored, field-tested approach had been around for thousands of years, but in Iraq it became an example of derived wisdom. An updated U.S. Army field manual was coupled with the proprietary relationship that some senior generals and researchers in Washington-based think tanks claimed for any and all ideas related to tactics and strategy in Iraq. In a country on whose ancient land the wheel had once been invented, in our vanity we were claiming the reinvention of other ideas in the cradle of civilization.

The only problem was that this so-called new weapon of war was fast drying up. L. Paul Bremer, whose civilian operation was in effect a wholly owned subsidiary of the military, had some $20 billion at his disposal for so-called reconstruction. Bremer was a civilian, a retired Foreign Service officer who had been dispatched to Iraq as the lead U.S. official when it was understood that the tasks would be more political than military. But during his one year in Iraq he still reported directly to Secretary of Defense Donald Rumsfeld, not Secretary of State Colin Powell, and his mission took on the character of a sprawling civilian component to the U.S. military rather than a Foreign Service post reporting to the State Department. Bremer's colossal budget was far more akin to the military's mega-budgets than to those the State Department was used to managing. As Bremer's Coalition Provisional Authority (of course, "CPA") became an American embassy accredited to a sovereign Iraq a year later in the summer of 2004, the downward pressure of funding a State Department operation began to be felt. As I sat in Nasiriya, the State Department was struggling to convince Congress to support less than $500 million in Iraq-related projects.

I tried to be as forthcoming as possible with my Iraqi hosts, but on the issue of the international airport, I took a tougher line, explaining the enormous funds that would be needed for construction of such an investment in Dhi Qar, that the citizens there need to create more reasons why more people should come to their province. I tried earnestly to explain the need to take ownership of their own problems, to work together, and to be realistic about what can come from outside. "The best thing I can do as an American diplomat is to be perfectly honest with you. We cannot solve all your problems." That was a formulation I had used in Albania years before, and it had been understood there as the country and its brave people struggled to emerge from decades of communist totalitarianism. But U.S.-occupied Iraq was different.

Indeed, Mohan was nonplussed, suggesting by his body language that part of what was going on was his effort to show the other members of the provincial assembly what a tough leader he was and that he was not afraid to ask for more, because the Americans always have more, and should give more. Watching this ambitious deputy, I took a measure of optimism in that as painful as some moments of this meeting had been, there was a spark of democratic life here. Mohan had a political interest in showing that he was a doer and a leader. I found myself liking him for that. As if to slow down any emerging comfort level on my part he returned again (and again) to the subject of why an international airport near Nasiriya would be what the doctor ordered. I held my ground on their airport, though flying away from there did have some appeal.

We parted amicably after he had graciously escorted me out of the building to our waiting vehicles; their exhaust fumes mixing effortlessly into the hot afternoon city air. It was late, and we had less than two hours of daylight remaining, with a dust storm on the way, as we headed back to the sprawling U.S. base at Tallil. The team started piling into the cars, including Greta Holtz of the Embassy Baghdad Provincial Reconstruction Team, who took a seat in the second row next to where I would be sitting. The other "limo" carried staff assistant Jen Davis, a former Peace Corps volunteer and now a Foreign Service officer embarking on a promising career that would soon have her in Chinese language training.

Also in her car was the embassy's military advisor, U.S. Air Force Col. Jeff Prichard, "JoBu" to his many, many friends. JoBu worked entirely for the embassy, was our liaison to the military, and went on all my trips throughout Iraq. A career officer, he understood the military, its strengths and its foibles, and had a capacity to explain those issues to those of us who had not spent two decades in uniform. A good military advisor—and JoBu was a great one—is invaluable to an ambassador in a country where the U.S. military is so prominent. Nothing ever seemed to faze JoBu, a former F-15 and F-22 pilot, except when the University of Alabama Crimson Tide would occasionally lose a football game. He was extremely quick and smart, as flying those complex aircraft would suggest, but he also had an emotional intelligence.

I said farewell to Mohan and turned to the vehicle that Lance Guil-lory, the lead security agent, motioned for me to use. Before climbing in I took one more look around downtown Nasiriya, marveling at how our security could have guaranteed our safety in that hardscrabble town. I looked over at JoBu, who was about to get into his vehicle, which would be ahead of mine, and whose opinion I always sought immediately after a meeting ("hot wash," he would call it, an Air Force metaphor that refers to cleaning a plane's tail section from the grit and grime while it is still hot from flight). "Hey JoBu, see you back at the base. We'll talk." He gave me a thumbs-up and got in his vehicle.

Fifteen minutes into the ride, Lance, riding shotgun in front of my seat, started speaking into his walkie-talkie in an agitated tone as he saw ahead that our Nasiriya police detail had inexplicably turned left onto another main road while the plan was to continue driving straight. The procedure for these motorcades was never to inform the police in advance which road we would take, but rather to tell them during the journey by radio what turns to make (or not to make). Lance, subbing for my regular head of security detail, Derek Dela-Cruz, who was on leave, was con-cerned that the trip go well under his command, and therefore seemed particularly annoyed with the police for turning off the route.

As we moved forward along the two-lane road, all wondering why the police car had turned left at the intersection, we heard a deafening boom and saw just ahead of us a massive plume of thick black smoke rise into the air from the right side of the road. The vehicle ahead of us carrying JoBu and others sped furiously through the wall of smoke. My vehicle began to slow down, the U.S. driver momentarily unsure whether to keep going through the smoke, which is a standard maneuver in such situations to foil the possibility that the bomb was a decoy designed to make a stopped vehicle a sitting target for a rocket-propelled grenade or small arms fire. Lance, his diplomatic security training and his personal leadership very much in evidence, immediately shouted at the driver, "Go! Go!" and the driver slammed the accelerator to the floor, violently flinging those of us who had been leaning forward, back into our seats as the vehicle surged ahead into the thick wall of smoke.

We braced ourselves in the expectation that our armored Chevy Suburban would hit something ahead hidden in the smoke, but as we emerged from the detonation area, I marveled that we were still roaring forward, as was JoBu's car in front of us, now only vaguely visible through the dust and smoke. Just then the road took an abrupt left turn that our skilled driver, even at an accelerating speed, managed (barely) to careen through, getting us safely onto a bridge and over a dry riverbed. A huge gasoline truck stood on the side of the road. Could this be the real bomb? We sped by it, holding our breath at the thought that everyone had but nobody dared utter. Greta Holz, sitting next to me, shouted to me, "Get your PPE on!" referring to personal protection equipment, a flak jacket, something I had neglected to do when we were departing Nasiriya. "It's too late, I'm going to be in trouble with Lance. He'll write me up for this," I responded, managing a lame joke.

We continued to drive at breakneck speed on through a small settlement, where nobody except for some young boys playing by the side of the road even bothered to look up at our speeding convoy. It took still another thirty minutes to get back to the base at Tallil, where we entered the safety of the facility, past the American soldiers on the checkpoint. We all wearily lumbered out of our SUVs, still feeling the brush with fate in our stomachs. Roadside bombs had claimed so many lives over the course of the Iraq War, but it was not a subject I wanted to dwell on that day. I felt fine and quickly checked the vehicles to see how others were doing.

Jen Davis, who had been sitting next to JoBu, was having serious headaches and some bleeding from her ears, an apparent concussion, and was whisked off to a medical facility. I moved away from the vehicles to telephone the embassy and tell them we were all fine. I told our public affairs team to try to downplay the attack in talking to the press, since we didn't need any panic buttons pushed. Just as I completed the call my mobile phone rang and it was the State Department Operations Center patching through a very concerned Secretary Hillary Clinton, who asked for details. I told her "it was nothing," and that we were all fine. I wasn't really sure that was true, having been through other such circumstances in the past and realizing that people are not always as okay as they appear.

After concluding the call I found myself momentarily reflecting on the fact that the purpose of the bomb was to kill somebody. Later I saw on the internet the creepy video belonging to a group calling itself the "Regiments of Promised Day," relating news of the incident with the voice-over, bragging that the intention was to kill me. Whatever the intention, I thought it was best not to dwell too much on that either. I looked up at the darkening sky and saw that a sandstorm was fast approaching and that we would probably be spending the night in Tallil, instead of returning to Baghdad. That was fine with me. I had had enough traveling for the day.

JoBu was also checking on how everyone was doing, with no shortage of his usual high energy.

"You good, JoBu?" I asked. He stood there, glancing around briefly at the scene of hastily parked SUVs, and took his helmet off. He ruefully shook his head in relief as he wiped his brow, and finally looked back at me.

"Jobu?"

"Sir, you should have said yes to the airport."

1

EARLY DIPLOMATIC LESSONS

There is a bleakness to Belgrade in the winter months, when snow instantly turns gray from the soot-filled air. So even on a clear day like that day in January 1961, everything seemed to have a dirty dampness to it.

The school bus that took me to and from the International School of Belgrade was a two-tone, pale blue and white VW Microbus with gray vinyl benches. Along with its dirt and grime and black ice clinging to its undercarriage, it fit in well with the winter landscape. The best part of the bus was the turn indicators. Incredibly, whenever the driver flipped the turn signal next to the steering wheel, an eight-inch, ruler-shaped stick would obediently snap to attention, flipping up and out from its hidden perch in the pillar just behind the front doors on whichever side the vehicle was to turn. I never tired of seeing that mechanical turn signal operate. As soon as Mrs. Brasich's class was over, I would race outside from the huge, old stone mansion that served as the school for children of diplomats to find the bus in the driveway and secure my seat behind the driver to have the best view of the indicator. The driver, Raday, a small man who was usually, though not always, in a good mood, sometimes would let me inspect the flipper up close while he would operate it from inside. One time the driver's side flipper wouldn't work and Raday started to pull it with his hand. "My dad," I said, "always tells me never to force something. If it isn't working, there's a reason." Raday, who by this time was pounding the side of the vehicle, didn't seem to appreciate the advice coming from an eight-year-old. I don't know if Raday ever remembered my dad's advice, but it stuck with me the rest of my life. Things work or don't work because of something else, so try to find out, if possible, what that something else is.

The school bus drive to my home from the International School was fifteen minutes at most. When we turned from Topcidarsko Brdo Circle onto Tostoljevska Street, I gathered up my books and papers, knowing I was only a minute away from home. Our house was located on a small cul-de-sac, Krajiska Street, opposite a wooded area. But that afternoon, as Raday turned to pull the microbus off the road and into the small woods on the left, I could see that everything was not quite right. As I got out and Raday began the careful exercise of backing the vehicle into Tostoljevska, I saw immediately that the sidewalk and high fence surrounding my house were covered with graffiti that included (in English) "Yankee go home" and "Lumumba," and something that ended with "CIA." I looked around, a little confused and concerned, as Raday drove the vehicle off, evidently not noticing what I had seen, because he presumably was focusing all his energies on backing out into the busy Tostoljevska Street. Two policemen in their long gray coats were talking to each other nearby, not an unusual sight for this area of town that housed many senior Communist Party functionaries. I hurried over to the rusted iron gate and pressed the doorbell, anxious to get inside to something more familiar and out of the January cold. But as I stepped back from the gate I could see the front of the house, the main floor of which sat up like a second floor with the basement and garage level underneath. Most of the front of the house—my house!—had almost all its windows broken, as if it were abandoned and no one was living there anymore.

When nobody came out, I shoved the gate with my shoulder and despite its rusty resistance it somehow opened. I stood there and stared into the cobblestone driveway below the house. I could see shattered glass everywhere. Instead of turning to my left to make my way up the stone staircase to the main entrance, I walked farther along the driveway and could see that not just some, but almost all the windows on the right side of the house were broken and the driveway littered with rocks that had bounced back off the stone siding of the house. Now far more scared than surprised, I ran up the stone stairs to the big, wooden front door and pounded on it to get inside. My mother, holding one of my two-year-old twin brothers in one arm, opened the door with the other. "What happened here?" I asked. And she responded calmly: "Chris, you won't be playing outdoors today."

What had happened on that day in January 1961 was that the Congolese leftist leader Patrice Lumumba had been killed at the hands of the CIA—a suspected targeted assassination that was finally confirmed as such years later. His assassination was a cause célèbre throughout the world, especially in communist countries, where he was seen as the vanguard of a new wave of communist expansion in sub-Saharan Africa. And what happened at 2 Krajiska Street in that heavily wooded suburb of Belgrade, Yugoslavia, where my father, the embassy's political officer, lived with his wife and five children was that an angry Yugoslav student mob, presumably with the knowledge of the Yugoslav communist government under Tito, had marched to a house they (somehow) knew to be occupied by an American diplomatic family, chanted epithets, scrawled chalk slogans, and threw rocks until the police, who had apparently stood by, finally chased them away.

But what did not happen was any sense of panic in the Hill household that afternoon. My father came home to see how we were doing. As if to explain that nothing much had really happened at our house, he told me what had been going on at the Belgian embassy that day. A mob broke into the Belgian compound, located just a few blocks down from the American Embassy, and threatened to come up the main stairway inside the building before the Belgian ambassador, wielding a pistol, yelled to the crowd from the top of the stairs: *"Ça suffit!"* That's enough! They left. My father enjoyed telling that story that night as he sat in the living room next to the fire, making his way through his usual evening pack of cigarettes. I'd often sit with my parents at night, getting my dad to tell me about the embassy while they both had their martinis, and I wondered how anyone could drink such a thing (though I did always lay claim to the olives).

My father had a special affinity for Belgians, having served his first assignment in Antwerp immediately after World War II, and admired them for the suffering they had endured in that conflict. Dad explained to me who Lumumba was, and why the connection with the Belgians, and for that matter the connection with Tito's nonaligned Yugoslavia. "Everything has a reason," he always explained. "Our task is at least to try to understand what that reason is, even if we don't agree with it." I couldn't understand why a Yugoslav mob was attacking our home over something we obviously had nothing to do with. "Well, not everything has an easy explanation," he said, as if to negate what he had just explained. "We'd probably have to talk to them."

"Talk to *them*?"

"Of course. How else would you find out what they are thinking?"

I don't remember my father ever telling the story about the pistol-wielding Belgian ambassador again. It just wasn't that big a deal. Stories like that had a short life span in the Hill household. We would get on to the next issue quickly.

Late that afternoon my mother was still dealing with some remaining shards of glass that had become stuck in her hair-sprayed hair when she had dropped to the glass- and stone-littered floor of the living room to shield Jonny and Nick. Embassy carpenters came the next afternoon to repair the windows (with my assistance in the form of passing them their cigarettes). Apart from those two policemen, who had seemed more interested in their own cigarettes than in protecting our home, there was no additional security and no routines altered or created. My father went to work the next day. I went to school, after the usual argument with my mother about what to wear to my third-grade classroom. I do not remember my parents ever talking about the incident again. It never became part of family lore. I talked to them years later, but it fell to me to jog their memories with my own.

Just two and a half years later, in May 1963, the seven Hills were living in Port-au-Prince, Haiti. François Duvalier had just declared himself president for life, and from our second-floor porch, which had a view overlooking much of the city, I could see fires and hear gunshots. As luck would have it, my dad, the embassy's economic officer, was the duty officer that week, meaning that he would make frequent trips to the embassy in the dead of night to check on telegram traffic that required immediate attention. This night he had gone to the embassy at 11 P.M., but now at 1 A.M. had still not returned. My mother radioed the marine guard (there were no phones) and was told he had left an hour earlier to make the twenty-minute drive home in an embassy car. She woke up my older sister, Prudy, and me to explain the situation, and we sat on the upstairs porch, our mother with her cigarette, and I with my worries.

He soon returned, to our great relief. He explained that he had been ordered out of the car at gunpoint by Duvalier's not-so-secret police, the dreaded Ton Ton Macoutes, and held there for some thirty minutes while the TTMs decided what to do with him and his embassy driver. The next evening Mother and Dad told me the situation was deteriorating, that we all might be evacuated, but wanted me—I was ten years old—to know that we had a revolver (with five shots) in the event it was needed. Dad showed me how to aim and fire, while I focused on the fact it had only five chambers and not the six that I assumed every revolver had. "Don't use it unless you have to," my mother helpfully told me.

Just a day later my dad came home to tell us that all families were being evacuated and that we needed to pack. "Where are you going to be?" I asked him anxiously. "I'll be fine," he told us.

The next morning we were at the airport, boarding a chartered Pan Am flight bound for Miami. My dad, and other Foreign Service dads, stood on the tarmac as we made our way up the stairs. He was waving at us, telling us all to take care of our mother, who was holding on to Nick and Jonny, now four years old, while my two sisters, Prudence and Elizabeth, and I followed. He was still waving at us when the plane pulled away. I was so struck by the fact that if he was worried about anything, he sure didn't show it.

2

PEACE CORPS

Eleven years later, in 1974, during my senior year at Bowdoin College, I knew I wanted to serve my country. The military draft was over. I decided to join the Peace Corps. Many Foreign Service officers trace their first jobs in diplomacy to their decision to answer President John F. Kennedy's challenge to spend part of their lives working in the developing world. In October 1960, at 2 A.M., in what he called the "longest short speech" he had ever made, one given to a University of Michigan crowd of five thousand, President Kennedy told students that on their willingness to perform such service would depend "whether a free society can compete." Generations of Americans joined the Peace Corps filled with a sense of Kennedy's idealism and many returned with an even stronger dose of realism about what we encountered, and how we needed to manage—and sometimes not—other people's problems. Whenever I am asked what my favorite Foreign Service job was, I invariably answer that it was my time as a Peace Corps volunteer, the position from which I entered the Foreign Service.

I waited a few weeks before receiving an offer to join a credit union project in Cameroon, West Africa. A few weeks after graduation I was in a credit union accounting training course in Washington, D.C., and on August 11, a day after my twenty-second birthday, with twenty other nervous and excited volunteers I boarded a flight from New York City to West Africa. The Pan Am Boeing 707 stopped at every coastal capital on its way to Central Africa. On the fifth stop, we arrived in hot and steamy Douala, Cameroon. We staggered down the stairway off the airplane into sheets of warm rain and headed to the terminal, where we collected our bags and went through customs, all the while wondering whether we could get a flight the next day to go home. A rented bus whisked us off to a hotel for late-night briefings by an endlessly cheerful Peace Corps staff. The next morning we got on that same dripping-wet bus and headed to a small airstrip in the town of Tiko to board a Twin Otter aircraft. It groaned audibly as it somehow managed to lift off the dirt and muddy runway and begin the one-hour trip to Bamenda in the highlands of the Northwest Province of Cameroon, where the temperatures were far more comfortable than in the coastal south. Our three-week training took place in a Catholic mission where we were housed in a two-room, whitewashed, cinder-block building, ten cots jammed into each room. We had our meals in a similarly austere cafeteria, where we received tips in Cameroonian culture and the basics for communicating in Pidgin English. At the end of the program I was assigned to supervise the credit unions of Fako Division in the Southwest Province, so I packed my bags for the trip to the town of Buea.

Buea had been an administrative capital in the latter half of the nineteenth century, during Germany's ill-fated colonial era, which came to an abrupt end at the conclusion of World War I, when Germany lost its entire colonial empire to the French and the British. The town is located some 3,500 feet up on the slopes of Mount Cameroon, a volcanic peak that rises from the shores of the Atlantic Ocean, the Bight of Biafra, to reach 13,270 feet. With its cool and pleasant weather, albeit with a long rainy season, it is easy to see why the Germans chose Buea at the turn of the century as an administrative capital for its vast plantation system in "Kamerun." The plantations, which were mostly within one hundred miles of the Cameroon coast, produced rubber, palm oil, bananas, and, in one plantation along the side of the mountain, tea.

Signs of the Germans' fifty-year stay were visible throughout the town, but especially in the form of the occasional two- and even three-story terraced stone buildings with red metal roofs that seemed so out of place in the lush green natural scenery.

Another volunteer, Jim Wilson, and I arrived there on the first day of September, having survived an eight-hour trip in a Peace Corps Land Rover. The roads in Cameroon would be familiar to anyone who has been to West Africa: a laterite clay, hard almost to the point of feeling like cement in the dry season, but soft like tomato soup during the rainy season. Four-wheel-drive vehicles used in rural Cameroon in the mid-1970s bore no relation to those parked in front of hotels today in Vail or Aspen, Colorado. The shock absorbers seem to have been left out of the undercarriage and a ride of longer than an hour made one feel like a jackhammer operator. Our driver seemed to be in constant road races with the "bush taxis," Peugeot 404 station wagons that seated nine passengers—two in the front, four in the second seat, and three people stuffed in the rear—and would carry them between towns. Luggage on those taxis (which included live goats and chickens) was stored on roof racks made locally of crude metal and covered with garish signage to encourage repeat customers. The names of the taxis painted on the front of the roof racks were quite varied, often a line from the Bible, or a movie character ("007"), or sometimes just a philosophical expression that the proud driver may have been inspired to make up himself, such as (my favorite) "Man Must Die."

Getting out of our Peace Corps vehicle was a welcome moment indeed. The driver helped pull our bags out of the back of the vehicle, wished us good luck and told us not to drink the water, and sped off. Jim and I looked at each other and then at our house and our waiting motorcycles sitting against the side of the house. A neighbor who had been watching over the property since the last volunteers had left a few months before emerged from a nearby house with our keys. Our house was made of cinder block and cement and sat incongruously in the midst of a patch of five-foot-high grass off a dirt road. With occasional running water, it was the lap of luxury for a Peace Corps volunteer, a cheerful thought I conveyed to Jim as we surveyed the mauve interior walls and the ubiquitous spiderwebs and, a first for me, a two-inch-wide ant column that had effortlessly marched its way under the front door to what presumably had been a feast of insects inside. Groups of small children started emerging from the tall grass to stare at us, a sight they never lost interest in during the two years we were there. There wasn't any furniture, but Jim and I used our Peace Corps allowance to build wooden bed frames for our foam rubber mattresses (which we both decided we didn't want to place directly on the floor) and to buy a few chairs and straw mats.

The best part of the house was its roof. Made of corrugated tin, it stubbornly, albeit loudly, withstood the pounding monsoon rain. Buea had 265 inches of annual rainfall, most of which fell during the summer months through the end of September. That first night in September, with the dry season still a few weeks away, the rain came down on the tin roof in a deafening torrent that I thought would punch holes through it. In the morning, however, a bright sun was up in a cloudless sky, the grassland slopes of Mount Cameroon had become an emerald green, and every insect in the world, it seemed, along with a few newly formed columns of ants, seemed hard at work on the cement stoop or nearby in the thick, green tall grass.

I was assigned to the Department of Cooperatives, under the Ministry of Agriculture, with duties to serve as a credit union field-worker. Catholic priests from the Netherlands had introduced credit unions about a decade before. They had studied the local "Njangi" savings societies, a system of monthly savings against an eventual payout of everyone's savings. Thus if each person saved a dollar a month and there were twenty persons in the group, that person would, every twentieth month, receive twenty dollars, which, less the funding for food and drink for the monthly party, was a substantial payout, almost like winning the lottery. The priests, carefully building on the Njangi system, created a rudimentary but effective standardized bookkeeping system that allowed people to take loans against their savings or those of a cosigner. The Cameroonian government supported the program and had asked the Peace Corps to send volunteers to help supervise the credit unions.

Credit unions were often the only access to credit that anyone had. And even though the word *microcredit* had not yet become the subject of Nobel Peace Prizes, loans from tiny credit unions in places were instrumental in helping people create small businesses (foot-pump sewing machines were a popular loan request), buy schoolbooks for their children, and replace thatched roofs (the smells and sight of which bore no relation to thatch roofs in the English countryside) with shiny corrugated metal.

My job was to get to each credit union over the course of the month to check the loan balances, tie up the individual accounts with the general accounts, meet the board of directors, and otherwise make sure that nothing unusual had taken place. The Peace Corps gave me a Suzuki 125cc dirt bike. It was large by local standards, and with its four gears and another four lower gears, activated with the click of one's heel, it could climb the steepest trails even with Mr. Timti, my Cameroonian credit union trainee, holding on to the rear seat for dear life.

In some villages, especially those up on the mountain, my arrival on a motorcycle was not so much an important event as it was the *only* event happening in the village that day or even that week. While most adults had at some point been down the mountain to the market towns of Tiko and Muyuka, most of the children had not. Thus dismounting the motorcycle also involved clearing a path to escape the circle of kids that would form around the bike, some interested in the machine, others simply fascinated by my white skin and determined, for a start, to cure me by rubbing it off my hands.

After a meeting with the village elders, with the help of the local schoolteacher, who translated local dialect into something between English and West African Pidgin English, I would make my way to where the credit union was housed, usually a tiny one-room hut with a table and two chairs, and not much more room than that. The bookkeeper, who was also the schoolteacher, would hand me the stacks of individual ledgers, probably about 150 of them, a cash book, and the "files" of monthly statements, with pretty much the last sign of any work traced to the last time I was there. I would get to work under the watchful eyes of the small children, who by this time seemed to include every child in the village, except for those still taking turns sitting on my motorcycle. The task was to update the transactions so that the sum of the individual loans would, together with money in the bank in Muyuka and the cash on hand, actually equal the total assets of the credit union. I would also add people's savings ledgers to make sure that together with some other issues they would prove out the actual liabilities amount showing in the credit union's statement.

In the early afternoon, farmers in from their coffee farms would drift over to the credit union to see what was going on. Some would bring their own paperwork, consisting of tiny scraps of mildewed receipts, received from the coffee cooperative and subsequently stashed in their homes, to see whether in having savings and loan repayments garnished from their coffee payments they were actually credited with them.

I looked at each of them, disrupting as it was to the task of adding long lists of numbers (in my second year I received a hand-crank adding machine with a roll of paper that I strapped on to the back of the motorcycle). I was pleased to see that the numbers added up, and most important that there were no signs of fraud. Fraud was rare. I can only imagine the bookkeeper's prospects in that village if the rest of the village saw him as cheating them out of their life savings. At around 4 P.M., I would wrap things up and once again tell the bookkeeper to try to stay up-to-date with postings so that I didn't have to do them all on my next visit a month later. He, of course, promised it wouldn't happen again, that his child had been sick, etc. I smiled and thought about where I was a year before: writing an independent study for Professor Vail, my economics professor, and coming up with all kinds of excuses why I hadn't finished it on time.

I walked back to the village elders, the number of accompanying children having diminished since earlier in the day (though I could see the motorcycle was still attracting a crowd, while a slightly older kid was now organizing the turn taking and how long each was allowed to sit on the seat).

People came up and thanked me in ways I had never been thanked for anything like that in my life before, and I thought what that had meant to me. I sat in the village chief's home, his several wives scurrying around to offer food and drink, the latter consisting of palm wine, a milky fermented liquid tapped from a palm tree. He asked how I thought the credit union was doing and told me how much he supported it because it was helping people in his village. He said it was more important than any single person because it would stay to help different people in the future. He never used the word *institution*, but I understood what he meant by something not made of any physical materials but made by people who were very real and might help others in the future. He suggested I come more often, not just to work or worry (he could see I was a little grouchy at having to do a month's worth of bookkeeping during that day), or even to address problems, but just to be there with his people. He then ranged further—a lot further—and asked about the moon landings, and how it was my country had decided to accomplish that. I told him about President Kennedy's vision, and he was very moved by that. He asked whether I thought a Cameroonian might go to the moon someday. I said I surely hoped so. We'll go together, I told him optimistically. He liked that idea. I felt a little troubled that I had come up with such an insincere thought so effortlessly, but its effect seemed to be to draw us closer and I was pleased with that. Besides, I don't really think he believed it, either.

But mostly he thanked me for my work that day. And then he

thanked America for sending me there, and thanked President Kennedy, whose picture sat in the corner of the room, for thinking of the idea in the first place.

He accompanied me to my motorcycle (whose seat by then needed a certain amount of cleaning off, having been sat on by every kid in the village with or without trousers). I headed down the mountain track, riding slow in the gathering twilight. I felt that in that far-off village I had been representing my country, and that people felt better about my country as a result of my visit that day. Heady stuff.

I signed up for the Foreign Service exam soon afterward and resolved to pass it, because I knew that was what I wanted to do with my life.

Some credit unions took more time than others, and Tole Tea Estate's credit union was one of those. There were about six hundred members, not unusual for a credit union whose membership was drawn from a plantation workforce. Unlike village credit unions, the plantation-based credit unions seldom had any loan delinquency problems because the corporate employer garnished the wages.

Tole had a "board of directors" that consisted of about twelve people. When I looked at the loan ledgers, I discovered that some 50 percent of all of the credit union's loans had been taken by those twelve people. The loans appeared to be cosigned, that is, covered by savings accounts, and I hadn't spotted any arrearage, or indication that they were not going to be paid back. Still, the concentration of loans with such a small group of people highlighted the fact that these leaders had abused their positions and needed to be replaced.

I raised the overall governance issue with Alex Lantum, Southwest Province director for the government agency that had broad oversight for cooperatives, including the Cameroon cooperative credit union league to which I was assigned. He looked at my report and agreed that something had to be done before there was lost or stolen money and other more dangerous threats to people's savings.

With the annual general meeting coming up, I worked fast to prepare my report to the general membership, and, most important, my recommendations for a fresh start with a new board of directors. Fortunately, Tole was located only thirty minutes from my home in Buea, which I could get to through a back road, a narrow dirt track that descended rapidly down the side of Mount Cameroon, a dense forest shading it on both sides. Approaching the estates, the forest would give way to tea fields, and refreshingly, as I looked back over my shoulder, to a view of the thirteen-thousand-foot mountain that often disappeared into thick rainy season clouds.

Tole Estates was a division of the Cameroon Development Corporation plantations system in the province, a German, then British, and now Cameroonian-owned corporation that produced rubber, palm oil, bananas, and, only at Tole, tea. Unlike in the other plantations, the bulk of the workforce was composed of women. All day, they worked along the rows of tea bushes, carrying on their backs enormous wicker baskets the size of a laundry basket, attached by a string that would loop around the women's foreheads, which were in turn covered with thick headbands.

At the annual meeting, held on a warm Sunday afternoon in March, the board and I sat in plastic white chairs set up on a green sloping hill, the view of Mount Cameroon behind us, and a thick forest below. When the time came for my report, I stood and delivered a cautiously optimistic version of events, but made very clear to the membership that the board of directors had entirely too many of the loans. Person after person rose in support of what I had uncovered. And while the board appeared sullen and upset, one of them saying to me, "You are destroying the credit union," I stood there in my khaki pants and excessively colorful Cameroonian loose cotton shirt, explaining that these loans exceeded our rules, should not have been approved, and needed to be reduced.

The reaction overall was positive and, more important, not panicky. I was calm in my appearance and presentation, though clear about the need for change, and the reaction could not have been more approving and supportive. I decided it was time to move on to the next phase of my plan. I had identified a group of people who were not associated with the previous board but had enough education and integrity to take over the union and run it properly. I proposed this new board be elected to replace the old one.

The reaction to the announcement of a vote was mainly positive. There were applause and smiles, although most of the members seemed to be more attentive to what each other were saying than to credit union speeches. Elections were accomplished by gathering the old board on one side of the grassy field, the new board on the other side. The logistics took a few moments to develop, but soon I had on my left the old board (not very happy with me) standing around and facing the large audience, and some fifty feet away from me on my right, the reform board, also not looking very happy, and standing around facing the crowd. At that moment the hundreds of members were asked to stand and file in behind whichever board they wanted to support.

There was no need for a count. The membership, men and women still talking to each other quite cheerfully and the latter still nursing their babies, pretty much (about 90 percent) all lined up in front of the old board. My reform board attracted a few votes, relatives perhaps, but the results were in. The board chair shook my hands, let bygones be bygones, and invited me to the annual general meeting party, an occasion that consisted of tons of beef, covered by tons of flies, lots of fruits (covered with still more flies), and lots of beer, soft drinks, and, for the hearty ones, palm wine.

Person after person came up to me to shake my hand to thank me for caring about the credit union. Small kids stared as they always did, with a few of them first gently holding my hands then doing what they really had in mind, which was to rub my skin to see if the white pigment would come off. I peeled the kids off me, said good-bye to the board members, pulled the half dozen kids off my parked motorcycle, and headed home to Buea. I acted nonplussed, deciding that the best way to behave through this humiliation was to pretend it never happened.

That night, sitting on the cement step on the back of my house, starring up at the giant grass slopes of Mount Cameroon illuminated by a brilliant night sky, I reflected that I had no idea what was really going on in Tole Tea Estate's Credit Union. I asked myself what I had missed, what I could have done better to understand the dynamics, the relationships, of the place. Had I talked to enough sources or did I just talk to people who already agreed with me? How could I have been so misled to believe that people genuinely annoyed with their leaders would have illogically, at least in my view, voted to put those same leaders back into office? Was it that I had chosen the wrong ones to replace them? Could there have been another group I could have identified?

None of the above, I concluded. I just needed to accept the fact that I didn't understand the place, that I had really overstepped my authority in thinking I could unseat an elected leadership and impose another. I had completely misread the support people gave to me during the meeting. They were thanking me for my sincerity and hard work, not for my solution. I resolved that even though I had twenty-seven other credit unions to deal with, I was not going to presume that I could make personnel decisions for them again, or ignore their own reasons, presumably based in cultural idiosyncrasies, most likely in the relationships that trumped my preferences for better credit union management. The first question I had asked myself when I saw the problem at Tole was how to get rid of the board. The question I should have asked myself first was how that board got there in the first place.

Years later, in the Middle East, in the Balkans, in Asia, I would see time and again systematized efforts on the part of the United States to pick winners in situations we understood little about. Like my efforts at the Tole Tea Estate's credit union, they never worked.

On a Saturday morning in December 1975 I got up at 4 A.M. and with another volunteer, Ed Diem, rode a motorcycle to the U.S. Consulate in

Douala to take the three-hour, three-part Foreign Service exam. We arrived at 7:30 A.M., cutting it close because along the way a truck carrying sap from the nearby rubber tree plantations had run Ed off the road into a water ditch.

A month later, I went to the post office and checked the mail. I had a thick envelope from the State Department.

3

FIRST MENTOR

I entered the Foreign Service in October 1977 and began the series of required training programs in preparation for my first assignment. The U.S. Foreign Service is a career in which advancement is not unlike many others. There is an entrance exam process, an entry class, followed by a scramble for first assignments that seem so much more important than they really are in the context of a full career. After all that, it becomes pretty much what the person makes of it: what area of the world one chooses, for example, Europe or Africa; what issues, such as refugees or helping businesspeople abroad.

Though the Foreign Service emerges on the stage every so often—Benghazi, Libya, being one of the most recent examples—it is not well-known outside Washington, D.C. Nor does the State Department have much continued resonance anywhere in the United States other than certain offices in Washington. "The state department of what?" is a question I would often get in response to my explaining where I worked.

The depiction of it in movies is especially disheartening. Usually, a

Foreign Service officer is shown sitting all too comfortably behind a large desk, an American flag on display in the background, and explaining rue-fully but firmly to a frantic American tourist why he (Hollywood has long concluded that only white males work in the Foreign Service) cannot offer any help. Most unhelpfully, the Foreign Service officer is sometimes depicted cravenly explaining that local laws don't allow him to do any-thing for that frantic tourist, often a parent trying to recover an abducted child.

Hollywood's view of the Foreign Service is in sharp contrast with its overall appraisal of the military as bold and unflinching from the vigorous pursuit of U.S. interests. The Foreign Service seems, to many Americans, to be more interested in the other country's interests than in our own.

I had the perfect model for what a Foreign Service officer should be when I arrived in Belgrade, Yugoslavia, in July 1978, for my first assignment. I met our ambassador, Lawrence S. Eagleburger, soon after my arrival in his office at the U.S. Embassy in Belgrade for my required "courtesy call," a stress-inducing event on every newcomer's ar-rival checklist. I had just arrived as the "assistant commercial attaché," a modest perch appropriate to a twenty-five-year-old junior Foreign Service officer, a couple of notches below the "fast track" political and economic officers.

When the opportunity to go to Belgrade came up, I worked hard to convince the assignment officers that I was the right person for the post. After all, I had been there when I was eight years old. Probably more in spite of my lobbying efforts than because of them (junior officer lob-bying is not well received by assignment officers), I got the assignment, and after six months of learning to speak Serbo-Croatian, I arrived in Belgrade and checked into a small two-bedroom apartment behind the embassy. There were no signs of any ant columns, and for a former Peace Corps volunteer, everything was perfect except for the oversized king bed in the tiny bedroom. (It was unceremoniously removed the next day when the embassy's logistical services realized it belonged not in Apartment C-22, but in the ambassador's residence.)

In the morning, I began my checking-in process, beginning with the call on the ambassador. Eagleburger offered me a seat on his couch and spoke to me in a way that made me believe that it was the first time he had ever given the briefing, such were the powers of his performance art. He explained what he was trying to do in Yugoslavia in the twilight of President Josip Broz Tito's life: to weave a "web of relations" with Yugoslavia in such a way that it would keep the country from going in another direction. He had, after all, first been assigned to Yugoslavia in 1963, and had become known as "Lawrence of Macedonia" for his masterly relief work after the earthquake in southern Yugoslavia that destroyed Skopje, the capital of the Republic of Macedonia, in August of that year. His energy and enthusiasm, sardonic humor, and apparent enjoyment of talking to a junior officer on his first day at work blew me away. I was in awe.

I listened carefully to his explanation of my role in the "web of relations." He linked my remedial tasks of assisting visiting U.S. businessmen with their hotel reservations and appointments to his strategic goal of managing the coming post-Tito Yugoslavia. I had been scared to death for the entire twenty-minute meeting, but I walked out a little taller. I felt instantly a sense of loyalty to him, maybe because I sensed that he would be loyal to me as well. I was going to be on the team, and he made me feel like he had picked me!

Of course, another reason I had been so frightened to enter his office was his legendary temper. I would see it many times on the tennis court. As one of the most junior officers in the embassy, I was often summoned as an emergency fourth player for tennis at the ambassador's residence. Eagleburger, who was short and somewhat hefty, would range over the court, not particularly mindful that he was playing doubles. He wielded a Wilson T-2000, an all-aluminum, state-of-the-art racket at the time, ugly (perhaps the worst-looking product that sporting goods brand had ever produced), unbreakable (though bendable), and potentially lethal when hurled at warp speed after a failed lunging shot. A couple of times I dove for my life to the clay to the sound of the menacing whir of the flying metal racket, accompanied by Eagleburger cursing at himself.

Tito, one of the last of the World War II leaders, had steered Yugoslavia along its tightrope between East and West. He fell ill in January 1980 and would remain in a hospital in northern Yugoslavia for five months, suffering from the terminal phases of circulatory and heart disease. News about his health appeared every day in a top corner of every newspaper, in the form of a short medical bulletin: "The general condition of Comrade Josip Broz Tito remains the same" (or, increasingly as the months went by, "has worsened"). "Intensive measures continue."

On Sunday evening, May 4, 1980, as I carried camping equipment from my car back into my apartment behind the embassy from a weekend trip to Kosovo and Macedonia, I could see lights had started going on in the upper floors of the embassy. I knew what that meant. Tito had died and the government had just made the announcement.

What would come next was the question of the hour for the future of Yugoslavia. The Soviet Union was beginning to show its frailties, but only six months after its invasion of Afghanistan, it still seemed ready for more. (The Yugoslav joke about potential Soviet intervention: *"Danas u Afganistanu, sutra u vašem stanu."* Today in Afghanistan, tomorrow in your apartment.) Since 1948, Yugoslavia had charted its independent way, a communist country that had left the communist bloc and assumed the mantle of "nonalignment." Could Yugoslav's Communist Party set a new course for Yugoslavia back into the Eastern Bloc, from which it had been expelled by Stalin thirty-two years before?

Or would Yugoslavia's restive nationalities—the Slovenes, Croats, Serbs, the founding members of this post–World War I state—each decide to go its own way? Dangerous as this course could be, it was seen as the less likely option in 1980, even though much of the internal deliberations in the embassy had to do with the growing frictions between the northern republics of Slovenia and Croatia and those in the south, including the autonomous region of Kosovo.

Eagleburger was agitated in the embassy staff meetings that followed as we prepared for the international event that the state funeral would surely be. He explained to us that he had argued forcefully but unsuccessfully with the Carter White House that the president should lead the U.S. delegation. Eagleburger had a special relationship with junior officers in the embassy, and those of us at the low end of the ranks often were treated to even more candor than sometimes his senior officers heard. I tried to spend as much time with him as I could. A close confidant of Henry Kissinger and a devotee of a realpolitik view of the world, he had no patience with President Jimmy Carter or his focus on human rights, referring to those views as "a mile wide and an inch deep."

And he never shrank from taking on Washington or letting officials there know what he thought. "I didn't come here to preside over a post office," he told me as I delivered a paper to him that he threw over to his inbox, then continued his rant about what he considered a feckless instruction he had just received from the State Department (*feckless* was a high-frequency word in Eagleburger's lexicon). Then he explained his preferred course of action to me, as I stood in front of his desk wondering why he was sharing all this. It was reminiscent of the way my father would talk to me during a home carpentry project, when in fact he was just talking to himself. I learned a lot being Eagleburger's faux audience. "Pique is no substitute for policy," he then told me. I nodded (having figured he wasn't really interested in my opinion), but I always remembered that line and had the occasion to use it now and then in my later career.

Vice President Walter Mondale arrived in Belgrade to represent the United States at the funeral, one of the only deputy heads of government to attend. He was accompanied by Jimmy Carter's mother, Lillian, who was wearing white. She explained to a puzzled group of embassy officers on the funeral day that when she had been a Peace Corps volunteer in India, white was the color people wore to funerals. That may have been true in India, but in Belgrade, people wore black. So in the sea of black that moved slowly up the steps of the parliament building to where Tito's body lay in state, our delegation, or at least one member, stood out.

President Carter's decision to send his vice president and his white-dress-clad mother didn't answer the mail, so to speak, in Belgrade, and so a month later the president of the United States himself rolled into Belgrade for a visit to express solidarity with a country in grief. He was concerned that it could become the next victim of the Soviet Union. Meanwhile, the people in Yugoslavia were busy pulling their long knives and other weapons out of the attic to use on each other. As we worried about the Soviets, they knew where the looming catastrophe would likely come from.

After Yugoslavia, Eagleburger went on to bigger and better things. He was undersecretary of political affairs in 1989 during the Polish and central European revolutions, overseeing and spearheading U.S. assistance, and soon was made Secretary of State James Baker's deputy in the George H. W. Bush administration. It was an extraordinary career, made so by the fact that he threw himself into each job as if there were no tomorrow—or for that matter, no next job.

His health, but never his sense of humor, had started to fail him. As the State Department's desk officer for Poland, I accompanied the intrepid Polish democratic revolutionary Jacek Kuron to Eagleburger's enormous seventh-floor office. Eagleburger, in a wheelchair because of his knees and phlebitis, coughing from his cigarette habit and asthma, instantly recognized a kindred spirit in Kuron. When Kuron asked if he could have a cigarette, Eagleburger, frustrated perhaps by his doctors' nagging advice and new State Department regulations, responded, "You smoke? Fantastic! I've got some." Whereupon he whirled his wheelchair 180 degrees and headed at breakneck speed to look for them in his desk, risking what I feared would become a bizarre workplace accident. He and Kuron lit up, and it took hours to pull them apart.

As I prepared to go to Iraq in early 2009, I visited Eagleburger at his home in Charlottesville, Virginia. He had grown very old since I had last seen him, some years before. He was now hugely overweight, his face even more puffy, perhaps from medication. I knew he didn't have much longer to live and I wasn't going to miss the chance to see him one more time. Two years before, when he and I were both made honorary citizens of Skopje, Macedonia, he for having helped rebuild it in 1963, and me for having been ambassador there during a difficult time in the late 1990s, I called him at his home in Virginia from the central square in Skopje to tell him I had just read his letter at the ceremony, as he had asked me to do. I also wanted him to know how much he was remembered there more than forty years later. The famously gruff Eagleburger seemed to choke up at that point. He recovered to ask how the city looked. "Better than when you were working here in the aftermath of the earthquake," I told him. He then asked, "What do you think? Are we going to get to use the city buses for free?"

In his home that afternoon two years later, we talked for a few hours, his thoughts lucid and rapid, and his sense of humor unfailing, as if it were his best and last companion. He wanted to know all about the negotiations with North Korea that I had been conducting during the four years of the second George W. Bush administration, when I had been appointed as assistant secretary for East Asian and Pacific affairs and also made the head of the U.S. delegation to the Six Party Talks on North Korea. He was skeptical that the North Koreans would ever follow through on their commitment to denuclearize, but he understood the necessity of working with the Chinese, and indeed, that working with China and other countries, including South Korea, was the main dividend of the process. "That's it," he said, after a puff on his asthma inhaler and before taking out another cigarette. "People who think China is there to be ignored or fought with understand nothing about what we are dealing with today," he added. I could see that his sense of pragmatism had also not abandoned him in his final days.

I gave him some details of the negotiations, including what I had been dealing with from not only Pyongyang, but also various quarters in Washington. I described some of the more theatrical moments with the North Koreans. He laughed between coughs and alternating puffs from his inhaler and his cigarette at my admitting that I had borrowed some of his performance art. "That's all right, Hill"—he never called me Chris and I sure never called him Larry—"glad you learned something from me."

"How do you think the Foreign Service is doing?" he asked. He worried that we'd surrendered too much of our role to the military. I told him that the Foreign Service would be fine, and that we would do our duty in Iraq and Afghanistan, military engagements about which he had great concerns.

"Just make sure our people show some guts," he responded, then lit another cigarette.

4

A FORCE OF NATURE

After my first assignment in Belgrade, I went back to the State Department in the summer of 1980 and worked as a watch officer in the Operations Center for a year, before transferring to the Policy Planning Staff as a staff assistant, also a one-year assignment. The Operations Center is the eyes and ears of the State Department, a twenty-four-hour facility on the seventh floor where telephone calls, telegrams, and news wires come fast and furious, some requiring alerts to senior officials in the department, often in the dead of night. One moment there is a call from someone in a distant embassy reporting a coup. The next, it is a senior department official asking to be put through to another. Though it's a glorified switchboard position, it is nonetheless considered a prestigious job requiring the recommendation of a senior officer, in my case Ambassador Eagleburger. But for anyone who joined the State Department to have an impact on policy, it was far from that. It is tough being a junior officer in the State Department. Pay is low, as is the self-esteem of someone so junior to everyone else and so distant from any decision making.

My duties in the Policy Planning Staff (an office created in 1947 and whose first director was the iconic diplomat George Kennan) included maintaining a looseleaf binder of "talking points" that covered virtually every subject in the world for use by senior officials in public settings. My job wasn't to write them, but to collect them from grouchy midlevel officers manning desks throughout the State Department who were responsible for writing them and getting them cleared by other relevant offices. In the era before email, the job involved logging a lot of miles running through the department halls to collect the latest versions of the guidance.

After Belgrade, my next overseas assignment was Warsaw, Poland. I arrived there in July 1983, after nine months of Polish language training at the Foreign Service Institute in Arlington, Virginia, with my growing family of a son, Nathaniel, and a daughter, Amelia, on the way. Poland in 1983 was a sad place indeed. The Solidarity era of 1979–81 was long gone after the imposition of martial law by General Wojciech Jaruzelski in December 1981 and the rounding up and imprisonment of Solidarity's senior leadership. It was a gloomy country that seemed painted in so many shades of gray. Trips to West Berlin, eight hours away on Poland's narrow, bumpy highways, were a welcome respite. As we would pull through the checkpoint, it was just like *The Wizard of Oz:* black-and-white would suddenly turn to color. Once on a Friday afternoon dash to Berlin, a Polish policeman stopped me outside Lodz, about halfway to Berlin, for speeding and asked rhetorically why I was going so fast. My explanation that I was "going west" was more than enough for him and he waved me on.

There was something indefatigable about Poland's people. Abandoned to their fate on the wrong side of the Iron Curtain in 1945, they never seemed to give up on where their rightful place should be, even if many of us—myself included—thought at the time that nothing could ever be done.

During those years in the mid-1980s, there was little to cheer for. The heady days of Solidarity had given way to Jaruzelski's martial law, which in the Polish language is literally translated as "state of war." Even the

Catholic Church, which for centuries had been the protector of Poland's independent nationhood, seemed exhausted by the lack of hope for the future. One Sunday in St. John's Cathedral in Warsaw's old town, I heard for the first time the expression "inner emigration," and the concern expressed by the priest giving the sermon that the Polish people were tuning out and otherwise giving up. In October 1984, a Catholic priest, Father Jerzy Popieluszko, was found murdered, a victim of members of the secret police. Hundreds of thousands of Poles turned out in the streets for his funeral.

The American embassy remained the proverbial beacon of hope, one that assured Poland that we would never abandon their aspirations. Back in the States, Poland under martial law became a main theme in Ronald Reagan's first term when the president uttered the expression "let Poland be Poland," but it was a sentiment shared on both sides of America's political divide. Trade unions, including the AFL-CIO, under Lane Kirkland, had embraced Solidarity, even though that Polish independent trade union was a political movement whose scope was far more than a trade union. The AFL-CIO kept Solidarity afloat financially and helped it maintain offices outside Poland, including in Brussels, Belgium, where the sometimes wobbly Europeans needed to be reminded that Poland was not giving up on its future as a free country.

Our science attaché, John Zerolis, was arrested in early 1983 in a setup by the Polish security services for giving assistance to Solidarity (which consisted of U.S. magazine literature, including a copy of *Newsweek*) and summarily expelled from the country. When I saw John after he had returned to the States, his future was unclear as the department scrambled to find him a new assignment. His advice on dealing with the Polish communist security services was very clear. "Whatever you do, don't look angry, because to some it will look like you are scared. Just smile, because in the end we are going to be proven right, and they will be shown to be wrong."

Despite optimistic expressions of the inevitable triumph of freedom by Reagan, Kirkland, and, for that matter, John Zerolis, by 1985 I had had enough of dark and gray Eastern Europe. I looked forward to pivoting to an assignment in East Asia, in South Korea, where I served as an economic officer from 1985 to 1988. Korea's future seemed as bright as Poland's was dim, and I marveled at the energy and bustle of its people. On my arrival I met the U.S. ambassador, a courtly gentleman professor and political appointee from South Carolina named Richard Walker, who went by the name Dixie. In my first meeting with Dixie Walker he asked me to compare what I thought of authoritarian Korea under the current president, General Chun Doo-Hwan, and Poland under martial law and General Jaruzelski. "In a matter of a few years, Korea's political system will be unrecognizable from what it is today. Korea is on its way to success, and nothing can stop it now," I told him. As for Poland, "Ten years from now, perhaps a hundred years from now, Poland will be sadly the same." If I had shown any wisdom in making the first prediction, I undermined myself in the second. Poland, in fact, was on its way as well.

By 1987, South Korea was moving fast. Demonstrations broke out in Seoul, less than a year before the 1988 Summer Olympics were to get under way. The Olympics were not a catalyst for change in Korea, but neither were they irrelevant to it. As a Korean friend explained, "We don't want the world to see us as a first-rate economy with a third-rate political system." He continued, "If we are to be accepted into the ranks of important countries (if nothing else, Koreans believe in rankings), we need to have a real democracy." I thought of the poor Poles, still mired with third-rate everything, and the fact that becoming a democracy was something that did not seem to depend on their aspirations alone.

In 1988, I returned to the United States for an excursion tour as an aide to New York congressman Stephen Solarz. Solarz's district was in Brooklyn, where he saw to the interests of a melting pot of hyphenated Americans, including those from Poland. His energy and enthusiasm were apparent in everything he did, especially traveling to distant countries and reporting back to those constituents who felt in Solarz they had someone who, like them, would not forget the old country. A year later I became the desk officer responsible for Poland. By the summer of 1989, Poland (only four years after my prediction to Ambassador Walker) was now the catalyst for a process that would sweep through Eastern Europe. Just before transferring to the department to take up my duties as the desk officer, I took a trip with Solarz to Yugoslavia, Poland, Hungary, and still-slumbering Czechoslovakia and East Germany. We met the pantheon of Solidarity figures who had been imprisoned when I served in Poland a few years before and who were now considering how to take over the government they had defeated in the June 1989 elections. I talked to Jacek Kuron, who had suffered in prison for many years but was now widely expected to be a member of a new noncommunist government, the first since World War II.

"How did you organize the elections in such a short time?" I asked him, noting that the communists had hoped that the short time between agreeing to elections and election day would ensure them some seats and therefore some legitimacy.

"Each candidate posed for a picture with Lech Walesa, which became each candidate's campaign poster," he explained.

"That simple?"

"Look," Kuron replied. "If a cow had had a campaign picture with Walesa, the cow would have won, too." How could I have ever bet against such people?

Being a desk officer is a step up the policy ladder from serving in the Operations Center, but there is a lot to aspire to after that: deputy officer director, office director, deputy assistant secretary, principal deputy assistant secretary, and assistant secretary positions. But being responsible for the day-to-day relations with Poland that summer and for the two succeeding years was an extraordinary opportunity. Poland seemed like the center of the universe that year. Lech Walesa addressed a joint session of Congress, famously starting his speech with "'We the People.' As an electrician from Gdansk I believe I am empowered to use that phrase." Prime Minister Tadeusz Mazowiecki made an official visit to the White House, preparations for which fell on the desk. I made several trips to Warsaw and Krakow during those two years, caught up with old friends from my time in Poland a few years before. They were now liberated from a system, as Czech president Vaclav Havel said at the time, "whose purpose no one can now understand."

I marveled at the changes that were under way. On a visit to Warsaw I witnessed the toppling of communist statues, including that of the first KGB director, a Pole named Felix Dzerzhinsky (who had a statue, so the communist-era joke went, because he had killed more Russians than any of his countrymen). I stood on the side of Dzerzhinsky Square with a junior officer from the embassy, together with many happy Poles, watching the construction crew remove the statue in what would soon regain its precommunist name of Bankers' Square.

The summer months in 1989 were a whirlwind of developments for Poland as I managed the day-to-day tasks in the department. With the Solidarity government set to formally take the reins of power in Warsaw, I got to my State Department office early that day to receive the first telegram reports (there were no live feeds) from our embassy in Warsaw about the speech to the parliament of the newly installed noncommunist leader of the government, Prime Minister Mazowiecki. At the start of his speech, he promptly fainted before he was revived to continue to describe the program this government was about to pursue to revive the country.

Two weeks later, Deputy Prime Minister Leszek Balcerowicz visited Washington to enlist support for his radical efforts to transform the economy from a command-style communist model to a wide-open capitalist system. I had known Leszek from my days in Warsaw when he was just another brilliant Polish academic, one who like many others had long understood the dead end toward which Poland was limping. Now he was charged with a program of transformation that would be known as the Balcerowicz Plan (a name that he had no part in creating). I met him at the main Diplomatic Entrance of the State Department and chatted with him as we made our way up the elevator to the waiting room just outside then acting secretary Eagleburger's office. Balcerowicz looked around at the oil paintings on the walls and asked who was in the largest portrait. "That's George Marshall," I explained. Balcerowicz then took a close look at the author of the Marshall Plan, the post–World War II economic program of assistance that had restored Europe. He stood back to take one more look and said softly, "A good omen."

Eagleburger greeted him warmly and made no secret that the United States was completely committed to the success of the new Polish government. As I watched Eagleburger's performance art, I almost forgot my role as the note taker. I marveled at the way he turned a person he had never met before into a close friend.

A year and a half later, in April 1991, I accompanied newly elected Polish president Lech Walesa on a trip to the West Coast. The visits included a meeting with former president Ronald Reagan at his presidential library, which was still under construction. The two men laughed and joked throughout the lunch, with Walesa playing the role of the skeptic as to the completion date of the presidential library as he pondered the batts of insulation hanging exposed from the ceiling and the unconnected wires sticking out of walls. A piece of the Berlin Wall stood on the grounds and the photographers asked the two men to pretend to be pushing on it. I stood back to watch this odd scene, but I found myself nodding in approval, realizing there was something very real in what I had been watching.

But by 1991 it was over. Eastern Europe, now redubbed by many Central Europe to highlight the fact that the Soviet Union's western republics were themselves beginning to change, became quiescent, more interesting perhaps to work on than the Benelux countries, but increasingly similar. The adrenaline of the summer of 1989 was finally wearing off, and in looking for an overseas assignment I looked for a place that like Poland in the 1980s was beginning to stir. That country was Albania.

One of the problems with accepting an assignment like Albania was how incomprehensible it is to people outside the service. "What did you do wrong?" was a common, only half-joking reaction. But I didn't want to miss the opportunity to open a post that had been closed since 1946, when Albania became the North Korea of Europe. Sealed off from the rest of the continent for forty-five years, it had slipped into a dark age and become a country that time forgot. A brutal dictatorship had kept it out of Europe, and out of the mind's eye.

I arrived at the airport carrying two suitcases that included MREs (Meals, Ready [or not] to Eat) and a sleeping bag. Officials from the Albanian Foreign Ministry met me at planeside as a rusted tractor-drawn cart collected the luggage from the plane, and drove me to our "embassy," located in room 215 of the Dajti Hotel. I checked into room 216. "The residence." I was on my own that night, as I was many subsequent nights. I got to know my new post, learned how to communicate with Washington with unreliable phones and faxes, hired Albanians to help us get networked and established, and began to put together an embassy. We had an embassy building and compound, built in 1931, that we had handed over to the French in 1946 and later the Italians for safekeeping, and had given notice to our Italian tenants that we were to move in on October 1, 1991.

Within a week of my arrival, I received a telephone call from Mother Teresa, who, unbeknownst to many, was an ethnic Albanian, and who was spending her summer establishing orphanages and a medical facility in Tirana. She asked if I would meet her at her office. I cupped the phone and asked our assistants whether it could be that I was really talking to Mother Teresa or was there someone else by that name and title in Tirana. I had learned not to be surprised by anything there.

I met her in a sitting room of the villa she was using for her clinic with her New York–based assistant. Mother Teresa spoke softly but directly. She thanked me for the food assistance from the U.S. Agency for International Development (USAID) that was to be given to the orphanages. She apologized for not having filled out all the forms, explaining that her main oversight indeed came from above, as she humorously pointed her finger up in the air. She asked if when we took back our embassy from the Italians, would we continue to store her medications for her clinic. I wasn't going to be the first person in the world to say no to Mother Teresa, and so I promptly agreed. Her assistant interrupted to ask if we would build a new gate in the back of the compound. "We can talk about that," I responded. I then asked Mother Teresa if she could do me the favor of meeting one of our transport planes bringing in food for Albanians and personally accept a pallet of canned products for her orphanage. She agreed.

The next morning I went out to the airport and met the C-141, a large, four-engine jet, whose cargo was being unloaded. I explained to the crew chief, based in McGuire Air Force Base in New Jersey, to expect a VIP. A few minutes later, a small white jeep pulled up to the plane. The aircraft crew stopped their activities and stared in disbelief as Mother Teresa, riding shotgun, slowly descended from the vehicle and approached the aircraft. All the crew members dropped to one knee in her presence. She went among them, giving small Virgin Mary medallions to each of them.

The pilot, a diminutive woman in a flight suit, her red hair pulled back in a tight bun, invited her on board. Mother Teresa slowly climbed the three or four steps of the ladder, and on entering the aircraft looked at the enormous cargo bay, telling the pilot, "This plane is too big to fly." The pilot assured her that was not the case, whereupon Mother Teresa said, "All the same, I will say a prayer." She stood in the hatchway, clasped her hands together, and prayed silently. The rest of us, though somewhat less anxious about the plane's capabilities, did the same. Never having seen anything quite like this in my life, and concerned whether anyone would ever believe me that this extraordinary moment which had many of us near tears had actually happened, I slowly backed out of the hatchway and took a picture from outside. The photo of Mother Teresa silhouetted in the hatchway of a MAC aircraft would later make its way from me to the USAID assistant administrator, Carol Adelman, to the office of the chairman of the Joint Chiefs of Staff, Colin Powell, and on to many offices and public areas of the Military Airlift Command. It symbolized, in 1991, a more gentle and optimistic moment for the United States, when there seemed to be no end to the capacity of our country to rise to the occasion.

What I was doing in Tirana, Albania, many of my colleagues were doing over the vast regions of the former Soviet Union, now being divided into newly independent states. From 1990 until 1992 more than a dozen new embassies had been established in places where there was virtually no infrastructure; even getting to these newly created countries, with their newly created national airlines, could be a lifetime adventure. Using a tired cliché from more recent times, it would be called a "civilian surge."

But the Foreign Service pulled it off. We found people who were prepared to go to these places, more often than not without their families and without any other creature comforts. Tirana had two restaurants plus one on the back balcony of the Dajti Hotel. Dining out in Albania was a culinary adventure then, the dimensions of which were sometimes not known until the middle of the night.

A few colleagues were to join us as the weeks rolled by, but the real company was in knowing that what may have been unique for me was typical for the Foreign Service. We got to know the Albanians, one by one, the way a good diplomat does. It is always about relationships, not transactions. My first visit with Deputy Prime Minister Gramoz Pashko was followed quickly by an invitation to his small home. He and his wife, Mimoza, welcomed me with everything they had, including a bottle of whiskey. Mimoza's brother, the new finance minister in the transitional government, Genc Ruli, stopped by. They asked about America, but mainly told me about Albania and made me feel comfortable so far from my own home.

At one point Gramoz took a music cassette from a shelf and before putting it in the tinny-sounding boom box asked, "Do you like Dire Straits?"

"My favorite," I replied.

We had interpreters, Kestrina Budina and Andi Dervishi, who had been hired a couple of months before by temporary summer personnel we had in Tirana, and a consular officer FSO named Bill Ryerson. Bill set the U.S. standard for deeply and passionately caring about Albania, even learning the language in his spare time. Appropriately, because there was no one remotely as qualified, he went on to become our first ambassador. I became his number two, that is, deputy chief of mission, in charge of running the inside of the embassy while the ambassador performed the outreach. I found a language teacher, Professor Ukë Buchpapai, to start teaching me survival Albanian. Meanwhile, I signed on many day laborers to help repair the embassy, Albanians who had somehow managed to learn some English from some source and could be useful as we moved into what was pretty much the skeletal remains of our embassy, built in 1931 and abandoned in 1946. One was Tony Muco, who showed up at the gate on the day we moved into our old embassy and said to me: "I need job. I will do anything. Work very hard. I good friend of Chris Hill."

"Funny," I told him, "he never mentioned you to me." I liked him instantly, invited him in, and put him to work. (Tony later rose to be the head of our local guard force.)

Small teams of U.S. government experts in economic assistance, humanitarian aid workers, and other contractors came through the embassy. They provided enormous help to this fledgling little democracy, though unlike Iraq later, here the contractors never dominated embassy life. We helped the Albanians privatize the agriculture sector. We had people working in their ministries of finance, foreign trade, energy, and food distribution. The U.S. Department of Commerce sent out a team led by a seasoned commercial expert, Jay Burgess, with whom I had worked earlier. The International Republican Institute, led by a dynamic North Carolinian named M. C. Andrews, and Tom Melia from the National Democratic Institute provided technical assistance to political parties. Also, a distinguished but thoroughly down-to-earth senior judge from the federal bench in Manhattan, Judge Robert Sweet, assisted the Albanian court system. He helped introduce a totally new concept of a "procedures code." The Albanian courts had heretofore been meting out death sentences and lengthy terms for the catch-all "agitation and propaganda," but the new code would be the centerpiece of a new country based on the rule of law. Judge Sweet's statuesque wife, Adele, a former newspaper publisher with a keen political sense, accompanied him, and we put her to work as well, advising Albania's nascent media outlets.

We were not experimenting, or using Albanians as a laboratory, because almost everything we were doing in Albania was being done elsewhere in the newly independent states of the post–Cold War period. In Albania, USAID funded still one more project. The Albanian dictatorship had created a gulag of prison camps located in some of the most remote places in this remote country. People sent to prison spent decades in these prison farms, as did their families, who had been evicted from their apartments for having had a "bad biography" (Albania's contribution to the lexicon of twentieth-century communist dictatorships). They lived in these rural barracks without schooling or any other amenities that would equip them for life in a modern state.

It was difficult to explain such systemic cruelty to American visitors. When Deputy Treasury Secretary John Robson visited, I asked our Albanian assistant to pull together a group of ex-political prisoners who had suffered internal exile in the gulag system. "We need at least fifteen of them," I told Kestrina. "No problem," she answered. "And I'd like that each has been in prison for twenty years to show the extent of the issue." "No problem," she answered, shrugging her shoulders at the simplicity of fulfilling the request.

Kestrina's group of twenty ex-political prisoners who had served twenty years apiece met with Robson in a small room in the embassy. The most senior was Osman Kazazi, who had been in internal exile for forty-six years and was now eighty-seven years old. Robson listened to all of them telling stories of their horrific lives. "We all need to think about the future," Robson concluded, while Kazazi nodded in agreement, albeit somewhat confused. USAID Deputy Administrator Carol Adelman then put together a training program for the victims and especially their families, teaching them to manage hotels that we believed were sure to come. With Robson serving as bureaucratic top cover, Adelman made clear to the cumbersome USAID bureaucracy (and perhaps with the aging Kazazi in mind) that we didn't have a lot of time. We needed to get this done now. Over the months and years, a country whose system had been based on terror was, thanks in part to U.S. assistance, being transformed into a country that could begin to live and breathe.

In a part of Europe where war clouds were gathering fast, despite the forecast of a sunny and warm post–Cold War era, Albania managed to stay out of trouble. It stayed on the right track with a modicum of foreign aid but with a great deal of support from the United States. Albania would later send troops to Iraq and by 2007 would be invited to join NATO. It wasn't the number one issue in Europe, but I had learned a lot about how to manage these situations.

After completing my tour in Albania, I returned to work in the State Department's European Bureau, with responsibility for all the countries of northern Central Europe, including the newly independent Baltic states and Hungary, the Czech and Slovak republics, and of course Poland.

In September 1994, the new assistant secretary for Europe, Richard Holbrooke, asked to meet me. I had never met him, nor had anyone explained to me why he had asked to see me. But given that we were in the first chaotic days of his tenure as the assistant secretary of the bureau (EUR), which oversees the primary implementation of U.S. policy in Europe, I thought it might be in connection with a reassignment, perhaps something to do with the Balkans. I was right.

Ambassador Holbrooke had taken over EUR two weeks before with a mandate to improve it in any way he could, to make it responsive to the problems now coming fast and furious in the post–Cold War world. He began to put together a strong leadership team to deal with these challenges. For his principal deputy he selected John Kornblum, an officer known throughout European policy circles for his work in helping to create that continent's post–Cold War multilateral architecture. For the newly liberated states of Eastern Europe, renamed Central Europe, he selected Bob Frasure, who had served as the first U.S. ambassador to Estonia. Bob, a negotiator at heart, had played a crucial role in the withdrawal of Soviet troops from that fledgling state.

The most urgent of these changes was to find a team that could work with Bob Frasure to help devise a policy to address the violence in the Balkans, which was making a mockery of international standards of human rights—the slogan of a Europe "whole, free and at peace." The ongoing fighting in the Balkans was also contributing mightily to the fraying of the transatlantic relations. The breakup of Yugoslavia was fast shaping up as a major post–Cold War crisis gripping the young Clinton administration.

But the complexity of it exceeded people's patience in trying to understand it. On the one hand, there was the interest of the northern republics, Slovenia and Croatia, to exit a state consisting of poorer regions and republics that they felt were holding them back. To want to leave seemed fair enough, especially when these aspirations were consistent with long-standing U.S. sympathy for self-determination. But changing of international borders was not something lightly regarded in Europe, or in the United States or anywhere for that matter. Croatian and Slovene nationalists regarded Yugoslavia as a conspiracy to enshrine the hegemony of Serbia. Yet the origins of the Yugoslav state were far more complex, and in fact in the early twentieth century those two republics wanted to join forces with Serbia to resist the Austro-Hungarian Empire.

From the Serb nationalist point of view, another narrative flowed, that of Yugoslavia being a conspiracy to make the great nation of the Serbs a one-eighth player among five other republics and two autonomous regions, in effect denying the Serbs their sovereign place in Europe. This latter narrative in Serbia, so cynically and shamelessly exploited by its leader, Slobodan Milosevic, ultimately worked with Croatian and Slovene nationalism to break up Yugoslavia.

But breaking up is hard to do, and with the internal political maps of Yugoslavia not corresponding to the internal ethnic map, war, a phenomenon well-known in the Balkans, was a present danger. When the European Union countries gave diplomatic recognition to Bosnia, having encouraged the Bosnians to hold a referendum, they hoped that diplomatic recognition would end the matter. Instead, the Serbs sharpened their pitchforks.

Many Serbs had lived in Croatia and Bosnia for centuries. When these republics seceded, Serbia claimed parts of each of them.

Amid all this history, the supply of which certainly exceeded the demand for it, the State Department's European bureau was far better set up to deal with the need for thoughtful, well-drafted, and typo-free memos to prepare senior officials for polite discussions with European senior officials than it was for the direct diplomacy required to deal with those responsible for murder and mayhem in distant Balkan villages.

Bureaucratically, the Balkans was still handled as a kind of backwater, the issues tucked away in the so-called southern tier of the Office of Eastern Europe and Yugoslav Affairs, located on a floor below that of the assistant secretary. Meanwhile, offices that dealt with Europe's "architecture," including NATO, the Organization for Security and Co-operation in Europe, and the European Union, were all located within shouting distance of the assistant secretary.

Holbrooke's first step was to make EUR more like the East Asian and Pacific Affairs (EAP) bureau, which he had run during the Carter administration—make the offices smaller and eliminate middle management, that is, the deputy directors, and thus remove the "layered look" and turn it into a bureau with an operational mandate capable of dealing with the real crises of the day.

A week before I had been enjoying my new role as the deputy director in the Office of Eastern European Affairs. I was responsible for the northern tier of countries, which included all the Baltic states and the upper tier of east-central European states, including Poland, where I had served just three years before. But as much as I was interested in working on these countries, I realized that by the summer of 1994 they had lost a lot of their luster. There were no crises to manage. Soviet troops were fast withdrawing from bases in the now-independent Baltic States, and some of the relationships were burgeoning—namely, with Poland—with the expectation that NATO membership might be extended to some of them. The lack of urgency, however, meant that these countries had become very much secondary in the minds of senior policy makers. In fact, a week before my summons to Holbrooke's office, I had learned that my position was slated to be abolished as part of his reforms.

The European Bureau is the proudest, one of the busiest, and, viewed from the rest of the State Department, the least-liked of the bureaus. Every Foreign Service officer wants to have a foothold there because that is where the good jobs are. The Latin American bureau can offer a position in Rio de Janeiro or Buenos Aires, but that is about it in terms of family-friendly assignments. The list of cushy assignments in Europe goes on and on. Of course, such a state of affairs does not necessarily attract the most agreeable staff, and the stories of Foreign Service officers trying to get into EUR are replete with examples of arrogance from their EUR counterparts. When I was preparing to leave Seoul, I had applied in 1988 to be the desk officer for Bulgaria, a modest perch if ever there was one. The deputy director of the office of Eastern Europe told me cheerfully about my chances: "You haven't done badly: you are fifth on our list."

I stood at Holbrooke's doorway and looked into the oddly darkened wood-paneled office, the ceiling fluorescents all turned off, with the only lighting coming from a couple of table lamps nearby that illuminated the couch and upholstered chairs for visitors. He motioned me in and I walked across the room. He rose from behind the desk to introduce himself and shake my hand, still keeping his eye on the *NBC Nightly News* on the small television sitting on the windowsill, the view of the Lincoln Memorial beyond. He offered me a seat on one of the two hard-backed chairs positioned in front of his large desk while correspondent Andrea Mitchell talked onscreen. The walls were covered with pictures of Holbrooke with famous people, often from his days of managing our country's relationships in Asia. I thought about the extraordinary career he was having, truly one of the giants of U.S. foreign policy, even though as a political appointee of the Democrats he had sat out the Reagan and Bush administrations in the private sector. What a country, I thought, that can afford to take a talent like this and sit him on the bench for twelve years. I continued to survey the scene of this larger-than-life figure who was in effect keeping me on hold as Mitchell concluded her story. There was a small door in the back wall that was left open, the toilet visible and the seat up.

Holbrooke finally asked me, one of his eyes still fixed on the television, now showing an antacid commercial, "What do you think of the changes I have made to EUR?" These reforms had, of course, included abolishing the deputy director job I had just started two months before, but before I could answer he held up his right hand as if directing traffic and went back to full-time listening to the news. He turned to me again, this time asking, "What should we do with Yugoslavia?" As I was about to answer, he raised his hand again, though this time he absentmindedly pointed the remote control at me. I didn't mute immediately, but I understood that he wanted to focus on the *Nightly News*.

At that moment Holbrooke, still watching television with his body turned to me as if we were in the midst of a conversation, managed to triple-task by motioning into his office Principal Deputy Assistant Secretary John Kornblum, who had appeared in the doorway. John walked into the room and sat down in the other hard-backed chair to join in the competition for Holbrooke's attention.

"Okay, I'll hire him," Holbrooke told John. He muted the TV, and then turning to me, he added, "In case you didn't notice, I just offered you a job." I found myself thoroughly enjoying the scene. I had never had a remote pointed at me before. Holbrooke added yet another task: opening his thin brown leather briefcase to find a clean pair of socks to change into in the middle of all this. I had been looking at John taking his seat and watching a little of Andrea Mitchell's newscast myself, still waiting for Holbrooke to reengage with whatever it was he had asked me to come to his office to discuss, then turned to him to ask, "That's wonderful, but could you tell me what the job is?"

"I want you to be the new director of the Balkans for the new office I have just created: the Office of South Central European Affairs."

I thought about insisting on a name change for the office before accepting (South Central Europe sounded more to me like Switzerland than the Balkans), but decided I could fight that one later. I accepted. He glanced at his watch to see that it was about 7:30 P.M. and that he was late for something. He threw some papers in his briefcase (as well as the dirty socks), explaining that John would tell me the details. Before he left, he encouraged me to make whatever personnel changes I wanted in the office and said, "See you in New York on Sunday at noon."

John and I walked into his office, next to Holbrooke's, where he filled me in on what would be happening in New York. The United Nations General Assembly would be starting its fall meetings. I was to accompany Holbrooke to meetings in New York that would take up most of the week and would be primarily focused on the Bosnian delegation, expected Sunday afternoon. The task was to convince the Bosnians, and others, that lifting the arms embargo on Bosnia, as many in the U.S. Congress were calling for, would not so much help the Bosnians as it would embolden the Serbs and increase the bloodshed.

However, the U.S. position needed to go beyond simply opposing the lifting of the arms embargo. We needed to show the Bosnians, starting with President Alija Izetbegovic, that we were serious about finding a solution to a crisis that had spanned two administrations, caused thousands of civilian causalities and human rights violations on a scale not seen in

Europe since World War II, and was ruining the transatlantic relationship just when it needed to become stronger in addressing post–Cold War challenges. Izetbegovic needed to know that America was committed to ending the war and achieving a just solution for the Bosnians. We would not abandon the problem, or leave the Bosnians to their fate. We would be committed to the end.

Since my time in Yugoslavia with Ambassador Eagleburger, things had not gone well there. Yugoslavia, relatively small though it was, was a symbol for both East and West, having defied Stalin, but never integrating with the West. It also was a leader in what was then called the Third World and was a key player in the so-called North-South dialogue. In the beginning of the twentieth century, south Slavic peoples came together to resist the Austro-Hungarian Empire, which was seeking to replace the Ottoman Empire, now in fast retreat. The collective interests of those south Slavic peoples had long given way to centrifugal forces as each republic, especially the more economic advantaged northern ones, looked for a way out of Yugoslavia. Slovenia's exit was relatively painless, but the fact that large Serb minorities had lived in Croatia and Bosnia for centuries would make the declaration of independence of those two republics far more problematic. The fact that Bosnia's population was some 30–35 percent Serb would make its own declaration especially difficult. Immediately after the holding of the independence referendum by the Muslim-dominated government, the Serbs, especially those in the rural areas of eastern Bosnia, rose up to declare their own right of self-determination so that they would not be a minority in a new Bosnian state.

Sitting with John after the "interview" with Holbrooke, I asked him if that was how most decisions were being made in there, pointing over at Holbrooke's now-empty office. He smiled and said, "No, most are far more chaotic than that."

John explained what had led Holbrooke to change directors earlier in the day. John had recommended me for the job in the morning, and Holbrooke agreed, with the proviso that he had to meet me personally.

I had met John Kornblum for the first time just the previous day, quite randomly. I usually walked to the Tenleytown Metro station from my home in Washington, D.C., but running a few minutes late I had hopped on the M-4 commuter bus, recognized John, and sat down next to him. He was absorbed in the sports page, and so I introduced myself as the deputy director for the northern tier of the soon-to-be-defunct Office of Eastern European and Yugoslav Affairs, several rungs below the principal deputy assistant secretary.

John was one of the great career Foreign Service officers, a person whose knowledge of Europe was unmatched. He had been in the center of many of the crucial decisions about Germany since the early 1970s: the Four Party Arrangements, which enhanced stability in Germany; and the East-West process in the mid-1970s, which created the Helsinki Final Act and in turn had created the Conference of Security and Co-operation in Europe, later the Organization for Security and Co-operation in Europe. These were the main elements of the political and security architecture in Europe that normalized relations with the Soviet Union and introduced the concept of human rights as an element of European policy. He was one of the great minds in NATO and understood the delicate balance of U.S. leadership and European ownership. He understood the threat that instability posed in the Balkans to all that had been achieved—and would need to be achieved—in the transatlantic alliance.

He also had flair and knew how to get things done—something that obviously had appealed to Holbrooke. A few years before, John was serving in Germany as the United States minister in Berlin. This was the senior civilian job in Berlin and it made John responsible for all U.S. policy in the city. He had proposed that President Reagan's 1987 visit for Berlin's 750th anniversary celebration be transformed into a political initiative. Against great opposition, John had worked out an agreement to have the president stand at the famous Brandenburg Gate on the border between East and West Berlin, and had proposed the key sentence in the president's speech calling on Gorbachev to tear down the Berlin Wall.

I thought about whether I should discuss the article he was reading on the Redskins and their quarterbacking woes at the time, whether
Heath Shuler, the Redskins number one draft pick that year, was the answer (he was not, though he did go on to have a career in politics), or talk
about the future of Europe.

Forty-five minutes later we walked into the State Department, and I
thought I had had the best D.C. mass-transit conversation on Europe I
would ever have. I was wondering when I would get to talk to him again.

At 8 P.M. I left Kornblum's office to meet with the Bosnian team
and introduce myself as their new boss. I stopped to call my family and
my dad in Little Compton, Rhode Island. I told him about what had
happened, that I was very pleased but could not be sure that Holbrooke
might not fire me the next day. "I doubt it," he said in his laconic New
England style. "He doesn't strike me as someone who likes to admit
making a mistake." I weighed how much of a compliment that was, but
decided that Dad probably had a point about my job security.

At 8:30 P.M., the Bosnian team was still hard at work in their offices. I
sat with a few of them: Sue Bremner, working on Bosnia; Chris Hoh, on
Croatia; and Phil Goldberg, on the Balkan humanitarian portfolio. They
were writing talking points for the secretary's meeting with Balkan leaders for the UN General Assembly meetings. I asked to see all the materials, explaining I wanted to know how they viewed the situation.

The Balkan unit of the Office of Eastern European and Yugoslav
Affairs had been a demoralized group. Several had quit in protest at a do-
nothing U.S. policy. George Kenney, Marshall Harris, and Steve Walker
had all resigned, and eight others in the Office of Eastern European Affairs sent a joint letter to Secretary of State Warren Christopher to protest
the policy. When Phil Goldberg, who later became the chief Bosnian
desk officer, listed his accomplishments at the end of the performance-
rating period (an assignment some officers take five pages to complete),
he did it in four words, "I did not resign."

I grabbed everything I could find on the Balkans and headed home for a weekend of nonstop reading that would help prepare me for Sunday in New York.

On Sunday at noon I was at LaGuardia Airport waiting for Holbrooke, who was arriving an hour later on the Washington shuttle. Twenty minutes before he was to land I began a frantic search for his Town Car. The driver seemed to be cutting things rather close. I called the EUR office at the Waldorf-Astoria hotel to make sure it had been ordered, and finally found the driver, who explained that he had been caught in traffic delivering his previous customer to UN-gridlocked Manhattan. The car arrived just as Holbrooke cheerfully emerged from the gate area. He never broke stride walking toward me and finally getting into the back of the car.

"How old are you?" he asked. I told him. "Then why do I have more hair than you?" I thought for a second, recalling especially the last twenty-five minutes tracking down his Town Car, and answered, "Because you don't worry nearly as much as I do."

Holbrooke chuckled, and then turned to business:

"What time is Izetbegovic arriving?"

"Two thirty, Kennedy, Austrian Airlines."

"Let's get out there and greet him at the plane."

Our car swerved onto the exit of the expressway and started making its way to Kennedy. Holbrooke reached for the car phone, his huge fingers somehow finding their target on the keypad.

"John, yeah . . . this will work out . . . gotta go."

I took it that I was not going to be fired, at least that day, and tried to concentrate on the briefing materials in the thick binder I was carrying.

"Tom, I'm on my way to meet Izetbegovic at Kennedy. This is crucial. We need to reach him first. I'll meet Chris [Secretary Christopher] and tell him to call Hurd [British foreign secretary Douglas Hurd] and brief him on what we are doing. Someone needs to talk to Sandy [Berger, Clinton's national security advisor] . . . no I'll call him."

Holbrooke started to place the phone back on the stand. It would not immediately comply, so he started grinding it onto the stand as if it were mill corn. I interceded and turned it ninety degrees to make sure it settled onto the cradle. I remembered my dad had told me never to force a mechanical object. As soon as I got it placed properly, it rang and Holbrooke reached forward to grab it. It was the State Department Operations Center.

"No, I can't talk to him now. I have another call. I can't hear you. We're going through a tunnel." There was no tunnel.

I handed him the briefing papers. He gave them right back to me.

"Is there anything here I need to know?" he asked, referring to the two-inch-thick papers, complete with lettered tabs carefully punched into a binder, the words DEPARTMENT OF STATE emblazoned on the cover.

"I think you might want to look at some of the background material on—"

The car phone rang. This time I grabbed it, realizing the plastic stand was beginning to show some distress. It was the Op Center again and he grabbed it from my hand.

"I really want to talk to him. Tell him I'm really sorry, but can't just now. Tell him I will call him in ten minutes."

I didn't know who it was, and at that point I really didn't want to.

The car turned onto the ramp for the international terminal area at Kennedy Airport.

I realized we were about to go through every security check at Kennedy to reach our destination and meet the Bosnian president at planeside. I turned to Holbrooke and asked: "Do you have your State Department ID?"

He looked at me with a mixture of contempt and pity, as if I had asked the world's dumbest question and combined it with a brain seizure. I never asked him about his ID again.

Within minutes, he had recruited a policeman and another security person to escort us through the airport. Many blurry-eyed passengers just getting off international flights had their New York wake-up call as they were unceremoniously cast aside to create a path for Holbrooke, who was power-walking with a stride that the diminutive police officer, sweat now beginning to bead on his forehead, could only match with a jog.

We marched through the metal detector exit, Holbrooke in the lead, making conversation with the wheezing police officer. Still clutching the precious State Department briefing book, I pulled up the rear, stopping a couple of times to check the boards to see whether the flight had already arrived.

We reached the plane just as the ground crew opened the front doorway. Izetbegovic stepped out.

"Mr. President, welcome to America," Holbrooke said, acting as if we had been waiting patiently for some time. Holbrooke introduced him to the police officer who was still at our side, as if part of an official welcoming party.

"Mr. President, I want you to meet my new deputy for Bosnia, Chris Hill. Anything you need to tell me you can tell Chris."

Izetbegovic shook my hand with even less enthusiasm than he had shown in greeting the police officer. The Bosnian foreign minister, the very media-savvy U.S. citizen Muhamed Sacirbey, stepped forward to greet me, saying sardonically, "Congratulations. Bosnia is the graveyard of diplomats."

Holbrooke and I made our way back to our car and headed through the Sunday afternoon traffic to the Waldorf-Astoria hotel. For decades, during the two weeks in the latter part of every September, the Waldorf houses several international delegations, including that of the United States, for the opening of the United Nations.

For most Americans, September is back-to-school month, or the start of the football season. But for international diplomats—as well as hapless New Yorkers stuck in traffic at all hours of day and night—it is the opening of the United Nations General Assembly during the last two weeks of the month. The General Assembly (UNGA) has 193 member states, and just about everybody is represented at the head of government level, or, alternatively, by the foreign minister. Midtown hotel rooms, booked months in advance, are at a premium as the world descends on New York, and every head of government or foreign minister gives a speech to the assembly, often to a sparse audience, but always to the television cameras.

Ignored as most of the speeches may be in New York, they are often headline news back in the home country, where the public may be unaware of the other 192 that will be given during the two-week opening. The international media picks up some foreign leaders' speeches—Fidel Castro, the president of Iran, and other notorious figures, of course—but others will have to resort to props to gather some limelight. Bolivia's President Evo Morales earned the attention of the U.S. media by carrying a coca leaf to the podium in an effort to explain that coca farmers in his impoverished country use the leaf for many purposes, apart from processing into cocaine. The champa-clad president had been known to consume coca leaves in front of bemused international delegations.

For the U.S. delegation, the UNGA is nothing short of a scheduling nightmare. Many of the delegations want an individual meeting for their head of delegation with the U.S. president, who can accommodate around ten such bilaterals, plus his reception, which turns into a two-hour-long grip-'n'-grin receiving line. The secretary of state is asked to take the rest of them, and since that schedule is also physically impossible, the under-secretary for political affairs meets many of them, as do the regional assistant secretaries, each of whom stays for at least a week in a suite in the Waldorf, meeting foreign ministers and heads of government representing smaller countries who did not rate a meeting with the secretary.

And then there's the traffic. Motorcades carrying heads of state crisscross New York's avenues and midtown streets, while New Yorkers not lucky enough to have headed out of town must endure the invasion. In 2009, the then Libyan dictator Muammar Qadhafi, seeming more buffoon than evil, endeared himself to some New Yorkers when he complained in his annual speech to a perplexed UNGA audience that traveling to New York caused too much jet lag for delegations from the Eastern

Hemisphere and proposed moving the UN headquarters somewhere else. He probably could have won some votes in New York for that suggestion.

Holbrooke and I pulled up to the curb on East Forty-Seventh Street, the side entrance to the Waldorf-Astoria that leads directly to the Waldorf Towers, where Secretary Christopher and his staff had set up their offices on the thirty-fifth floor. The Towers are inadequately served by just a couple of elevators, a fact that Holbrooke was aware of. As I stood there on the sidewalk with him just outside the building, he promptly recruited an unsuspecting security person to escort us up a service elevator. We arrived on the thirty-fifth floor, squeezed our way past carts full of towels, sheets, and small shampoo bottles and began to head down the corridor to the secretary and his staff. While still in the service area, with Holbrooke in the lead (where else?) followed by the security person, he spotted some canapés on a tray being staged for an event. Not having eaten all day, he indelicately reached for one of them as an on-the-go snack. Not noticing they were all covered by tightly stretched clear wrap, he pawed at the canapés, barely breaking his stride in the process. By the time I walked past the tray, all was still intact, save for the pawlike scratch marks on the clear wrap. It looked like a bear was on the loose in the hotel.

We were met by Special Assistant Bob Bradtke, who tried to explain to Holbrooke that the secretary could not see him because he was studying his briefing book. At that moment, the irresistible force met the quite movable object and Bob, like so many other people that day, was unceremoniously pushed aside as Holbrooke kept moving. I turned back to Bob with my palms up, trying to apologize without falling too far behind Holbrooke, who by then had knocked perfunctorily on the door to the secretary's study and entered.

Secretary Christopher, impeccably dressed in a gleaming white shirt and silk tie, just as I had seen him in numerous photos, looked up from his desk without expression (which I suspected was the best he could do in the circumstances) and greeted us languidly. Bob had followed us into the large study, as had another aide. Holbrooke said to the secretary,

"Chris, have you met Chris?" Holbrooke chuckled at his own "Chris meet Chris" line. Christopher seemed less amused.

"No, I don't believe I have met Chris."

"Well, Chris is my new director for the Balkans."

I shook hands with the secretary, while briefly contemplating leaping out the thirty-fifth-floor window.

"Chris," Holbrooke said to Secretary Christopher, "you need to call [British foreign secretary Douglas] Hurd immediately. There is lots of speculation today in the press that we are prepared to give in to the Congress and support the 'lift and strike' resolution."

"Lift and strike" was a proposed measure in the Congress to unilaterally amend the UN-imposed arms embargo on the countries of the former Yugoslavia by exempting Bosnia, generally understood to be the victim in the wars. Since it was widely believed that lifting the embargo on Bosnia would trigger a massive Serb and Bosnia-Serb response, the idea was that the United States would then "strike" Serb forces and buy the Bosnians time to procure arms from abroad and defend themselves better. There was another serious problem: the Europeans had troops on the ground as part of the UN peacekeeping mission. They were concerned that the violence that would surely follow the resolution would endanger their troops. Thus "lift and strike," whether it actually helped the Bosnians or not, was almost certain to cause a major rift in the Atlantic relationship.

"You need to speak to him before he says anything publicly."

"Okay, Dick, but what do you want me to say precisely to the foreign secretary?" I was wondering that myself.

"Chris will do up some talking points for you." Turning to me Dick said, "Chris, do up talking points for the secretary."

It was a good thing the window was closed. I went over to a hard-backed chair nearby, put down my two-inch binder briefing book, thought for a second what I would want to say to Douglas Hurd, and began in the best handwriting I could muster to write five pages of talking points on what the Clinton administration's strategy was to resist the "lift and strike" congressional resolution but how public comments by allies would be counterproductive to our efforts. I tore the pages off the spiral, careful not to allow any flecks of paper to fall to the floor, and handed them to Holbrooke. He took about one second per page to look at them and handed them over to the secretary.

Christopher, fastidiously removing some of the remaining specks of paper I had missed from the jagged top of the pages, placed them on his desk in a row, and with his left index finger pointing at each point (there were three or four per page in block letters, with lots of space between them), read them all under his breath. He placed the call to Hurd.

Hurd could not be reached at that moment, but the call was set up for later in the day, and Holbrooke, with me in tow, left the room telling the secretary he would be meeting with Izetbegovic.

During the coming days, we did what good diplomats do. We began building relationships with all the parties, and in particular we created trust with the Bosnians where little had been before. We didn't offer them pity, or even claim to be on their side as the aggrieved party in a war, gaining trust as someone who wouldn't ever give up. The Bosnians had had plenty of sympathy in the years before. What they had lacked was a diplomatic team that would stay with the problem until it was closed.

5

FRASURE

Eleven months later, at about five thirty on a Saturday morning in August 1995, the telephone rang. The State Department Operations Center was on the line with a call from our ambassador in Sarajevo. In a very agitated voice, John Menzies told me to get down to the Operations Center.

"What happened?" I asked.

"There has been a terrible road accident," John replied, and explained he was not at liberty to say more on the telephone.

"Is everybody okay?"

"No," he answered. "Just come to the Op Center."

It was August 19, 1995, and after months of joint U.S. and European diplomacy, what the international press and other critics were calling "feckless" and "dithering," a serious, and we hoped decisive, U.S. effort was under way to bring the parties—the Serbs, Bosnian Serbs, Bosnians, and Croats—around a peace plan that had been outlined more than a year earlier by Britain, France, Germany, Russia, and the United States, countries known collectively as the Contact Group. Violence was escalating over the summer. It started in the spring with successful tactical cooperation between the Bosnian Croat and Bosnian Muslim forces in the Livno Valley (itself a product of U.S. diplomacy some two years before under Ambassador Chuck Redman, which put these two entities together in a "Federation"). It continued with a brutal Bosnian Serb response, culminating in the capture of the Muslim enclave of Srebrenica in July. That in turn led to the hunting down and murder of many of its male inhabitants in the forests between Srebrenica and the Bosnian lines near Tuzla. Finally, Croatia's own "Operation Storm," a swift and decisive military assault that kicked off on August 1 against the Serb enclave of Krajina, where Serbs had lived for centuries, culminated with the spectacle of long lines of Serb refugees leaving Krajina for the last time, after burning their homes so that Croats could not move into them. Murderous as much of the fighting had been (it usually pitted one side's military against another's civilians), the map of Bosnia, which had been 70–80 percent held by the Bosnian Serbs, was beginning to appear more like that envisioned by the Contact Group countries in the summer of 1994, a 51–49 percent split, with the Bosnians and Croats to possess the 51 percent majority share.

Those of us who had worked on Bosnia during the past year welcomed the Bosnian and Croat advances, a payback for all the Serb brutality of the previous three years. The Bosnians began to succeed more on the battlefield due to cooperation with the Croats and a more regular flow of arms despite the UN embargo. But with every success, they became less interested in peace or in cohabitating with the Serbs in an eventual federated state.

Fifty-one percent seemed out of reach only months before, but now it seemed too modest a share given the battlefield advances that had begun to pile up. Moreover, it was increasingly clear that Milosevic was fast losing interest in the fight.

U.S. interests were essentially twofold: 1) protect human rights and end the conflict by finding a political arrangement acceptable to all the parties on the ground (Serbs, Bosnians, and Croats), and 2) prevent further corrosion of the transatlantic relationship.

Making U.S. policy goals possible would require convergence of U.S. and European aims. That process accelerated in 1995 as Europeans realized that the entire mission of the UN protection force, known as UNPROFOR and led by the French and the British, was becoming untenable and might require evacuation, even under fire.

There was enough concern about a humiliating departure that in July the European Union dispatched a quick reaction force to Bosnia to help protect the mandate of the UN forces.

There had been a growing chorus of complaints and outrage from the international media about the role of the European-led UN forces in Bosnia. The UN was broadly perceived as failing to protect the Bosnian civilian population from attacks by armed groups often instigated by the Bosnian Serb government.

In fact, the UN forces were in Bosnia to enforce a weak, so-called Chapter VI mandate to deliver food, not to take "all necessary means," the much more robust mandate of the UN Charter to enforce a UN Security Council Resolution and which includes the use of force against any party to the conflict.

The difference between a Chapter VI (peacekeeping) mandate and a Chapter VII (peace-making) mandate was well-known to anyone working from the inside. But it was completely misunderstood by the general public, which could not understand how the international community's response to genocide and ethnic cleansing could be to send soldiers in traditional UN powder blue helmets and white vehicles (to distinguish the peacekeepers from warring sides) with a mandate that they could not intervene with force or take sides except to protect themselves. The UN forces were taking a beating in the international press, even though, as their British commander tried (not so) patiently (but accurately) to explain, "One doesn't go to war in white tanks and wearing blue helmets."

Not all the blue helmets and white tanks were so passive and accepting of the limited rules of engagement. The British UN force commander, General Sir Michael Rose, despite his notoriety with the pro-interventionist international press, was no flower child. He told me of an incident when a Danish unit was attacked by Serb gunmen outside Sarajevo in early 1995. The Danish commander reported to Rose that they had robustly returned fire with seventy-two tank rounds.

"Why seventy-two?" Rose asked.

"That was all we had."

The failure of the British-led and largely European-composed UN force to go to war with the Bosnian Serbs was often explained in conspiracy circles as a result of historical alignments: the relationships in World War II between the Serbs and the British and especially the French, whose senior leadership could remember the war, meant that the latter were somewhat sympathetic to the Serbs, if not necessarily to their behavior. Meanwhile, the Germans were perceived as much more "pro-Croat," and their diplomacy (Germany at the time had still not committed troops to any peacekeeping missions) supposedly reflected it.

The dispatch of a European Union rapid reaction force was thus Europe's effort to recoup an image harmed considerably by participation in a UN mission that looked weak in the eyes of the world. The UN force also began to regroup the small units deployed throughout the country and put them into more defensible redoubts. This would ensure that a decision to employ NATO air strikes would not be thwarted (as in the past) by the threat of hostage taking by Serb militia. A new British force commander, Major General Rupert Smith, was sent to Sarajevo. Smith, a thoroughly professional and no-nonsense general, had no time for public relations and set to work tightening up the security of UNPROFOR and preparing it for even tougher times.

As the situation deteriorated on the ground, the diplomacy in the spring and summer of 1995 was going nowhere. Bob Frasure spent weeks on end in Belgrade trying to bring Milosevic around to supporting the implementation of the 1994 Contact Group plan. Milosevic, however, continued to insist he could not speak for the Bosnian Serbs, and that any progress on the ground would depend on our direct negotiation with them. Bob sent back cable after cable explaining that there was nothing more that could be accomplished in Belgrade and that he needed to leave.

Unbeknownst to Bob, as far as diplomacy was concerned, he was it. If his mission was determined to be at an end, there would be loud cries. Neither the Europeans nor the U.S. administration was prepared at that point to support a military approach. As long as Bob was in Belgrade, the answer to any suggested new approach was that we had a diplomat in the field working the problem. Bob was ordered to stay.

When Bob was finally allowed to depart ("The lambs of Serbia will not miss me," he wrote in a telegram from Embassy Belgrade, a sardonic reference to his being force-fed enormous traditional Serb lunches), the Europeans were prepared to launch their new peace mediator, an energetic, tough-minded, and very capable former Swedish prime minister named Carl Bildt. Carl came to Washington for a round of meetings and met Holbrooke and me in the La Chaumiere restaurant, across from the Four Seasons Hotel. He listened as Holbrooke explained the politics of Washington in the late spring of 1995, and how U.S. policy was likely to evolve in the coming months. Holbrooke was aware that if the twenty-thousand-member UNPROFOR force were to be evacuated under deteriorating security conditions, it would be the U.S. military that would take the lead in organizing the departure.

In May 1995, just before the dinner with Carl Bildt, Lieutenant General Dan Christman, the director of the Pentagon's "J-3," responsible for U.S. military plans and operations, had come to Holbrooke's office to outline the UNPROFOR evacuation plan to us. Christman unfurled maps on Holbrooke's coffee table in his dimly lit office that showed an extraordinarily well-endowed force of some twenty-five thousand U.S. troops that would swoop in wherever UNPROFOR personnel were. For example, a Bangladeshi battalion (the Bang Bat, as it was affectionately known) was located in northwestern Bosnia and would require assistance in their extraction. Holbrooke and I looked at the map and the accompanying charts detailing the strength of the mission, including the airpower that would be available.

I glanced over at Holbrooke and said to Christman, "My God, General! With that force you could take Belgrade."

Christman began rolling up the maps and gathering the charts.

"Heck, with this force we could take Moscow."

I stayed behind with Holbrooke. That briefing had made clear to us what we had been thinking for some time. No matter what, we were going to be militarily involved in Bosnia, so why not do so in a way that enforced a peace agreement rather than simply assisting in a humiliating withdrawal? Early on in the UN deployment, U.S. allies, including the Canadians, had asked for specific assurances that the U.S. military would be available were it necessary to withdraw under fire. We had declined to draft anything (not wanting to be obligated for every unit in Bosnia, or establishing a new practice of providing U.S. guarantees for units on UN deployments), but we knew that a failure to come to the rescue of an ally would be the end of that alliance.

Some months before, the issue of UN extraction had come up during a Contact Group meeting with Milosevic in Belgrade. The British representative made the point that if things got worse the UNPROFOR mission would have to be curtailed. Milosevic shot back that if things got worse the mission would not be able to get out. I interjected at that point that if our allies needed assistance of that kind we would help them.

"And we would help you," added Milosevic. There were times when Milosevic's insincerity was just too much. I shook my head and responded directly.

"We wouldn't need your help. You just need to stay out of the way." The British and French representatives nodded their approval.

While the public in most Western countries was focused on human rights, the concern within governments was the impact Bosnia was having on alliance relationships. European elites regarded U.S. reluctance to serve in UNPROFOR as reflecting an unwillingness to accept our role as a great power. We saw UNPROFOR as a flawed and ultimately doomed mission. Moreover, U.S. policy-making circles were beginning to look ahead and contemplate the future of NATO and whether "out of area" missions—and Bosnia was such a mission—could be envisioned for the future.

The summer of 1995 brought new challenges. NATO air strikes in the spring resulted predictably in the taking of UN hostages. Serb militia groups chained UN peacekeepers to a fence in the presence of international media in an effort to humiliate the European powers and dare them to support further NATO air action. In July, the Serbs overran the eastern enclave of Srebrenica in reprisal for ambushes conducted by the tiny force of Bosnian Muslim militia there. Within days, reports began to emerge from refugees streaming into Tuzla that the Serbs had murdered thousands of Muslim men, often in a macabre sport of hunting and chasing them down in the forest. Others were executed and thrown into mass burial pits, the likes of which had not been seen in Europe since World War II. The mass murder was preceded by a filmed encounter between the Bosnian Serb commander Ratko Mladic and the head of the lightly armed Dutch UN unit guarding the Srebrenica safe area, which was incapable of halting what was to happen.

Meanwhile, NATO began to flex its muscles and the alliance members began to come together with the understanding that the future of the alliance, and indeed of the entire transatlantic relationship, was being put to the test. We gathered at a conference in London in July and established the "Gorazde Rules," designed to expand the scope of NATO air action beyond "pinpricks," as the press had come to describe the use of NATO airpower, or the symbolic bombings in retaliation for real Serb atrocities.

Amid the deteriorating situation on the ground and the weight of NATO alliance deliberations, Bildt's mission began to founder as both the Serbs and the Bosnian Muslims made clear they wanted to deal with an envoy who actually represented the United States, the country whose eventual direct involvement was seen as the guarantor of any peace settlement.

The person they wanted was Holbrooke, but as the winter and spring months had worn on in Washington, "le Bulldozer," as the French described him, was beginning to amass too many detractors within the bureaucracy. One of the reasons had to do with his penchant for speaking on the record with the press. Holbrooke took the view that "on the record" was far preferable to the Washington practice of providing background material, or "deep background," by which an unidentified "senior official" is at liberty to think out loud or even predict the future with impunity. It would involve the use of ground rules for each thought conveyed, for example, "now this next point cannot be for attribution to a senior U.S. official, so please make it 'a senior diplomatic official' or just 'a person with direct knowledge of the deliberations.'" Worse yet, statements and insights would often be made not for any attribution at all, as if the reporter simply knew the information without any sourcing, such as "Holbrooke is distrusted by a number of senior White House officials."

Dick Holbrooke told me many times that he preferred speaking on the record so that there would be no question as to who said it and what was said. The trouble with his approach was that it ran contrary to "message management." On-the-record comments make much more publicity than ones attributed to unnamed sources. He may have had another motive. As an assistant secretary, a rung below undersecretary, two below deputy secretary, and rungs below the secretary and the U.S. representative to the UN, Holbrooke was fast becoming a household name around the world. "What's he doing on CNN?" was being asked as he became the face of the administration's foreign policy. And Holbrooke was good at it, so the more he did it, the prouder I—and everyone else in the European Bureau—was to work with him, even if it meant we sometimes got caught in the middle of things.

People got annoyed and then got even, and as the spring turned to summer, Holbrooke became increasingly frozen out of internal council meetings. Even his friends tired of defending him, especially in inter-agency meetings that no one wanted to attend in the first place, where Holbrooke often took the stage to offer his lengthy, professorial sweep of nineteenth-century European history. Twentieth-century Europe was fast becoming history, while nineteenth-century Europe, with the breakup of the Ottoman Empire, was fast becoming current events. Holbrooke un-derstood that before anyone else.

I was constantly in the middle of Holbrooke's disputes with other parts of the bureaucracy, and even with other Contact Group delegations, as when the British representative, Pauline Neville-Jones, blew up at him when he opened up a copy of the *International Herald Tribune* while she was speaking. (Thankfully, she didn't notice that he was reading the sports page.) Frequently he would ask me to go "fix a problem," usually one set in motion by his expressed impatience with the person in question. Often it was a no-win situation for me, because if I sided with his adversary, I would inevitably hear it from Holbrooke and that would undercut my influence with him.

In summer 1994 the national security staff tried to coordinate policy by convening a morning teleconference for representatives of different agen-cies to touch base and assess what had gone on in the Balkans the previ-ous twenty-four hours, and what needed to be done about it. Dick saw this basic National Security Council function, governmental coordination, as an insidious effort not only to coordinate but also to direct the policy, and he would have none of it. Whenever he detected NSC fingerprints on an instruction to one of our embassies, he would pounce:

"Why are we doing this, Chris? Why are we asking Embassy Sara-jevo to approach the Bosnians about this situation in Bihac?"

"It was something that came out of this morning's teleconference."

"'Came out of the teleconference'! What does that mean? Did you suggest this at the teleconference?"

"Well, no. But everyone thought it was a good idea."

"Who do you mean, 'everyone'?"

To make a point about the NSC-chaired morning meeting, Holbrooke refused to allow me to attend any more of them. I started sending my deputy, Jack Zetkulic. When Holbrooke heard that Jack was going, he forbade him from being there as well. Trying to salvage our relationship with the NSC staff, I then sent our Bosnian desk officer, Phil Goldberg. Desk officer is a fairly junior level, but since Phil had gravitas that made him a real player and he was acceptable to the NSC staff. But when Holbrooke heard that Phil, one of his favorites in my office (Holbrooke knew all fifteen officers in my office by name), was going, he outlawed it. ("You sent Phil Goldberg?" he asked, as if I had dispatched Henry Kissinger.) Finally, on a summer day when many people were out, I sent the summer intern with the instruction just to take notes and not speak. At that point, the NSC staff complained up the line to the national security deputy advisor, Sandy Berger, who called over to Deputy Secretary Strobe Talbott, who took up the issue with us. Holbrooke allowed me to go once, and then it started all over again. As Talbott took the irate phone calls from Berger, I became the go-to Holbrooke handler for this kind of problem.

Dick was on thin ice with National Security Advisor Tony Lake, his deputy, Sandy Berger, and others around Washington, including even Secretary Christopher and UN Ambassador Madeleine Albright. Strobe had fought hard to keep Dick ("our thermonuclear device") from being fired, or worse, sidelined, but his support was increasingly becoming a lonely struggle. In early summer of 1995, Dick had heard about a meeting in the White House Situation Room, only to learn on arrival at the Southwest Gate that he was not on the list of attendees. Dick had quite worn out his welcome with old friends and colleagues from the 1960s and Vietnam days.

My approach to Holbrooke was to protect him from himself. I'd often try to convince him it wasn't worth the fight, a comment that always earned me the favorite Holbrooke put-down. "What a typical Foreign

Service officer reaction. I thought you were better than that." He bright-ened up when I assured him we never did what the national security staff wanted us to do. The staff was often out of touch with the situation on the ground, and I would regale Holbrooke and Bob Frasure with stories of the gap between the staff's constant confusion of memos and talking points, and the situation on the ground. Frasure, no fan of senseless talk-ing points, would mimic a Balkan warlord receiving a memo and hit the side of his head with the palm of his hand, saying, "Oh, now I understand. Now I get it, thank you, thank you."

Sending talking points to be delivered by our embassies to various warlords reflected the limited Washington bureaucratic understanding of what motivated ruthless factional leaders. Frasure, whose laconic and ironic style had a way of defusing a problem, including an outburst of Holbrooke temper, added, "A wheelbarrow full of those talking points wouldn't work with Milosevic unless you hit him over the head with it."

Accomplishing something on the ground in a war zone and managing Washington anxieties were often two very distinct skill sets. Some people were good at neither, while many had one and not the other. Bob Frasure was a master at both. Being effective at the Washington end involved first of all never panicking. But it also required a keen understanding of exactly when others in the vast interagency world of Washington bureau-cracy might be inclined to push the panic button. "Tell the embassy to come in with something on this ASAP" (meaning send a cable about it), he would often say, having just seen an intelligence report suggesting that an initiative of ours was about to be rejected. "This might be a problem today."

While the Balkans were a distant part of the world, far removed from the centers of power and authority, their explosion, to say something of the human rights calamity graphically detailed by CNN's coverage, meant that this tiny, obscure region of the world became the locus of all our fears. If Washington's senior foreign policy leadership had learned anything in school it was how to prepare for big problems (for example, the behavior of the Soviet Union). It was ill-prepared for the issues coming out of the scruffy edges like the Balkans. Even the proxy wars of the 1970s and '80s, which took place in odd, faraway places such as Angola, had organizing principles attached to them, such as Soviet aggressive behavior. The Balkans was a constant stream of bad news that seemed impervious to any efforts—certainly not those cooked up in Washington interagency meetings—to make it better. The resultant frustration was a tendency to blame our diplomats in the field, or more immediately, those not in the room.

After one of those meetings where nothing was decided and the administration seemed content to allow the situation to continue forever, Frasure walked back in his office and, as he often did after a frustrating encounter, headed over to the window and looked out on the Lincoln Memorial.

"What happened, Bob?" I asked him as I entered his office anxious for a report of the meeting. I knew that it was another desultory, unproductive discussion, but I still wanted to hear the details. He had his hands in his pockets and barely turned to see me in as he gazed out the window. I could tell he was very unhappy with what had just transpired. He answered still looking at the Lincoln Memorial.

"In the Civil War, troops in the field assembling for battle would always want to know the identity of the units in the battle formation on their sides to give a better sense of whether they could be expected to be flanked or not. So you can imagine you are out there, battle drums sounding, and you yell to your sergeant: 'Sarge, who's that yonder to our right?' And imagine the fear that must have swept through the lines when the answer came back, 'Don't worry, boys. That's the Interagency Brigade.'"

Bob had become very special to all of us, both in the State Department and out at Embassy Sarajevo, where John Menzies was now calling me that Saturday in August at 5:30 A.M. I sped down to the department through Rock Creek Park, listening to the radio news in my car for anything about our team in Bosnia. Earlier in August, the president and secretary of state had overruled the objections of many and decided to name Holbrooke as the negotiator, sending him to the region at the head of an interagency team. Bob Frasure had accompanied Holbrooke primarily to introduce him to Milosevic, whom Dick had never met, and then to accompany him to Zagreb and to Sarajevo, the other two stops on the circuit, both places that Holbrooke had visited within the last year.

Frasure had been on the road constantly in the past year, often with me in tow, but always with one of the officers from my office, including Phil Goldberg. This was to be Frasure's last trip. In the future, I would travel with Holbrooke, and Frasure would cover our back in the interagency process, where the real combat was. Given that Holbrooke would be the one in the field, Bob's job would be a tough one. I was excited at the prospect of serving on Holbrooke's team. It was everything I ever wanted to be as a U.S. diplomat, and having served in the Balkans, once in Belgrade and another in Albania, I felt prepared.

I drove into the State Department garage at breakneck speed, barely stopping to show my ID to the security guard. I parked as close to the elevator as possible and didn't stop pressing the elevator button, as if it operated pneumatically, until the doors slowly opened. I entered the Operations Center on the seventh floor.

There were now press reports that there had been an accident on the dirt road that came up from the south and over Mount Igman into Sarajevo. Bosnian Serb soldiers manning checkpoints and taking bribes controlled all the other roads into the city, and "tolls" (bribes again) were often levied, raising the price of the goods. UNPROFOR commander Rupert Smith had once remarked to me that "every boy in this country grows up wanting to run his own checkpoint."

I took the telephone from the watch officer and got back on the phone with John Menzies.

Before he could say anything I asked: "What about Bob?"

"He's dead."

I paused.

"Who else?"

"Kruzel and Drew," referring to Joe Kruzel, the representative of the Office of the Secretary of Defense, and Nelson Drew, the representative from the National Security Council staff's European Directorate.

I was horrified about Bob, a daily companion whose company I missed whenever he was out of town. But the report about Nelson Drew was also terrifying in its randomness. Nelson had hardly been involved with Bosnia, a last-minute add-on to the trip when the senior director of the Europe Directorate had decided not to go.

I wanted details. "Anyone else?" I asked.

"I don't know." There were some injuries. Some bad.

"Holbrooke and Clark [three-star general Wes Clark, director of the Joint Chiefs of Staff's J-5, for Plans and Policy] were in a Humvee in the front. The French armored personnel carrier was behind and couldn't keep up. It went over the edge of the road. That's all we know now."

"Are you sure about Bob and the other two?"

He paused. "Yes, I'm sure."

I called John Kornblum, who was the acting assistant secretary in Holbrooke's absence, to alert him, but he was already heading to the department. It was now after 7 A.M. and other members of the Bosnian team were arriving at the Operations Center. We set up shop in a small room with a table and telephones and began to plan our day, such as it was. We kept an open line to the embassy in Sarajevo and fed what information we had to the watch team.

The watch team that morning was extremely busy putting together conference calls involving National Security Advisor Berger, Deputy Secretary Talbott, and many others. There was a good deal of frustration at not getting more details about what had actually happened. I mentally replayed my calls with John Menzies and within seconds he was pulled into the conference call himself to repeat what he had told me earlier.

After making his way down Mount Igman, Holbrooke was patched into calls with the president and the secretary of state. Later in the morning, press reports started coming in with short quotes from Holbrooke that appeared to provide additional information, inflaming people in Washington.

Soon thereafter, John Kornblum and I drove out to Falls Church, Virginia, to tell Katharina Frasure that her husband was missing and feared dead. It was a typically sultry, humid August day in Washington, with no sign at all of any early fall. We drove in John's car through leafy Northern Virginia and arrived at the Frasures' home. Katharina answered the door, already looking stricken, and led us into the living room. One of Bob's teenage daughters walked into the kitchen, staying away from the brief discussion in the living room. John took the lead, explaining what we knew, not wanting to pass on unconfirmed reports but also avoiding speculation that Bob was okay. His body had not been recovered, or at least the recovery had not been confirmed. At the same time, John had been very clear that Bob had not survived.

Back in the Operations Center, details were now flowing in, and all of the Balkan team had arrived. We were staffed up, manning the phones, writing memos, and beginning some of the technical tasks of getting the delegation home. Holbrooke insisted that the surviving team members accompany the fallen. I took a walk out of the Operations Center down the corridor to be alone for a second. I stopped for a moment and Deputy Secretary Talbott walked up to me. Strobe, whom I had never really talked with, said some kind words about our team's efforts on this tragic day. He had just gone out to Katharina Frasure's house to confirm to her the recovery of the body.

A few days later the delegation returned together to Andrews Air Force Base with the bodies of Bob Frasure, Joe Kruzel, and Nelson Drew. President Clinton came to the memorial service at Arlington National Cemetery a few days later and afterward huddled with the reconstituted negotiating team that I was part of, along with Jim Pardew from the Office of the Secretary of Defense and Don Kerrick from the European Directorate at the National Security Council staff.

I visited with Katharina once more, a few days before heading out on our first trip after the funeral and memorial services. It was the first week of her loss, and she was visibly pained. She told me that her two teenage daughters had shown no signs yet of recovering from the shock. We reminisced a little more about Bob, and I told her that I had brought my three young children, Nathaniel, Amy, and Clara, into the office one Saturday morning to meet him. Clara, then eight, told Bob what we needed to do about Milosevic and the Serbs, and Bob had run over to his desk to get a pencil and paper to write down the suggestions, such was our need for fresh ideas. As I headed a few steps down the front walk, Katharina stood at the door and her expression turned very dark. She called out to me, "How can you do this to your family?" I stopped and looked back at her. While I had asked much of my children, the idea that they could lose their father was too much. I told her I would be careful. She nodded slightly, as if she had heard that before, and gently closed the front door.

6

A PEACE SHUTTLE

Early in the morning on Monday, August 28, 1995, I arrived with Dick Holbrooke and the rest of the team at a military airport in Paris, nine days after losing our colleagues on the Mount Igman Road. The mood in our six-person interagency delegation was of grim determination to pick up where Bob and the others had left off. But what were we doing in Paris? A number of us asked each other. We had landed in the French capital apparently for no other reason than for Holbrooke to hang out with Pamela Harriman, the intrepid socialite ambassador and scion of Democratic Party politics, whom Holbrooke described as "brilliant" and insightful. The stop seemed to have little to do with our mission. We had preliminary meetings arranged with the French, one of the Contact Group members, so no harm there. We also had arranged for Bosnian president Izetbegovic, who was on a visit to Paris, to meet us and discuss what an eventual peace document could look like, as well as, most important, the shape of the map of Bosnia.

Holbrooke, as I knew from being at his side for the past year, was not at his best around people like Pamela Harriman. He was effective at many things, but pouring unreciprocated flattery on someone whose approval he was desperately seeking was not one of them. As Harriman, the wartime wife of Winston Churchill's son, the mother of Winston Churchill's grandson, a mistress to numerous men of power and wealth, and the widow of Averell Harriman, put it to Bob Owen, "Dick is very affectionate, but he still hasn't been housebroken."

Both on the airplane and as we settled into our rooms on the second floor at Harriman's residence, I was getting to know Roberts "call-me-Bob" Owen, our team lawyer, team player, and a close friend of Secretary Christopher. Bob was extremely accomplished in his field, the State Department's legal advisor to Secretary Cyrus Vance in the late 1970s, negotiator with Iran for the hostage release in 1980, and a man whose legal mind was coupled with a refreshing down-to-earth modesty. More recently Christopher had him working on the vexing problems within the Bosnian Federation, a shotgun alliance between the Croats and the Muslim communities in Bosnia that required constant marriage counseling. Rumor had it that Secretary Christopher wanted Bob on the reconstituted travel team as his eyes and ears. It was probably true, but Bob also brought to the table a very sensible, straightforward drafting style that would eventually form the basis for the entire Dayton Accords. "It's like writing wills," Bob said about many of the document's provisions and their need for absolute clarity. And while Holbrooke did not choose Bob, he was pleased to have him on the team.

Holbrooke was keenly aware of Bob's closeness to Secretary Christopher and often turned his clumsy efforts at flattery on him. They worked about as well as they did on Harriman. "Bob, this is brilliant!" "Dick, it's not brilliant, it has nothing to do with brilliant. It's not even close to being brilliant. In fact, Dick, it's fairly basic stuff. . . ." Bob kept Dick from using the word *brilliant* for at least twenty minutes, something for which we were all very grateful. Like the rest of us, though, Bob did eventually fall prey to his charm. Such was the Holbrooke force field, where, if nothing else, people would begin to sympathize with this imposing figure who seemed also to possess equally imposing vulnerabilities and insecurities.

I was struck by how carefully Holbrooke selected his small interagency team, going over with me names of people as if the future of the world depended on his choices. He looked for loyalty, or potential loyalty, but he was also on the lookout for particular skills, especially those that he did not have, such as organization, follow-up, and timeliness. He realized that his laserlike focus on an issue at a given moment might leave other crucial problems completely unattended. I was keenly aware of Holbrooke's detractors in Washington and the fact that a negotiator in the field needs backup in the capital, especially when things go wrong. And when it came to Holbrooke, backing him up wasn't always people's top priority.

Dick was particularly cautious about the choice of a representative from the National Security Council staff. When the NSC staff proposed army Brigadier General Don Kerrick to join Holbrooke's team, Holbrooke agreed only after several of us gave Don glowing personal references for his restraint, during the dreaded morning teleconference. "Dick, he never tasks the department. Never!" I lied. I added: "He's a great admirer of yours" (thinking that he could *become* a great admirer), if only Holbrooke could get over the issue of the NSC representative so the rest of us could get back to work. I started getting somewhere with him. "Dick, he thinks you're the only person who really understands what to do in the Balkans," I lied again.

"Okay, I'll try him out." Dick and Don went on to be the closest of friends.

In Paris, Dick was very much in the saddle and enjoying every minute of the ride. He turned Pamela Harriman's ambassadorial residence into the salon of salons, holding court in various rooms of the mansion with different personages. An upstairs drawing room was converted to a map room. General Wesley Clark, accompanied by several junior military staffers, spread an enormous map of Bosnia from wall to wall, "actual size," I quipped to Bob Owen as we walked in for a discussion along the fringe of the map with President Izetbegovic and his foreign minister Muhamed (Mo) Sacirbey.

With his American-accented English and media presence, Sacirbey had become the spokesperson for the Bosnians on CNN and other networks. Sacirbey had played linebacker for Tulane University, apparently without a helmet, as Holbrooke would quip to me after many difficult meetings with him.

Some people could not stand to be in the same room as Sacirbey. But not Holbrooke. As I explained to him, "When we see a problem person we see a problem. But when you see a problem, you see an opportunity." For what opportunity, of course, Holbrooke wasn't quite sure, but he knew that he would need every asset, every relationship he could muster for the battles to come.

On Monday afternoon, CNN broke into its regular programming to report what became known as "the market bombing." A 120mm mortar shell had hit a line of civilians in a Sarajevo market, resulting in heavy casualties; the Serbs claimed the Bosnian had done it to their own people to gain sympathy. CNN's live footage brought the scene not only into Americans' living rooms but also into every senior official's office in Washington. There would be a response.

Our team began manning phones to Sarajevo and Washington. Holbrooke made numerous calls to Strobe Talbott and Sandy Berger while Wes Clark kept in close contact with the Joint Chiefs. It was clear that President Clinton was not going to punt on this one, and Holbrooke saw an opportunity—albeit a high-risk one—in having bombs fall on the Serbs in Bosnia as we met with Milosevic on Wednesday night, two days away. Holbrooke asked each of us, as if we were a lobbying firm ahead of an important congressional vote, whom we had called to make sure the bombing would happen. I did not have anyone I could call to ensure that President Clinton's response to the market attack in Sarajevo would be in the form of air strikes against the Serbs.

"Who were you talking with?" Holbrooke asked, having noticed me on my cell phone.

"I was talking with Phil Goldberg," I replied. Keeping our team in Washington up-to-date on what we were doing in Paris was one of those chores that had to be done.

"Chris, I love Phil. You know that. But there is nothing he can do from his position to . . ."

A few hours later, U.S. fighter-bombers were in the air out of bases in Italy, hitting Serb targets with a sustained force that had not been seen before. The UN peacekeepers, under British General Rupert Smith's command, had been pulled into more defensible positions, thus minimizing the possibility that Serb militias, as they had done in the past, would grab peacekeepers and use them as "human shields."

We discussed the onward leg of the mission to Belgrade and whether it would be feasible while NATO aircraft, mainly American, were hitting Bosnian Serb targets as never before. My own view, and Holbrooke's, too, was that there was never a better time to go to Belgrade.

Milosevic greeted our delegation warmly as we filed into his large, ornate receiving room. Standing next to him was his foreign ministry advisor, Bojan Bugarcic, who spoke perfect English. Milosevic directed us to a large circle of heavily stuffed brown chairs and couches gathered around two glass-topped coffee tables. A waiter in a white jacket appeared almost instantly to offer us the choice of mineral water or numerous Balkan fruit drinks. Holbrooke, thirsty from the plane ride in from Paris, looked at the selection of waters and other drinks and asked Milosevic: "May I take two?"

"Ambassador Holbrooke, please take three."

Milosevic began with expressions of condolences on the death of Bob Frasure, with whom he had spent many hours over the course of the spring. The Serb leader was dressed in a double-breasted blue blazer and red tie. I sat next to Holbrooke, occasionally looking over at him as

Milosevic continued his sorrowful eulogy for Bob. I knew well that Bob would not have reciprocated the kind words, because, like the rest of us, he held Milosevic accountable for the destruction of Yugoslavia and its peoples. Listening to Milosevic I realized how successful Bob had been in building a relationship with such a person, and how that relationship, even after his death, was now going to help us get to yes.

Holbrooke introduced each member of the delegation: Jim Pardew from the Pentagon, Wes Clark from the Joint Chiefs, General Don Kerrick from the NSC, Bob Owen, and me, whom he described to Milosevic as someone close to Bob Frasure. Milosevic looked us all over carefully. I'm sure he recalled my previous meeting in the fall, when in response to his point that the United States could not maintain sanctions against Yugoslavia because of lost business opportunities, I responded somewhat curtly that the United States could keep up the sanctions against Serbia for decades if need be. Look at Cuba, I said, thinking perhaps that finally we had discovered a purpose in the Cuban embargo. That comment had not been well received, but, on the other hand, Milosevic seemed to have a pretty thick skin.

Milosevic, as Bob had long believed and I was now convinced, was ready to settle. He had not lifted a finger for the Bosnian Serb forces during their defeat in the spring and summer months, and now he wanted to get on with the challenge of implementing the Contact Group plan that essentially split Bosnia into two entities, giving the Serbs living there much of what they had wanted. Our concern about Milosevic all along was not whether he could coerce the Bosnian Serbs, but whether he could actually be accepted as their representative when the endgame came. The relationships between the Serb nationalists in Bosnia and former communist power structure types like Milosevic was far more complex than anyone in the West could understand. Milosevic was no one's favorite among the Serbs. For the nationalists, he was a former communist, and for the former communists, he was a nationalist. In fact, Milosevic's loyalties stayed very close to home, but he wanted respect from us, and was clearly prepared to pay to get it in the form of a Bosnian settlement.

Though NATO bombing of Serb positions was front-page news throughout the world, Milosevic never mentioned it in our initial discussions. He turned the subject to the negotiations:

"I have been busy," he said, reaching inside his blue blazer to pull out a piece of paper. Its contents were astounding. Milosevic had reached an agreement with the Bosnian Serb leadership, witnessed by the patriarch of the Serbian Orthodox Church, to make him, Milosevic, their sole representative for the purpose of the negotiations. I was shocked at the sweep of what had just happened. Milosevic gave the Serbian-language documents to Holbrooke; I was sitting next to him and took it from his hand to see what was actually in it. The one-page paper was extraordinary and I knew immediately it meant that our negotiation would succeed where others had failed because Milosevic had finally acknowledged or at least created via the patriarch the linkage to the Bosnian Serbs that was necessary for negotiation.

A sustainable peace process, which had eluded us for years, was now at hand, and in fact in my hand. A war that had claimed so many lives, and was claiming more lives that very night, could really be brought to an end. As I made my way slowly through the brief Cyrillic text and studied the scrawled signatures to try to decipher whose was whose, I thought about Bob. Holbrooke listened as I read out a translation (with Milosevic trying to help me) and finally said to me: "I wish Bob were here to see this." I knew I would choke up if I tried to say something. I just nodded. After years of this war, we were going to be the ones to end it.

The meeting continued for hours, until well after midnight. Conversations with Milosevic never followed a linear course. They flowed into historical discussions about the Ottoman occupation of the Balkans, World War II, then New York City, where he spent his youth as a Yugoslav banker. Milosevic would then describe his (always grandiose) plans for the Yugoslav economy, drift back to New York, and so forth. Side conversations began to ensue and I got to know Bojan, the son of a diplomat, as we talked about attending international schools around the world.

Dick ducked out for the occasional phone call, which he would invariably describe as coming from the White House, though most of us suspected they were from his wife, Kati, in New York. Milosevic was at pains to differentiate himself from the Bosnian Serbs, at one point to our amusement calling them "shit." That was a reminder for me that no matter how well one learns a foreign language (and Milosevic's English was pretty good), swearing in it can never be mastered.

When the meeting finally adjourned, we left for the Hyatt hotel on the other side of the Drina River and were met by the first of many gaggles of reporters that would follow us through the entire shuttle. The press was always curious about the marathon meetings with Milosevic and what was really being discussed. Were we giving away Bosnian towns to the Serbs? I watched Holbrooke deliver his lines and marveled at his capacity to speak in complete paragraphs without pause, while saying so little about the talks that had lasted eight entire hours with Milosevic. He would also give the press some memorable lines that would drown out everything else, such as "We come on a mission of peace at a moment of war." It was a line he had not rehearsed nor to my knowledge used in any of the meetings with anyone. In a stroke, it captured the essence of our endeavors and of our mission. When someone has a line like that, who cares if he reveals nothing else?

What Holbrooke did not tell the press that day was the plan hatched with Milosevic to have the three foreign ministers go to Geneva and announce an agreement of some kind. To Holbrooke the exact kind of agreement was secondary. He would figure out that detail later. "Remember, Chris, logistics are always more important than substance. That will come later." Milosevic had pressed Holbrooke for a conference to decide the entire issue of Bosnia, but Holbrooke, having just met with

Izetbegovic in Paris, knew that the Bosnians were not ready for a high-wire act of that kind.

After Belgrade we dashed off to Zagreb, Croatia, where we met President Franjo Tudjman to brief him on the discussions in Belgrade and to convince him of the value of holding a foreign ministers' meeting in Geneva. Unlike Milosevic, who would be accompanied by a maximum of two or three people in his meetings with us, Tudjman would assemble his entire cabinet, including a formal arrival ceremony at the presidential palace. The ceremony never came off the way Tudjman's protocol staff planned. Each time we arrived at the front entrance, manned by guards in uniforms that resembled something from an overbudgeted version of *The Wizard of Oz*, Holbrooke would step into the entryway, Tudjman and his retinue visible far ahead in the palatial greeting area, and immediately turn left to use the men's room while the president and the entourage stood waiting. After Holbrooke answered nature's call three visits in a row, the protocol chief implored me to suggest that he use the facilities at the airport, even though our cars pulled up to the plane on the tarmac, thus requiring another stop in the terminal building. It wasn't going to happen. I gave it a shot with Holbrooke, but he wasn't interested. "Chris, I appreciate your attention to detail. But this is too much."

Airplane flights always allowed for the best staff meetings even though there was no table and people had to perch on seats facing the wrong way or sit on the floor of the aircraft to hear. As we departed Zagreb that first visit, Holbrooke discussed how we had secured agreement from all parties to hold a foreign ministers' meeting, but there was no agreement on what was to be done at it. Holbrooke turned to Bob Owen and said, "Let's do up a document. We'll call it Agreed Principles, and it will list the elements of the Contact Group plan, that is, things that have really already been agreed." Thinking about the agonizing Washington clearance process, I asked how we could get that cleared in just a couple of days, moreover while we were on the road. "Don't be a typical Foreign

Service officer," he said. This was a favorite epithet of Holbrooke's. "You know the only thing worse than not having guidance from Washington is having guidance from Washington. Draw it up, Bob," he said. With a glance at me he added, "I'll take care of Chris's concerns about Washington clearances."

7

UNFINISHED BUSINESS

Since arriving in Paris on August 28, the team had already visited Zagreb, Belgrade, and Sarajevo as well as Geneva, Berlin, Paris, and Brussels in a frenetic effort to gain support for the "Agreed Principles" that we intended to announce in Geneva on September 8. But on Labor Day, September 4, 1995, with only three days until Geneva, I convinced Holbrooke to add two more stops en route to Ankara, Turkey. Based on a visit that the DOD representative Jim Pardew and I had made to Skopje on Friday, September 1, we were also going to stop in Athens and then Skopje to try to close the "interim accord," a set of mutual obligations to be agreed to between Greece and Macedonia that would result in an end to the Greek economic embargo on Macedonia, which was strangling that small and troubled country in the south Balkans.

The problem between the two countries might seem like a joke in the heads of a late-night comedian, but in the Balkans there was nothing funny about it. Greece objected to Macedonia's use of a name that first appeared in Greek antiquity and had since served as a place-name for an area that included northern Greece and southernmost Yugoslavia. Macedonia was the name of Alexander the Great's home kingdom, the Macedonians his tribe. When Tito fashioned Yugoslavia, he recognized that the Slavic people living in that southernmost part since around A.D. 700 (a thousand years after Alexander the Great) were not Serbs, as the Serbs were inclined to insist; however, neither were they Bulgarians, as the Bulgarians insisted. They were Macedonians, that is, people living in a region known as Macedonia.

The Greeks accepted the creation of a "Republic of Macedonia" as long as it was a part of Yugoslavia. But when Yugoslavia broke up and the Macedonians like other republics created their own state via a referendum, the Greeks objected that an independent Republic of Macedonia was in effect a heist of intellectual property rights from ancient Greece and might imply a territorial claim on northern Greece, also a part of geographical Macedonia.

The Macedonians were having their own bout with nationalism and did not help matters by the adopting of a flag that was based on a symbol from ancient Macedonia unearthed some years before in an archaeological dig near the northern Greek city of Thessaloniki. They were stirring up bitter memories among Greek-Americans, many of whom had been driven from their homes during the Greek Civil War in 1947. It was a war that had engaged a (largely) Slavic minority in northern Greece, in line with Tito's ambitions to stretch his communist Yugoslav state all the way to the Aegean Sea. Whether it was a fight that dated from Alexander or represented a modern territorial dispute, the problem was not going away on its own. Meanwhile, Greece had imposed a blockade aimed at forcing the Republic of Macedonia to change its name and constitution and to abandon the symbols from the time of ancient Greece.

By 1995, the issue had been mediated for some two years by both former U.S. secretary of state Cyrus Vance, representing the United Nations, and Matthew Nimetz, a New York–based lawyer representing the United States. The two distinguished negotiators had worked tirelessly to get Athens and Skopje to negotiate an interim accord, one whose purpose was not the final resolution of the "name issue" but to put to rest other issues that made the narrower question of the name so intractable.

The United States had a special interest because Macedonia was the one country in the Balkans in which the United States had agreed, primarily as a gesture of solidarity with beleaguered Europeans who were already deployed in Bosnia and Croatia, to station forces under UN command. Progress in Macedonia's relationship with its southern neighbor would strengthen Macedonia's stability and viability, and help it overcome its status as the most fragile new state in the Balkans.

Vance and Nimetz had taken the talks as far as they could, but they now required an endgame. However, there was a serious problem. Macedonia would not sit down with the Greeks to negotiate the final points of the plan unless the Greek embargo was lifted. The Greeks would not sit down with the Macedonians unless the embargo remained in effect. For some two months, little progress was achieved.

Just before we were to head to Paris and on to the Balkans, I had gone to see Holbrooke late at night, knocking perfunctorily on his door and walking in. It was the usual dark and forbidding office, with the table lights on and the overheads off. I told him I had an idea for how to break the Greek-Macedonian impasse. He was reading a memo on Bosnia.

"Chris, I don't have time for Macedonia now." He was tired of listening to me about Macedonia. Admittedly, I had become a little obsessed with the idea that Macedonia-Greece was the low-hanging fruit of the Balkans, a place where most pickings seemed to require an extension ladder, but Dick didn't mind people taking another run at him. He did it all the time to them.

"Dick, we could solve this. Can you imagine what it will look like if our delegation swept into Skopje and Athens and came away with an agreement, a breakthrough that would really give us momentum for Bosnia?"

He looked up from what he was reading. I think I had him on the words *momentum* and *Bosnia*.

"Go on," he said cautiously.

"Here's the idea: During our trip to the Balkans Jim and I will break off from the delegation to go to Skopje and offer the Macedonians to arbitrate the last few issues, based on consultations with them and the Greeks. The Macedonians and Greeks would then meet in New York for what would essentially be a one-day signing ceremony. No one, given the time zone differences, would remember whether the embargo was lifted in the morning or the afternoon. The sticking point is [Macedonian president] Kiro Gligorov. If he agrees, I would propose you head to Athens and Skopje and seal the deal."

"How will Matt and Cy react?" said Holbrooke, his wheels turning.

"I've talked to Matt. He told me we are down to a few issues in the text, none of them deal breakers, really small items."

"Chris, if there is one thing I thought I had taught you, it is that there is no such thing as a small issue in the Balkans. Okay, what are they?"

In seconds Holbrooke's laser focus took him from barely knowing where Macedonia was on the map, to being a full-fledged expert on the minutiae of the Vance-Nimetz interim accord.

"The problem is that every time Matt and Secretary Vance"—I could not refer to the former secretary of state, one of the most distinguished Americans alive, by his first name—"receive a proposed solution from the Greeks, the Macedonians object, and vice versa."

"So you would arbitrate it?"

I leaned over from my chair and put both my hands on his desk: "No, not me. *You!* Based on conversations with the parties that *you* would have on the next trip. They would know what the ideas are, where we were heading with them, and accept them when presented with them at the negotiation-signing ceremony."

"Marshall okay with this?" Holbrooke asked, referring to Marshall Adair, head of the Greek office in the State Department. I told him he was (which he was, sort of). I asked Holbrooke whether I should brief Matt Nimetz. He thought for a second, tilting back on his chair behind his desk, his hands behind his head, and his elbows spread from what seemed like one end of the room to the other.

"No, I'll handle that."

On September 1, 1995, I went to Skopje to meet with Macedonian foreign minister Stevo Crvenkovski and President Gligorov. Jim Pardew from the Office of the Secretary of Defense, who was also a bit of a Macedonian enthusiast, accompanied me on the two-hour flight.

I always enjoyed going to Skopje. I had visited it on several occasions since becoming the office director for the Balkans a year before. It was a quiet town, an outpost of the Ottoman Empire whose downtown was dominated by a hill and a Turkish fortress, much as it had been for four centuries. A stone bridge connected the older part of the town with the newer section, built after an earthquake had devastated the city in 1963. The bridge had survived for centuries, a testimony to Turkish engineering. Grainy old photographs on display in the ethnographic museum revealed its multiple uses. During late-nineteenth-century uprisings the Turks hanged insurgents off the sides, a warning to potential recruits to the cause.

Macedonia was truly off the beaten track for journalists and officials alike. Under the steady leadership of its octogenarian president, Kiro Gligorov, it had managed to gain its independence without a shot being fired. But its serious issues included an unhappy ethnic Albanian community in its western regions, bordering Albania and Kosovo; an unmarked border with Serbia proper on the north; Bulgarian neighbors to the east who maintained that Macedonians were Tito-ized Bulgarians and spoke a language which was a slightly Serbianized Bulgarian; and, of course, the issue with its southern neighbor, Greece.

Jim and I arrived at Gligorov's downtown office, part of the parliament building. It was a large, musty structure with red carpets that slid with every footstep over the marble floor. I went over the remaining points in the text with Foreign Minister Crvenkovski and President Gligorov, explaining how I would propose to resolve them, one in favor of them, the other in the Greeks' favor, and so forth. Gligorov said very little, but both men agreed to the approach—provided, of course, that the Greeks would, too. I assured them that we had worked with the Greeks and would have them fully on board. President Gligorov explained the risk for his government, which had made it clear it would never sit down with the Greeks and negotiate under the pressure of an economic embargo. To do so, even for a day, would be politically risky. I assured him that the Greeks wanted to get through this as much as he did. "How can I trust them?" he countered. "You don't have to," I explained. "That is our problem, not yours. Your problem is whether you trust us." I was rather proud of that line, and thought I might file it away for future use. So far, so good, I thought, as we headed back out to Skopje Airport.

Jim and I flew on to Belgrade, where a U.S. Embassy car was waiting to drive us to Milosevic's office to catch up to Holbrooke. We walked into the middle of a session and Holbrooke asked how it had gone. "We got it," I answered. Milosevic was left to wonder what I was talking about.

During a break I gave Holbrooke more details and reminded him that he had to call Nimetz and Vance, that we didn't want to look like we were poaching, worse yet have them hear anything on the news. Vance's and Nimetz's sensitivities aside, an announcement on the interim accord would be a powerful signal that our team meant business. It would set us up as different from the parades of negotiators that came before us. Greek-Macedonian issues did not amount to much in the international press, but everyone in the Balkans would take notice.

As the evening came to an end after dinner, Milosevic heard Holbrooke and me talking about the next day's travels. He approached us in his usual emphatic way: "You are completely wrong if you think you can solve that problem."

"Watch us," I replied.

"Take it easy," Holbrooke told me. "It's not over till it's over."

We arrived in Athens and went to see the elderly prime minister, George Papandreou, who looked older than anyone I had ever seen. His young wife, a former flight attendant from Olympic Airlines, attended to his needs as he agreed to our proposal, all the time telling us how untrustworthy the team was in Skopje. Holbrooke turned to me to then explain our reading of the outstanding issues and how we would solve them. I laid out the issues as the prime minister gazed at a wall, seemingly uninterested but reiterating that we could go ahead as proposed. Neither he nor his younger and feistier foreign minister commented on the remaining items. They seemed to want to get out from the embargo they had imposed, perhaps, I speculated to Holbrooke, because it was harming commercial interests in northern Greece.

As we drove back out to the airport, Holbrooke turned operational, wanting to make sure he knew exactly the whereabouts that afternoon of the U.S. chargé d'affaires for Embassy Athens so that he would be available if we needed to get back in touch with the Greeks while in Macedonia.

In Skopje, we went to President Gligorov's residence, away from the downtown, at the foot of Mount Vodno. Holbrooke was in full deal-closing mode as he laid out all the good things that would come with the Greek-Macedonian interim accord, an arrangement that would create a broad foundation for the two countries to normalize on all issues except for Greece's insistence on a name change for its tiny northern neighbor. He said that he would personally make sure an American ambassador was quickly named and dispatched to Skopje. He tried to interest Gligorov in a more direct relationship with Prime Minister Papandreou. Gligorov ignored the offer while he continued to look at Holbrooke carefully, as if sizing him up. I thought at that moment of the asymmetry. For us it was a deal to jump-start our Bosnia shuttle; for Gligorov it could be the future of his country.

The president quickly turned to his favorite set of talking points, his government's strongly held position that the Greek embargo was illegal and would be determined as such in international law. Holbrooke, for whom references to international law never led to any good, immediately returned to the subject at hand, that the Greeks were prepared to meet in New York City in September and sign the interim accord. The Greeks promised the remaining issues would not hold up a signed agreement that day. If Gligorov's government was prepared to do the same, this would be the long-awaited breakthrough.

Gligorov would not allow himself to be hurried, despite Holbrooke's theatrical looks at his watch as he explained the need to leave for Athens and, to a perplexed host, the fact that we could not be late because of the U.S. Air Force's strict rules on crew rest time.

Gligorov would not be pushed, and he began a point-by-point discussion of the issues, and why it would be problematic to expect them to be resolved in a single session. Holbrooke turned to me seated on the couch and in an exacerbated tone whispered: "Chr-is," somehow turning my name into a two-syllable word with the second part slipping into a higher pitch. I motioned with a rolling gesture of my hand to keep at it, that it would be okay. Foreign Minister Crvenkovski, sitting on a couch opposite ours, interjected to say that he knew the text well and that if the Greeks were really ready to accept these points as we had laid them out, then this could indeed be wrapped up in a single session. Holbrooke, who hadn't paid the slightest attention to the foreign minister, turned his full attention to him as if he were a bona fide BFF. He talked about the modalities of the agreement, expressing his personal sympathy and respect for the Macedonian position and for their skepticism about the Greeks. He had instructed our chargé in Athens to stand by the phone and at a minute's notice to go to the Greeks if there was any confusion.

The president, not sure what to make of the fact that some hapless American diplomat was standing by the phone in Athens, nodded approvingly. After forty-five minutes of sizing him up, he had concluded that Holbrooke was a closer, and was not going to allow this one to slip by. He got back into the conversation by agreeing to the plan. Holbrooke turned back to Gligorov, leaving his BFF in midsentence.

And then Gligorov said, "Mr. Holbrooke, I have one more request. Could you leave Mr. Hill here?"

I was slow to pick up on that, since I had been working on a heart attack for most of the meeting. But Holbrooke understood immediately.

"You want Chris as your ambassador here?"

Crvenkovski confirmed that that was what the president had in mind.

"Okay, you got him. I need him for a couple more months on Bosnia, then he'll come here as the first U.S. ambassador. Chris, you have your next assignment!"

"Um, sure, Dick, that would be great," I managed to say, but the craziness had started to get on my nerves. "Would you mind mentioning this to our secretary of state or president, what with them both having a role in this sort of thing? And, by the way, did you ever call Nimetz?" Holbrooke ignored me and turned back to Gligorov and Crvenkovski, dismissing me with a downward chopping motion of his hand.

"Mr. President," he said, "with your permission I would like for Foreign Minister Crvenkovski and I to go out and announce that there will be a meeting on September 13 for the purpose of signing the interim accord."

President Gligorov shot an admiring smile Holbrooke's way and told him to go ahead, still shaking his head in amusement and realizing he had been totally won over.

"Do you have time for lunch?" Gligorov added, mentioning that Holbrooke had talked about needing to get back out to the airport and on our way to Ankara.

"Of course, Mr. President. I would be delighted. As much time as you can spare."

As Dick made the announcement in several quick calls to senior Washington officials (though not, to my knowledge, to Nimetz), I talked to Gligorov and his aides in a reassuring tone. Buyer's remorse is an ever-present danger to a diplomatic deal. The ambassadorship seemed distant and unreal to me, and I felt I knew more about the laborious process of being selected than Holbrooke did, that it might have been one of those last-minute points in a negotiation that helps the atmosphere but is never actually realized. Indeed, it wasn't until mid-November 1995 that the secretary offered me the position. Of course, I was delighted.

8

ON TO GENEVA

The trip to Greece and Macedonia was only part of the itinerary that busy September 4. From Skopje we headed to Ankara for an overnight visit to meet with Bosnian president Izetbegovic and his team and secure his support for our agreed principles, then back to Belgrade to get the same from Milosevic. Nothing was easy.

We were trying to achieve agreement on what was essentially a repeat of the previous summer's Contact Group plan on how Bosnia would be divided 51–49, and spelling out what kind of autonomy the two elements of the federal structures would have would become the first objective of the shuttle. We called the paper that we intended to announce in Geneva on September 8 the "Agreed Principles." Those principles, however, weren't so agreed at first. Izetbegovic reluctantly agreed to the two entities—the Federation and the Sprska Republic—but objected to the name for the latter, since the use of the term *republic* implied sovereignty, or at least the possibility that the Bosnian Serbs would someday achieve it. For his part, Milosevic objected to calling Bosnia a republic and preferred a weaker formulation like *union*, which could suggest more of a confederation than a unitary state. He also insisted that the Serb entity be allowed to refer to itself as a republic, which would give him far more latitude in dealing with the Bosnian Serb leadership.

But Milosevic had also agreed to Bosnia's "present borders" (that is, no land grabs to be given over to Serbia) and "continuing international recognition," a concession to the fact that Bosnia was indeed in existence and that the Serbs recognized this fact.

In Ankara, Izetbegovic agreed to participate in Geneva by sending his foreign minister, Mo Sacirbey, to join the Yugoslav foreign minister, Milan Milutinovic, and the Croat foreign minister, Mate Granic.

As the hour of 10 A.M. on September 8 approached, there was no sign of Sacirbey and Holbrooke was going into full-scale panic mode. Unbeknownst to me, he had had a rough telephone conversation earlier in the morning with Sacirbey, who had just insisted that in the document "Bosnia-Hercegovina" must be called the "Republic of Bosnia-Hercegovina," a change that would be a bridge too far for the Serbs (especially at this late hour).

After that morning phone call—which at the time I knew nothing about—Dick asked me calmly around 9 A.M. to make sure Sacirbey arrived okay. This wasn't the sort of request Holbrooke usually made of me, but I agreed to do so and asked if he would like me to do the same with Milutinovic and Granic. He said no need, so I immediately called the Bosnian mission in Geneva and reached Sacirbey, who assured me he was getting ready and would be there soon. Around 9:30 I called again and was told he had left for the U.S. mission. A few minutes before 10 A.M., there was no sign of Sacirbey and Holbrooke approached me in a rage.

"I asked you to do one thing. One thing. One thing only, to deliver Sacirbey, and he's not here!" His shouting was audible throughout the room as people looked over to see what was going on. On the one hand I thought that at forty-three I was a little too old to be screamed at in a way that I hadn't heard since childhood. His behavior was particularly egregious in that he had not bothered to tell me that he had had a shouting match with Sacirbey minutes earlier over the inclusion of the word *republic*. On the other hand, I composed myself long enough to think about the unimaginable pressure he was under. The press was already there, and if for some reason Sacirbey were not to show it would strike a potential deathblow to his management of the process. A Geneva meeting without the Bosnians would have been a fiasco, and I knew Washington would turn such a disaster into a blame-Holbrooke moment. I had already learned—and would again later—how lonely the position of a special envoy can be. And besides, as Strobe Talbott had told me earlier, "when dealing with Holbrooke, one has to accept the good along with the bad. It is a total package." I decided to stand there and take it, and to assure him I would find Sacirbey.

A minute later Sacirbey walked in, apologizing for being late due to the Geneva traffic. Holbrooke greeted him as a long-lost family member, and I took my seat immediately behind Holbrooke. Holbrooke chaired the meeting, starting with his insistence that Sacirbey, Granic, and Milutinovic shake hands for the assembled press while representatives from the Contact Group, nine seats in all, gathered around a small table.

Holbrooke moved the meeting along quickly, not wanting to give anyone time to think of some way to mess it up. By prior agreement, there was no discussion about the Joint Agreed Principles, while each participant made a short statement. A member from the Yugoslav delegation, the "vice president" of the Bosnian Serbs, Nikola Koljevic, rose to make a statement from the backbench to protest the proceedings, but he was ruled out of order. The press was allowed to photograph the event, and it was over almost before it started.

The shuttle continued for almost three weeks before all the delegations were to head to Wright-Patterson Air Fore Base, near Dayton, Ohio, for still another three-week process, which would finally conclude the "Dayton Peace Accords." Just days after Geneva, on September 13, we were back in the field to negotiate a halt to the bombing in return for lifting the siege of Sarajevo.

Milosevic had asked us to come to his hunting lodge north of Belgrade, in the hilly part of Vojvodina known as Fruska Gora. In this meeting he got right to the point about the ongoing bombing campaign against Serb forces in Bosnia. The campaign had continued since Paris with only a short pause to allow for what turned out to be fruitless conversations between UN commanders and the Bosnian Serb general Ratko Mladic. Milosevic was adamant that the bombing needed to stop if more progress was to be achieved toward a peace accord. He proposed a general cease-fire on the ground. Cease-fires in Bosnia, as in many other places, seldom held for long if no political arrangement quickly followed. We were not ready with a political arrangement. The Joint Agreed Principles had begun the process, but there was much to be done. We proposed instead that Bosnian Serb forces withdraw from around Sarajevo, lifting a siege of that city that had become the longest siege in Europe since World War II.

Milosevic explained that he could not negotiate this on his own. Mladic and Bosnian Serb president Radovan Karadzic would have to do it.

"And they are here."

"Where?" Holbrooke asked in astonishment.

"Over there." Milosevic gestured over his shoulder. "In a villa."

Holbrooke asked for a break and huddled with the team.

"Should we talk with them?"

Everyone agreed with should.

"Should I shake their hand?" Holbrooke asked. I thought it was about as inappropriate a question as I could imagine. Given how far we had gone in just two weeks, that we were standing on the cusp of ending years of brutal killing in the Balkans, and of lifting the siege of Sarajevo, how could he ask whether to shake the hand of people we knew would eventually be in prison if there were any justice in the process?

"Dick, for Christ sake, do it, and let's get on with this and go home." No one disagreed.

As Mladic and Karadzic walked in, each with his own awkward gait, they both looked to me like the Serb peasants they were: Mladic a short, murderous one, and Karadzic a tall, murderous one—the banality of evil, as Hannah Arendt observed at the trial of Nazi Adolf Eichmann in the early 1960s. Holbrooke greeted them as stiffly as possible, though he did shake hands with both. Later a journalist would ask me whether he shook hands with them, and I responded I hadn't noticed.

Mladic acted as though he had been brought there under duress, with Karadzic acting as the conciliator, urging Mladic not to leave and occasionally offering his considered opinion that all the violence was caused by the Muslims and Croats. He explained that the Bosnian Serbs were the victims while maintaining a stranglehold on the lives of two hundred thousand people living in Sarajevo. He frequently invoked the name of Jimmy Carter, who had met with him and other Bosnian Serbs in their "capital" of Pale and made a statement after his talks that had convinced the Bosnian Serbs that he was their friend.

With no progress, the discussions broke for dinner, and I found myself sitting across from Mladic, who remained hunched over his food, chewing on a bone held in his hands, having dispensed with the knife and fork. We talked a little, but he was not interested in substance, asking me gruffly how it was I could speak some Serbian.

After dinner the delegations sat outside on a large veranda. After what we assumed was some prompting from Milosevic, Karadzic surprised us with a proposal that the U.S. side work on a document. If for no other reason than to get away from this miserable Bosnian Serb delegation, all of us—including Bob Owen, Don Kerrick, and Jim Pardew—worked on a statement that in effect meant the Bosnian Serbs would pull their forces from Sarajevo. Discussions over the document went to deep into the night, with Milosevic playing a passive role and Karadzic urging his military colleague to participate with General Wes Clark on defining the weapons to be withdrawn. Holbrooke explained that the bombing would continue unless there was an agreement on Sarajevo. In fact, Admiral Bill Owens, vice chairman of the Joint Chiefs of Staff, had told us a week before that almost all the targets had already been struck, and that at best there were just a few more days before aircrews would in effect be asked to "bomb rubble." Holbrooke had asked for the pace of the attacks to be slowed, a gross interference in operations that was not well received within the military. We knew that unless there was a major decision to start hitting infrastructure and other targets, the bombing was going to be over soon. But Holbrooke wasn't about to reveal that to the delegation.

At 2 A.M. Wes Clark reported that the document was agreed to. Holbrooke had wisely resisted the Bosnian Serb demand that he sign; he did not have Washington's authorization to negotiate such an instrument in the first place. If he tried to send it back for the dreaded clearance process in order to get permission to sign, it would have been returned with numerous proposed changes. But when it was done and sent in as final, no one in Washington, not even the wordsmithing NSC staff, tried to argue.

The Bosnians, however, were another story. When we met with them two days later in the war-torn city of Mostar, some two hours south of Sarajevo, President Izetbegovic and Prime Minister Haris Silajdzic were visibly angry that the bombing had been halted. I told Holbrooke that I thought they were not convinced that the pullback would be for real, and that their opposition would cool in the days ahead. Holbrooke was sufficiently alarmed that he asked Bob Owen and me to accompany Silajdzic back to Sarajevo over the same road that Bob Frasure and the others had been killed on a couple of weeks before. As we walked to the vehicle, Holbrooke gave Bob and me tips on how to handle Silajdzic, seemingly oblivious to the fact that we were being asked to go over a mountain road whose condition had caused the fatal accident involving our colleagues.

Bob and I sat with Silajdzic in the backseat of the SUV and talked about everything under the sun—his time in the United States, his interest in Turkey, even his academic work on Albanians, a subject on which

I was able to keep up my end of the discussion. We slowly made our way up to Mount Igman and then down to Sarajevo below, and stopped at the spot where the French armored personnel carrier had fallen off the road. I looked around at what a prosaic place it was; nothing special, as we looked at the scrub pine. The Bosnian leaders did not have much good to say about Frasure, because in trying to get something done, Bob had also talked to the other side. Reflecting on our conversations in Mostar, it looked like we were in for some of the same treatment. That evening we had dinner with Silajdzic at a Sarajevo restaurant where the U.S. ambassador, John Menzies, who had lived for months under Serb shelling, joined us.

Sarajevo was a proud city, one of the great sites of European civilization, a meeting between East and West; in less than thirty minutes one could have walked from the Habsburg Empire to the Ottoman Empire. But now whole parts of it lay in ruins. The old Turkish library was a pile of rubble after a direct hit by Serb artillery. The Hotel Evropa, my favorite place to stay when I visited during the 1970s, also was a ruin. I wondered if it would ever be rebuilt. The Holiday Inn, where I had spent a couple of days the previous January, was shot through by snipers firing automatic weapons from a street known as "sniper alley." The president's building, a stately old stone edifice built in a grand Habsburg style, was surrounded by sandbags and barriers. Nothing in the city had been painted in years, and many of the trees that had adorned its boulevards had been cut down for desperately needed firewood. Like a city hit by a natural calamity, it begged the question of whether it was worth rebuilding.

The next morning, an embassy vehicle drove us out to the airport, across the empty runway, still not cleared for aircraft use, and then back onto the dirt road, and finally up to the top of the mountain, where a French helicopter was waiting. We flew down from the mountain, hugging the tops of the trees as we made our way out to the Drina River valley and then the coast to meet up with a small military plane that would catch up to Holbrooke and the rest of the team, now arriving in Belgrade, whom we could debrief about our conversations with the Bosnians.

Owen and I accompanied Holbrooke and the rest of the team back into Sarajevo two days later on the first plane to use the newly opened airport. With the cease-fire implemented, supplies began flowing into the city. As we emerged from the cars in front of the presidential building, a crowd had begun to form and we could hear applause as we made our way inside. By the time we emerged after a lengthy and again disagreeable meeting with Izetbegovic, who was demanding more NATO air action against the Serbs, the crowd outside roared its approval. We all were moved, Holbrooke almost to tears. I told him to wave at them, and he finally did, awkwardly and reluctantly. He knew, as did the rest of us, that there was much to be done before taking any bows.

By the end of October we had secured still another document: Further Agreed Principles. The document was similar in its brevity to the Agreed Principles, but instead of showing how Bosnia would be divided, this one demonstrated how the country would be united by joint institutions, including a collective presidency and a national parliament. The Serbs hated the draft, and the Bosnians were not enthusiastic either (largely because with every document the chance of restarting a bombing campaign receded), but by the time we had brought them all around a table, this time in New York, they had agreed. All that remained was to agree to a cease-fire and head to Wright-Patterson in Ohio, our chosen site for the peace talks.

The story of the Dayton Peace Accords, the cliffhangers, the all-nighters, has been told and retold, most authoritatively by Holbrooke himself in his book *To End a War*. The endgame in the Bosnian war that took us most of September and October to secure agreement on included the lifting of the siege of Sarajevo and a cease-fire as we got ready to head to peace talks in Dayton. In Dayton itself, we worked out the constitution to allow the agreed principles to be implemented, and finally agreed on a map and a unified Sarajevo.

Dayton had its painful moments. Holbrooke, to everyone's consternation (especially Warren Christopher, who visited the talks several times), had invited his journalist wife, Kati Marton, to attend the negotiations, often sending her on walks with Haris Silajdzic and other senior interlocutors. And when David Rohde, a U.S. journalist back in Bosnia, had rented a vehicle to head into Bosnian Serb territory to look for mass grave sites, he was arrested by members of a local Bosnian Serb militia unit. We approached Milosevic for help in releasing the journalist, and he made calls back through his security services to find the hapless journalist and return him to Sarajevo. Holbrooke brought Kati to see Milosevic and seek his help in the name of the Committee for the Protection of Journalists.

At one morning staff meeting, after a particularly short night of sleep, Holbrooke mentioned an idea to which I responded, "We'll put it in Kati's talking points." This sarcastic comment earned me a trip to the woodshed. As Holbrooke excoriated me, I did nothing except bite the inside of my cheek, shake my head, and walk out. He was in charge of the talks, and their failure would not be laid at anyone's doorstep except his own. I respected that fact, but some of his actions were becoming hard to take.

Dayton was Holbrooke's signature work. One of the greatest diplomats of his time would be known for an agreement among warring factions in a Balkan country no one had ever heard of before or has much since. Yet Holbrooke understood, and had the capacity to make others understand, the importance of what he was doing in a broader context. With Europe and the United States drifting apart, he brought them closer together. With questions emerging about U.S. leadership in the world, he demonstrated it was alive and well. With concepts of universal justice emerging on the international stage, he brought them to the practical world, where they have to live. And to diplomats everywhere, he showed that the profession was also alive and well, and that courageous and driven individuals like Dick Holbrooke could make a huge difference.

An hour before the initialing of the agreement, Holbrooke asked me to make sure all was good with the Serb delegation, which had made the most last-minute concessions. I went over to Milosevic's suite and asked him how the Serb delegation was holding up.

"Well, I'm very happy," Milosevic said, "but [the head of the Bosnian Serbs, Momcilo] Krajisnic is not."

"Where is he?" I asked.

"In a coma," he said with a shrug. "It's all right, not your problem."

I told Holbrooke that everything was a go. Krajisnic was not pleased, but Milosevic would initial for the Serb delegation and he acted like he couldn't care less what the Bosnian Serb leader was thinking. The deal was done. A war that had seen hundreds of thousands of people killed and wounded and millions displaced from their homes was over.

"Then let's get over to the ceremony," Holbrooke responded while putting his tie on, fumbling with it in the anticipation of something we had waited so long for.

We walked out excitedly from the building that housed our delegation. "Are we late?" Holbrooke asked as we picked up the pace. The day-in, day-out tension of the last few months wouldn't allow us to relax. We began to jog the three hundred yards to the building, and then, for no apparent reason, with a hundred yards to go we started sprinting, racing each other until we got to the entrance, exhausted again.

9

"YOUR BEAUTIFUL COUNTRY"

Holbrooke kept on running and soon left the government after Dayton, waiting for another job in the Clinton administration, which finally came when he was named U.S. ambassador to the United Nations in 1999. I remained as the director for the Balkans in the State Department and turned my attention to preparing for my next assignment as the first U.S. ambassador to Macedonia. I began reading everything I could get my hands on about Macedonia, truly an example of what Churchill had once said of the Balkans, that it has produced more history than can be consumed. I started a Slavic language course, the purpose of which was to convert my Serbian into Macedonian, but the consequence of which seemed more that I lost my Serbian without gaining an equal amount of Macedonian. But as the implementation of the Dayton Peace Accords got under way, my office and I were pulled into helping the team turn hastily drafted accords into a functioning agreement on the ground, and shepherding visitors.

Since the United States was a major part of the agreement, contributing the largest troop contingent and providing key civilian personnel, soon planeloads of members of Congress and staff delegations began to descend on Bosnia, especially on Tuzla, where most of the U.S. troops were based.

Tuzla is a historic Bosnian town, an industrial city some two hours' drive north of Sarajevo. Many of its Ottoman Turkish roots are very much exposed in the form of medieval architecture, narrow stone streets, high walls and large mosques and tall minarets. During Ottoman times it was a major producer of salt. It was not far from Serb lines to the east, now renamed the inter-entity boundary line, but unlike Sarajevo, Tuzla had not been damaged during the war. The U.S. chose to make Tuzla the main base for several technical reasons, but primarily because of its long airstrip, a legacy of the Yugoslav air force. I had been there two months before, in January 1996, when President Clinton came for an early visit with the troops and to meet the Bosnian government leadership. During that visit, he sensed the bleakness of the base and its immediate surrounds on the outskirts of the city, recalling for the troops the movie *Groundhog Day* to express empathy for the boredom they must all be enduring at seeing every day pretty much as the previous. What I saw in January was a military base that was very much a work in progress. It was abuzz with the sound of truckloads of gravel being dumped on the ubiquitous mud that seemed knee-deep everywhere, augmented by a midwinter thaw. The mud was a metaphor for the quagmire that many pundits and opposition politicians believed that our participation in Dayton Peace Accords would become. The administration had assured critics of Dayton that U.S. troops would remain in country for only twelve months (a departure date that would have conveniently coincided with the November 1996 presidential elections), but a quick glance at the buildup in Tuzla made clear that we were planning to stay much longer.

On March 26, 1996, I was the State Department representative accompanying First Lady Hillary Clinton who was making her own visit to Bosnia. Her plane was filled with an assortment of White House aides for whom adventure travel to places like Bosnia was not something they did every day. She was also accompanied by well-known print and television journalists including Andrea Mitchell, an abundance of U.S. military escorts, lots of security agents, her daughter, Chelsea, and entertainers Sheryl Crow and Sinbad, who had donated their time to come along and entertain the troops at USO shows. The first lady's primary agenda was to visit the troops, but she also was scheduled to meet with leaders of Bosnia's emerging civil society, including some of Bosnia's nascent women's groups, among which were the widows of the Srebrenica massacre who barely nine months before had staggered across Serbian lines from that eastern enclave, their husbands having been rounded up and executed by Serb paramilitaries.

We overnighted at Ramstein Air Base in Germany and early the next day boarded a C-17 military transport for the final two-hour leg to Bosnia. Having visited there during the war, I didn't think much about security now that the fighting was over. I was more curious about what the Tuzla base would look like after two months, the first U.S. military presence in Bosnia, and most importantly whether Ambassador John Menzies had been successful in bringing the Bosnian women's groups onto the base for the meeting with the first lady.

As our descent began, I could feel the g's associated with a corkscrew landing. Typical of a military flight, there was not the same level of discipline in fastening seat belts as there is in a commercial flight. Despite the turbulence of the landing pattern, people were standing around in the enormous cavern of the aircraft's hold, excited at the prospect of soon landing in Bosnia. I ventured over to listen to a member of the security detail briefing the first lady and her team on the situation we would likely encounter on the ground. As she did for every briefing she received, she listened attentively, glancing at her reading materials as he talked and talked. I found myself almost rolling my eyes as the briefer went on and on about the possibility of snipers and what the plan of action would be (essentially, making a beeline to the armored vehicles parked nearby). As the briefing continued for what seemed like half an hour, one of the journalists, a little worried, asked me if it was going to be that dangerous. I explained I was not going to contradict the briefer, but, whispering, I told him I seriously doubted we would encounter any such threat. For heaven's sake, I explained, it was a U.S. military base with thousands of troops, where there had not been a single such incident in the three months they had set up camp. He was relieved, but those more attentively listening to the briefer were not, as they contemplated that soon they could be running for their lives across an open tarmac à la "sniper alley" in Sarajevo.

There of course were no snipers, and as the nervous passengers exited from the rear of the aircraft off an enormous steel ramp that could handle tanks and other tactical vehicles, we were greeted by a group of Bosnian children in colorful native dress. Hope none of them is a sniper, I thought. They presented Mrs. Clinton with bright bouquets of spring flowers that were quickly gathered up by aides while the first lady patted the children on the head. She wanted to spend more time with them, but was urged to keep moving by her security detail, which was bent on getting her to the safety of an armored SUV. The U.S. troops' commander General Nash was there, as was Ambassador Menzies, and having delivered the women leaders to the community center, we soon began a packed schedule of meetings: first, the Bosnian women's groups, then soldiers, then a helicopter ride to another base to see more soldiers, a demonstration of remotely guided robots that could inspect potential bombs and booby-traps, a visit to an empty but thoroughly prepared field hospital whose doctors briefed her on their capabilities for handling complex surgeries. Finally, under an enormous green tent, we were treated to a Sinbad comedy monologue and a Sheryl Crow concert that culminated in several of her top hits, including a rendition of "Strong Enough" that she serenaded to the senior enlisted NCO as the soldiers roared their approval. The visit seemed over before it began by the time we made our way back to the airstrip and boarded the C-17 for the flight to Germany. But the threat of snipers seemed to be all most people could remember.

The U.S. Senate confirmed me as the first ambassador to Macedonia in June 1996. The procedure had gone smoothly even though the

Greek-American community had its continued reservations about sending an ambassador to Macedonia. As the Senate was about to clear the nomination, Senator Mitch McConnell (R-KY) placed a hold to protest the administration's decision to put U.S. troops in Macedonia under the command of the United Nations. It was, so I was told, "nothing personal," and therefore something the administration could work to have lifted.

The problem with a "hold" is that no one can be sure when the senator will release it. Senator McConnell did not have a record for keeping holds indefinitely, but the reason for the hold took some time to decipher, starting with the fact that at the time Senate rules did not require that a senator acknowledge placing a hold. When it was finally revealed after a few days that McConnell, via one of his staff members, had done it, the State Department's Congressional Office went into action, first by blaming the victim: me.

"Do you have some problem with Senator McConnell you have not revealed to us?" they asked me.

"Um, not that I am aware of," I answered, racking my brain to recall whether I had ever met the senator on a congressional delegation and whether I could have done anything to offend him.

My father was in Massachusetts General Hospital with pancreatic cancer fighting for his life. He wanted to see his son become an ambassador and there was no way of knowing how long McConnell would continue to place his hold. My family and I remained in limbo. We had half the things in our house packed in anticipation of moving, but we had no idea of when or if we would move to Macedonia. Moving to a different country is bad enough in the best of circumstances, but not knowing was not easy on my kids. As one of my daughters said to me during the ordeal, "Dad, I'm very proud of you, but you have ruined my life."

Three weeks after the nomination was supposed to clear, a deal was struck that involved Senator McConnell lifting his "principled hold" (meaning, nothing personal about me!) in return for the deputy floor leader reading a bloodcurdling speech about the evils of United Nations peacekeeping, followed by a voice vote to approve my nomination. I was in Boston with my dad, now in intensive care with an elaborate oxygen mask and throat tube covering most of his face. He had barely survived an operation on his pancreas, a procedure in which he contracted a life-threatening infection. I leaned over and told him, not knowing if he could hear me. He lifted his right arm off the bed slowly with a clenched fist. Two weeks later his cancer was in remission for what turned out to be two more years.

I arrived in Embassy Skopje, housed in a former nursery school building to which very few ordinary security upgrades had been made. There was no security officer and no marines. It was one of the new embassies that had sprung up like mushrooms after the rains of change washed out both the Soviet Union and Yugoslavia five years earlier. There were only a handful of staff members, including just one officer to manage all the political and economic and commercial relations with Macedonia. There were a couple of administrative officers to oversee the myriad tasks associated with transforming a nursery school into a U.S. embassy, and there were consular operations.

I selected a deputy chief of mission from a list given to me by the State Department's human resources personnel. Paul Jones was in his mid-thirties and had already worked in Latin America, Moscow, and, most recently, Sarajevo. He had wisdom and instincts well beyond his years. I interviewed Paul for what was to be an hourlong meeting. But after hearing him out for a minute, using an old Holbrooke trick I told him, "You're hired. When can you get out there?"

The United States had not recognized Macedonia's constitutional name, the Republic of Macedonia, and instead followed the absurd moniker "the former Yugoslav Republic of Macedonia," or FYROM. It was not only absurd, but most Macedonians found it insulting as well, an excessive effort to placate the Greek public (and Greek-Americans as well). Use of the name Macedonia out of the context of the FYROM absurdity by any U.S. government official would provoke a swift protest against our State Department in Washington, or the U.S. Embassy in Athens.

Often the State Department spokesperson, Nicholas Burns, would be blindsided by a question from a Greek journalist about the use of the name Macedonia by an obscure U.S. official at an obscure international conference somewhere. The journalists would ask, "Does this represent a change of policy?" which of course it did not, a fact that Burns would always confirm. The obscure official would then be hunted down and admonished for such careless nomenclature. With the U.S.-Greek relationship always burdened by Greece's frustrations about the U.S.-Turkish relationship, and by U.S. frustrations with Greece over a wide range of issues, including Greek management of its own terrorist problems, the last thing those working on Greece wanted was still another issue to complicate the relationship. The consequence was that the embassy in Athens became one of the primary enforcers of the name issue.

Meanwhile, in Skopje, I could hardly go around calling the country to which I had been accredited by the name FYROM if I was to have any relationships or influence with anybody in the country. Nobody in Macedonia had any intention of changing the name of the country over Greek sensitivities. I started avoiding using the word FYROM by referring to "your country" or, better yet, "your beautiful country." People liked that at first, but soon understood the gymnastics I was employing to avoid the name issue. "So, Mr. Ambassador, thank you for thinking our country is beautiful. But could you tell us what exactly is the name of our beautiful country?" Finally, after a few months of this, I gave in and started referring to Macedonia as Macedonia. Our embassy in Athens immediately objected, asking whether perhaps the Greek press had misquoted me. I told them no, I was correctly quoted, and that I was done using FYROM. The protests went away, and the press spokesman in Washington began to give such a dry, formulaic response to the Greek journalists that even they got tired of asking. The Greek desk at the State Department ignored the issue, and no one in the front office of the European Bureau complained to me.

Deputy Secretary Talbott came out to Macedonia in March 1998 and gave a serious and scholarly speech at the Academy of Sciences in which he referred to Macedonia. A few protests ensued in Greece, but it was over. I explained to Deputy Chief of Mission Paul Jones, "Sometimes the best way to change a policy is neither to ask for permission or forgiveness, but to just do it."

No embassy works well without its locally hired staff, and in Skopje we had some of the best people I had ever worked with in the Foreign Service. One of them was Mitko Burcevski, who had been hired a few years before when the embassy was a U.S. office run out of our embassy in Belgrade. He had applied for a position as interpreter/fixer while he was an elementary history teacher in Gostivar, a two-hour bus ride from his home in Skopje. When the American Foreign Service officer asked how much notice he needed to give his school, he answered, "Do you have a phone I can use?"

Life in Skopje was remarkably quiet for the first two years. There was good family time as I took my two daughters, Amy and Clara, thirteen and ten, ice skating and skiing in the winter, and in the summer my son Nat would visit from his boarding school in the States. We spent as much time as we could on the shores of Lake Ohrid, a mountain lake in the south of the country whose towns and villages date back to antiquity.

It was a tightly knit embassy, but like many embassies around the world the issues we grappled with seldom seized anyone's attention or imagination in Washington. Rarely did anyone more senior than a desk officer show much interest in the post. Our requests for physical upgrades to what had been a nursery school were politely accepted and filed, as was our request to have marine guards.

10

KOSOVO

"Where It Began and Where It Will End"

In the spring of 1998, the Balkans was set for another convulsion, this time in Kosovo, the Serbian province whose majority population of Albanians chafed at being ruled by Belgrade. Serbs often describe the Battle of Kosovo in June 1389 as the crucible of the Serb nation. They lost to a superior force from the Ottoman Empire, but in the retelling of the story, complete with a martyred Prince Lazar, Serb identity was supposedly born. The actual history of the battle is, of course, more complex. For starters, it is not clear who fought on whose side, though most historians agree that what are now called Albanians almost certainly fought alongside the Serbs and others resisting the Ottoman invasion of the Balkans, not the other way around, as is often explained by the Serbs. Indeed, in the middle of the fifteenth century, Albanians, under the leadership of George Skanderbeg, fought battle after battle against the Ottoman occupation. Every Balkan nationality had its stories of struggle against the Ottoman Empire, but for the Serbs, their struggles seem in their mind's eye to eclipse all others. Outside the town of Nis, four hours southeast of

Belgrade, there sits atop a grassy knoll a round tower some twenty feet high, built by the Turks entirely out of porous concrete—and thousands of skulls belonging to the victims of a Serb uprising in 1805.

The Dayton Peace Accords of November 1995 had reconfigured what was left of Yugoslavia to a rump state consisting of two republics, Serbia and Montenegro. Within Serbia were the autonomous provinces of Kosovo and Vojvodina. As the centerpiece of Serbia's historical narrative, the Serbs would not allow Kosovo to be its own republic, so that it would stay within the Serbian republic.

Yugoslavia's longtime leader Tito, to square the circle of Kosovo's inhabitants having their own rights, had created autonomous provinces. Kosovo would have all the rights and responsibilities of the six republics of Yugoslavia, but those rights and responsibilities would be expressed from within a province belonging to Serbia. As if not to make Kosovo the only such province in Yugoslavia, Tito also gave Vojvodina a similar status. Vojvodina is the part of Serbia north of the Danube and is historically linked to neighboring Hungary, with a substantial Hungarian population. With the departure of German landowners after World War II and the influx of Serbs looking for better agricultural land, Vojvodina had become more Serbianized. The solution: Vojvodina would also enjoy autonomous province status and would, like Kosovo, become one of the eight constituent parts of Yugoslavia.

But Kosovo was having none of it, and pressure for a separate republic intensified as the Dayton Peace Accords, taking up Bosnia, reduced Yugoslavia to a kind of Serbo-Slavia. When Milosevic abolished the Yugoslav constitution and began to centralize powers that had previously been given to the republics and provinces, Kosovo began to stir again.

Albanians were also upset that their issues had not been raised during the Dayton talks, an expectation that had no basis for being met as the Bosnian peace process had never envisioned including the Kosovo situation. I was more aware of Kosovo than some others because I had served in neighboring Albania, but as concerned as I was from several trips there in 1994 and in 1995, I realized that compared to the brutal ongoing war in Bosnia, the issue of Kosovo could not be included in already complex talks. When Albanian-American demonstrators came to the gates of Wright-Patterson Air Force Base to protest that Kosovo was not on the agenda and demanding to meet with the U.S. negotiating team, Milosevic asked Holbrooke to keep me from meeting with them. Not to my surprise, because he was so focused on Bosnia, Holbrooke agreed to Milosevic's request and sent instead the chargé of the U.S. Embassy in Belgrade, Rudy Perina.

By the spring of 1998 it was clear that Kosovo's time in the Balkan Wars had come. As a Kosovo Albanian leader said to me, "It is where it began and where it will end." The proximate cause was the growth of a Kosovar armed resistance movement that was fast looking to remove the Gandhi-like presence of Ibrahim Rugova as the leader of Kosovo's independence aspirations. Holbrooke's first successor in the Balkans was John Kornblum, but by the start of Kosovo's crisis the reins had been handed to Bob Gelbard. Gelbard was a smart Foreign Service officer whose professional experience was primarily in Latin America, dealing with leaderships tied to the narcotics trade. Gelbard had a passion about his work, but in dealing with Balkan leaders, he fell back on his experience in Latin America and treated many as drug lords.

Gelbard's approach to his interlocutors was straightforward and brutally honest, excessively so. In the United States, honesty and clarity are often considered virtues, especially on the public speaking circuit. But to people on the rest of the planet, it can be a mixed blessing at best. And in diplomacy, especially involving mediation, a stray comment can become deadly.

In February 1998, the Kosovo Liberation Army (KLA) was a fast-growing force in the countryside. It had a historical grievance to be sure, but it also had been armed to the teeth with military weaponry looted the previous year during Albania's "pyramid scheme" meltdown. In Albania's case, financial institutions took money from the public and at first paid out enormous dividends. Soon those dividends began to shrink, and within months they had disappeared. When the United Nations imposed trade sanctions against Yugoslavia in 1992, the Italian mafia moved in and the oil companies, complying with sanction resolutions, moved out.

Enormous quantities of gasoline were shipped up the Albanian coast, arriving in the port of Vlora and departing Albania through Lake Shkodra, en route to Yugoslavia. The mafia-controlled oil shipments created other business opportunities, and soon Albania, no stranger to organized crime, was in the clutches of the international mafia. They were not so much Ponzi schemes, which was what the international press had concluded, as they were money-laundering facilities, a fraud committed against naïve Albanians experiencing their first taste of capitalism.

After the Dayton Peace Accords in November 1995, normal international trade was reestablished with Yugoslavia, and the underpinning of those money-laundering facilities in Albania, principally from gasoline smuggling, began to decline through 1996 and 1997 as the big money moved elsewhere. When the larger investment schemes completely collapsed in early 1997, civil unrest broke out in several of Albania's cities. By March, Albania was in complete chaos, as cities began to fall into the hands of well-financed gangs. Government armories were looted and Western embassies began to evacuate their citizens. The U.S. ambassador in Tirana delayed ordering the evacuation in the hopes the situation would improve. Ultimately, the delay resulted in an eventual helicopter evacuation of nine hundred U.S. citizens on what turned out to be one of the most violent days of the disturbances.

From neighboring Macedonia I could see that Albanian government stood on the brink of collapse. By the time order was restored with the help of Italian troops, an estimated three million weapons had been looted, many of them sold to gangs in Kosovo, many of which in turn would soon reemerge as elements of the Kosovo Liberation Army.

The KLA operated sporadically in Kosovo in 1996, but in 1997 attacks on Serb security forces grew more numerous and more deadly. Serb forces responded, and soon Kosovo was engulfed in war. In Macedonia, the public watched with increasing alarm as Kosovo began to descend into chaos.

The KLA, whose ranks of Kosovo patriots also included former smugglers and armed gangs, was careful to keep the identity of its leaders a secret and its politics tightly controlled. Such a level of secrecy helped frame myths that the KLA fighters were Islamic terrorists, Marxist guerrillas, or, in the fertile imagination of Albania haters, both. One fact was clear: Ibrahim Rugova's leadership did not impress the KLA. In part, that was based on Kosovo's clan structures. There were also regional issues at play, but more fundamentally it reflected a growing popular feeling that Rugova's Democratic League of Kosovo (LDK) had become corrupt and unresponsive to the needs of the public, a reputation that also started catching on with Western nongovernmental organizations, which were now done with Bosnia and facing a steep learning curve in Kosovo.

The United States had long considered Rugova the leader of Kosovo's political aspirations. I first met him at the U.S. ambassador's residence in Belgrade in July 1989, just days after Milosevic's infamous visit to Kosovo for the six hundredth anniversary of the great battle, an event that helped drive the Serbs to war. A quiet academic who would not be easily identified as a politician, he spoke in measured tones about the step-by-step process the Kosovars were on, explaining the underground school system his movement had started and funded. Rugova saw little hope in Milosevic but was prepared to meet with him if it could lead to a better outcome.

There are no secrets in the Balkans—it's too small a place—but it was clear that Rugova's aim was complete independence, nothing less. He was nonetheless strategically patient about how and when he could achieve his goal. More fundamentally, he shared with most Albanians in Kosovo a deep trust and abiding faith in the United States.

In February 1998, Special Envoy Gelbard, in a misplaced effort at evenhandedness, condemned Serbian police activities in Kosovo but went on to say that the KLA was a terrorist group, remarking after meeting two members of the KLA, "I know a terrorist when I see one and these men are terrorists."

Gelbard's remarks about terrorism spiked tensions within Kosovo and caused huge concern that the Serbs would view them as a green light to attack the KLA wherever they could find them. In fact, Serb authorities had long viewed the KLA as a terrorist organization, and whether Gelbard's comments had any bearing on the situation is doubtful. But within weeks, the Serbs moved aggressively into the Drenica Valley, the heart of the KLA, and attacked the compound of a known KLA commander, Adem Jashari, where they killed him and his entire family of sixteen, including children.

The Serb action was universally condemned, but Gelbard's own vigorous denunciation of the Serb action, perhaps influenced by his frustration at being blamed for contributing to the Serb rampage, was particularly hard-edged against Milosevic.

An envoy, for which access to all parties is essential, does not always have the luxury of speaking out publicly. That task can be left to all sorts of people in Washington, many of whom rarely travel, let alone have exclusive access to Balkan dictators. I was told that Gelbard compounded his problem during a meeting with Milosevic, his last, when he pounded his fist on the table. He was praised in Washington for his directness, but in Belgrade was shown to the door and never granted another meeting on his own.

With the situation on the ground now deteriorating fast, the Clinton administration had no one who could meet with Milosevic. For many in both the "liberal hawk" and the growing neoconservative movements, lack of access to a dictator was hardly a disadvantage. But Secretary of State Madeleine Albright, who had replaced Warren Christopher in 1997, knew all too well from her days as the U.S. ambassador to the United Nations what her European colleagues thought of intervention on behalf of the Kosovars, whose case they viewed as straightforward separatism, with all that implied in many such situations on the continent, whether in Spain or Northern Ireland. Albright, who personally found Milosevic repulsive, knew that like it or not, we needed an envoy who could talk to him and vigorously follow the negotiating track until it was obvious, or could be made obvious to our allies and partners in the process, that no progress was possible.

In early May, Secretary Albright called me in Skopje and asked if in addition to my duties as ambassador to Macedonia I could take on the full-time job of Kosovo envoy. I was not surprised by the call, having been tipped off that it was coming. I knew it would mean that in splitting my duties I would be spending more time in Kosovo than in Macedonia. I worried whether being a peace envoy between the Serbs and the Kosovo Albanians held much prospect for success. Diplomacy is a little like hitting in baseball. If you succeed one out of three times you are probably doing well. Nonetheless I told the secretary I would do it. Besides, her request didn't seem like an offer I could refuse.

After explaining the impossible situation Gelbard had put himself in with Milosevic (Holbrooke had already done so in great detail and with great zeal), Albright told me she had asked Gelbard to focus full-time on the upcoming Bosnian elections. She requested that I go to London to meet with Holbrooke, who, although now in the private sector, was acting as a consultant with the administration (and would within the next year become the UN ambassador, replacing Bill Richardson). After meeting in London, we would fly to Belgrade, and Holbrooke would reintroduce me to Milosevic.

Dick had been out of the game for two years. He had made lots more money in the private sector, "client skiing," as he explained his duties to me. It was clear that he relished being back and was looking forward to the meeting with Milosevic.

Milosevic greeted Dick and me as if we were long-lost friends. As we walked into the White Palace in Belgrade, he offered a stiff handshake to our highly capable chargé d'affaires, Richard Miles. Milosevic always blamed the local diplomat if he had a problem with another country, and he knew he had a problem with us.

Milosevic gestured to chairs we were familiar with and began to recall all the great times we had had together in Dayton; meanwhile, Dick and I wondered how Richard Miles was taking all this in. We practically fell out of those chairs when Milosevic tried out a joke in his article- and preposition-deprived English: "You know what was most important accomplishment of Dayton?" He was recalling the difficulties we had had with Izetbegovic during the last hectic hours. "Americans," he said, "finally learned what is like to live with Muslims!" The Serb leader then chuckled at his own line.

Holbrooke and I ignored it, and Dick got going: "Mr. President, President Clinton, Secretary Albright, and I"—huh?—"have decided to name Ambassador Hill"—I didn't have that title when I last had met Milosevic, and he looked over at me, nodding approvingly at my new status—"as our new envoy to assist in finding a solution to the Kosovo crisis." I glanced at Milosevic.

Leaning forward, his right hand on his knee, Milosevic responded, "Mr. Richard Charles Albert Holbrooke"—Milosevic enjoyed being one of the only people on earth to know Holbrooke's full name—"there is no crisis. There are just a few Albanian separatists that the American media is fond of talking to, and our security services are dealing with. Do not concern yourself with a crisis."

"Nonetheless," Dick continued, "we believe the situation is becoming more serious, and needs to be addressed, and I hope we can—"

"Mr. Holbrooke, I do not need an envoy. Kosovo is a part of Serbia. It is a *domestic* problem. Serbian people could never accept a foreigner dealing with their own internal problems. Did you not notice that on April twenty-third there was a national referendum and ninety-five percent of Serbs completely rejected any foreign mediation to solve the Kosovo crisis? But I can say to you that Ambassador Chris"—he paused to look at me, and smiled as I cringed—"is welcome anytime to see me, and can go anywhere he wants in Kosovo."

I was on as the mediator despite Milosevic's disclaimer that no mediator was necessary, but I had no great sense of accomplishment. I took over the conversation from there, believing it was not in my interest or anyone else's that Holbrooke be perceived as the envoy, especially as he was not even working for the government at that time.

Our next stop was Kosovo itself. Holbrooke did not know the players there, so it fell to me to introduce him. We visited Rugova in his ramshackle LDK offices, along with other LDK leaders, including Fehmi Agani, the vice president, as well as Rugova's interpreter. Rugova visibly lit up at the prospect of an American envoy based in nearby Skopje and devoted entirely to Kosovo, not Bosnia. We met with Rugova again that afternoon in his home. Rugova always had his television on while he received people in his home. At first I thought it was a precaution against Serb wiretaps, but I later concluded he just liked having the TV on all the time.

Holbrooke proposed an idea we had pursued with Milosevic the previous day: "Would you be willing to come to Belgrade and meet with President Milosevic?" Rugova clearly was not interested and started to express his reluctance, but before I could make the case for the meeting, Holbrooke blurted out another idea: "And after visiting Belgrade, I know that President Clinton would be very interested in meeting you at the White House."

It was the old negotiator trick, to package an unpleasant element with something much more palatable. But, of course, nobody in Washington knew that Holbrooke was going to offer a presidential meeting. Those meetings are the coin of the realm and are not offered lightly. Presidential schedulers—people for whom saying no comes very naturally—are almost as powerful as the person whose schedule they control. But Holbrooke was riding high in the years following Dayton and had no doubt that he could pull it off.

On May 15, I went to Belgrade to be nearby when Rugova met Milosevic for an inconclusive meeting. On May 28 Rugova met with President Clinton in the Oval Office (for another inconclusive meeting).

Meeting people, as I tried to explain to Holbrooke, was really not the issue here. The problem remained that Rugova was fast losing influence on the ground to the KLA. His meeting with President Clinton, taken together with his meeting with Milosevic, was not going to change that situation.

In June I began to shuttle between Kosovo and Belgrade in an effort to find common ground between the Albanians and the Serbs in the form of a joint statement that would restore (and then some) Kosovo's autonomy, and establish the basis of a negotiation. The State Department sent me Tina Kaidanow, an extremely capable officer, fluent in Serbian from her recent assignment in Belgrade. I also included in the team Embassy Skopje's skillful press attaché, Phil Reeker. Tina and Phil came with me on almost all trips, while Deputy Chief of Mission Paul Jones ran the embassy in Skopje.

The European Union also appointed a negotiator, a knowledgeable, intelligent, and all-around good diplomat, the Austrian ambassador in Belgrade, Wolfgang Petritsch. Whether it was because he was from neighboring Austria or that his descendants were originally from Slovenia, Wolfgang knew the Balkans well. He was also a pleasure to work with. He understood the complex history, the effects of the Ottoman Empire and of the national churches on national identity, the mythologizing of the Serbs about Kosovo, but at the same time the importance of Kosovo to the Serbs. He was bright, dedicated, moderate, and worked well with everyone. I was delighted to have him as a colleague and to have the Europeans as partners in the entire process. If the endgame was to join the Balkans to Europe, a project that had been somewhat delayed by four hundred years of Ottoman occupation, it was obvious that the European Union needed to be a partner throughout.

The negotiations Wolfgang and I were conducting (usually with different daily itineraries, but always coordinated with frequent meetings and telephone contact) took place against the backdrop of a seriously deteriorating situation on the ground. Within days of the meeting with Clinton, up to twenty Kosovo Albanians were killed in apparent retaliation for the killing of a Serb policeman in Glogovac. Despite the fact that it had been the Dayton peace process that brought the war in Bosnia to an end, many people believed it was the NATO air attacks and could not understand what diplomacy we were waiting for in Kosovo when air strikes would do the trick.

Our diplomacy was viewed as just an extension of our raw power. In Washington the unholy alliance of liberal interventionists and neoconservatives demanded action. In one meeting I found myself in front of Paul Wolfowitz, who rarely encountered a problem in the world that couldn't be solved by dropping a few bombs, and Mort Abramowitz, a former head of the Carnegie Foundation who rarely encountered a village in the Balkans he didn't want to see turned into an independent state. They were combining forces to pressure the U.S. government, even though philosophically they came from very different perspectives.

The triumphalist mood in the United States in the 1990s was palpable. No problem, no matter how gritty and entrenched in decades or centuries of miserable and sordid history, was outside our capacity to solve, usually by force. Those who did not subscribe to this worldview were supposedly trapped in the past, unable to understand the new paradigm of the "new American century."

Thus the Balkans with its historical legacy would be the crucible of this instrument of might and right. Rwanda would be, according to this view, the last chapter of the previous era, where old concepts of sovereignty and national interests had yielded to disastrous consequences. Rwanda would live on as a brutal reminder to those who could not embrace the future.

The trouble, of course, was that not every country embraced this future of Pax Americana. The French, for starters, had concerns, especially with a country (a "hyperpower," as then foreign minister Hubert Vedrine was calling the United States) that eschewed UN Security Council imprimaturs on armed interventions. The free ride we had had in the early 1990s with the new Russian government had come to an end, especially when the Russians came to understand that our respect for their interests did not include keeping former Warsaw Pact countries from joining NATO.

Americans on the left and right increasingly asserted an American exceptionalism that seemed to many across the globe to put us above the law. Our tendency to reduce enormously complex historical issues into Manichean morality plays did not sit well with Europeans. There was no question the Dayton peace process had been a success, thanks to American leadership. But as much as we had tried to share the success with all the Contact Group members from Europe, we paid a price there, too, for solving a European problem for them and then—as we did in the post-conflict reconstruction—sticking Europe with the bill while we looked for another war.

We were not going to be successful in ending the Kosovo violence unless we first worked with the Europeans. And if it came again to war, we needed the Europeans at our side.

As the dusty Balkan summer of 1998 wore on, I realized that bringing the Serbs and Albanians around a table to end the violence was looking more and more remote. The Albanians had one thing on their minds: get NATO, that is, the United States, to intervene militarily. What was low-intensity conflict in one way became low-IQ warfare in another when Serbs time and time again retaliated for often minor provocations with brutal and excessive force, which would be thoroughly documented and increase worldwide sympathy for the Kosovar cause.

To help protect the civilian population from Serb attacks I began an effort with Milosevic to convince him to accept an international observation mission. He refused.

"But you allow diplomats accredited to your country to visit Kosovo," I pointed out.

"Yes, but they are diplomats accredited to our country. They are not international monitors."

"But aren't they allowed to report what they see when they are in Kosovo?"

"Of course."

"Can they go in a group?"

"Yes, of course. That is up to them."

"Well, then can we call them the 'Kosovo Diplomatic Monitoring Mission'?"

"That is your business what you call them."

Thus the monitoring mission, KDOM, which would eventually number some two thousand diplomats, was born. I was one of the first to visit Kosovo in this capacity. And as I walked down a street south of Peje, a large town in the west of Kosovo, I sensed that much had been accomplished in the creation of KDOM. But as I continued on past a row of abandoned Albanian homes, whose inhabitants had fled to the mountains, I heard a small explosion in the back of a house some twenty feet away. I jumped back and saw the house go up in flames. It was as if the Serbs were saying, "Hey, KDOM member, monitor this!"

Rugova had been the de facto leader of the Kosovo Albanians for more than a decade and, certainly in my view, deserved to be treated with respect. But he was increasing being dismissed in Washington as ineffectual, and more tellingly, as not in charge of the men with guns.

In late May, Gelbard stole a march on this issue by meeting with a KLA group in Geneva at the time that Holbrooke and I were meeting with Rugova. The implication was that Holbrooke and I were with yesterday's news, while Gelbard was with the people who counted. But as Dick and I journeyed out into the Kosovo hinterland before he returned to the United States, we came to a small town in the southwestern part of the province called Junik, which had been the site of violence. Village elders invited us to a farmhouse where we sat on the floor with glasses of strong, sugared Turkish tea to listen to what twenty villagers sitting with us had to say. A few minutes into the meeting a KLA fighter looking like Che Guevara joined us, in a full store-bought camouflage uniform, and sat down next to Holbrooke. There was very little room, and to anyone looking at the wire service photo that was shown around the world the next day he seemed to be sitting in Holbrooke's lap.

Holbrooke realized that even though this more than evened the score with Gelbard, it could cause him the same problems with Milosevic that Gelbard had incurred a few weeks before. Holbrooke asked me to go back to Belgrade the next day to meet with Milosevic and assure him that Che's entry into the room was entirely unexpected.

The next day Milosevic rose grudgingly to greet me and, as we sat down, threw the newspaper picture at my lap and said, "Do you know the problem this is for me? I want to work with you and Deek," as he called Dick, "but the Serbian people are very angry now. Very angry."

I explained to him that notwithstanding the photo of the KLA guerrilla sitting in Holbrooke's lap, we had no part in it. I pointed out that mediators should talk to all sides. He interrupted to point out something we already knew, which was that this wasn't going to help Rugova, either.

But he finally seemed ready to let it go. He had seen the report of Gelbard's meeting as well, and figured (correctly) that there was some level of competition going on between Gelbard and Holbrooke. His last comment on the issue: "I like Deek. But for the sake of career he would eat small children for breakfast."

11

UNFINISHED PEACE

Phil Reeker, Tina Kaidanow, and I continued to make the rounds in Kosovo through that brutal summer and fall of 1998, meeting with Albanian politicians and visiting areas hit by the violence. An early trip south of Pristina, the Kosovo capital, in our armored SUV earned us a mortar round fired overhead that landed harmlessly but ominously some fifty feet away. We agreed that the chance of hitting a moving vehicle with a mortar round was fairly remote, but we got on out of there quickly anyway. On another occasion, with our car packed with three Kosovo Albanians as we drove south from Pristina for a hoped-for encounter with the KLA leadership, we turned right at the town of Lipjan. We continued south to Shtime, where the highlands begin. We drove through the strangely quiet town and had an eerie sense that something was amiss. As we exited on the western side, we found a group of Serb security forces lying on the ground firing their automatic weapons into a distant tree line. One turned back to us while still lying on the ground in a firing position, and motioned with his left hand for us to get out. Our driver immediately began the three-point turn to reverse the vehicle. At that point our back bumper took several rounds that pinged into the metal. We sped back through Shtime, all of us thinking that this trip to find the KLA might have been a bad idea.

Fehmi Agani, the usually taciturn vice president of the LDK, was first to comment from the second row of seats, "It is a Serb provocation." (I guess Fehmi was suggesting that Serbs were pretending to shoot at each other in order to derail our mission.)

"And a very good one," I replied. "We are heading back to Pristina." Veton Surroi and Blerim Shala, also sitting in the second seat with Agani, did not protest. Neither did Phil and Tina, the kids in the third seat of the SUV.

By June, my team had still not had any serious encounters with the KLA, the men-with-guns whose cooperation in any peace process needed to be enlisted if we were to forge an inclusive Kosovar negotiating team that would have a broad enough mandate to reach a deal. The representatives Gelbard had met in Geneva were indeed KLA sympathizers, but they were not fighters in the field. In early June, KLA fighters moved into a small village along the Pristina-Peje road, the main east-west line that could divide Kosovo if controlled. KLA fighters set up roadblocks and announced rebel control of the area, while establishing the customary tolls, a very old habit in the Balkans.

Milosevic got word to us that if the KLA did not clear the road he would have his forces clear it for them. Holbrooke, with total seriousness, described the area to an amused gaggle of press corps in Pristina as "the most dangerous place in Europe." His point was that the prospect for a pitched battle between Serb security forces and Kosovo rebels was real.

But since Kijevo checkpoint was the most dangerous place in Europe, I went out to see it, a scant ten miles outside Pristina. Taking a U.S. embassy car from Belgrade, I hoped to meet the KLA, get a direct look at how they were controlling the road, and ask them to take me to their leader. Kurt Schork, an intrepid war correspondent from Associated Press (who was killed in an ambush in Sierra Leone some two years later), asked if he could come along. An interpreter, a junior officer from Dick Miles's staff in Belgrade, and the Serb driver of the embassy car accompanied us.

A line of cars with frustrated motorists awaited us as we approached the checkpoint. The waiting cars added to the banality of the whole scene, with armed young KLA fighters, cigarettes hanging loosely from their mouths, dressed in store-bought fatigues. Using a technique I had learned in Albania years before, I determined that the most senior person to talk to was the one with the most expensive pair of sunglasses. I asked him to tell his leadership that the United States wanted to be helpful to the people of Kosovo, but that checkpoints and the prospects of conflict were not conducive to our efforts, and that we expected a Serb effort to break through the checkpoint here, with possible loss of life. The soldier I spoke with directed us to pull up along the grass and promised to get back to us; then he retreated to the surrounding forest.

An hour later (a long time on the outskirts of Kijevo), another fighter (my sunglasses rule may not have worked that day) approached us to explain that his was a unit belonging to the Drenica command of the KLA, and that was all he was authorized to tell me. There would be no further conversation. I thanked him, but as we headed back to our vehicle, he called to say we were to stay put. We had attracted a bit of a crowd by then, and while I thought of ignoring the fighter and his colleagues and continuing to walk to the cars, Kurt (with more experience than I) indicated that we should not leave. I told the fighters that we were leaving, and in broken Albanian that I needed to report to the American government.

The fighters huddled up and the leader returned with the mixed news that we could leave, but that the embassy driver could not. I told them that that was not going to work for us, that it was unacceptable; we would all have to leave together. The fighter told us to wait and headed back to the tree line above. I smiled over at the embassy driver to reassure him that all was going to be okay. He did not smile back. The fighters had already taken his documents, something that also needed to be reversed before we left.

Thirty minutes later the fighter returned finally and said we were free to leave. I told him we needed the documents back, and he reluctantly supplied them. I lingered as the others got into the car. I shook hands with a couple of the fighters and jumped in the car as we drove off back in the direction of Pristina, wondering how I could have been so reckless as to drive to a checkpoint and try to find a negotiating partner that way. I reached over the front seat and patted the driver's shoulder.

"I owe you a beer for that." He kept his eyes on the road, driving at breakneck speed, and said softly in a very sober tone, "Bottle of whiskey."

Later that summer, we would finally succeed in making our way into Drenica along dirt roads, eventually finding the KLA headquarters in a mountain town called Likove, high above the KLA-controlled Drenica valley. It looked like a military camp one could find anywhere. There was a makeshift Albanian national flag, the black, two-headed eagle on a red background, mounted on a crude flag pole. There were some Yugoslav national army (JNA) vehicles, obviously found somewhere in one of the JNA's many depots. In Yugoslavia's heyday, the JNA was a well-equipped army with a doctrine of citizen-soldiers, reserves, all fully trained from stints in the army, with orders—and regularly drilled—to report to local assembly areas in the event of a foreign invasion, which was usually understood to mean a Warsaw Pact move. As the crisis deepened at the start of the 1990s, these depots became the origin of the fighting between local reserves and the locally deployed regular JNA units. Kosovo was no exception to this pattern of violence that began in Slovenia in 1991.

We entered a drab, ugly cement building that had been built with another purpose in mind years earlier, during Tito's reign, when central authorities tried to bring the accoutrements of large-town living to small villages.

Our conversation with KLA members—young men in beards, their camouflage uniforms with KLA insignia sewn onto their sleeves—did not reveal much, and certainly no interest in participating in a negotiating process. I learned that this KLA unit was implacably opposed to Rugova and deeply suspicious of Pristina's intelligentsia. This fact was brought home to me when Veton Surroi, the editor of Pristina's main newspaper, who was a consistent Rugova critic and a vocal and courageous voice for Kosovo's independence, was led off and banned from our meeting. We didn't see him again until we were ready to get into our Chevy Suburban and head back in the gathering dusk to Pristina. The basis of suspicion about Surroi was the fact that he was the son of a former Yugoslav diplomat who had represented Tito's Yugoslavia around the world, including in such far-off places as Latin America. There did not appear to be much else against Surroi, except that he was not from Drenica.

These desultory encounters did help begin a process where the KLA began to reveal more about itself. It was often clannish, as the exclusion of Surroi had suggested, with most senior leaders coming from the Drenica area, but in the summer of 1998 its ranks had swelled with new recruits who joined whatever local structure existed. Whoever was leading the KLA, it was becoming less a Drenica affair. The KLA became a fixture not just in Drenica, but also throughout the province.

The search for a KLA leadership structure, as Gelbard had discovered in Geneva, uncovered many such self-described leaders. That search was fast coming to dominate my time through the summer and into the fall. Rugova's LDK was not immune to such war fever, and in areas out in western Kosovo, armed units loyal to the LDK began announcing themselves, usually in the form of checkpoints in the middle of nowhere, or in the killing of local Serb police, followed by a proud announcement of the event and then the inevitable retaliation against the population in the area.

As difficult as it was to recruit the KLA into the peace process, things were equally problematic back in Pristina, where resentment against Rugova and his LDK was building. Rugova became increasingly detached, unwilling to engage except to repeat slogans about Kosovo's right to independence. I met with him weekly and experienced some of the same frustrations, though I retained my respect for his personal integrity and his vision for Kosovo and its role as a part of Europe.

Rugova was a Kosovar nationalist, but not a sectarian with any interest in Muslims in Europe, as Izetbegovic had sometimes been seen as in Bosnia. In addition to being a serious writer, poet, and thinker, he was also an amateur geologist. At the end of each visit to his upstairs living room, I would leave his home with still another "Rugova rock," often some kind of magnesium ore sample rich in interesting colors from Kosovo's geological endowment. The rocks began to weigh me down as I realized that Rugova seemed more interested in describing them than in telling me what he was prepared to do to reach out to Rexep Xosia or other opinion leaders in Pristina. As visitors tried to talk with him and engage him on Kosovo's politics, he would flip through cable television channels, absentmindedly stopping sometimes on the cartoon channel.

I realized that my efforts to forge consensus around negotiating a peace document were increasingly divorced from Washington's sentiment of getting on with military action. As the Serbs carried on their counterinsurgency operations and casualties rose, human rights organizations and activists were beating the war drums, which was putting more pressure on our relationship with the European Union, which was still suspicious of the value of any military intervention. Longtime human rights and peace activist Bianca Jagger arrived on the scene late one morning. After a few meetings in Pristina and before getting back on a plane in Skopje early that evening, she told me we should be supporting the KLA, and as for Rugova, "he's finished." Nobody in this part of the world is ever "finished," I thought.

On a late summer morning on September 9, Serb police pulled bodies out of an irrigation ditch near the village of Glodjane. All told, some thirty bodies were found. The victims were evidently killed by fellow Kosovars, although that account was disputed. I didn't think it much mattered to those villagers, but it was a reminder that these conflicts seem always to be fought not between armies but between civilians, or often one side's army and the other side's civilians.

I became more of a monitor to noncompliance than a mediator in a peace process, because neither side seemed interested in reaching an agreement with the other, a reminder that the odds of finding a solution are often very long. While many major European countries were not prepared to give up on peace in the former Yugoslavia, the country that counted the most, the United States, had clearly done so. My efforts became relegated to demonstrating that we had tried and failed to force through a peace deal.

In early fall the Serbs began a new tactic: clear out the villages along the main trunk lines, a move that bought them the enmity of the world while doing nothing to enhance their own security. The overall dynamic of the war soon became clear enough: KLA would move into a village and fire an automatic weapon at a Serb police vehicle driving by. A reinforced Serb unit would return, often with a 20mm cannon originally designed as an antiaircraft weapon, now used instead on mud huts. Rounds would be emptied into peasant homes, and the inhabitants would take to the hills behind, fleeing for their lives. When the Serb forces moved on, the KLA would tell war correspondents to come and have a look at what the Serbs have done.

This brutal tactic on the part of the Serbs, quite apart from whether it was justified by any provocation, or subsequently exploited by calls to foreign media, was too much for Western capitals to stomach, even those terrified at the precedent that an independent Kosovo might mean for their own country's internal divisions. On September 23, the UN Security Council approved Resolution 1199, demanding a cease-fire, Serb withdrawal, and return of displaced people. The resolution also called for further measures, an ominous warning to the Serbs of the cost of noncompliance. Three days later the Serbs gave a reply of sorts: they killed thirty-five villagers, including twenty-one members of a single family in the village of Goren Brine.

In early October, on a drizzly day, Tina, Phil, and I went up to some of the mountain areas, where we understood displaced persons had gone to escape the onslaught near Ostrozub and Malishevo, in east-central Kosovo. We journeyed up a small dirt road in our armored Chevy Suburban, encountering a couple of KLA checkpoints before finding the camp. There, throughout a dense mountain forest, we saw thousands of people huddled under sheets of plastic and in makeshift plastic tents, with blankets and clothing covering the cold ground. I met with several groups to hear their stories, which seldom varied much in the central plot line: they heard automatic rifle fire, followed sometime later by the louder sound of Serb weaponry. Did the Serbs order them out? No, they just knew they were supposed to get out of there or face the consequences.

I told the villagers that we were working hard to get them back in their homes, that it was our top priority. At that point, a young man spoke up to say that the people didn't care about getting back to their homes. They wanted independence for Kosovo.

An old man with no teeth stood up and stared at the political commissar in disgust before turning to me and saying: "I want to go home. Zoti Christopher, can you get me back in my house?"

"I promise to do my best," I answered, with little confidence that my best could come even close.

We drove down the mountain track, horrified by the sea of humanity we had just encountered, especially at the sight of the ill-clad children in the cold, wet mountain air. Tina, Phil, and I were deeply concerned about what would happen to these people when the winter finally settled in. We drove south along the road, past the larger village of Rahovec, near Malishevo. There we saw Serb forces busily, but unhurriedly, setting the town on fire.

The next day, I took a flight to Belgrade and confronted Milosevic about that village burning. I also told him about meeting villagers on the side of a mountain, omitting the part about the possible KLA presence, since I didn't want them to become a further target for his forces. Gone was the bravado of the past, along with the humor, albeit sardonic, that he had used to amuse his guests. He stood up and paced the room, very uncharacteristically, called for a telephone, and made a call to what I presumed was a military aide as I sat waiting.

"That unit had been transferred. They will be gone today," he said firmly.

"Good," I responded. "I'll be back there tomorrow."

The unit was indeed gone by the next day, but it didn't matter at all. Another unit took its place, and the violence continued.

By this time in the fall I had succeeded in bringing Rugova together with the "independent intellectuals" in Pristina to discuss what an autonomy arrangement could look like. I was assisted by Jim O'Brien, a State Department lawyer with close ties to Secretary Albright, and by Jonathan Levitsky, a political appointee lawyer who worked with Jim in the State Department's policy planning office. They were putting together drafts that carefully threaded the needle between Serb sovereignty of its territory and complete autonomy for the Kosovars. The drafts were ever more favorable to the Kosovars, but in the absence of an independence provision I knew that I could not convince the Kosovars to accept them, nor would the Serbs go along. It became more of an effort to show the other members of the Contact Group that we were doing all we could to find a diplomatic solution. At best, it would be an unfinished peace.

As the war on civilians wore on, nobody in Kosovo was interested in autonomy anymore. They wanted complete independence, and with every documented example of Serb excess, they felt correctly that they were getting closer to their goal. Those prepared to work on autonomy were denounced as weak or pro-Serb.

On October 12, NATO ministers approved an "activation order," or "ACTORD" in NATO-speak. The ACTORD, in effect, became the "further measures" noted in the Security Council's Resolution 1199. Dick came back to the region after a three-month absence as a "private consultant," having long since left the government, to deliver the tough message to Milosevic that he must either pull back his forces and allow the return of displaced people, or otherwise face NATO bombing. Milosevic complied, at least for the time being, but the Albanians, like the Bosnians three years before, had no interest in a cease-fire. They wanted a bombing campaign. Nevertheless, Milosevic's compliance allowed the ACTORD to be suspended, though not rescinded.

I urged Rugova to come with me for a swing through Malishevo, Ostrozub, Rahovec, and Suharek and meet people returning to their homes. Rugova had increasingly become a shut-in, either for security reasons (and they were always present) or for psychological reasons, which I worried about more. Rugova, more than any conceivable leader who might emerge from the still-opaque KLA structure, had national and popular appeal in Kosovo, and I feared for the day when the Kosovo people dismissed him, as he had been by Bianca Jagger and other instant experts on Kosovo. I could see that whether Kosovo gained independence through constantly expanding autonomy plans that would allow time to thicken the institutions of democracy, or instantly through a general war, it was coming, and a person of Rugova's stature and commitment to moderation had to be part of it.

I took him in my car on November 3 first to what had been a scenic small village, Banja Malishevo. The minaret of the local mosque had been toppled by a very accurate tank round, and the carcasses of livestock that had belonged to the village inhabitants were still rotting in the fields from a month before, when the Serbs used them as target practice. We continued out to the small village of Ostrozub, where we also got out on the main street, now teeming with returned inhabitants carrying and dragging their belongings back from the mountain forests where they had hidden for weeks. The reaction to the sight of Rugova was extraordinary. People, hesitant at first at the sight of their leader of more than a decade, approached him and draped their arms around his neck, kissing him on his cheeks. Some hugged him and dropped to their knees, kissing him on his hand as if he were the pope.

I stood back to absorb the totality of the scene. For those who had written him off, I wished they could see him now. What makes some politicians charismatic and others not has always been an elusive concept for me, but on this day I saw that Ibrahim Rugova was a force to be reckoned with—perhaps the reason the KLA and others were so harsh on him.

As I stood watching him, his soft and gentle voice obviously of such comfort to those gathered around him, people who had gone through so much, an old man approached me as fast as his limp could bring him. He started calling for me as he got within earshot, "Zoti Christopher, Zoti Christopher!" I didn't know who he was, but I put out my hand to shake his (I guess I thought I should press the flesh as well that day), but he ignored my hand and ran into me, hugging me with all the force he could. As he slobbered kiss after kiss on my two cheeks, saliva pooling on the sides of my face, I recognized him as the man whom I had met in the mountain camp. "Mr. Hill, I am in my home just as you promised. I am back home." I hugged him and kissed him back.

I knew, however, that his torment wasn't over, and that it may have just begun. If Milosevic had thought he was intimidating the Kosovars, he was doing quite the opposite, and in so doing was making any type of negotiated process more difficult. The team back in Washington under the supervision of Jim O'Brien and Jon Levitsky continued to make revisions to the autonomy proposal, but as the Serbs continued their rampage the revisions continued to be in favor of the Albanians and less and less acceptable to Milosevic and the Serbs. Milosevic lost interest in making any concessions on the document, as did the Albanians.

Unlike Bosnia, where Milosevic had displayed an interest in settling, Kosovo was a different matter. "You might as well ask for my head," he said after reading drafts that banned the Yugoslav military from stepping foot in Kosovo. And when the entire project became known as an "interim accord," because the Albanians could not negotiate on the basis of giving up their aspiration for an independent Kosovo, Milosevic was done negotiating.

I kept presenting updated versions of what, unfortunately for my reputation, became known as "the Hill Plan." Each version had the dubious characteristic of being less than what the Albanians wanted and more than what the Serbs said they were prepared to accept. Serbs and Albanians rejected two more updated drafts in November. "Well," I told Tina and Phil in mock optimism, "at least they agree on something."

In early January 1999, the KLA captured eight members of the JNA and demanded a swap of prisoners, a normal procedure in wars, but not one that had ever been accomplished in the Kosovo conflict. The Serbs promised only that retribution would be swift and furious.

I met with Milosevic in his office in Belgrade. He was angry, indeed barely able to contain himself. After two hours I got him to accept a prisoner swap, but there was a catch. Insisting that to agree to a swap would be to invite more such "kidnappings," as he called them, he agreed to the swap provided the Serbs were released ten days before the KLA soldiers. Having worked the issue for hours, I knew it was the best I could get, so I made sure that in ten days the KLA were to be released.

"This is our agreement. Is that correct?"

"Of course," replied Milosevic. "You have my word."

That was a comforting thought, I muttered to myself. But I agreed based on the following: If he released them after ten days as he promised, it would be the first such agreement in the war and offer a tiny bit of momentum to the process. If he didn't, I would immediately resign. I started finding myself rooting for the latter outcome.

I journeyed back up to Likove, this time in winter, the dirt roads having long since turned to mud. Phil and Tina, and also then Colonel Dana Atkins, who was representing General Clark's staff at NATO, accompanied me. Along the drive we could see scores of displaced people. It was hard to tell where they were coming from as they walked in the open fields alongside tractors and trailers, presumably looking for a place to spend the night. I brought Bill Walker, the very newly appointed head of the international monitors, a veteran of all sorts of conflict and revolution in Latin America. We had dispensed with the "diplomatic observer mission" chapeau as of October and now had an appropriately titled mission, the Kosovo Verification Mission. (*Verification* was seen as a stronger, less passive concept than merely *monitoring* compliance, although these distinctions sound more important in Washington meetings than they do on the ground in Kosovo.) Our mission was under the mandate of the Organization for Security and Co-operation in Europe (OSCE). Bill was a senior U.S. ambassador with a number of tough assignments in Central America. That did not mean, however, that he had necessarily ever seen the inside of a Balkan history book; but he was a gruff and tough character who could be relied upon as such with all parties to this very fragile cease-fire.

In Likove, we sat across the table from the "KLA spokesman," a position I suspect had been created the moment our vehicle pulled into the driveway. In any case, CNN's Christiane Amanpour had interviewed Jakup Krasniqi a few weeks before.

Krasniqi took a hard-line position on the ten-day delay, insisting that the swap be in perfect symmetry, with strict and complete reciprocity, a concept and condition that was the refuge of all Balkan officials, high and low. Bill Walker, seated on my left, said "enough of this" and stood up as if to leave. I grabbed his right sleeve and pulled him back down to his seat while I continued looking Krasniqi in the eye across the narrow wooden table.

"Mr. Krasniqi, why won't you accept this proposal? Ten days is not very long."

"How could I ever trust Milosevic?" he replied.

I was working through an interpreter, and wanting Krasniqi to understand everything, I spoke in short sentences to allow the interpreter to render each statement literally while I thought of the next line.

"Trust Milosevic? Mr. Krasniqi, that is not your problem. That is my problem. Your problem is not whether you trust him, but rather whether you trust me. But before you answer whether you trust me, you need to understand something. If you don't trust me, it means you don't trust the American government. If you don't trust the American government, you don't trust the American people. And if you don't trust the American people, you do not trust America. And Mr. Krasniqi"—this was the most fun I had had in months—"if you don't trust America you are in very big trouble. So, Mr. Krasniqi, let me ask you. Do you trust America?"

The Serbs were released the following day, and the Albanians nine days after that.

That proved to be the last piece of good news we were to have. A few days later forty-five inhabitants of the small village of Racak were massacred, their bodies left in a drainage ditch. The massacre, the worst in months, was likened to the one carried out in Srebrenica, Bosnia, which had been the proximate cause of NATO action. The killings at Srebrenica, which totaled some seven thousand, were far greater in number, but the effect was similar. The Racak murders were denounced throughout the world and helped put military intervention on an inexorable path. Bill Walker, as head of the monitoring mission, went to the site and pronounced the Serbs guilty. Some criticized him for preempting the findings of the forensic team, but one doesn't always need a forensic team to know the gist of what has happened, and Walker did the right thing, even though his candor earned Milosevic's denunciation and expulsion (an order the sometimes-practical Milosevic later rescinded as NATO planes began to fuel up on their runways).

While Washington had long been ready to commit NATO airpower, other partners in the process and near to it, the Italians, wanted to give negotiation one last chance. Secretary Albright called me and asked what I thought of a face-to-face negotiation somewhere in Western Europe, one last try at it. I was no more enthusiastic about the idea than she was. Most concerning was the fact that while the Serbs were prepared to inch toward more autonomy, the Kosovo Albanian side would have no part of the A-word. That had been the reason I had added the word *interim* to the plan I had been working to sell. Milosevic had not reacted well to the idea that the agreement should be a five-year plan, but I pressed for it as the only feasible approach given that Albanians were not prepared to give up on the historic mission to gain a Kosovo homeland.

Meanwhile, the Serbs made clear that they could negotiate many aspects of a new quality of autonomy for Kosovo but were not going to agree to a "republic" status for Kosovo, which would in effect take it completely out of Serbia. Nor were they prepared to accept "foreign troops" in any kind of implementing role.

Secretary Albright and her close advisors, especially her spokesperson Jamie Rubin, had long come to the conclusion that NATO would be involved, but she knew far better than others in Washington, including Rubin, that getting the Europeans on board was going to be difficult. Refusing to hold a negotiation on the basis that it would not work was not an option.

On January 29, the Contact Group foreign ministers summoned representatives of Serbia and the Kosovo Albanians to attend peace negotiations at Rambouillet, France, a chateau just outside Paris, and to appear by February 6. The Contact Group set the time parameter at seven days, with an option to extend for another week. "Where did that [the time frame] come from?" I asked Phil Reeker, recalling that at Dayton we never set a time frame. "They have to know how much food to order," he responded.

The parties arrived in Rambouillet on February 6. Whereas the Dayton talks took place at a large military base, surrounded by barbed wire, Rambouillet is a fourteenth-century château complete with turrets; from a distance it looks like a large Lego project. Not every room had its own bathroom, and many that did had been modernized some time around 1890. The French ambassador in Macedonia, my colleague Jacques Huntzinger, who also knew a thing or two about the Balkans and had been a key conduit to understanding French thinking on the Kosovo crisis, was tasked by his government to assemble the Kosovo Albanian delegation and deliver them to the talks. Given the degree of antipathy that existed among the three-headed delegation—Rugova, the KLA, and the "independent intellectuals" from Pristina—I did not envy Jacques's duties that day, herding them onto a plane and enduring the three-hour trip to Paris.

The morning the negotiations were to get under way, a front-page story in the *International Herald Tribune* reported that Holbrooke was giving the talks a fifty-fifty chance of success, odds I would have been pleased to have. I called him:

"Dick, I understand the fifty percent you have on failure, but I would be very interested in what your basis was for the other fifty percent."

"Chris, you may have a point."

No kidding. As we got under way, I saw little chance it could work, and decided that what we really needed was an Albanian approval of a document, and a Serb refusal. If both refused, there could be no further action by NATO or any other organization for that matter.

The Albanians, fractious as they were, nonetheless understood the need to negotiate, and the need to get to yes. The Serbs, in the absence of Milosevic, did not engage and seemed all ready to go into a fatalistic stall. The chief of the delegation was Milosevic's former foreign minister, now prime minister, Milan Milutinovic, or as members of the U.S. delegation, especially those not speaking Serbian, called him, "Tuna." Nikola Sainovic, Milosevic's representative in Kosovo, was the deputy of the delegation.

I had spent considerable time in Kosovo with Sainovic, seeking to clear roads of Serb security forces and ensuring a flow of displaced persons back to their homes, as well as humanitarian access. He was intelligent, straightforward, and highly capable. But at Rambouillet he was a broken man. Just two weeks before, intercepts of his cell phone calls, leaked to the *Washington Post*, appeared to implicate him in ordering security forces to commit the Racak massacre. Sainovic understood what those intercepts, now public knowledge, meant. Sooner or later he would be arrested for war crimes. (He was arrested on May 2, 2003, and was subsequently found guilty in 2008.)

The Yugoslav delegation did not negotiate, instead maintaining their fixation that there could be no foreign implementation of the agreement. "If the agreement is good and fair . . . no foreign force is necessary to make them implement it." It was an internally logical statement, a classic Milosevic high school debater's point, except that it made no sense at all. For their part, the Kosovo Albanians engaged but demanded that the document provide a path to independence.

With little or no progress to report in the first week, I met with Secretary Albright and her spokesman, Jamie Rubin, who was emerging as a substantive advisor on Kosovo. Madeleine asked what I thought of possibly making a trip to Belgrade to tell Milosevic that he'd better get serious on the negotiations.

It was the first I had heard of the idea, though I didn't think it was a bad one and wished I had thought of it myself. It would have the advantage of showing that we were prepared to go the extra mile to warn Milosevic, and would have the added benefit of making clear to him what we thought of his delegation's behavior. I had always found that Milosevic was at his worst when he hadn't seen us recently and received a dose of reality. I told the secretary I would think about it, but thought it was a good idea.

Just thirty minutes later, I, along with Wolfgang Petritsch and the Russian envoy, the affable, intelligent, but somewhat irrelevant Boris Majorsky, were seated in front of the press for our weekly press conference. The venue was a large indoor gymnasium, a basketball and volleyball facility in the village of Rambouillet. The reporters numbered into the hundreds. Phil Reeker, who had become the spokesman at Rambouillet (or, as I never tired of calling him, "the grim Reeker"), introduced us and called on the rock star of correspondents, CNN's Christiane Amanpour, who also happened to be the wife of Jamie Rubin, to ask the first question.

"This question is for Ambassador Hill. Ambassador, have you given any thought to making a trip to Belgrade to meet with Milosevic?" I realized that this idea was gaining currency.

On February 16, I flew to Belgrade in a U.S. military aircraft with Petritsch. Milosevic had long since lost any confidence that the process could lead to an outcome acceptable to the Serbs, but his inability to think strategically meant that he was going to make the job easier for us. He loudly rejected any role whatsoever for NATO, a sine qua non for any conceivable solution. He had never quite gotten over the inclusion of the word *interim*. To Milosevic, it felt like the eastern Slovenian agreement during the first week of Dayton, which had led to the imposition of Croatian sovereignty in that region. Interim was simply a means to give the Serbs in Kosovo "time to run away."

To the extent I ever had any ability to reach Milosevic, it was fast depleting that winter. For the first time he tried to insist that I also see his new foreign minister, a clear sign that the Milosevic channel was coming to an end. I objected to seeing Foreign Minister Vladislav Jovanovic at all, pointing out to Milosevic that he did not seem to me in the loop, and, without being too tough on the foreign minister, questioned whether he was intellectually up to such issues. For a second, Milosevic showed a sign of his old self.

"You know, Serbian people are very proud that their foreign minister is a genuine Serbian peasant."

But as uncooperative as the Serbs were being—and conveniently so as the goal increasingly became an effort to convince doubting Europeans and Russians that there was no other alternative—the Albanians were not much better.

Jamie Rubin was of the view that the real leader of the Kosovo delegation was Hashim Thaci and that Albright should focus her efforts on him. Jamie had begun to pay attention exclusively to Thaci, even going so far as to recommend combinations of suits and ties for him to wear. For all the time I have met and worked with foreigners, it would never have occurred to me to tell one of them how to match a shirt and a tie, such was Jamie's attention to detail. But Jamie had a definite point about focusing on Thaci as an eventual leader, a point that would be validated some years later when Thaci was elected prime minister.

I had no problem with a focus on Thaci, especially the need to get him on board, but given our reluctant European allies, on whose continent this war was raging, I believed we should play it straight with the others as well, and not put ourselves into domestic Kosovo politics, favoring those who engaged in violent resistance over those who for decades had not. I knew Rugova had enormous popularity (he would eventually be elected president in a free Kosovo) and that a tilt toward the KLA leadership might not serve us well, especially as we knew very little about Thaci at the time, whether he was a leader or a front for someone else. American foreign policy is replete with stories of supporting the more aggressive player in a civil war, only to find that that aggressive player was not at all our player. Since the Peace Corps I knew how fraught the process of picking someone else's leadership could be.

Getting tough with the Albanians to get them to yes was not made any easier by their use of cell phones, a device that had not been as prevalent at Dayton in 1995. Tough talk with them would often result in someone calling one of their many supporters in Washington, who in turn would call the State Department and complain. Life in the big city, I explained to Phil and Tina.

The Kosovo Albanians allegedly did not really believe that NATO would come to Kosovo; instead they suspected the entire negotiation was a ruse of some kind to induce them to accept autonomy rather than independence; then, for whatever reason, NATO would not come to be part of the implementation. Wes Clark called to tell me he understood that this lack of trust was an enormous problem within the Kosovo delegation, but that he was willing to help by coming to Rambouillet whenever I needed him. "Just say the word and I'll be there," he told me. Other acquaintances of mine in Washington sent emails and suggested the same.

"Bring Clark to Rambouillet," I told Tina and Phil. "There is something fishy in Brussels."

American generals do not get four stars on their shoulders by accepting no for an answer (something I was to learn again when I was assigned to Iraq), but the French, who wanted no part of it, were resisting mightily Clark's "send me in, coach" campaign. I said to Clark that, given that U.S. forces in Europe had well over one hundred thousand troops, surely someone, say a colonel doing planning for the Kosovo mission, could meet with the doubting Thomases of the Albanian delegation? No, the answer kept coming back from Clark. "I'm the only one who can put their concerns to rest."

Finally, the French agreed that Clark would meet the Kosovars at a nearby French air base, which he did on February 22. That was as close as Clark was going to get to Rambouillet.

Just before the recess that was set to be called two weeks into the process, Thaci, to our great concern, left the conference on February 18, returning two days later with even tougher demands. He never said where he had gone, though the suspicion was that he went to see Adem Demaci, the firebrand self-appointed political leader of the KLA, who had refused to take part in Rambouillet. For months, Demaci had made outlandish and outlying pronouncements to the press in Pristina, so much so that the Serbs never interfered with him, such was his contribution to their argument that the KLA was simply a group of crazed radicals.

"Why can't you agree to this?" I asked Thaci, truly not understanding whether he comprehended the near-fatal consequences for the Kosovars of a "no" answer.

"It is you who doesn't understand," he replied. "If I agree to this, I will go home and they will kill me."

The Rambouillet conference was extended for three days at the request of the Contact Group ministers, who were spending more and more time at the meetings, between their duties managing their countries' affairs in every other part of the world. I marveled at the amount of time busy senior officials had for the problems of Kosovo, whose total population could fit into a small section of Beijing, Seoul, or Tokyo.

On the last day of the extended session, the Contact Group ministers met with the Serb head of delegation, Milutinovic. Tuna danced around as best he could but finally had to admit his country could not accept the presence of foreign troops on its soil and therefore could not accept the agreement.

The Kosovo Albanian delegation was completely split as the hour drew near. Thaci had become incommunicado; nor was Rugova prepared to take the lead. With hours to go, we were in a situation where both sides were saying no, an excuse for some of the assembled Contact Group ministers to wash their hands of the entire affair. Wolfgang and I went into the Albanian delegation room, an ornate, refurbished lower-floor room made of granite and wood paneling, richly appointed with tapestries. As I began my plea a cell phone started ringing, and an embarrassed Kosovar struggled to find the mute button.

"Turn that thing off," I said, "because whoever is calling you cannot possibly have something more important to tell you than what I am about to say."

My interpreter, Bix Aliu, an Albanian-American who had been living in Skopje and had accompanied me through many experiences in Kosovo, delivered my lines with great precision. Although an American through and through (he would soon go on to become a Foreign Service officer), Bix could not help but feel a sense that Kosovo's moment had arrived, but that its leadership, all assembled in that room, was failing it.

"We have come a long way together, but this is the end of the road. If you do not accept this agreement, there is nothing I or anyone else can do for you. So now it is your choice."

Wolfgang made a similar plea and we left the room. I slumped down on a stair step outside the room and accepted a cigarette from Jamie Rubin, as if taking up Jamie's smoking habit would help. We waited.

After a half hour, Veton Surroi emerged. Veton was one of the nonaligned group members, neither KLA nor LDK, whom I had never found all that enjoyable to deal with over the past nine months, and who hadn't seemed to have much support among the others in the delegation. I was aware of that when he was banned from my meetings with the KLA leadership in Likove a few months before. He told Wolfgang and me that he had been asked to speak for the Albanian delegation to the Contact Group foreign ministers. His word was good enough for me, since there didn't appear to be any other approach on the table.

I escorted him into the room where the Contact Group foreign ministers were meeting and told them that Surroi had an announcement for them. He said that the delegation accepted the plan but would need time to return to Kosovo to build support among the people there, since some aspects of it, namely autonomy rather than independence, would be problematic for them. That the delegation had to return to Kosovo did not please all the foreign ministers, but Secretary Albright made sure they understood that Veton's message was a yes.

Outside the foreign ministers' room I approached Veton. I told him that I had doubted him for many things he had done in the past, but that I would never forget what he had done on this day. He thanked me for my efforts, words that never came easily to the crusty journalist. I put my hand on his shoulder and told him we had much to do, and that the future might be as complicated as the past. He gave an understated nod and we parted.

The Kosovo Albanian delegation returned to Kosovo to prepare for peace, and to get others in Kosovo to do the same. The Serbs went home to prepare for war. Violence took another upswing, the expected spring fighting season coming early that year, as Secretary Albright had observed. I went to Kosovo to meet with KLA commanders west of Pristina, making our way cautiously through KLA checkpoints. By March 8 I was able to report that the KLA had definitively accepted Rambouillet.

Emissaries to President Milosevic all returned with the report that he had definitively rejected the Rambouillet Accords.

On March 19 in Paris, the entire leadership of the Kosovo Albanians signed the accords as Wolfgang Petritsch and I and others stood behind them. It was a bittersweet moment because everyone, but especially Wolfgang and I, knew that in the absence of a Serb signature and given the continued violence there would be war. But there was also something uplifting. After months and months of trying to encourage the Albanian leadership to work together, we had succeeded. I thought this might be a good omen for the future, but the gathering was mainly a repudiation of Serb propaganda—which I had heard many times from Milosevic himself—that the Albanian leaders could never work together. I looked over at Tina and Phil, two young Foreign Service officers who would both go on to make ambassador, and smiled. They had also put everything they could into the agreement. I was so proud of both of them.

Washington in its collective judgment decided that we needed to make one more try, and asked Holbrooke to return to Belgrade and meet with Milosevic. My own relations with Milosevic had deteriorated further in light of Rambouillet. The visit to Belgrade that I had made at the suggestion of Secretary Albright and Jamie Rubin had gone poorly. Later I was sent back again to Belgrade for the sole propaganda value of having Milosevic refuse to see me, which he obligingly did, sending me to his peasant foreign minister.

Holbrooke and I and a small delegation from Washington met with Milosevic the evening of March 22. He was in a fatalistic mood, to say the least.

"You are superpower. If you want to say that Tuesday is Thursday, you can do that. It doesn't matter what the rest of us think."

We spent hours and hours trying to find a way forward on the critical issue of NATO's implementation of the Rambouillet Accords, but it was not possible. Milosevic—and many other Serbs—were not prepared to host foreign troops. Milosevic had told us that the question of NATO involvement in a Kosovo settlement was up to Serbia's parliament, the Skupstina, and it would meet the morning of the twenty-third. That night

Holbrooke and I discussed whether there might be a way forward, but we both concluded that nothing would happen. Still, we decided to stay through the morning.

After scores of bloodcurdling anti-NATO speeches by parliamentarians, the Skupstina took no further action on the question of inviting foreign troops. We went to the airport late on the afternoon of March 23. Tina, Phil, and I prepared to board a small jet to Skopje, where I would resume my duties as ambassador. Holbrooke and the others boarded a flight to Budapest; from there they would go on to the States. Our embassy in Belgrade was evacuated that same day. Tina, who had previously served in Belgrade and knew many of the airport workers, had many tearful farewells that night. Ninety minutes later we arrived at the Macedonian capital, where previously friendly faces of airport workers had turned sad and sullen at the prospect of outright war on their border.

The next morning we buttoned down the embassy as best we could, reviewing our procedures and requesting more local police support. I sat down behind my desk to place a call to Milosevic's foreign ministry aide, Bojan Bugarcic, to check one last time. He told me, "We will not be in contact again for a long, long time. I wish you well."

On March 24 the bombing began.

12

THE SAFE ROOM

Early in the afternoon of March 25, 1999, I snuck out for a jog in a park across from the embassy in Skopje. There were no signs of expected demonstrations. About a dozen student-age protesters were serenading us in front of the embassy with an off-key version of John Lennon's "Give Peace a Chance," the only intelligible words of which were the title (over and over again). They paid no attention to me as I crossed the street in shorts and a sweatshirt, wearing a Red Sox hat pulled down over my head. I was giving a local television press interview that afternoon and had met with foreign ministry officials in the late morning to give my daily pep talk and briefing to them on why things were as they were in Kosovo. Our administrative officer, Greg Slotta, had been in touch with the interior ministry to introduce our new, but very temporary, security officer and to seek assistance.

The withdrawal of the KDOM observer mission from Kosovo over the weekend meant orange SUVs everywhere in town, pulled up in front of Skopje's many restaurants and cafés, a scene that I knew from my Macedonian friends was not welcome, even though it meant more business for the bar owners. The now totally unemployed monitoring mission members, several hundred, had filled the hotels, especially the deluxe Aleksandar Palace Hotel, about a twenty-minute walk from the embassy. There monitoring mission members competed for rooms with the international press now streaming through Skopje's tiny airport. Like spectators at a sporting event, everyone was surging through the turnstiles looking for their seats. Room rates were shooting up, another temporary dividend for a crisis. Senior members of the international monitoring mission were giving interviews to the gathering international press about the deteriorating situation in neighboring Kosovo.

The war correspondents, many of whom had cut their teeth on the Balkans in Bosnia, were now assigning identities to the new players. ("Serbs are still the Serbs. Albanians, they are the Bosnians, and the Macedonians, are they maybe like the Croats?") They would inquire about Macedonia, a country whose people had never been enthusiastic about the growing crisis on their border, and both the journalists and the members of the monitoring mission didn't find much to like about their reluctant new hosts.

The Macedonian concern about war was increasingly taken as a lack of support for Kosovo independence (a fair inference), nostalgia for the former Yugoslavia (less fair), and tacit support for Milosevic's policies (not fair at all). For those who did not understand Macedonia's historic and contemporary predicament—and Skopje was fast filling up with such people—all this, including Macedonia's troubled internal relations with its Albanian community and its failure to sort out its problems with neighboring Greece, was being tossed into a blender out of which came a not very digestible narrative of a country that seemed incapable of working together or with anyone else.

By the late afternoon, I could see from the window that the young singing group, having repeated "give peace a chance" about a thousand times, had retired, presumably to find some throat lozenges, and had been replaced by a somewhat larger crowd less interested in singing than in throwing eggs over the fence of the embassy. Along with eggs there were now occasional rocks as the crowd brought in reinforcements and new ammunition.

Our temporary security officer was busy giving updates to Washington, but the main problem continued to be the Macedonian government's lack of interest in providing greater police presence. Busloads of protesters were being let off nearby at the heavily guarded Aleksandar Palace Hotel. According to the telephone reports we were getting, the crowd, on seeing the menacing police lines, was turning back and heading in our direction down Ilenden Street.

By about 5:15 P.M., embassy windows in the front had begun to give way as heavier rocks crashed against them. A Mylar coating on the windows prevented the glass from shattering but the rocks themselves started to crash through the windows and land on the floor.

At that point, Charlie Stonecipher, who had been on the phone calling for more police help, came to me. "Mr. Ambassador," he said, "I can't see that there are any police out there at this point. It is a matter of time before they get through the fence and into the compound. We need to get to the basement *now*."

I ordered all hands down to the vault in the basement and checked all offices and rooms to make sure everyone was accounted for. There were forty-two persons, mostly local Macedonian workers in the embassy. Accompanied by Bix Aliu, I went into the security control room to get one more look through the camera at the growing crowd. The front fence had been knocked down. The crowd was in the compound. Others were climbing the walls in the back. Bix and I went to the back entrance, a security door with five-inch-thick ballistic glass that had been magnetically sealed with several dead bolts. The scene outside was horrific. Demonstrators were everywhere and in the process of torching our vehicles. I saw one person, not particularly young, in a long wool coat and not appearing to have set out that day with the idea of attacking the

American Embassy, take a large rock and pound it on the rear window of a hatchback car until it broke. He lit a Molotov cocktail and threw it in the backseat. I was seething. I looked at the huge switch that would open the door. I was thinking about that Belgian ambassador in 1962 and how he had essentially frightened a mob away from his embassy in Belgrade. As if reading my mind Bix said, "We need to join the others in the vault, now!"

By about 5:45 P.M., all staff was accounted for and locked up with me in the basement safe room. The vault had an enormous steel door that sealed it off from the rest of the embassy's basement. Behind that door were several small rooms, some furniture—consisting mainly of folding metal chairs—broken computers and computer monitors, and some provisions including bottled water. For most of the forty-two employees there was little to do but wait. Thankfully, there were telephones that allowed us communications with Washington in the form of an open line to the State Department Operations Center, while on another line we were in touch with the head of the embassy guard force, Ljubco Bajevski, who had ripped off his embassy uniform, melted into the crowd, and continued to give us telephone reports with his cell phone. On another line we monitored progress with the Macedonian government in providing the necessary riot police.

You can tell a lot about people in a vault, I thought. Some, such as Phil Reeker, remained totally calm, retaining a sense of humor while making sure others were all right. Some seemed lost in their thoughts. Nobody was panicky, but I told Phil and Tina Kaidanow we needed to keep an eye on those not doing well, and above all keep them busy. Tina gave people things to do, usually in the form of logs and lists. All but three in the vault were embassy employees. One exception was my eleven-year-old daughter, Clara, who had come to the embassy earlier that day before any signs of the crowds. Clara, the ultimate Foreign Service trouper, who a few years before had visited me in Dayton and urged Holbrooke and Bosnian prime minister Haris Silajdzic to bomb

Milosevic (what Holbrooke would later describe to people as "the Clara plan"), was fine and chatted up some people to keep their minds off the situation.

The other two were a cameraman and Biljana Sekulovska, a reporter from A-1 television network, who had come in the late afternoon for an interview arranged by Phil but which had to be cut short when rocks started coming through the windows. My answers to her were in a tone of calm resolve. At one point I had actually talked through the sound of a rock that landed on the floor between our chairs. Before we finally stopped it, the interview had begun to resemble a Monty Python skit. As we got everyone in the vault, Biljana seemed nonplussed, other than continuing to ask, "Can I smoke now?" "No!" we all replied.

I reached Secretary Albright through the State Department Operations Center line. She asked, "Chris, are you okay? What can I do? I've talked to Wes [Clark] and they are preparing a force to come help you." I assured her (against any evidence) we were all going to be okay and briefed her on the situation. By this time the line on the other end in Washington involved numerous people receiving updates from us and asking questions, as if my answers were going to help us get out of our plight. The Pentagon command center was on the line, as was Wes Clark, who, as Secretary Albright informed me, had ordered a quick reaction team of some seventy-five soldiers from the U.S. logistics base out at the airport. He told me they would be in the vicinity within ten minutes. I told him we needed to coordinate very closely on any further moves by these troops. But when he said they were minutes away, I thought, Thank God.

I made my way through the four rooms, telling people we were going to be fine and assuring them that U.S. forces were nearby. Though I did not tell anybody, not even Phil or Charlie or Tina, I was particularly worried about one aspect of what I had witnessed a few minutes before, when I saw the cars being burned. What would happen if bottles of kerosene were thrown between the thick iron bars of the windows and the broken glass into the embassy? Could the embassy burn? There is a sprinkler system, right? And if the embassy did burn, what would happen to the air supply in the basement, where we are? I walked around as if I were on an inspection tour to make sure of people's comfort, though I was really looking for whether there was any air supply in the event the air ducts started pumping smoke. I saw a trapdoor in the lower part of a rear-facing wall and asked Mitko as calmly as I could if he knew where it led.

"That is the door to a tunnel that leads out to the middle of the parking lot. But I wouldn't try to use it now." We laughed at the thought of coming up through a manhole in the middle of the parking area with hundreds of demonstrators and blazing cars all around. But I thought, Okay, we could get out, albeit to some uncertain circumstances.

I racked my brain for anything else I should be doing; I'd run through checklists in my head, trying to remember various courses in the Foreign Service Institute about crisis management. Instead I remembered something someone had once said to me about leadership: it is about imparting a sense of optimism to the others. I tried to do that but all the while worried about fire and smoke, and about some of the quiet types who appeared lost in their thoughts. I asked Phil, Tina, and Mitko to stay engaged with them.

At about 6 P.M. we all heard a steady but slow noise above us. Boom (ten seconds) . . . boom . . . boom. Like a scene in a submarine movie, we all looked up and then at each other. No one spoke. I turned to Greg Slotta, who was on the phone with Ljubco. "Greg, find out from Ljubco what that noise is." Part of me didn't want to know.

"It's the flagpole," he told me. "They are using it as a battering ram on the embassy front door. But, it's holding, no problem." I sighed. "Medieval," Phil remarked.

At about 6:15 P.M., the heroic Ljubco was reporting to Greg that riot police were entering the compound, and about that time we heard what sounded like a knock on the vault door (it turned out to be some piping that had fallen from the ceiling). I was on the telephone with Undersecretary Tom Pickering and the Balkan office director, Jim Swigert. I told them we were hearing that riot police were entering the compound and that the knock came maybe from them. On the other hand, I continued, it might be Land Shark, referring to a particularly absurd *Saturday Night Live* episode. "Should I open the vault?"

"Wait!" Pickering and Swigert, presumably both *SNL* fans, said in unison. "Not yet!"

I briefed Wes Clark, who was still on the line. He confirmed he was hearing from our quick reaction unit nearby that police were beginning to enter the compound. I told him we were going to venture out from the vault.

We started turning the crank to open the door and sent a small party out to survey. Bix Aliu came back to say that the compound was empty of demonstrators and full of police and now U.S. soldiers. As I started up the stairs, Biljana, still holding her unlit cigarette between her fingers, asked, "Can I smoke my cigarette now?"

We opened the back door of the embassy. The smoke was still thick from the carcasses of the vehicles and burning tires. I saw a U.S. soldier in full battle gear, and as he approached I could see two stars on his helmet.

"General Craddock, I presume." I had always wanted to say something like that in such circumstances.

"Mr. Ambassador, I think we are okay now."

He explained the situation, and I then toured the compound as the riot police left and the U.S. troops took up positions. They strung large bales of razor wire across the front where the fence had been taken down, and were starting to string wire on top of the walls in the sides and back. I approached a U.S. soldier standing nearby at the side wall.

"What are your orders?" I asked.

"Well, sir, if a few come over the wall, we cuff 'em, and turn them over to local authorities. If more than that start coming over, we fire warning shots in the air. If even more than that comes over, well, sir, they won't want to do that."

And they didn't. The next morning I got to the embassy early. All the wrought-iron bars had held, as had the thick, though cracked, ballistic glass in the doors. But most windows were broken and glass lay everywhere in the compound. Outbuildings, including the guard posts, were destroyed and burned out, as were some twenty vehicles in the rear parking area, some still smoking. Greg Slotta's motor scooter had been reduced to a puddle of plastic on the pavement, and his Hyundai car to a burned-out wreck. Our General Services officer, Rudy Kyle, a rock of a person, as steady as they come, had begun to organize a cleanup staff consisting of about twenty dispirited Macedonians. I told Rudy I wanted to speak to them all. They gathered around me in the parking lot. I asked Mitko to translate and wondered whether anyone had given a motivational speech to an embassy cleanup crew before.

"I want the embassy open to the public tomorrow, so we have much work to do today. We need to remove all these cars, and clean the parking lot so we can park new cars here. We need to sweep up all the glass so that we can begin to install new window glass. We need to clean the front walls so that painters can paint over the graffiti. We"—I don't know why I kept saying "we"—"also need to clean up the front of the embassy so we can get the flagpole back up and the flag up, and up today. I don't want people to see us looking like this. Okay. Let's move!" Like a football team breaking a huddle they went to work with looks of grim determination.

At five that afternoon Rudy appeared at my office door with an anxious look on his face.

"Rudy. What's the matter?"

"Sir, we just raised a new flag. Come see it." Several of us ran out to take a look. I had never seen such a beautiful sight in my life.

The deputy chief of mission, Paul Jones, returned late on the night of the attack from a road trip outside the city and took over much of the internal operations of the embassy, chairing our "emergency action committee" and providing Washington with frequent "Situation Reports" to reassure them that our eyes and ears were open and we were on top of things. I focused on the Macedonian government to reassure officials that we would remain open, while also convincing people in Washington that remaining open was a workable plan.

A team of about seventy-five marines arrived that first morning to take over for the army's quick reaction force. Paul urged nonessential personnel to leave so we could be down to an absolute minimum in the event we had to evacuate. The Macedonian government, realizing its mistake, had begun to cooperate by sending far more police than we needed. They also blocked the road in front of the embassy, a rather classic instance of closing the barn door after the horse has fled.

After a few days, Washington agreed. We were staying. All the European embassies, watching carefully for our cue, had also decided to stay. We had no idea how or when the Kosovo War was going to end, but we were going to stay in Skopje.

The war dragged on and on. It was a very strange war in that it consisted of the U.S. bombing targets in Serbia every day to convince Milosevic to change his mind and allow NATO forces into Kosovo. Bombing to change someone's mind is a new one in the annals of war. To change someone's mind, do you bomb bridges? Factories? Villas? Ministry buildings? We bombed them all, and still Milosevic would not change his mind. European allies began to worry that he would never give in, while liberal and conservative hawks in the United States began to call for a ground invasion. I accompanied Wes Clark to see President Gligorov. Wes asked the president for permission to pre-position equipment in the event a decision to invade Kosovo was made. Gligorov asked Clark, "If I agreed to your request, will you allow us to join NATO?"

Clark explained that such a decision went beyond his authority, that he understood there were problems associated with Macedonia's entry into NATO, including technical issues involving the readiness of its forces to work with NATO, and a continued foreign policy problem with NATO member Greece over Macedonia's name.

"Because, General Clark," Gligorov continued calmly in his measured voice, as if having ignored Clark's answer, "we are Serbia's neighbors and expect to be for many years. And the Serbs, as you might know, have long knives, but even longer memories."

Clark refocused on Albania as a place to build up equipment in the event of a decision to invade with ground troops.

Macedonia continued to fill up with Albanian Kosovo refugees, at first those simply sitting out the conflict in the Albanian communities in western Macedonia and later, starting in April 1999, those forced out of Kosovo by Serb paramilitaries. As the numbers grew, the Macedonian government began to panic. Macedonia's total population was barely 2 million and there was already a population of some 450,000 Albanian citizens of Macedonia. With the prospect of another half million Albanians from Kosovo's 1.7 million population, and potentially even more, the specter of Albanians actually outnumbering ethnic Macedonians loomed in the minds of the latter.

The Macedonian government began what was in effect a slowdown at the border, thereby reducing the flow of Albanians southward to a trickle as thousands of frightened refugees, without food, water, or sanitary facilities, and without any place to go, stacked up north of the border.

The international community's response was by and large to accuse the Macedonian government of not living up to its international obligations to take in refugees. Soon, tiny and frightened Macedonia became in the eyes of the international community an accomplice to Serb ethnic cleansing policies, a kind of little brother to Milosevic's reign of terror.

The embassy went to work. I met often with Prime Minister Ljubco Georgievski to urge him simply to open the border and not to try to process individual refugee cases there. These demarches usually worked for a day, but were then followed by more delays.

Charlie Stonecipher and Mitko came up with a plan. On the way back from the border station where they were checking the flow of refugees, they identified an underused sport plane airstrip halfway between Skopje and the border, ten miles away. What if we proposed to the Macedonians that it become a refugee camp, with tents and food provided by the UN? Charlie and Mitko suggested in my office. I asked how many refugees could be housed there. "A lot," answered Charlie. "Maybe upwards of fifteen thousand." Probably not enough, I thought, but it would make a good start.

It was definitely worth a try, but the prime minister was growing tired of my daily call, and responses from his office were coming as slowly as the refugees were getting through the border. I kept seeing the prime minister because it was essential to keep his door open to us. No one else in Washington was doing that. Keeping communication with the local government is probably the most important duty of an ambassador. It is far more important than making tough pronouncements and criticisms that impress people back in Washington but complicate communication.

That afternoon, Deputy Secretary Strobe Talbott called. I told him the Macedonians were not keeping the border open and that we needed to do something quick. He asked what could be done, and I told him about the idea for a large refugee camp near the border that would be fenced and where refugees could be sheltered. He told me he was in Italy and would check with me in the morning about a possible visit.

The next morning, as Strobe got ready to head for a day trip from Italy to neighboring Albania, he called to ask whether I still wanted him to stop in Macedonia. I had just heard that the border was again closed overnight and told him by all means to come, that I would arrange for a meeting with the prime minister.

That afternoon, Talbott and his interagency delegation arrived in a C-130 at Skopje Airport, the aircraft having popped chaff and flares to thwart antiaircraft missiles. The C-130's sensors had detected being "painted" by fire-control radar from nearby Serbia on its final descent into Skopje, a fact that made Strobe and the group especially happy to greet me on the ground.

We arranged for the fifteen-member group to stay at my house and some nearby government villas, not wanting to use downtown hotels.

Prime Minister Georgievski, whose villa was close to mine, agreed to come over to the residence, together with Deputy Foreign Minister Boris Trajkovski making sure he actually showed up.

At the end of a one-hour meeting we had a deal with the prime minister. Macedonia would allow for the creation of a large "transit" camp in which refugees could catch their breath before being evacuated temporarily to third countries, where they would sit out the war. I recommended we get this out as soon as possible, preferably to the journalists waiting outside the house.

Strobe Talbott accepted a pair of underwear and socks and got some well-deserved rest that night. In the morning, en route to the airport, he stopped at the embassy to address the Macedonian and U.S. staff who had worked so hard, with such dedication, through the crisis.

"I have never felt so close to Embassy Skopje," he began. "Because having arrived here last night without a suitcase, I am this morning wearing Ambassador Hill's underwear."

That afternoon, the trickle at the border became a flood. Under the expert supervision of British Brigadier General Tim Cross, widely known as a logistics genius, NATO troops, principally Italian and British with some U.S. help at the airport, immediately started erecting large six- and twelve-person tents, building sanitary facilities, and organizing food operations. By Monday afternoon there were twenty thousand refugees, and by Thursday the number had grown to sixty thousand. They were weary, frightened people who had been driven from their homes in Kosovo, sometimes at gunpoint, and had just spent days stacked up at the closed border. Now they were safe.

For more than two months, my family and I heard the rumble of fighter-bombers overhead as they completed their runs over Serbia and Kosovo and made their turns back to NATO bases in Italy. At one point, an A-10 Warthog jet landed at Skopje International Airport, having been hit by a Serb missile, its tail section looking like Swiss cheese and its pilots feeling lucky to be alive. For those passengers landing at the airport on Austrian Air and other airlines that continued service through the war, the sight of a U.S. ground attack jet was a reminder that all was not well in Macedonia.

The Kosovo bombing campaign continued through the spring. It is often cited in the fullness of time as a brilliant effort that created the independent and peaceful Kosovo of today, a model for the future. In fact, once it was clear that those who had predicted Milosevic would immediately capitulate were completely wrong, the bombing campaign became increasingly unpopular, especially when, inevitably, targeting errors mounted. I woke up one morning to learn that a train in central Serbia was hit, killing many civilian passengers. On another day I arrived at the embassy to discover that we had inadvertently targeted Kosovo-Albanian refugees on the road between Jakove and Prizren, killing many of them, mistakes that caused some of the international nongovernmental organizations to start offering advice through the media to NATO war planners as to the altitude at which they should bomb their targets.

The most notorious targeting mistake took place on May 7, 1999, when U.S. precision guided bombs struck the Chinese embassy in Belgrade from three sides, killing several Chinese inside. The night before I had spoken with General Clark, who told me that we had a "big package" going down that night. I turned on CNN in the morning and learned the news. I sat on the end of the bed clutching the sides of my head between the palms of my hands. "Oh my God, is this what he meant?" Of course, the targeting of the Chinese embassy was a total mistake, though the Chinese never seemed to believe that. It had been misidentified as an Interior Ministry facility. The bombing continued, but no one was feeling very optimistic.

There was, however, an important diplomatic track at work. Strobe Talbott, in addition to bucking up the morale at my embassy, was also making his way between European capitals, especially Moscow, to keep the pressure on Milosevic and make him understand that there would be no respite until he agreed to open Kosovo to NATO troops and to what in effect was to become an international protectorate. Without the diplomatic work of Talbott and his team, the bombing would not have been effective. "Diplomacy without force," as Frederick the Great of Prussia is reported to have said, is "music without instruments." He could have gone on to say that bombing without diplomacy is just systematized violence.

Per our agreement with Prime Minister Georgievski in April, some of the refugees were indeed being transferred to other countries, including the United States, but most were still there seventy days later, still without hot meals due to concerns about fire in the hot and dry environs of the camp, which consisted of thousands of green and brown tents. They still had no idea what the future held for them. Rumors substituted for news.

June 4, 1999, the day Serb military commanders agreed to allow NATO's entry into Kosovo, was a happy one, not only for the refugees, but also for the Macedonian people, who had seen their economy collapse due to a war on its border that seemed to have no end. Our embassy had done all we could for the Macedonians. When an official realized that our transit camp did not have a fence around it, I offered to finance it provided he could find a Macedonian contractor to build it. He found one very quickly. Our economic officer, Anton Smith, organized a trade fair for Macedonian suppliers of goods needed for the camps to substitute for imports. I toured the trade fair with British General Sir Michael Jackson as NATO purchasing officers trailed behind us, exchanging their contact information with Macedonian producers of such items as bottled water, cheese, bread, and camping equipment. A few business transactions were completed, though most were not. Nonetheless, we had helped transform Macedonian public opinion, which had been so implacably hostile to NATO, the UN, and the international community in general for bringing "their war" to Macedonia. Deputy Foreign Minister Trajkovski (who would later become president of Macedonia, only to die a few years later in a plane crash) became the embassy's closest interlocutor. Trajkovski and I hosted what were at first daily meetings in the Macedonian Foreign Ministry to address the mountain of mistrust between

Macedonian agencies on the one hand, and the international nongovernment organizations, UN organizations, and NATO on the other. Seated at a long table with some thirty people gathered around it, we dealt with practical problems. When the Macedonian electrical agency representative complained that the UN had failed to pay its bill, I asked, "Is there a representative here from the UN who can answer that?" A person from the other end of the table said, "Of course we will pay, but they never sent us the bill!" I turned to the Macedonian and asked, "Have you sent a bill?" Before he could answer I directed him and the UN rep to meet in the corner of the room, work it out, and report back to the group. And so on.

Macedonia had endured its worst months as an independent state, though it learned much and developed some self-confidence in the process. Visitors from Washington, at first only Strobe but later planeloads of congressmen and senators, saw firsthand what war was doing to this tiny country whose only ambition was to stay out of it and survive.

When the bombing stopped and the announcement was made about the first meetings between the Serbs and NATO commanders, I went out to Uranija Restaurant, located in a park in the center of Skopje. It was a clear, beautiful June night. With a group of Macedonian friends, including the Gruevskis and Peshevs, we celebrated the expected end of the war and the ordeal. "I never thought our little country could ever survive a war in Kosovo," one said to me. "You mean 'your beautiful little country,'" I joked as we toasted again.

I returned to my home that night to turn on CNN and check for the latest developments. The relief I felt was overwhelming. For the first time in three long months I could watch the news without a sense of foreboding. Anyone who today suggests that the Kosovo War was an inexorable march toward an inevitable triumph, a model for resolving future such conflicts, simply was not there at the time.

But just then my cell phone rang. It was our refugee coordinator, Ted Morse, who asked in a very agitated voice if I would tell the Macedonian interior minister not to use the riot police currently at the camp. I told Ted to slow down and explain why there were riot police at the camp in the first place. He explained what had happened. An Albanian had seen a young boy he believed to have helped the Serbs burn his home. He gave chase, and soon many of the camp residents were hunting down the Roma living in the vast camp. The Roma family took refuge in the offices of Catholic Relief Services (CRS), a prefabricated structure that sat on cinder blocks in the center of the main Stenkovac camp. The hostile crowd began to gather around the office compound, at which point CRS called the Macedonian police for help. With the situation momentarily stabilized, Ted called me to ask that I use my contacts in the Macedonian government to prevent the police from entering the camp. I then spoke by phone with the CRS official, who told me the situation remained fluid. The Albanians had not returned to their tents and were milling around to see what would happen next. I told her I would get there immediately.

When I arrived I could see in the dim light the Macedonian riot police sitting outside the camp fence waiting for orders. Ed Joseph, the Catholic Relief official in charge of the camp, met me at the entrance and asked that I talk to a group of camp elders whom he had brought outside the gate. I agreed, though it was clear to me that the camp elders were hardly the problem, nor could they be much of a solution. I spoke about the need to restore order in the camp, and most important, to get the crowds of young men away from the CRS offices. One spoke up: "You need to enter the camp and speak directly to them." I looked over into the camp through the crude fencing and saw the large crowd. I didn't want to do it—it seemed a little risky, to put it mildly—but I certainly couldn't see what talking to a pleasant group of septuagenarians outside the camp gates was accomplishing, either. I also thought a camp riot involving Macedonian police would undermine much of what we had accomplished in the past two and a half months. I asked Joseph what he thought. "Worth a try," he responded.

I could tell that Brad, a member of the two-person security detail who had accompanied me out from Skopje, was not very enthusiastic.

"It'll be okay, Brad. We'll stay close to the gate in case we have to leave in a hurry."

Brad smiled wanly and agreed. I told him, "Let's do it."

Charlie Stonecipher, DCM Paul Jones, Ed Joseph, Ted Morse, and Ed's interpreter accompanied me. Brad and his colleague followed, carrying semiautomatic rifles. A couple of the younger of the camp elders led the way, calling out to the crowd with a battery-powered bullhorn to make way for us.

The crowd opened for us as we made our way through the gate and toward the administrative area, surrounded by young men. The camp elder on the bullhorn was really doing his job, demanding room and calling on people to sit down to listen to me. Paul Jones had the presence of mind to grab a plastic Coca-Cola crate for me to stand on, and Charlie had somehow found an American flag, albeit a beach towel, but nonetheless a welcome sight to the crowd.

Paul planted the crate on its end in the mud and said, "Good luck." I climbed onto it, holding the bullhorn in my right hand while raising the other to signal for quiet and hoping the crate wasn't going to tip over. I had no idea what I was going to say:

"Mir mbrema. Une jam Hill. Une kam liame sot. Generale nga NATO sot keni takoj me Serbise." (Good evening. I am Hill. I have news today. NATO generals have met today with the Serbs.)

I looked down at the interpreter, who I suspect had listened to as much butchery of the Albanian language as he could take in a lifetime and so said to me, "Please let me help." I started speaking in English, passing the bullhorn down to him for interpretation.

"The NATO generals have not met with the Serbs to negotiate. They told the Serbs and the Serbs have agreed to allow NATO to enter Kosovo."

The crowd erupted into a loud roar. If my plan was to calm them down, it wasn't working at all. The advantage of using the interpreter was that I could think of my next sentence while he was rendering the previous. I started to get on a roll.

"This means that soon all of you and your families will return to Kosovo. And when you return you will find that much has been destroyed. But we will go back together, and together we will rebuild Kosovo brick by brick. The rule of law in Kosovo has also been destroyed, but that also must be rebuilt. But we will not wait until we have returned to Kosovo to rebuild the rule of law. We will start now!" I added in Albanian language, "tani" (now), "sot" (today)!

By this time the crowd, seated on the ground and stretching as far as my eyes could see, lit up by one klieg light, coming from a Macedonian television station, had become an audience. The danger had passed, but my adrenaline was flowing and I was in a good rhythm with the interpreter:

"I know there are people here who you believe have committed terrible crimes. Give them to me and I will see that justice is done to them. You know me! Give them to me! I will do right by you. We have been through too much together to shame ourselves by making a terrible mistake." It was a little dramatic, but it seemed to be working.

At that moment, two VW Microbus ambulances pulled up to the back of the offices and the two Roma families who had been falsely accused (it turned out) were put into the vehicles and taken out of the camp. A father and son had been beaten mercilessly. The fourteen-year-old had both arms dislocated in an effort to dismember him.

"Now, please go back to your tents. Rest, and get ready for the next part of our journey together." Again, a little melodramatic, I thought, but why not, given the circumstances?

It had worked. One of the camp elders came to me as the crowd began to disperse and explained that some of them had not been able to hear and wanted me to repeat my message. I looked over at Charlie and ruefully shook my head to the effect that I simply couldn't do it again. Always the Foreign Service officer, he said in mock seriousness, "Maybe just an executive summary."

After the encore performance, we got ready to drive back to town in a Chevy Suburban. Nobody said much about what we had just seen, nor did we want to talk about the risks we had all just run. I mentioned to Ed Joseph my concern about what the future of Kosovo would be like. "Maybe that was a taste of things to come," Ed answered.

Within weeks the camp was gone, and what had peaked as a city of more than sixty-five thousand people was now an empty space, as many had followed NATO convoys into Kosovo. President Clinton came to visit two weeks later. The day before, I was back out at the camp, this time pleading with people not to leave quite yet, so there would be enough refugees for him to meet there.

13

PATTERNS OF COOPERATION

Macedonia survived, and as NATO troops and convoys, with helicopters overhead, poured up that familiar valley into Kosovo, trailed by cars and tractors carrying returning refugees, even that troubled land also calmed down. Leaders such as Veton Surroi, Hashim Thaci, and Jakup Krasniqi emerged from hiding. I accompanied Ibrahim Rugova, who had sat out the war in Rome as a guest of the Vatican, on his return to a hero's welcome to contend with a new political landscape in a Kosovo unrecognizable from before. Many towns and neighborhoods had been burned to the ground by Serb paramilitaries taking reprisals on the Albanian community for the NATO bombs. None was worse than in the town of Jakove, where during a visit in July I saw row upon row of shops that had been torched by departing Serb troops.

The Kosovars began to rebuild, an activity that never seemed to slow down to this day. I also visited the United Nations building in Pristina and met with the new special representative, Sergio de Mello (who almost a decade later would be killed in the bombing of the UN headquarters in

Iraq). He had experiences in many parts of the world, and together with the representative of Organization for Security and Co-operation in Europe, had already started the preparations for free elections. Kosovo may have a unique history, but its postconflict challenges of getting the economy moving, and of forging political consensus and legitimacy, were far from unique. De Mello's experience elsewhere made him the right person to begin the tasks there. Meanwhile, Kosovo's Serb community, already small, became smaller as many packed their own cars and tractors, and like the Serbs of Croatia, some dug up the graves of their ancestors and headed north into Serbia. Those who remained grouped themselves into a few enclaves, expecting the worst from their Albanian neighbors. Fortunately, despite some score settling, an age-old issue in the Balkans, the worst never came.

In Macedonia, people picked up where they had left off before the war. Textile orders from international buyers abroad started trickling in again. First Lady Hillary Clinton had made two visits during the war. On the first visit, she heard about the problem facing the textile industry—their loss of contracts due to the conflict and to a flexible and globalized garment industry, which can switch suppliers on a moment's notice. But when she returned a month later with her husband in June 1999, she brought with her several garment purchasers, including the CEO of the American apparel maker Liz Claiborne. She announced to a packed auditorium of mostly women textile workers who had previously been laid off that they would be working again.

"She really cares about Macedonia. She is so sincere in trying to help us," a Macedonian friend said to me. There was no question that she had followed up. I was deeply moved.

On one of my final days in country, a businessman approached me on the street and put his arms around me and thanked me for my work. He was a milk producer from Bitola, in southern Macedonia, who had actually received a real contract from the U.S. military to supply our troops. "Thank you, thank you!" he continued. "I never knew Americans could drink so much milk!"

"You're welcome," I responded, still in his embrace and somewhat overwhelmed by this emotional outburst of affection. I wasn't sure what to say. "We also use it on our cereal."

I left Macedonia in August 1999, sadly, because I could not imagine my life without a daily life-and-death crisis, such is the addictive quality of adrenaline. I returned to Washington to begin a one-year assignment at the National Security Council staff as a senior director for the Balkans, responsible for advising the president on the Balkans and for making sure the interagency process of government stayed focused on the tasks ahead. Kosovo had been a traumatic experience for all, and there was a very real sense that we may have just been lucky at the end, when Milosevic gave up. "It was such a great experience, we should never repeat it," a British diplomat commented to me.

I wasn't really in the mood for Washington's trench warfare, nor for a climate of polarization and recrimination that seemed increasingly similar to what had caused the Balkans wars in the first place. Secretary Albright and President Clinton had selected me, at my request (sometimes it helps to ask), to become ambassador to Poland when that position opened up in the summer of 2000. Earlier in June I had arranged an academic year in Boston to organize and collect my thoughts, intellectually calm down, read a few of the books that had piled up unread throughout the crisis, and jot down some thoughts about what I had just experienced. But National Security Advisor Sandy Berger instead asked if I would take on the task of coordinating U.S. government agencies working on postconflict operations in the Balkans, especially Bosnia and Kosovo. Berger had asked me during President Clinton's visit to Macedonia in June 1999, just a week after people had begun to return to their homes in Kosovo. We were visiting Stenkovac, where the refugees were busy packing up whatever belongings they had to begin another phase in their uncertain future. In every respect, it wasn't really an offer I could refuse.

The national security staff broadly consists of a national security advisor to the president, a deputy or two, and senior directors of "directorates" that roughly correspond to geographic and functional bureaus in the State Department. Working for each senior director are "directors," a kind of entry-level position where much of the work of the NSC staff is done. These can be members of the career Foreign Service, career military or career CIA, and political appointees who are experts from academia. This last group will sometimes spend the rest of their professional lives talking to the media with the inflated role of "the director," as opposed to one of several. When Berger asked me to take the job, he also asked if there was anything he could do. "I need Tina," I told him. She became a director of the office and proved as adept a Washington player as she was in the field during the conflict in Kosovo. Foreign Service officers who are effective in Washington and in the field are not easy to find, and I didn't want to let Tina go elsewhere.

When the president hosts a foreign leader, the senior director joins the national security advisor as the briefer, note taker, and participant in the debrief meeting. It's heady stuff, but only for the few minutes the president is actually focused on the issue before he turns his attention to something else. A foreign policy meeting may be sandwiched between events involving domestic issues, like greeting a winning baseball team or signing a bill. I always marveled at President Clinton's ability, indeed at any president's ability, to remember which meeting he was in and who he was talking with.

Where the president does become especially focused is on overseas trips. I accompanied President Clinton to Bulgaria and Kosovo just before Thanksgiving 1999, and his capacity to absorb the briefing materials and then hold cogent discussions with his starstruck interlocutors was remarkable. His conversations with the Kosovo leadership in particular showed his sweep of the issues, and his advice was particularly on target: "You are in the world's spotlight today, but it won't last. Take advantage of it. Demonstrate progress in building your institutions, because at some point that spotlight will move elsewhere." That was very good advice for a region that was already becoming yesterday's news. As I took notes of the meeting, I saw the puzzled looks on the faces of the much-divided Kosovo leadership as they sat across from the president in a makeshift, austere meeting room at the Pristina airport. It was as if they could not understand that there might be issues in the world more compelling than their own and that could eventually divert the president's attention.

As relieved as the administration felt about the "victory" in Kosovo, the continued presence of a defiant Milosevic in Belgrade, like Saddam Hussein in Iraq almost a decade before, remained a bitter aftertaste of the war. Some European countries, such as Italy, seemed prepared to move on, though most did not. At the NSC I chaired numerous meetings aimed at finding stiffer, more personalized sanctions that would target family finances hidden in third countries or otherwise restrict Milosevic's travel and that of his family, so-called smart sanctions. Despite the promise by sanction experts, the sanctioneers, to create financial havoc for Milosevic and his family, no evidence ever emerged to suggest they were anything more than a momentary nuisance, a fly at a picnic. Milosevic seemed to be fully recovered from the war and, if anything, more self-confident than ever.

It would not be until the summer of 2000, just as I was preparing to leave for Poland, that Milosevic, one year after NATO's entry into Kosovo, optimistically called for early presidential elections in September. He had every expectation of winning, just as he had in every other election. But this time, as I was settling into my new life in Poland, he overreached. By October 5, amid the "Bulldozer revolution" (all transfers of power during that era seemed to require a catchy name, this one deriving its own from a striking factory worker who plowed an industrial vehicle into one of Milosevic's party buildings), he relinquished power. That night in Warsaw, I was hosting U.S. participants in the Chopin Piano Competition together with Polish guests for a large dinner at my home, the U.S. ambassador's residence. I'd sneak away from the sixty or so guests seated at small round tables and go to the study to watch the latest CNN coverage, at last returning to announce to the guests that Milosevic was finally gone. They applauded politely and went back to their dinner. I was now living in a different country.

I had arrived in Poland in July 2000 on a hot, sunny day, my family and I anxious to begin our new lives. The city of Warsaw was unrecogniz-able from the time I lived there fifteen years before. Construction was everywhere. Miraculously, it seemed, the dull grayness was gone, replaced by bright colors. What I remembered as grim, heavy buildings were now freshly sandblasted to reveal a textured brightness that had been covered by decades of communist grime and soot. Even the weather seemed better than under communism. Somehow out of Poland's ashes had emerged a vibrant entrepreneurial class of young people whose collective memory of the communist years was fast fading and who seemed uninterested in looking back. They were focused on Poland's future as a European Union country, a status that would complete the country's journey of a thousand years, to be in every way a Western European country.

Just a month before I arrived in Warsaw, the ruling coalition split when the junior partner to the government, the "Freedom Union" (UW, by its Polish acronym), walked out of the government. Freedom Union was the party that represented many of the Warsaw-based intellectu-als who had in many cases borne the brunt of Jaruzelski's martial law crackdown a few years before. Its leadership had been a who's who of communist-era prison inmates. They were replaced by lesser-known Soli-darity figures, who by the summer of 2000 were understood to be tempo-rary, given the expectation of a victory in 2001 by the Left Alliance Party, the former communists. "You're really unlucky to come to Poland when you did," one Polish watcher told me. "No more fun!"

Actually, I relished as any diplomat would the challenge of doing my part to keep Poland on track. Poland in 2000 seemed safely out of the communist woods in which it had struggled ten plus years before, but in the meantime, a new form of nationalism had begun to engulf the region. With its large rural and disaffected population Poland seemed to be a prime candidate to catch this new disease. Poland had succumbed to dic-tatorship in the 1930s after enjoying a democracy of about a decade. Of the new democracies in the northern tier of former Eastern Bloc states, Poland was the one deemed least likely to succeed.

The embassy needed to be close to the opposition, the former communists now social democrats, which had high expectations that they would take over the government, as well as to the Solidarity government, now on its last breath. "Don't lose track of anyone," I told the political officers. "Today's opposition will be tomorrow's ruling party, and so on." When Solidarity, as predicted, lost the election in 2001 and went into the wilderness as the opposition, they accepted their role but were back in government in 2005. Poland's democracy continued to work.

I did what U.S. ambassadors have done in Warsaw for decades, plunging into its complex social and political scene, turning my house into a salon of senior politicians and artists and writers. General Jaruzelski, still wearing his trademark dark glasses from the time he ran the country during martial law, returned my visit to his modest home in the neighborhood. Adam Michnik, a writer who had been imprisoned by the communists and later forgave them (earning considerable criticism from those who had never been near a prison cell or even paid a fraction of the price that he did for Poland's democracy), became a frequent visitor. There were many others: Helena Luczywo, who brought Poland's top underground newspaper into the open and made it Poland's newspaper of record; Wanda Rapaczynski, a teenage refugee in 1968, who returned to help turn that newspaper into a media giant.

Though the Poles had their own thriving democracy, they seemed just as interested in the U.S. elections in November 2000. As embassies do worldwide, we hosted an election party. The Marriott hotel ballroom was filled to capacity as the animated and boisterous crowd carefully watched the coverage, holding drinks in their hands, unworried by the outcome. Poles loved George H. W. Bush and had been equally fond of Bill Clinton, though less familiar with George W. Bush and Al Gore and had no reason to think that anything would change. As the voting returns began to come in at midnight, I stood on the stage and assured the audience that we would not close down until a winner had been declared.

I didn't keep that promise, and as the weeks rolled by Polish friends would ask: "Are things there going to be all right?"

Joining Europe (the EU) and keeping the United States engaged in Europe were two pillars of Poland's emerging foreign policy, positions that enjoyed consensus across Poland's raucous political divide. That effort to keep close ties with the EU and the United States seemed to be getting a tad more difficult as the Bush administration began an unceremonious and relentless review of many U.S. commitments to multilateralism, including in arms control and climate change. The Poles shared some of the skepticism about agreements that also seemed to them to have dubious enforcement regimes, but they did not want to be put in the position of choosing between the United States and the Europeans. The Europeans, a Pole complained, sometimes define being a European as not being an American. Differences over such issues as the Kyoto Protocol on global warming helped them to do that. The Poles watched helplessly as the U.S.-European relationship worsened. They tried to play the role that Britain also tries to play, that of a transatlantic reconciler. But while the Europeans had long since grown used to the British playing that role, an EU aspirant trying to do the same was less tolerated.

Even when the Poles tried to do the right thing with the United States, they sometimes felt out of step with the new administration. Deputy Secretary of Defense Wolfowitz arrived in Warsaw in March 2001 for a visit. The Poles explained their decision making on the acquisition of F-16s, a multibillion-dollar program that would make their air force compatible with the United States and one of the most modern in Europe. They outlined their thoughts on possibly joining a consortium for the next-generation Joint Strike Fighter. Wolfowitz brushed them off on tactical aircraft acquisition, explaining that the new administration was reviewing the entire Joint Strike Fighter program and was far more interested in reviving missile defense as a top priority.

In damage control mode, I made numerous calls to the Pentagon to make sure the Poles didn't believe they were receiving mixed messages, and at one point asked President Bush to raise the subject in the Oval Office with Prime Minister Miller to ensure that the Poles understood that buying our tactical aircraft was also a top priority. "You want me to talk about airplanes in this meeting?" the president asked as he got ready to host the prime minister. "Sir, we need to show a level of effort. Tony Blair talks airplanes when he meets the Poles, and I really can't stand the thought of them flying around in a Swedish-British thing called a 'Grippen.' Can you?" He raised the issue with the prime minister and the Poles got the message that we cared.

As if to stress the bipartisan commitment of the United States to its ally Poland, Bill Clinton made a private trip to Warsaw to make a well-remunerated speech in May 2001. At his request, we took a walk through Warsaw's old town streets, greeting shocked passersby who were not sure they were seeing a street entertainer or the former president (or both, as I watched his performance). We ducked into a restaurant and the former president ordered just about everything on the menu as he surveyed food being carried to other tables. "That looks good, let's have some of that, too . . . Oh my, what is that? Polish apple pie?!" After the lunch we continued to walk through the streets, stopping for an ice cream ("It looks sooooo good!"), the crowds thickening by the minute as he shook hands with everybody in reach, saying in that raspy voice, "Hah there, how yah doin'?" Finally an antiglobalization demonstrator (proof that Poland was a member of Europe!) threw an egg that found its mark on the president's blue blazer. While shaking another hand he quickly removed the jacket and handed it to an aide, never missing a beat. "Hah there, how yah doin'?"

George W. Bush arrived in Warsaw on a brilliant mid-June day, and the Poles loved him. He had just come from a particularly desultory meeting with the Europeans in Copenhagen, where he felt he had been treated to one too many lectures from the Danes and others as to the need for the United States to build more windmills. In Warsaw, nobody pressed him about windmills. They just thanked him and the United States for being a friend.

We stood outside the Presidential Palace for the playing of "The Star-Spangled Banner." I noticed the eyes of Bush's national security advisor, Condoleezza Rice, who was standing next to me, brimming with tears as the music played. Rice's entire academic and professional career had been dedicated to achieving the end of the Soviet Union, the end of the long and bitter division of Europe, so I decided to cut her some slack for shedding a tear or two at the playing of the U.S. national anthem in Warsaw. Later in the morning the president visited Poland's Tomb of the Unknown Soldier, a monument that sits amid the decapitated remains of a nineteenth-century palace destroyed by the Germans in 1944. It doesn't take too much time at that site to understand why Poland wanted to be in NATO. For lunch, Prime Minister Jerzy Buzek hosted Bush at an eighteenth-century palace built on a lake and took him on a tour of the frescoes and statuary. The president quipped to everyone's amusement, "We don't have anything like this in Texas."

In the afternoon he spoke to a large audience in the Warsaw University library about America's enduring commitment to Europe. In an important statement given all the rethinking that was going on in Washington, he announced his support for further NATO enlargement. It was music to the ears of the Poles, who did not want to be NATO's northern and eastern flank and looked for the day when countries north and east could also join NATO. In the Balkans I had been accustomed to urgent and gut-wrenching, life-and-death issues of war and peace. Here I just enjoyed the show. After the library speech, the president plunged into an enthusiastic crowd, who didn't want to let him go. Many Poles, not quite able to reach the president, tugged at me to congratulate me on the speech. I gave credit to my predecessor, Dan Fried, who after leaving Poland had started working in Condi Rice's NSC, but I finally learned just to say, "You're welcome." Over the course of a career where one is blamed for many things one never does, I thought it might be some payback to get credit for something I had little to do with, too.

After the event, President Bush asked me what was next on the schedule. I told him we had arranged for a brief walk in the old town market square, where he could duck into a shop and buy a small pastry.

"That seems a little phony," he replied. "Don't you think so?"

"Well, yes, sir. I guess you have a point."

He returned to the hotel.

The September 11 attacks took place at 3 P.M. European time, and by 4 P.M. the front of the embassy along Ujazdowskie Street began to be lit up by candles placed there by passersby. By late in the evening, crowds, many carrying candles and flowers, stood in front of the embassy, maintaining a vigil as the police closed two lanes of traffic of the four-lane road to allow enough room for the displays. The next morning I went out to thank them for their support. I was mobbed as people held up their private photos of New York City and held my hand as if to provide personal support to the country that had for so long symbolized their hopes and dreams. Huge crowds remained in front of the embassy for days, replacing flowers and relighting candles. Polish churches held mass after mass. Some countries are known for weddings, but Poles know how to do funerals as well.

The Polish government immediately offered to send blood to New York and anything else we might need. A few weeks later, the Polish defense minister, Jerzy Szmajdzinski, called me to his office and offered to send Polish forces for the expected attack on Afghanistan, complaining ever so slightly that he couldn't get much attention from Secretary of Defense Donald Rumsfeld. Sending troops to a place like Afghanistan would be a major commitment by Poland, he told me, as if to help me try to raise some interest by the secretary of defense.

In the coming year, as the United States got ready for Iraq, Poland continued to be supportive, even as public interest in war began to wane. I worried about what invading Iraq would lead to. I believed the reports about Iraq's weapons of mass destruction, but I could not see the link between 9/11 and Saddam Hussein, nor could anyone who understood the region.

Wolfowitz's visit to Warsaw and focus on missile defense, as if to try to reverse what he felt were the lethargic policies of the Clinton administration toward defense of the homeland, highlighted the growing divide in Washington. As he dismissed the Polish interest in F-16s and the next-generation Joint Strike Fighter as not "transformational," that is, as fighting the last war rather than the next (even though the real Polish interest was very much on the next set of challenges, that is, maintaining the U.S. in Europe), I could not help but think that new policy wonks in charge were more interested in repudiating the activities of their predecessors than in focusing on future threats. And even when the future threats came, in Afghanistan and Iraq, these issues too seemed more in the context of settling old scores, and in this case not just scores with Clinton as with the first Bush administration.

The run-up in 2002 to the Iraq War had me and every U.S. ambassador around the globe making the case for the undertaking. I spoke on Polish television, radio, in newspaper interviews, to international affairs groups, everywhere about the dangers of inaction. Even during the country's years in communist captivity, Poles were world travelers with opinions about every region of the globe. While they did not dispute the concern about Iraq's WMD, they were less convinced about our plans to replace the Saddam regime with a democracy. "You will win the war," one journalist said to me. "But then what? That is what I worry about." The tone was generally supportive, unlike the mood in Western Europe. And again, as in Afghanistan, Poland offered troops.

When the request came to train Free Iraqi Forces (FIF) in Poland, Polish officials were skeptical. "Where did you say you found these people?" Marek Siwiec, President Kwasniewski's national security advisor, asked me, somewhat incredulous of the entire endeavor. But the Poles, in the interest of their relationship with the United States, pulled together a plan and a place for the training. Ultimately, the decision was made to train the FIF elsewhere.

Visitors from Washington were impressed by the Polish élan during the preparations for war in Iraq, but in fact the Poles were interested not because they thought it was a good idea, but because they wanted to show the United States that it had good allies in Europe. "We are doing this for our relationship with you, not out of any belief that Iraq is necessarily the right thing to do." Indeed, when President Kwasniewski visited the White House in the winter of 2003, just weeks before the invasion, his questions to the president were full of skepticism. "How will you manage the people's needs after you take over the government?" he asked. "Food supplies? Medicine? The schools, the hospitals?"

When the invasion began, Poles joined Australian, British, and American troops in the first assaults on Saddam's forces. Polish commandos in rubber rafts attacked offshore oil facilities to prevent Saddam from blowing them up, as he had in the Persian Gulf War twelve years earlier. A day later, the office of the chairman of the Joint Chiefs, General Richard Myers, called to ask if the Poles would allow him to describe the actions of their troops on that first day, but when I checked with the Polish ministry they asked that I not do so, given the shakiness of public opinion throughout Europe. The next day, however, every Polish newspaper ran the story, with photographs of Polish commandos and U.S. Special Forces standing in group portraits, both countries' flags fluttering behind them.

I departed Poland in July 2004 for my next assignment, South Korea. Nestled between Japan and China, Korea had a historical experience not entirely dissimilar to that of Poland. It was an easier transfer to make than one would think. After only a few weeks in Washington I arrived in Seoul in August against a backdrop of a deteriorating relationship between a right-leaning U.S. administration and a left-leaning Korean administration. I set to work making sure that our public messaging emphasized the need to modernize the relationship and set it on a positive footing for the next fifty years. We needed much more "public diplomacy" than had been practiced in the past. Greater public diplomacy became the cure for why the popularity of the United States had fallen so precipitously during the time after the Iraq invasion. Even though it was the policy that needed improvement, there was no question that our diplomats needed to do a better job of explaining and reaching out to nontraditional audiences.

Defining a new relationship required a lot of listening, which was not a problem because getting to know Koreans is to learn how expressive they can be. Younger Koreans were particularly skeptical of the special relationship with the United States because it represented something from the past rather than the future. For starters, I asked a group of online editors what they thought about the embassy website. There was a brief silence before one finally spoke up in as diplomatic a way as she could muster:

"It is not good." The other eight guests giggled at the understatement.

"How can we improve it?" I asked.

"Make a new one," someone else answered, politely but earnestly (but also eliciting nervous giggling). I realized we were now going to have a good time bashing the embassy website.

"What if we added an interactive feature?"

"That would help," still another editor answered. I turned to Don Washington, our press and culture counselor, and asked him if we could do it.

"We looked into it, but because of security concerns that cost could be enormous, maybe thousands of dollars," Don said.

Still another editor spoke up, "I could do it for five dollars. But for you, no charge!" The table roared with laughter. These young Koreans had become totally at ease sitting at a small round table at the home of the U.S. ambassador. What a fabulous assignment I had stepped into.

We fixed the website and it turned out to be easy. Our Internet guru in the embassy, a young Korean employee named Ahn Chanmo, came up with the idea to have a link to the Korean portal, Daum. We called it "Café USA." About a week later Ahn and Jason Rebholz, a public affairs officer, came to my office for approval of my first posting to Café USA.

It was three-quarters of a page long and discussed the importance of democracy. I read it and asked, "Mr. Ahn, don't you think this is boring?"

No answer.

"Mr. Ahn, I think this is boring. What do you think?"

"Mr. Ambassador, you are right. It is very boring. Actually, it is extremely boring."

"Mr. Ahn, could you come around to my computer here, log onto Café U.S., and put in Korean my first posting, which I will now dictate to you in English?"

I got up and asked him to sit in my chair. He hesitated but was soon seated and typing out my message, about my first impressions of Korea. It was also boring, but at least it came directly from me and it gave the audience a sense that they were communicating with the U.S. ambassador. With that we started the first U.S. embassy Web chats. As Café USA gained an audience we began to schedule live Web conversations in a section of the embassy where we could use more than one screen to monitor the incoming calls and I could dictate my answers to Mr. Ahn as he typed my words into Korean.

When Koreans trace the legacy and lineage of their democracy, the narrative passes through the southwestern city of Kwangju. In August 1980, in response to the declaration of martial law by the military regime of General Chun Doo Hwan, antigovernment demonstrators in Kwangju had declared their city independent of the military regime. With thousands having joined the protests, the local police lost control of the situation. In response, Chun Doo Hwan ordered a paratrooper brigade to enter the city and restore governmental control. The brigade, with no training in civil disturbances, did so with predictable results.

The brigade had been originally assigned north of the Han River, where it was under U.S. command. Once south of the Han, the brigade was solely under South Korean authority. Only under actual conditions of warfare could it be ordered by the U.S. military commander, whose prerogatives extended in peacetime just to forces north of the Han River.

Korea's democratic foundation grew through the 1980s, with elections

in 1987, a fast-liberalizing press, greater attention to problems of corruption, and, finally, the development of a multiparty system. It is virtually
impossible to place a date or an event on when Korea's democracy actually was born. Economic liberalization even during the military regime
of Park Chung Hee in the 1960s and '70s played a vital role in bringing
Korea along the path to democracy. When I first arrived in Korea in 1985,
I went to the eighth floor of the embassy to have my courtesy call with
Ambassador Dixie Walker. As I sat on the couch in the waiting room
area, a Korean military drill began in the street below. Helicopters appeared at eye level and soldiers rappelled down ropes to "secure" government buildings across the six-lane boulevard.

In the 1990s a cemetery was constructed where victims of what was
sometimes called the "Kwangju Massacre" were buried. No U.S. ambassador had ever visited the cemetery, nor would such a visit have been
welcomed.

I thought it was important to do so. Not because I believed we were
culpable in any way, but because Kwangju had become the crucible of
Korean democracy and we should not be seen as on the wrong side of
democracy in Korea. Democracy came to Korea because of us, not in spite
of us. I was determined to make this point to Koreans.

I began by asking as many Korean friends as I could what the reaction would be to such a visit. In particular I asked a Korean friend, Sohn
Myong Hyun, to come to the residence on a Saturday morning and
discuss it. I had known "Mike" Sohn since 1985. I had met him at an
embassy reception soon after my arrival at post. At that time he was the
chief of cabinet to Deputy Prime Minister Kim Mahn Je, the chief official
responsible for coordinating the Korean economic ministries. He came up
to me at my arrival reception, hosted by the embassy economic counselor,
and had said very simply, "My name is Sohn Myong Hyun. Please call me
Mike. I have to get back to my office, but I wanted to introduce myself.
We will see a lot of each other."

Nineteen years later we were still close friends.

Mike believed strongly that the United States needed to reach out to nontraditional audiences. "The wealthy classes in Korea, 'the sorts of narrow audiences that American ambassadors had often spent a great deal of time socializing with,' are a dime a dozen," he explained in his excellent English. Mike explained that visiting the cemetery could indeed be the powerful symbol of a new era that I had hoped for, but that it was all in how it was done. He said that if the visit were announced ahead of time, all the anti-U.S. protest groups would descend on the place and then be joined by pro-U.S. groups. The effect would be to create controversy and could come to define my experience in Korea. He proposed that I go there alone, place ashes on the monument, and leave. No propaganda show. Just do it.

I arrived in Kwangju that day to attend the opening of a small American culture center within the local university (the rector of the university wanted to keep the announcement low-key). I then spent two hours at Kwangju's art "Biennale" admiring modern sculpture and multimedia painting, but I was thinking about the cemetery and hoping that the secret had held. At about 5 P.M., accompanied by a single police car, we drove to the cemetery.

The embassy staff assistant, Matthew Cenzer, was waiting at the entrance and had told the cemetery director to expect me. When we arrived, the sun was fast setting behind the hills, and no one else was there. I took a tour of the cemetery, paid respect at the main memorial, and in the visitor book left a message: "I am here with great respect—and great sorrow—for the memory of these brave victims. May they always be remembered and may their memory inspire us all."

Well, almost no one else was there. A "citizen reporter" from the leftist online news outlet *Ohmy Daily* had followed our car and learned of our destination by monitoring the police radio. He had a small digital camera.

The next day, *Ohmy* had the scoop, and by Saturday morning all Korea's major dailies had *Ohmy*'s pictures of an American ambassador paying respect to the victims whose deaths are remembered by many in Korea as part of the crucible of democracy. Many other factors had helped put the United States on the right side of history in Korea's democratic transition, but this example of what would later be called by the much-hackneyed phrase "public diplomacy" helped. Mike Sohn told me, "I think this has helped Korea and the United States turn an important corner."

Several months later, in early December 2004, I stood in a narrow West Wing hallway waiting to meet with Steve Hadley, the incoming national security advisor, who would soon be moving to the office previously held by Condi Rice. I was visiting from Korea, and Washington was in the midst of its quadrennial changing of the guard known as a presidential transition. It was a transition between terms but there was a sense that the second term would be very unlike the Bush first term, perhaps as dramatic as from one president to another. The administration was adrift in a sea of crises that seemed to offer no respite. There was an understanding that despite the supposed mandate President Bush had won over John Kerry a month before in a bruising campaign, the administration might have taken on in that first term more than it could chew. The Iraq War was proving to be a far more difficult undertaking than its supporters and cheerleaders had suggested. And while the Afghan War seemed to be going as well as could be expected, our continued investment there in blood and treasure and more blood had failed to bag Osama bin Laden, much less put Afghanistan on a better path.

Iraq was foremost on everyone's minds. The "historic" (a favorite word of any administration) elections there had gone reasonably well. Pictures of smiling voters holding up their ink-stained index fingers were supposed to attest to that. But in fact, these iconic images of nascent democracy were inspiring only to those who did not understand what was actually going on or where the true fault lines in Iraq lay. Iraq was on its way to becoming a thoroughly divided society. Those who understood those forces knew well what was in store during the second term.

Steve Hadley emerged from his office and explained that we would have the meeting in Condoleezza Rice's office, because she wanted to join us when she returned from another appointment. I was in Washington doing what many of my ambassadorial colleagues were doing during the lull after an election. I was to give an update on the fast-changing scene in South Korea, and to offer some thoughts and perhaps advice about the desultory pace of the North Korean negotiations from the point of view of Seoul. I was planning to share my ideas of how the negotiations could be improved. I had no idea that the incoming secretary of state wanted to take part in such a routine meeting with a visiting ambassador. I soon learned.

As Steve and I sat down on the couch and side chair, Rice entered the office, apologizing for being late (the apology rather unnecessary, I thought, as I had never expected to see her in the first place), and sat across from me. She got quickly to the point:

"This administration has fought two wars, and now we are looking for a few diplomats."

What a nice way to start a meeting, I thought, my mind racing ahead to try to figure out what this was all about.

Within about thirty seconds she slipped into her first sports metaphor. Given what I knew about her love of sports, I was surprised it took that long. I enjoy sports metaphors, with the understanding they have to be buried when one is overseas. Expressions like "can't get around on a fastball anymore" don't really work with a Kosovo insurgent. But I was back in Washington, and understood quickly what she was getting at when she deployed an expression from the NFL draft day.

"We are looking to draft and sign the best athletes regardless of their position," Hadley added, though I had the impression that Rice knew a lot more about the NFL draft than he did.

Condi then asked, "So what would you think about becoming assistant secretary of East Asia and being the U.S. negotiator to the Six Party Talks?" Assistant secretary for East Asian and Pacific affairs is one of the best jobs in Washington. The pictures that adorned the front office of the

East Asian and Pacific Affairs Bureau in the State Department, showing the thoughtful officials who have held the job since it was created in
1908—Averell Harriman, Dean Rusk, Philip Habib, Richard Holbrooke,
Winston Lord—were a who's who of superb diplomats whose work had
been instrumental in defining America's relations with that part of the
world. What an honor to be thought of in such terms.

In a perfect world, I like to think overnight about job offers. But sitting with the incoming secretary of state and incoming national security
advisor didn't seem like a good time to say I needed time to think about it.

"I'd be very honored to serve in that position," I said, my heart momentarily sinking as I thought about all the friends and contacts I was
making during my first few months in South Korea. Seoul is one of the
most vibrant cities in the world, full of political and economic life, and
fast developing a cultural life that is the envy of Asia. My family and I
loved living there, but I knew that sooner or later I would leave anyway.
The beautiful residence wasn't my own home, and though pleasant, it was
a little like living in a hotel suite. My mind quickly moved from life in
Seoul back to the conversation with Rice and Hadley.

I told them, "We have paid a price among the South Koreans for
what is perceived as a reluctance to negotiate. I'm a huge supporter of the
Six Party approach, but in that framework we need to be willing to sit
down and talk with the North Koreans. It is not all about our relations
with North Korea; I doubt we'll ever have one or even need to have one.
It is about our other relationships in the region, especially with the South
Koreans, where based on what I was seeing in Seoul, it could use a little
refreshing." I stopped to gauge the reaction.

"That won't be a problem," Condi said. "The president understands
that and understands that we also need to develop some more effective
patterns of cooperation in the region."

She had me at "patterns of cooperation." It was an expression that
summarized for me much of what diplomacy was about. I loved the
idea of sitting with these two key figures in the Bush administration, a

presidency that for many critics symbolized what was wrong with our country, still heady from the triumphalism that followed the victory over the Soviet Union, and more recently engaging in what to many critics was a classic case of imperial overreach. Both Hadley and Rice were warm, modest, extremely well mannered, and thoroughly committed to diplomacy as the way forward. I could definitely sign on to this new term, I thought.

Importantly, it seemed even then in December 2004 that the era of the neoconservatives, the aggressive, America-as-empire group of foreign policy specialists, led by John Bolton and Paul Wolfowitz, was receding with every policy failure. Wolfowitz himself, a cerebral policy maven who had a reputation as an expert on the Middle East, was the author of the fantasy that an imposed democracy in Shia-majority Iraq (the only Shia-controlled country in the Middle East) would start a democratic brushfire across the region, eventually creating a benign environment for Israel. He had help in creating these fantasies. The number three at the Pentagon, Doug Feith (famously dubbed by U.S. Central Command [CENTCOM] commander General Tommy Franks as the stupidest person in the world), was another card-carrying neocon. I had met Feith in Dayton during the final days of the negotiations, when he interceded as a consultant to the Bosnian government negotiating team, cheerfully advising the Bosnians to hold out for more military assistance before they signed. Feith was replaced early in the Bush second term by Eric Edelman, a former Foreign Service officer who while working in Vice President Dick Cheney's office arranged to be named as U.S. ambassador to Turkey, where his ideological opinionating appeared to do little to endear himself to that difficult regime.

The neocons were aided and abetted by Cheney and Secretary of Defense Rumsfeld, neither of whom was known to have an ideological cast, but believing as the neocons did in a U.S. manifest destiny. Rumsfeld seemed to me to be an old-fashioned Midwestern conservative, with one huge difference: he had an ego the size of Mount Rushmore.

I had seen Rumsfeld in action when he came to Poland. First, he told his advance staff he didn't want the ambassador to greet him at the airport, a normal courtesy that an ambassador would dispense with at some personal peril. When I told his advance team that I did indeed plan to meet him at the airport, I could see the looks of panic descend over their faces: "But, sir, he doesn't want you there," a formulation that could have used some refinement.

"But I must be there," I responded. "Did you know," I continued to the three advance persons as I sat behind my desk on the top floor of the U.S. Embassy in Warsaw, "that as the president's representative I actually outrank the secretary of defense so long as he is in Poland?" I could see their looks of panic as it began to dawn on them that I might in fact be as arrogant as their boss. "If I want to be at the airport to greet the secretary, I'll be there. It's as simple as that," I said, trying to remove from them any thought that they had the power to convince me otherwise.

"Now that we have resolved that," I went on, "could you tell me what the plan is for lunch?" In fact, Rumsfeld's entire visit to Poland, one of America's only fighting allies in the Iraq War, would take less than twenty hours, from late-night arrival to early evening departure.

"Sir, we have five scenarios for him to choose from."

"Five?! Name 'em!" I had met many advance teams for senior official visits, including presidents, but never one that was unable to limit the number of options for lunch to some reasonable number, such as two. It was pure fear on their part. Either that, or Rumsfeld sure cared a lot about how he had lunch.

"Well, sir," the advance staffer said, glancing at his notes, "he has the option of having lunch alone in his suite. He might also enjoy lunch with his senior staff. Or he might have a private lunch with the Polish defense minister. That's number three. Alternatively, he might make a visit to a Warsaw restaurant. We have several places in mind that we have identified as suitable. And finally, there might be a large early evening banquet hosted by the Poles." I tried to think of a sixth or seventh option, but I left it at that. (Rumsfeld eventually chose to have lunch in his suite with his senior staff.)

Condi and Steve were cut from entirely different cloth, and I could see that the second term would consist of a far more pragmatic group of officials, starting with them. There would continue to be neocon dead-enders, but their day was very much over. Little did I know then how hard they would continue to fight. With Iraq and Afghanistan policy largely shifted over to finding the pragmatic identifying endgame strategies for getting out, they would essentially try to make North Korea their final battle.

I left the West Wing realizing that I hadn't nailed down the next steps. Would they call me? Was I supposed to call someone? I decided to let things run their course. It is never good to look unctuous or anxious. I had indicated my willingness to serve in any position they wanted, and that was the impression I wanted to leave with them. Besides, if I stayed in Korea, that would have been fine as well. I walked from Seventeenth Street over to the State Department on Twenty-First Street, where I had a string of appointments starting with Secretary Colin Powell.

At the State Department, already feeling bludgeoned by the first term of the Bush administration, there was a fear and foreboding that the worst was yet to come with the departure of Colin Powell and the arrival of Condi Rice and an expected retinue of staff from her National Security Council.

During his four years at State, Secretary Powell had endeared himself to the Foreign Service as few before him. He knew how to earn loyalty and respect with an easygoing manner, walking around the building and casually dropping in on stunned but delighted desk officers, as well as venturing down to the first floor to stand in the cafeteria line and, in army tradition, making jokes about the food. Foreign visitors were in for a treat when they visited Secretary Powell. He welcomed them like long-lost friends he had been anxiously waiting to meet again (when in fact he sometimes barely had had a second to glance at the briefing materials ahead of time). Powell often exceeded the time allotted for a meeting (visitors enjoyed recording that fact, since running long suggested Powell had enjoyed the meeting), and then he would personally escort the foreign visitor down the elevator to the C Street ceremonial exit of the building, the way most foreign ministers would treat their own guests, but which until then was done only for very special senior visitors to the State Department.

Powell worked budget issues in the Congress with briefing skills that he had honed through his decades of military and public service. He looked after the "troops," personally taking it upon himself to make sure everyone had access to the Internet on their own desks, a technological breakthrough in the State Department. It may have been on its way to being done anyway, but he got the credit for it, and why not? He seemed to care. Apart from a few friends he brought with him from military days, he made sure he signed up the best and the brightest—and placed some of the most operationally gifted of Foreign Service officers in key positions. He also unfailingly found time to meet with visiting U.S. ambassadors in from their far-flung posts. That was the reason I was there.

Despite his enormous popularity, there was a perception among many senior Foreign Service officers that Powell was not as influential with President Bush as his experience and talent should have made him. In turf battles with Defense Secretary Rumsfeld he often seemed to come out second best and was viciously attacked in the conservative press. The liberal media liked him but damned him with faint praise by bemoaning that he was outnumbered and outflanked. I had noticed during visits back from Poland that Powell seemed frustrated and felt marginalized with the president and his team. Once I saw Powell in private conversation with the president defending Assistant Secretary Jim Kelly, his North Korea negotiator, against accusations that he had somehow been too soft in his dealings with the North Koreans. Kelly was still in the field and was already being criticized for the work he was doing. I thoroughly admired Powell for sticking up for him (not every senior official always does in Washington), but I had to reflect on the fact that he felt he had to do so directly with the president.

Two years before, in 2002, when I was back from Poland with President Kwasniewski, I told Powell that Kwasniewski planned to use some of his precious time with the president in the Oval Office to warn him about the dangers of the planned invasion of Iraq. I sat next to Powell in his car as we made our way over to the White House for the meeting. Powell made clear his own strong misgivings about the war and in particular his disgust at the war fever then raging in Washington. This was a man with an understanding of something most people in Washington have no idea about, but on Kwasniewski he could only offer the somewhat cynical observation that many come to the Oval Office with plans to be bold, but once in front of the president they behave quite differently. I felt while listening to Powell that there was also a note of his own frustrations dealing with elements of the government busily applying war paint. When Kwasniewski actually followed through I looked over to Powell during the meeting. The Polish president expressed friendship and solidarity with the president, but forcefully laid out his concerns about the plethora of logistical issues our troops would encounter after the inevitable military triumph. Powell's only postmeeting comment was to remark that the Polish president had indeed followed through, but that it would do no good anyway.

Later, I could not help but recall his strong view that the war in Iraq would be a mistake, against the light of his February 2003 speech to the United Nations Security Council, in which he used his extraordinary communication skills to make the case for war as he held up a vial of anthrax. He had deployed his persuasive powers to make the case for something I knew he did not believe in. I wondered if I could do such a thing with such persuasiveness. I hoped not. Powell would later explain that he had rejected 85 percent of what he had been told by the briefers preparing him for the United Nations appearance. It is a useful reminder that when someone tells you something that you know is already 85 percent inaccurate, there is not much reason to be confident in the remaining 15 percent, either.

As I entered his office for my farewell call, Powell was behind his desk and motioned me in. There was a melancholy look to him as he sat there. I offered an update on Korea and asked how things were going. He told me he had asked the president to allow him to stay longer as secretary of state, but that President Bush had told him that he could not. I thought it was an astonishing thing to tell a visiting ambassador in from the field, but it was typical of Secretary Powell's casual honesty and directness. I babbled some words about his service to the State Department and the fact that he would always be remembered for his loyalty to people. I asked how he thought things were going in Iraq.

"We can't even clear the road from the airport to the embassy," he responded glumly.

I left feeling very sorry for Secretary Powell. I always thought a leader should impart a sense of optimism to the troops. Powell had certainly done that for four years, but it was clear that day in December that he was done. His deputy, Rich Armitage, was equally composed, but in contrast to Powell it seemed he couldn't wait to exit the administration. Armitage offered some criticism of rumored personnel changes.

"Do you realize they are talking about *you* for EAP?" referring to the State Department's Bureau of East Asian and Pacific Affairs. I had long come to an understanding in my line of work that one should not be offended by anything. But then he added: "You would be great for EUR, but not EAP. Besides, you are doing a great job where you are in Seoul." I felt a little better, as the European Bureau was hardly a dumping ground, and the compliment about Seoul seemed sincere, but I said nothing of my discussion with Rice and Hadley.

From Armitage's office I walked down a flight of stairs to the Bureau of East Asian and Pacific Affairs (EAP) for my meeting with Assistant Secretary Kelly. East Asia was hardly an abandoned part of the world during the first Bush administration, but as important as it is, it certainly didn't pass the urgency test. Worse yet, in the wake of 9/11, it had come to be defined as a region whose importance was seen in terms of the role it could play in the Global War on Terror—the GWOT. And while the various challenges there often did touch on the broader issue of Islamic fundamentalism, whether in the southern Philippines or in Indonesia, the world's largest Muslim majority state, there was a rhythm that ran through that part of the world. Seeing the region as simply another battlefield in the Global War on Terror was not the best way to reach out to the people there.

The problem of dealing with the region was even deeper than just preoccupation with international terrorism. There was a body of opinion that the administration, at least in that fraught first term, seemed to want to run East Asia and Pacific policy through three key allies, Japan, Singapore, and Australia, and viewed others in terms of their relationships with those three. Other countries could be important in and of themselves—China, obviously, and Korea as the key player on the peninsula where U.S. troops were stationed—but our enduring, region-wide strategic interests would be routed through three countries. It was by no means a completely fair analysis, but it would stick, so much so that when the Obama administration was to announce a "pivot" to Asia, or, more delicately, a "rebalancing" to Asia, the move was taken as a substantive change of policy from one administration to another. After all, the Bush administration spent great effort to cultivate the South Korean government. But in contrast to the special relationship with Japanese prime minister Junichiro Koizumi, and Japan's critical role in the Indian Ocean with regard to the U.S. investments in the Middle East, South Korean president Roh Moo Hyun was perceived as not being helpful on the North Korean nuclear issue. Key Bush administration officials such as Undersecretary of State John Bolton (a person whose senior position at State was actually in the chain of command under Powell and Armitage) openly criticized the Roh government as soft on the North. Accusations of that kind sent from the safety of Washington, D.C., to people living next door to North Korea did not sit well with any Koreans. The Roh government, which for good measure was also busy downgrading relations with Japan, offered plenty of criticism of its own about the Bush administration's approach and its supposed lack of willingness to engage in dialogue with the North. The out-of-sync alliance, clearly showing its age at fifty, took its toll in the public mood, where Korean opinion surveys revealed an increasingly negative view about U.S. policy in the region. Impatience with Roh's administration began to boil over in Washington.

Secretary Rumsfeld, never one to be sentimental toward a fifty-year ally, increasingly challenged South Korean sensitivities with U.S. troop drawdowns about which the South Koreans were barely informed or consulted. Rumsfeld, the "transformational thinker," understandably had to consider more urgent needs in Iraq and Afghanistan and had been busy making cuts to forces in Europe as well as repositioning forces there for more strategic, "out of area" missions. In Korea he was doing nothing more than that, but given the North Korean threat (in contrast to the depleted threats to Europe), the Pentagon's moves in Korea angered our detractors and discouraged our friends.

In 2004, Rumsfeld started letting it be known that forces in Korea should have a strategic role, not just the tired old mission of acting as a "tethered goat" in the unlikely event of (another) North Korean thrust southward. The strategic role came across to the South Koreans as a desire to use their bases as part of war planning against China, and to do so without a South Korean vote.

14

CALLING AN AUDIBLE

The most serious problem festering in the U.S.–South Korean relationship was North Korea's nuclear aspirations and divergent opinions about how to deal with them.

The Bush administration's decision to withdraw from the Clinton administration's Agreed Framework, in which the U.S. side held direct talks with the North Koreans on a set of agreements whose essence was to provide North Korea with two light water reactors in return for dismantling their existing nuclear program, and the absence of any new mechanism took a heavy toll on our reputation in South Korea. The loose and uncoordinated talk in Washington criticizing any and all arms control negotiations, a neoconservative argument overheard by the rest of the world, alarmed many Koreans, who saw in the new Bush administration a radicalism that was disconnected from reality on the ground. By the time the U.S. administration had agreed with the Chinese on a six-party format for future negotiations, the U.S. reputation had already plummeted among the South Korean public.

This is not to say the Koreans necessarily had a more effective approach. Paying for summits between the two Koreas, paying for visits by ordinary South Koreans to North Korea, paying for any form of cooperation with the North gave South Korea a reputation as an appeaser.

That was not an approach that was going to work with the Bush administration, or any administration for that matter. I was convinced that the real problem was that as long as the United States tried to go it alone in negotiating with North Korea, no one else would take any responsibility and would blame the United States for the lack of progress. By 2004, the administration understood that the United States was paying a high price for its efforts with North Korea, while South Korea and China stood on the sidelines. It was time that those two countries took their places at the table.

South Korean public opinion was turning against the United States, but many were still unhappy with the Roh Moo Hyun administration for not maintaining a good U.S. relationship. As the U.S.–South Korean alliance seemed to be going into free fall, Roh began to look for ways to work with the United States.

Foreign Minister Ban Ki-moon made that possible. As he sensed a renewed interest in the administration to negotiate in the Six Parties, he appointed Song Minsoon, a friend of mine who had been the South Korean ambassador in Warsaw during the time I was U.S. ambassador there, a fact presumably known to Ban. He had also been Mike Sohn's deputy at the Korean embassy in Singapore years before.

I took over as negotiator for the North Korea talks in February 2005, a couple of months before I was to leave Seoul to take up my duties as assistant secretary for East Asia and the Pacific. Minsoon and I began to meet privately in the café on the top floor of Seoul's Plaza Hotel. It was close enough for each of us to walk from our offices ten minutes north on Sejong-ro Boulevard.

Minsoon had a reputation as a tough negotiator. That was the good news. The bad news for us was his reputation for toughness came from negotiations with the United States over basing rights and other difficult issues, a reputation that had had a positive effect on Roh's willingness to go along with Ban's choice of him as the representative to the Six Party Talks.

"We need an 'early harvest' of ideas that will show that the talks have life to them," I told him. "As you recall, there were only a couple of sessions last year, both short and neither showing much progress. I'm thinking that if we can take points already agreed on even in Washington, we can put them into a short statement of principles that we can get some agreement on from the North Koreans. The real problems will come later, when we move to implementation."

Minsoon didn't know I was channeling Dick Holbrooke from the Dayton Peace Accords. But he was on board.

"Let's work on them, together," he suggested.

We raised our beer glasses.

"I'll get you a draft"—I was hoping he wouldn't get the unintended pun—"tomorrow."

I was thinking about how the United States and the Republic of Korea could really begin to fix the damage being done to the relationship, if we could only work in this way on North Korea. In fact, South Korean and American diplomats had done many things together over the years, but neither the Korean people, not to speak of the U.S. public, understood how close the relationship had become. Sometimes we had taken each other for granted. With my ambassador to South Korea hat still firmly on my head, I thought that nobody believed that in the current state of relations we could really work closely on an issue of such fundamental importance as the North Korean nuclear crisis. I thought, maybe we could. I set about to meet the rest of the Six Party representatives, starting with the Chinese.

Wu Dawei, the Chinese vice minister who headed China's delegation to the talks, walked into the conference room on the eighth floor of Embassy Seoul. I had welcomed him at the elevator, pausing to show him some of the artwork on the eighth floor, including the pictures of all the past U.S. ambassadors to Korea. The collection of mug shots of U.S. ambassadors, typical in any U.S. embassy, had an added twist. At that time, all the former ambassadors whose pictures were in black-and-white were deceased. Those in color: still kicking. The ambassadors had all died in the order that they were ambassador, and while it was not true (as I had joked to many visitors) that the photos would fade to black-and-white on the news of a death, it did not take much of a sense of philosophy to recognize that our time in office is short.

A retinue of aides and note takers accompanied Wu as he sat across from me, his interpreter seated next to him. While Wu did not speak much English, one could tell that his staff certainly did as they dove into their notebooks before the interpreter had even started. The Chinese staff seemed bright and buttoned down, a credit to China's successor generation. Many had gone to U.S. universities, and I thought that if we could manage things with China during turbulent times, we could surely have a great future together.

I heard that Wu was a heavy smoker, and I thought briefly of suspending the smoking ban in the embassy, a move that could, in one way at least, improve the atmosphere, but looking at the smoke detectors above, patiently waiting to do their duty at the whiff of a cigarette, I decided not to.

From reading Wu's biography I knew I was sitting across from someone who had seen a lot over the years in China. He looked to be bracing for an unpleasant meeting and I was going to try to disappoint him on that score. As with the South Koreans, I knew that the purpose of the Six Party Talks was not just to deal with North Korea, but also to find common platforms with other countries and develop "patterns of cooperation" (Condi's phrase from two months before).

I had noticed something else in Wu's bio. He had a reputation for earning the loyalty and the affection of his staff, something I could also see on their faces. They liked their boss. He was quirky, engaged in shifting subjects, and I did my part to keep him off balance as well. Our official talking points tended to talk past each other. He called for more patience from the Americans toward North Korea, and I called for less patience from the Chinese. At times we both laughed at the impossibility of harmonizing our two approaches, but we agreed on where we should end up: with a denuclearized North Korea.

"I hope you don't mind if I sometimes recall something from Chinese history," he said.

"I would be disappointed if nothing from your four-thousand-year history ever came to mind. After all, this is a historic problem we are dealing with."

Kenichiro Sasae was the Japanese representative. Like Wu, he had long experience dealing with Asian neighbors and working with the United States. He was a problem solver, a pragmatist. He understood Japan's difficulties in the region: the internal Japanese politics churned over the thirty-year-old issue of the North Korean abductions of Japanese citizens, the competition with China, the problems dealing with Roh Moo Hyun's administration.

He came to my home for breakfast and promptly endeared himself by congratulating me on the Boston Red Sox winning the World Series. I recognized the good staff work that had gone into that comment and wished I had something as irrelevant and personal for him as well. We talked about how the negotiations might unfold. I told him we were interested in some kind of early harvest that would show the world that the process had some possibilities. He agreed and methodically went through Japan's negotiating history with the North Koreans, especially on the issue of the abductions. I assured him that the United States would remain engaged on the question, but that I was concerned whether the other participants shared that view. He understood but was pleased with my assurances.

I escorted Sasae to the front of the house, waving as he got into his car and waiting for the wheels to turn, the Asian custom for the precise moment when a visit ends. I had met the South Korean, Chinese, and now the Japanese representatives and was looking forward to meeting Aleksandr Alekseyev from the Russian Federation, about whom I had heard good things from other U.S. diplomats, including those in U.S. Embassy Moscow who had worked with him. I wondered, how hard could this be? All .300-plus hitters and with great personalities as well.

I hadn't met the North Koreans.

It was Wednesday, June 29, 2005, and I was at RFK Stadium in Washington, D.C., watching the Nationals play the Pittsburgh Pirates. It was the fifth inning, a tie score, and the Nats were about to come up. I had a great seat on the third-base side, but instead of enjoying the action of a close game I was anxiously looking at my cell phone. Finally, it rang.

"Chris, it's Joe DeTrani. I think we have a deal."

"Okay, Joe. Tell me exactly what they have agreed to."

Joe DeTrani, whom I inherited as my deputy in the Six Party process negotiations, was up in New York and had been meeting with the North Koreans at a nongovernmental meeting, a so-called Track 2 conference sponsored by the National Committee on American Foreign Policy, to which several North Korean negotiators were invited. He had just had a conversation with his opposite number in the North Korean delegation, Ri Gun. Ri had told him that if the U.S. side were to meet the head of the North Korean delegation, he was sure the North Koreans would be willing to go back to the Six Party Talks.

"Joe, it sounds encouraging, but, nonetheless, Ri being 'sure' is different from actually agreeing to return to the talks."

Joe understood that if I was to sell the idea to Secretary Rice, I needed to say that if we met them, they would announce their return to the talks. Being "sure" was not enough.

"I understand, but I think we are good. Do you want to speak with him?"

I went up the stairs of the stands to get away from the noise. But the Nationals were in first place at the time, and the stadium was pretty full that night despite a rain delay. I told him to put Ri on as I blocked one ear with the palm of my hand and pressed the cell phone against the other to try to hear him.

"Mr. Ri," I said—not quite sure how to address him. "Good to talk with you. I want to make sure we have an understanding that if I meet Mr. Kim [Gye Gwan] in Beijing, your government will announce that you are returning to the Six Party Talks."

"Yes. That is our understanding."

I thought of parsing the word *understanding*, but his answer was good enough for me, or at least good enough to try out on Secretary Rice. I knew that she would share my skepticism but would want to try. Iraq and Afghanistan were not getting any easier.

The next morning, I explained the proposed deal to the secretary. She listened carefully, and didn't seem concerned that Ri might be getting ahead of himself, except to comment that officials in communist/totalitarian societies usually have developed a survivalist sense of not getting out ahead of their talking points. She told me she'd get back to me later in the day.

When we met again, she told me I could proceed, but that the meeting had to be in a Chinese government facility, with the Chinese present. I responded that I understood the instructions, but that it might not work. The whole point of the North Korean boycott of the talks was that we don't meet with them the way we meet with all the other parties.

"Do the best you can. Those are the instructions," she responded. I tried to get more details on what she meant by a "Chinese government facility." A military base? Conference center? Their foreign ministry? A government-owned hotel? And what does it mean to have the Chinese present? Should it become a three-way talk? At what level do the Chinese have to be present?

"Do the best you can," she repeated.

I returned to the Bureau of East Asian and Pacific Affairs and went to the office of Kathleen Stephens, the principal deputy assistant secretary. I had known Kathy since my first tour in Korea and was delighted when she agreed to take the deputy position. Kathy and I started a facetious list of what could constitute a Chinese government facility in China. "There are a lot of them," she observed in mock understatement. I then walked over to my own office and asked my assistant Stasia Miller to get the Korea team up to my office.

There was a sense of excitement as desk officers, who would soon be asked to work twelve-to-thirteen-hour days in preparing for the negotiations, not to speak of weeks away from their families, rushed into my office, led by the desk director, Jim Foster. Everyone knew that the failure to get a negotiation going was hurting our reputation in Asia, even though, objectively speaking, the fault lay squarely at the doorstep of the North Koreans. But now all that was about to change.

The first thing we needed to do was to fix a date for the meeting. I turned to Jim Foster for the best way to communicate with the North Koreans, and most urgently to suggest a date, which we had tentatively agreed should be July 9, just a little more than a week away. He suggested the so-called New York channel, our contact with the North Korean United Nations office. I asked our China desk to send a message to the U.S. ambassador in Beijing, Clark T. "Sandy" Randt, to inform him that we had proposed that date to the North Koreans, and to ask whether it would work for the Chinese and our embassy.

We decided to hold off informing the other members—Russia, South Korea, Japan—until preparations were further developed, as well as to avoid leaks. A day later, the North Koreans got back to us through New York and agreed to the July 9 date. Sandy Randt also got back to me, pointing out that he would make it work, noting something that I had completely overlooked: Secretary Rice would be in Beijing, on a previously scheduled trip, later the night of July 9. That will sure add to the drama, I thought. I could meet the North Koreans that day, report to the secretary that night, and she could meet with Chinese foreign minister Li Zhaoxing the next day, then they jointly make the announcement following their meeting. Not bad diplomatic choreography, I thought.

I arrived in Beijing on July 8, accompanied by our Chinese-speaking staff assistant, Nolan Barkhouse. The summer heat had already set in and the dust and pollution were terrible. "Welcome to Beijing," Ambassador Randt said as he met us at the end of the jetway along with his North Korea watcher, Deputy Political Chief Edgard Kagan, who had taken charge of the preparations for the meeting. The "Chinese government facility" the embassy had chosen was to be a dining room, tucked away in the Chinese-government-owned business center, located immediately behind the Chinese-government-owned St. Regis Hotel.

"We should be able to slip in there without any press, as they will all be at the China World Hotel waiting for Secretary Rice," Kagan explained.

"The Chinese government owns the St. Regis?" I had asked Kagan when I first heard of the selection of venue. "Bit of a stretch as a 'Chinese government facility,' no?" (I was anticipating some eye rolling from Condi, who since coming over to the State Department was getting very good at rolling her eyes.)

"Hey, the Chinese own lots of buildings in Beijing," he responded cheerfully. "In fact, they even own the American Embassy building, but we didn't think that was appropriate."

Edgard Kagan was a solid professional and a real talent. He had served in Jerusalem and understood high-stakes diplomacy. In serving in different parts of the world, in jobs always close to the action, Edgard had a better understanding of each because he had a point of comparison. As for our condition that the Chinese had to be there, Edgard explained that negotiations for getting the Chinese to take part in the meeting had not been going well. At our request, the Chinese proposed to the North Koreans that Wu Dawei take part, but the North Koreans vetoed that on the basis that what we had agreed to was a bilateral meeting, not a trilateral. The Chinese countered by offering their director of peninsula affairs, Yang Xiyu, but that too looked to the North Koreans like a trilateral meeting. We agreed to the Chinese suggestion as a fallback that Yang take part only in the beginning of the meeting, and then leave, but as of the morning of July 9 we had not heard back from the Chinese.

It was a Saturday, late morning, and with nothing more to do in preparation for the meeting except monitor our cell phones, Edgard proposed we drive the forty-five minutes out to the Great Wall. In all my trips to China that spring, I hadn't yet seen the Great Wall, and with nervousness building up in my stomach and my head starting to throb at the thought that the Chinese might not show, I agreed.

It was a bright sunny day when Nolan, Edgard, and I joined the thousands of Chinese tourists on the wall. I wasn't sure what fascinated me more: the thousands of tourists or the thousands of miles of wall. I asked Edgard every few minutes to call the Chinese, which he did each time, sticking his head out between parapets to gain some privacy for the call. The Chinese never picked up. Edgard called his contact in the North Korean embassy, who confirmed they would be there.

"I'm not sure the Chinese are going to show," I said, wondering what I should do.

"We can cross that bridge when we get to it," Edgard said, not wanting to think about the unthinkable.

As I got back into our car and took one more look at the Great Wall, I thought about the work that went into the construction of something 5,500 miles long, almost twice the breadth of the United States. To all the think tankers who believe conflict or enmity is something we should consider inevitable with China, I thought: Who would ever want to get into a fight with a people who built a thing like this?

I arrived at the business center with Edgard, Nolan, and Beijing political counselor Dan Shield. We waited. There were no Chinese, but neither were there any North Koreans. I asked Edgard, for about the fiftieth time that day, to try all his numbers at the Foreign Ministry again. No answer. I then asked him to call his contact at the North Korean embassy to ask where their delegation was.

"He's asking if the Chinese are there," Edgard said, holding his cell phone against his chest.

"Just a second," I responded, trying to get some time to think.

Of course, there were no Chinese, and based on my instructions I should call the whole thing off. I glanced at my watch and realized that Secretary Rice was on her way to Beijing, probably just finishing the refueling stop in Alaska, meaning I could never reach her through the air force's telephone operator in time for guidance.

I thought about what would be the best outcome: We cancel, because going through with it would violate my instructions, or we proceed with the meeting and get the announcement of the resumption of the talks—and who in the world is going to care whether the Chinese were actually sitting there or not? After all, we were in Beijing, the venue for the Six Party Talks, and the whole purpose was to restart those *multilateral* talks anyway. All our partners wanted this to happen and were anxiously awaiting word. Besides, what's the worst that could happen to me? They fire me, and given the state of my head and stomach, I wouldn't have minded at all. I thought of past mentors: Would Holbrooke have canceled the meeting? How about Eagleburger? Bob Frasure? What would my dad have told me to do? I knew Condi wanted the meeting; she understood more than many people the world of hurt our foreign policy was in and the need for a breakthrough somewhere. And I was sure she would not have appreciated my canceling it without having asked her first. However, neither was I sure she would have wanted even to be asked that question. I took one more look at Dan, Nolan, and Edgard, who by this time was gesturing with a finger of his free hand at his phone clutched in the other, and with an exasperated look all for the purpose of reminding me that I didn't have all night to answer a simple question. I decided that if there was ever a time to call a diplomatic audible, it was now.

"Tell them the Chinese are not here and ask them if they are going to come or not."

Edgard gave the answer to his North Korean contact in his fluent but American-accented Chinese, and I'm sure that if China had a version of late-night comedy it would qualify for a pretty good skit.

"They are coming now."

My thought that no one would ever remember whether the Chinese had been present would, alas, not turn out to be wrong. My "audible" made its way to the press, at first in positive terms, and later as an example of a diplomat "gone rogue," a theme that would resurface with some senators during my ambassadorial hearings for Iraq, almost four years later. It was the right call. It was really the only call.

Kim Gye Gwan, Li Gun, Choi Son Hui, and a note taker walked through the elevator door, peering left and right as if to make sure there were no Chinese. I reflected on what must have been their instructions, and what would have been the consequences for them of not following them, or of calling an audible, not a concept known in the North Korean foreign ministry.

We sat down at a long, thin table, Kim Gye Gwan directly across from me, his interpreter to his right, and mine to my right. He and his entire team looked as nervous and uncomfortable as anyone I have ever encountered across such a table. I kept repeating to myself the question, the answer to which I already knew: what is the outcome of this meeting that I am trying to produce? It was, of course, to get the talks restarted. Simple. Stay on task and make sure that is indeed the outcome. Nothing else matters.

"Mr. Kim. It is a pleasure to meet." (Of course it wasn't anything remotely a pleasure, but I was focused on the hoped for outcome.) "I hope we will have the occasion to meet many times in the coming months. There is much that needs to be done. Our countries are adrift in a sea of mistrust, and we need to do something to overcome that."

Kim liked the maritime metaphor, and before I knew it he had us all "in the same boat" sailing to an agreement, I guess.

I told him we would need to manage expectations. These talks have either been characterized by pessimistic expectations, or wildly optimistic ones. We need to take out those highs and lows and manage steady progress.

Who knows if he understood what I was talking about, but his note taker seemed to be taking it all down. I found myself more interested in addressing their note taker because those who read those notes would be the decision makers, not Mr. Kim Gye Gwan.

I told him that the United States does not have a hostile policy to North Korea and its people. But we do have a "hostile policy" to many North Korean policies including its nuclear programs. We cannot accept these weapons of mass destruction, and will look for a political and diplomatic solution to achieve the end of these dangerous programs.

Again, not much of a response from Kim, but his note taker was busy. He seemed to appreciate my comment that we do not have a hostile policy toward North Korea, even though it may have seemed to him a distinction without a difference.

I found Kim, and would always find Kim, hard to read. On the one hand, he was quite willing to engage in conversations, and any expectations I had that he would be dumbly reading talking points to me did not pan out. He was intelligent, and self-confident, and thoughtful in his responses. But he was certainly not about to describe any personal opinions, or step outside his brief for even a second. And not reading talking points could have been because after more than a decade of doing this, he had actually memorized them.

Talks with the North Koreans were all business. Unlike in the Balkans, there was no discussion of raising difficult teenagers, or sports or hobbies. We rarely strayed from the subject at hand and hardly got to know each other.

15

PLASTIC TULIPS

I slipped back down the elevator, then through the long corridors to a garage where I got into an embassy black Ford Crown Victoria and headed to the back entrance of the China World Hotel. On the way I learned that Secretary Rice had just arrived with her huge entourage and passed through a gauntlet of well-wishers and fans in the hotel lobby, and was waiting in her suite with her senior staff for me to arrive and give a briefing.

When a secretary of state travels he or she brings along the entire staff: administrative assistants, advisors, spokespeople to deal with the press, regional experts, numerous security personnel, and a support staff that would be busy into the night preparing morning press clips and other papers, as if the operation were back on the seventh floor of the State Department. This one-night stand in Beijing was no exception. I went to the seventeenth floor and was stopped by two marine security guards borrowed from Embassy Beijing, who demanded my ID. As I began to look for my State Department ID, which I had chosen not to wear around my neck for the meeting with the North Koreans, one of the secretary's security agents walking down the corridor recognized me and waved me through. I walked down the hall, marveling at all the duct tape used to cover wires for the State Department telephone system that would join all the rooms where her staff was to stay. Two more agents stood in front of her suite.

Secretary Rice was in one of the sitting rooms, beyond where the elliptical machine, installed for her visit—and every one of her visits, wherever she went around the world—stood. She was sitting on a couch with a few members of her staff, enjoying a glass of wine after a long flight.

"I've got good news and bad news," I announced. "I met with the North Koreans, went through our approach. They have agreed to come to the next round of Six Party Talks, which we tentatively agreed would take place later this month."

"And the bad news?" she asked.

"The Chinese didn't show. I thought about canceling the whole meeting but decided to go through with it, hoping the Chinese would appear. They never did."

"I'll have to take that up with [Foreign Minister] Li tomorrow," she responded. "They knew they were supposed to be there. I talked to him. You talked to Wu. Sandy [Ambassador Randt, who was sitting with her] talked with his contacts. They should have been there. Take a seat and have a glass of wine. It has been a long day." She had that right.

The next (long) day, I accompanied Rice to her meeting with Foreign Minister Li Zhaoxing at the Foreign Ministry. Minister Li was a friendly sort of person, with a hobby of writing poetry whose quality and depth was not always apparent to those who heard it through an interpreter. The meeting was held in a large conference room on the ground floor. As we took our places in the brightly upholstered chairs arrayed in a semicircle, Secretary Rice and Foreign Minister Li in the center two chairs, a small table with flowers between them, we could hear the considerable preparations going on outside in the large hall for what would be an enormous press conference with banks of television cameras. The North Korean announcement that they would come to the Six Party Talks had reached around the world and the excitement was palpable. After opening pleasantries, Condi got right to the point.

"Why weren't you there?"

"The North Koreans didn't want us there. But it was a good outcome. You have succeeded in bringing the North Koreans back to the table. This is a great success. Congratulations!" He was very pleased and cheerful and was trying to get Condi to be the same.

"But you were supposed to be there," she snapped, not quite in the mood that the minister (and I) were hoping for. I started getting worried that she was overplaying this. At that moment Ambassador Randt turned slightly to me and gestured lightly with his right hand that all was going to be okay. Perhaps, I thought, this was all an act that she had rehearsed in front of Sandy. But whatever it was, I appreciated his concern for how I was taking all this, as I was getting more sick to my stomach by the moment.

Li continued in a very pleasant tone, "You should focus on the outcome, and not just the process."

"The outcome was good," Condi, in her petulant best, shot back, "but the process was bad." Oh, give it a rest, I thought. Not everything can be put into categories of good and bad. I started riffing in my mind. Okay, got it. Lots of politics back in Washington, but, really, time to move on. I emerged from my inner dialogue in time to hear her finally drop the issue and focus on when the Six Party Talks would take place, and how we should try to make progress.

At the conclusion of the meeting, the foreign minister and the secretary of state went out to meet the press. There were at least a hundred journalists from the United States, China, Japan, and other countries. Banks of cameras were set up in the back, and while there would be the required questions about Taiwan, the main issue was North Korea, and especially the news that the North Koreans would rejoin the talks after so many months.

I stood over to the side of the atrium along with some of Rice's aides.

Condi was very good in press conferences—gracious, smart, detailed, articulate, one of the best I had ever seen—so I didn't worry too much about any "bad process" comments (although the Chinese looked a little anxious). She made the obligatory and accurate comment that the resumption of the talks was "only a start," and that the goal of those talks would be to make progress on denuclearization. She spoke of the need for North Korea to "make a strategic choice" to give up its weapons.

I agreed, although my own view was that North Korean dictator Kim Jong Il was unlikely to fall out of bed one morning having made a "strategic choice." More likely, a strategic choice would only follow a series of less-than-strategic choices to join in talks, agree to some give-and-take, and finally, when the direction was clear, agree to move forward to the ultimate goal. But I knew that day was many months, perhaps years away. On that bright Sunday morning in Beijing, I had no idea how fraught the future would turn out to be, nor did I understand how difficult it would be to achieve even consensus within the Bush administration. All I knew then was that the secretary of state and the president wanted what I was doing to succeed and were going to back me up.

The "Fourth Round" of talks was scheduled for July 26, 2005. There had been three other rounds, in 2003 and 2004, but none had led to the slightest signs of progress even though the U.S. negotiators, led by former assistant secretary Jim Kelly, had worked hard (and fought hard within a divided administration) to come up with new proposals more in line with an effort to achieve a give-and-take negotiation. These internal battles were fought along several fronts. The East Asian directorate in the NSC, in the very capable hands of security scholar and Japan expert Michael Green, battled the Counterproliferation Directorate under the well-mannered but strongly opinionated Bob Joseph, who never saw a problem in the world he did not want to use some form of coercion to solve. Mike prevailed with the president (and with Condi) and so the U.S. position going into the talks was quite a reasonable hand to try to play. My job, in the summer of 2005, was to get some credit for the United States for taking such a position, demonstrate to the parties that we were committed not only to a process of dialogue but also to success, and especially to arrest the slide in U.S.–South Korean relations that our differences over North Korea had caused. We were not just going to give this the junior college try, as Bob Frasure used to say. We were going to emerge with something.

The first issue was to gain more time for the actual negotiations. One of the main reasons that the previous three sessions had made so little progress was the fact that their preset duration was so short. Delegates would arrive on a Tuesday, talk on Wednesday, and allow the Chinese hosts to issue a nonbinding statement on Thursday as everyone made their way through Beijing traffic out to the airport. I had raised the issue with Wu during a trip to Beijing in April, explaining that I thought we should leave the time frame open until we had an achievement in the form of something that everyone agreed to. Wu paused for a moment, perhaps contemplating potential food budget problems at the Foreign Ministry's negotiating facility in the event the stay were left unlimited, but he agreed.

The next issue was the need to come up with a joint statement that would strongly suggest progress in the negotiations, albeit not a final document, and not just a Chinese statement. Everybody at the talks needed to agree, hence joint. Recalling the Dayton Peace Accords, which were preceded by the two documents known as "Agreed Principles" and "Further Agreed Principles," I thought it was a good way to jump-start a moribund process and gradually bring the North Koreans into some kind of envelope of negotiation.

Several of the parties, including the Russians, were in favor of a statement of principles because they understood the difficulty of getting agreement on anything, let alone a full page of negotiation-guiding principles. The Russians also had vast experience in international negotiation and had a realistic sense of what was possible and what was not. That said, the Russians rarely took the lead in any phase of the upcoming negotiations except to support a process of dialogue. Their diplomats were talented and experienced, but they were unable to hide their cynicism and even disgust about the process. Aleksandr Alekseyev was typical of their stable of skilled but jaded diplomats. His body language conveyed someone who given enough time might have thought of a worse place to be than the Six Party Talks, but in the meantime he acted like he was in a living hell.

In our meetings at the Seoul Plaza Hotel and in long sessions on the telephone, Song Minsoon and I had put together several ideas that could serve as a basis for a joint statement. The basis, we agreed, would be North Korea's willingness to do away with its nuclear programs, but we understood that if that goal were achieved it would be worth something to get.

Song wanted to take a tough stand against Japan's efforts to include the issue of abductions in the document, and had gone public with his concerns about the Japanese, an opinion that certainly didn't lose him points in the Blue House but caused problems for the Japanese. I pushed back with Minsoon, arguing that Japanese negotiators had a serious public opinion problem back home and could hardly be expected to ignore what was really the issue for the Japanese: the abduction of several of its citizens by the North Koreans in the late 1970s and early '80s to use these hapless people as language teachers and other cross-cultural lessons for North Korean spies. Originally there were thirteen people confirmed to have been abducted. But that number grew to be seventeen, which drove Japan's diplomacy further into isolation. Song's retort was telling: "Do you have any idea how many hundreds, perhaps thousands, of our citizens have been abducted by the North Koreans?"

Ultimately, what became known as the Japanese abduction issue became the rallying cry for those who opposed the Six Party negotiations, or really any negotiations with the North Koreans in the first place. Japanese groups including families of abductees, but often just supporters of one kind or another, descended upon Washington to spread the word about North Korean perfidy. The groups from Japan, often carrying pictures of abductees, targeted congressional offices, think tanks, National Security Council staff, and offices in the State Department to press their case that nothing should be done on North Korea's nuclear arsenal until the abduction issue was to be solved—often in the form of gaining release of people murdered years ago by the North Koreans.

Japanese prime minister Koizumi had taken up the abductee issue in his meetings with Kim Jong Il in 2002, a meeting that resulted in the jaw-dropping admission followed by the equally jaw-dropping oral apology that they had indeed abducted thirteen Japanese during the period of 1977–83, just as the abductee groups had claimed. Five of the thirteen were released a month later, but of the remaining eight, Kim claimed that all had died (the North Koreans provided death certificates at the time, but later admitted that these were not originals and had been drawn up to respond to Japanese demands to see the documented causes of death). One of the eight was the youngest of the abductees, a then thirteen-year-old girl named Megumi, who, the North Koreans told Koizumi's delegation, had tragically committed suicide back in 1994. In late 2004, the North Koreans provided what they described as Megumi's ashes. But when the Japanese tested the ashes (in a controversial process that critics claimed was amateurishly conducted and politically tainted), they were found not to be those of Megumi, a finding that was to further exacerbate the issue. Since 2004, the North Koreans had refused to engage again on the issue.

One day I was asked to come to the office of Florida congresswoman Ileana Ros-Lehtinen and brief her on North Korea. Representative Ros-Lehtinen was a strong-minded Cuban-American and a senior member of the House Foreign Affairs Committee. Maintaining the Cuba embargo, combating human trafficking, and tormenting the State Department were her priorities, and not necessarily in that order.

I found her standing in front of her desk, smiling as always, with about fifteen Japanese gathered in the room, of whom many were photographers. She held out a list of abductees and ceremonially handed it to me as the cameras clicked away. I had met with the abductee supporters on many occasions in my own office, and I even knew several of the Washington-based Japanese photographers, so there was nothing unpleasant or embarrassing for me in meeting these Japanese again. What was, of course, unusual to say the least was that an American member of Congress would try to set up an American diplomat for the apparent purpose of embarrassing him in front of foreigners.

Ros-Lehtinen, as she always was with me in public and in private, was very affable as the Japanese filed out of the room, and even chatted for a few minutes before rushing off to her next appointment. Briefing a member of Congress is a matter taken seriously by the State Department. Indeed, Senate confirmation is always provisional on the basis of the nominee's willingness to brief the Congress, an obligation I thought I was fulfilling that day.

The encounter with Ros-Lehtinen highlighted a fact that was to be increasingly clear over the months and years of dealing with the North Koreans: nobody liked the idea of talking with them, but nobody had a better idea, either. Since Bosnia I had long since come to the realization that policy can have different, even contradictory elements. During the run-up to Dayton, the British representative, Pauline Neville-Jones, had said in a meeting, "We can bomb and talk at the same time."

But bombing and talking are elements of a strategy that can be controlled. One can talk, or not talk, depending on the situation. One can bomb or not bomb. In the case of some of the sanctions envisioned, these became doomsday machines that once imposed could not, at least not in any timely way, be unimposed. They also became weapons in the hands of those who did not want to see the negotiations continue.

The fact was that North Korea was the most heavily sanctioned country in the world, and it was unclear that any additional imposition of sanctions would yield a different result.

Managing the Japan relationship proved to be a complex process. As competent and pragmatic as Kenichiro Sasae was, I found, especially after Koizumi retired in 2006, that the Japanese had lost their way in dealing with others and, as the Six Party meetings unfolded, were often the delegation least in line with the others. What we anticipated to be a five-on-one frequently became far more muddled as South Koreans openly complained about Japanese behavior, especially in subsequent sessions when all parties—except the Japanese—were working on their domestic political authorities to provide heavy fuel oil to induce the North Koreans to shut down their plutonium plant and accept international inspectors in their facilities.

By that time I had made numerous visits to Tokyo and had a great deal of sympathy for what Sasae was dealing with. It was not unlike what I had to wade through in Washington, with attitudes toward government at an all-time low. Sasae invited me to dinner and drinks with senior Japanese politicians, perhaps in an effort to show them what he had to work with in me, but I like to think it was also to show me what kind of difficult people he had back in Tokyo. In these sessions over sushi and whiskey, I told the politicians how hard Sasae had beaten me up over inclusion of abductee issues in the talks. All true, except that some of them would have been disappointed to hear how pragmatic and reasonable Sasae was in dealing with it.

One of the expectations of the East Asian security club in Washington, of which NSC Asia director Mike Green was a charter member, along with many other think tankers and academics, was that in anticipation of Six Party sessions I should take part in three-party meetings with the Japanese and South Koreans. But rather than formulate common positions, I found these sessions represented more opportunities to have me hone the mediating skills I had forged in the Bosnian crucible. As reasonable as Song and Sasae were individually, their reasonableness did not project in these larger meetings. As I told Secretary Rice after one session: "I never knew Asians could be so sarcastic with one another." Frequently, after one got finished eviscerating the other's point, he would look over at me as if for approval. I tried every icebreaker conversation I knew—convincing teenagers to take useful courses in college, complaining about former diplomatic assignments, and baseball, a subject that united the three countries certainly more than positions at the Six Party Talks.

In Bosnia, the equivalent problem was our creation of the Bosnian-Croat Federation, a shotgun marriage consummated during the worst years of the war. Those sessions usually went horribly, but at least the United States had some real clout in dealing with the other two. Japan and Korea were not to be confused with constituent parties of a fledgling Balkan state. The last straw was a lunch in Beijing in which Song Minsoon had refused to emerge to go in front of the cameras with Sasae and me. It was left to me to explain that Minsoon had been called away from the lunch urgently. Actually, he was hiding out in the restaurant waiting for the Korean and Japanese journalists to leave. I told Secretary Rice I couldn't take it anymore. Give me the Bosnian Serbs any day! Each trilateral session left us worse off than we were before, and I would rather meet the Japanese and South Korean separately. She agreed.

But back in Washington, D.C., a town known not so much for second chances as for second-guessing, I was criticized for not being dedicated enough in taking advantage of this opportunity for trilateral cooperation.

As we filed into the grand hall at the Diaoyutai conference facility, I was struck by the extraordinary preparations the Chinese had made for the occasion. I thought of all the books I had read about multilateral conferences, the grandeur of the European venues, the more plain functionalism of the American sites. The Chinese erred on the side of grandeur more than functionality, but what the facility conveyed was that China was giving these negotiations its best shot, while imparting a sense of its power. If this all failed, it would not be because China did not make an adequate effort.

I took my seat at the U.S. side of the enormous hexagon table structure, with each of the six table sides (the tables themselves were only some three feet wide) containing five seats, the center one reserved for the head of the delegation. Behind each green felt-covered table side were some twenty to twenty-five chairs reserved for additional members of the delegation. The diameter of the circle of tables was some sixty feet, with a large floral arrangement in the center, access to which would have been possible only by crawling under one of the sides of the table.

The floral arrangements contained five large plastic tulips, which I soon discovered had a mundane but very functional purpose: each of the five represented one of the languages in the conference (Korean, Chinese, Russian, Japanese, and English) and was being used as part of the consecutive interpretation system. Thus when Wu Dawei spoke, each tulip would dutifully light up and remain lit until each interpreter was done interpreting his statement in the other languages, at which point the speaker, surveying all the extinguished tulips, could move to the next paragraph. Some interpreters were faster than others. The English tulip, for example, lit up along with the others, but went dark again somewhat more quickly than the Japanese tulip, which was often the last to be extinguished because the interpreter was trying to get it exactly right. How would one know which tulip represented which language? Easy. The tulip representing the language being spoken did not light up. Thus, when I spoke the English tulip stayed unlit.

As the above suggests, this venue, impressive as it was, was no place to get any real work done. Wu would convene the day's meeting. Each of the other delegation heads would have an opportunity to say something, usually not very positive, at which point Wu would thank us all and adjourn the so-called plenary. Then the work would begin.

Typically, I would start with bilateral meetings with the Japanese,

South Koreans, and Wu's Chinese delegation, and then my delegation would sit down for a session with the North Koreans. Generally, attendance would be limited to the principal plus six or seven. In that summer of 2005, I would make sure that Victor Cha, representing the national security staff, was present, plus Jim Foster, our Korea desk director, and Joe DeTrani, my overall deputy for the talks. I would try to rotate in as many technical staff as possible. Staff who did not get into a meeting would spend their time in the corridor using their cell phones to call back to their offices in Washington, often to complain that they were left out of meetings.

Sessions with the North Koreans would be fairly stiff affairs, although I was struck again by the fact that Kim Gye Gwan did not seem to need to refer to notes or talking points, despite the North Koreans' reputation as robotlike negotiators.

In talking with Kim I made sure that his own note takers were getting it all down, since I assumed what was important was what people back in Pyongyang were hearing about the talks. I noticed that he, as many diplomats are prone to do, would occasionally posture for his note takers by going into a diatribe about our supposed hostile policy to his country. I would respond in kind, pointing out that "hostile policy" is something for which the North Koreans have no equal. But mainly I tried to keep them on task by going through the elements of the draft joint statement that the Chinese had put together—largely on the basis of the draft that Minsoon and I had worked out months before.

After meeting with the North Koreans, I would immediately brief the South Koreans and Japanese (separately, of course), and would touch base with Condi Rice back in Washington often very early morning or late at night, when she seemed always, no matter when I called, to be getting on or getting off her elliptical machine. I needed to speak with her because in the meantime she would have been receiving phone calls from members of "my team" complaining that I was violating instructions by talking to the North Koreans. It was perfectly within my guidance to be speaking directly with the North Koreans, but many people found that anathema, besides which they had a literalist view of what constitutes a multilateral conference.

After one week of the conference I took score of how many bilateral meetings I had had with the five other parties, so as to set the meetings with the North Koreans in the context of the organization of the talks. Of course, I had more issues to talk about with the North Koreans than I did with our allies, the Japanese and South Koreans, with whom we were also having evening social events (separately), but I did not want a situation to develop in which I was meeting more with the North Korean delegation than the delegations of our allies, so in order to make the numbers look good I would add more meetings with the others. This prompted Minsoon at one point to be one of the first South Korean diplomats to turn down a bilateral with the Americans:

"But Chris, I just saw you an hour ago. We had breakfast this morning and we are on for dinner tonight. Why do we have to meet this afternoon again?"

"Never mind that, Minsoon. I just have to see you."

Whether it is in their manual of negotiation or not, the North Koreans would have an annoying habit of agreeing to something, then coming back and not agreeing to what they had just agreed. This was a habit that simply needed to be broken.

On one occasion, Kim Gye Gwan returned to talks after an hour break (I always suspected he was using these numerous breaks for taking a nap) to inform me that he had "new instructions from Pyongyang," that his position had changed. I called my own break, left the room, and did not deal with him for another three days, until Wu Dawei patched up the difference. I told Wu that meeting directly was a tactic, not a policy (a line I borrowed from Secretary Rice), and that if meeting with them was not going to yield any results I was happy not to meet with them and confine my contacts to the plenary (and the tulips). That sufficiently upset Wu that he said he would immediately work on it. I told him I was willing to be the good cop (a concept that Chinese cops-and-robbers movies had long since mastered) but that he needed to be the bad cop, and that the next time I saw him I wanted to "see some blood on the floor." Wu gave me a concerned look, as if to assure himself I was speaking metaphorically, and again told me he would address the problem with Kim.

Within what were presumably narrow marching orders, Wu managed to keep things going, and my respect and affection for him grew with every passing week. Our bilateral sessions at the end of the day were packed with Chinese and U.S. staff who jammed into the room to watch our repertoire as we discussed the day's events. I played the role of the exasperated and impatient American, he the calm elder Chinese whose wisdom was tempered by concerns that things might not actually work out.

Once at the end of a particularly long and unproductive day I said to him: "Over the years I have traveled throughout South Korea, up and down. I noticed how many monuments there are for the foreign troops who came to their aid. There is a monument for Canadians, one for Turks, Greeks, British, Australians, New Zealanders, the list goes on. But I understand if one visits North Korea one can hardly find any such monument to the Chinese, what you called the people's volunteer army. So my question, Mr. Chairman, is this: I know why they hate us. I know why they hate the Japanese. What I cannot understand is why they hate you."

I glanced around the room to find the Chinese aides purposefully writing in their notebooks, several of the younger ones nodding as if to agree with the premise of what I was saying. Wu, smoking heavily that night, said nothing, took a long drag from his cigarette, and offered me one. I took it as a gesture of friendship and let him light it for me. I knew he was not going to comment, much less answer my question, but I also knew that the Chinese–North Korean relationship was far more complex than often portrayed in the Western press. That relationship, forged in another era but now a burden for China and its international aspirations, goes to the heart of what China will become in the future. As the old motivational speaker line goes, you are who your friends are. China, surely, has to outgrow this friendship, and as I looked around that room, trying not to cough on Wu's cigarette, I felt that most people there that night understood what was running through my mind.

The complexity that is inherent in a four-thousand-year-old civilization of some 1.3 billion people cannot be underestimated, and I knew that the Six Party Talks would not change China. And even though the talks were such a dominant feature in my life, in the lives of all the negotiating teams, the policy makers back in the capitals, the journalists covering the events, I knew that just a block away from the Diaoyutai life went on exactly as it had before those talks and would after the talks. So much of what is said about this breathless country is so true yet so incomplete. The admonishments in Western newspaper editorials that usually focus on one issue—for example, human rights, or China's bullying of smaller neighbors in the South China Sea—usually begin and conclude with the formulation that "China *must* do something about something." It is as if the issue was a transaction gone wrong that can be righted with another transaction, guided by the sage advice of an editorial conceived and written thousands of miles away in a context that is in effect millions of miles away.

There is something in China for everybody—those who want to live life in fear can find much to be concerned about there. Every comment by every Chinese security official is a treasure trove for those with such a disposition. But similarly, those who try to look out over the sweep of history, and anticipate what may lie ahead, can see a far more nuanced picture of what China's rise could mean for itself and the world. And as that picture comes into better focus—as it does every day—we need to establish and maintain a cooperative relationship with the Chinese and understand that we cannot change them any more than they can change us. Building part of that relationship, and reinforcing some of those patterns of cooperation, is the best my generation can do. China's relations with North Korea go to the heart of what China is in the contemporary world. The linkage is not just about a historic fact, the Korean War. It is far deeper and goes to the questions of this civilization's relations with neighboring states, habits that were long learned and will take a long time to break.

Traditionally, the Diaoyutai facility has been where foreign leaders (Nixon comes to mind) are housed during visits, and since the 1950s it has been a site for conferences and negotiations. Its high walls and the extensive security presence around its perimeter suggest that what happens at the Diaoyutai stays at the Diaoyutai.

Our delegation would usually stay at the St. Regis Hotel, in the eastern part of Beijing, about a twenty-minute drive from the conference. Every morning I would start out from my hotel room, usually greeted by Ambassador Sandy Randt for a quick discussion before we headed down the elevator and out to the waiting cars and minivans. The press, mainly Korean and Japanese, would have set up a "stakeout" near the front entrance. My predecessor, Jim Kelly, used to walk past the gaggle of some thirty reporters with a brief wave on the assumption that anything said would be parsed in their own newspapers and often shredded in the unforgiving world of Washington's press cycle.

I found that just walking past them was uncomfortable, but more important, it was both unnecessary and a missed opportunity. Why not tell them what we planned to do that day? Much of what we were trying to accomplish was to demonstrate that we were doing what we can to address this issue through negotiation and through cooperation with regional allies and partners, and that we were open and prepared to work with others. I started answering their questions.

"Hi, how are you? Well, I just got off the plane from Washington and I've got a huge team here from Washington. We are really looking forward to these negotiations. It's going to take a little time. It's going to take a lot of work. But we come here in a real spirit of trying to make some real progress. As Secretary Rice said when she was here a couple of weeks ago, we're really going to roll up our sleeves and do the best we can to make sure we achieve some progress. It's obviously a very important negotiation, something we're very much committed to, and I look forward to meeting all the other delegations and to working with the members of my team and see what we can do. So, I will try to brief you all from time to time and keep you all informed. As for how long this is going to take, I have no idea. I did pack a few extra shirts. I suspect some of you may have done the same. So, thank you very much. Great to see you all."

"What will progress look like? What is the ticket to a success?"

"Well, I don't know. It's tough to say at this point, except that we are going to work very hard and we are very committed to seeing if we can make some very serious progress here."

"What will progress look like? What can we expect?"

"Well, you know I wouldn't expect this to be the last set of negotiations. The negotiations have been in suspension really for over a year. So, we have to see where we go with these. We would like to make some measurable progress, progress that we can build on for a subsequent set of negotiations. But at this point it is hard to tell until we really sit down. The Six Party negotiations will get going sometime tomorrow night. So, thank you very much."

"So, what's your plan for the next two days? Will you be meeting the North Korean delegation?"

"Well, we will be doing a lot of consultations and begin the overall negotiations tomorrow night at some meetings. I think the foreign minister of China will get us all together tomorrow night. Then the plenary, I think, begins Tuesday morning. So we'll be having consultations with all the parties. Thanks a lot."

And with that, press stakeouts began, a twice-a-day schedule, sometimes more if I happened to return to the hotel in the middle of the day. The effect was to develop relations with these mostly Japanese and South Korean press members, and to reverse the reputation of the United States in the region as a go-it-alone player, uninterested in the interests or the opinions of others.

Meanwhile, back in Washington, I got word via Mike Green that the president wanted me to keep up the daily briefings and to be, in effect, my own spokesperson.

Whether to be on the record or to transact in the Washington currency of "backgrounders" was really not a choice for me in Beijing. If I was going to be misquoted or somehow lost in translation, I much preferred that it be in the context of a public press conference rather than a backgrounder that would inevitably be traced to me anyway. Besides, even though there was far more self-discipline in making a public statement than in discussing sensitive issues over drinks with a reporter, in fact that which is classified is really a very small percentage of what one would have to say anyway. Certain basic rules apply: Avoid citing what the other side is saying in negotiation. They could simply deny it or say something even more difficult to live with after you have called them out on it. And don't talk specifics and certainly don't engage in speculation or hypothetical questions. Beyond that, there is much that can be discussed publicly without getting close to any inappropriate divulging of information.

The press in the region and in the United States had a field day describing a new U.S. approach to dealing with the opinions of others. While some cynics explained it in terms of being overwhelmed by two simultaneous wars and the need to quiet down one area of the world (an observation not altogether inaccurate), others saw relief in a second term now dedicated to a new approach to problem solving.

But within the extreme conservative camp in the administration, some neoconservatives, such as former Democrat Paul Wolfowitz and others, thought the United States should simply roll over and crush its critics. Secretary Rumsfeld and Vice President Cheney were allies to that camp. Ultimately, neoconservatives and hard-line conservatives made common cause over their view that to negotiate with an adversary is an act of weakness and a failure of resolve. Worse yet, to make progress in such talks would be to violate the theory of the case that dictators will never give up weapons and therefore any progress must be shown to be illusory, or undermined.

My instructions, a telegram sent to me at the start of the talks, were a case in point. The instructions essentially allowed for no leeway in achieving North Korea's denuclearization, and included such gems as instructing me not to engage in any toasts at official functions that included North Koreans. I thought, and Secretary Rice agreed, that the image of the American negotiator sullenly sitting with hands folded while the other five delegations raised their glasses would not serve any useful purpose.

My own view was that the negotiation was necessary if we were going to stop the plummeting of our reputation among friends and allies in the region, and that we needed to use the multilateral process to establish some patterns of cooperation. This was dismissed as diplomatic inside baseball with little relevance to the threats facing our country. Ironically, these views were a kind of mirror image of the North Korean one, to the effect that security, according to North Koreans and hard-line conservatives, must be 100 percent homegrown and can never rely on the efforts or attitudes of others.

As the hot and humid days and weeks of July gave way to the even hotter and more humid days of August, it was clear that the process was moving, and that North Korea was under increasing pressure to join the other five countries. Every day I returned to the hotel praising the work of the Chinese in getting the conference to yes. It was praise that I honestly believed was warranted, but it was also to remind the Chinese that they were in the chair and bore the ultimate responsibility for success or failure.

The North Koreans clearly began to feel the pressure to agree to disarm, and began instead to focus on their right to have a civil nuclear program. Needless to say, a country that had so grossly abused that right had no business expecting others to support them, but being North Korean is not to worry about what others think. With the Russians and Chinese very much supporting international structures, namely the Nuclear Nonproliferation Treaty, the North Koreans received a surprising amount of sympathy for its "right" to have a civil nuclear program.

Meanwhile, as much as I had support from Secretary Rice and from President Bush, it was clear that there was considerable unhappiness about going forward in a process that, in the eyes of the conservative wing of the Bush administration, was somehow legitimizing the North Koreans. Even on the team at the negotiation there was considerable mistrust at every stage. When the North Koreans invited my team to dinner, something I had avoided for the first two weeks but finally accepted in the third, I could get only a couple of the members to attend with me. When at one point Joe DeTrani and Jim Foster stayed behind at the talks for some side discussions with the North Koreans, other members on the delegation found out and had the bus return them to the site so they could join and make sure Joe and Jim were not somehow making concessions.

As Holbrooke had done at Dayton, I tried to insist on seeing all written reports sent back to Washington, but emails from mobile devices and cell phones had evolved considerably in the intervening ten years since Dayton and even Rambouillet. Thus I suspect I saw only the reports sent through official telegram channels while the real messages were sent via email.

The talks were grueling and tempers flared at times as fatigue took its toll on everyone. I had little flexibility on the North Korean insistence on receiving light water reactors as compensation for dismantling the weapons program, but this supposed stubbornness on my part simply masked the hypocrisy of other delegations who wanted to see the provision put in the agreement for the agreement's sake, but had no intention of ever paying for such a project. China, in particular, was very focused on the bottom line for any assistance programs and had absolutely no intention of providing light water reactors. Nonetheless they thought nothing of pressuring me. At one point Wu threatened to take my supposed intransigence to the press. I responded with a line I had always wanted to use in a negotiation: "Make my day!" After a little pause for the interpreter to figure out what I was saying, Wu and I got back on track.

Negotiations in the field are often double-tracked with discussions at the foreign minister level, and this one was no exception. Secretary Rice, taking advantage of the short overlap in working days between two parts of the world twelve time zones removed from each other, was frequently on the telephone with her counterparts, especially Korean foreign minister Ban Ki-moon, who helped Song and me keep the U.S.–South Korean position solid. Song and I often took long walks on the Diaoyutai grounds. At one point we looked up and realized that Korean reporters standing just outside the fence, without, we hoped, any lip readers, were filming our whole discussion.

We thought there would be opportunities for some forms of recreation, but just as in Dayton, nobody wanted to run the risk of a press story back home suggesting we were having a great time. So we continued discussions and drafting sessions, and a lot of waiting around, deep into the night.

Efforts to get off the Diaoyutai campus were rare, due mainly to the fact that the Japanese and South Korean journalists were prepared to follow us paparazzi-style, whether we went to a restaurant in the evening or did mundane chores like shopping for toothpaste and shaving cream. On one occasion, Edgar took me to a Chinese indoor market to buy some socks, among other things I needed. He would not let me buy anything at the sticker price and so began bargaining in his fluent Chinese while I nervously looked around to make sure there was no Japanese film crew capturing the event. Finally, with the merchant simply wanting to give away the socks for free, having been already sufficiently compensated by the opportunity to listen to Edgard's Chinese, we ran out just as a South Korean television crew arrived at the front of the market on the busy city sidewalk, having found us. I nonetheless gave a brief interview:

"Why are you here."

"I was shopping."

"What did you buy?"

"Personal items."

"Will you meet the North Koreans?"

"Not here. Sorry. I have to go. . . ."

September 19, 2005, came amid expectations that we had finally reached a deal. Washington had agreed to a formulation that skirted but did not slam the door on a light water reactor. We agreed "to discuss the subject of the provision of a light water reactor at an appropriate time."

I thought it was a judicious turn of phrase, apparently created by Steve Hadley, who, unlike the vice president and some others, was trying to support President Bush in making progress.

But as we got ready for the announcement, Secretary Rice called me to say there was another problem.

I sighed audibly as I took out my pen, the Joint Statement less than an hour from being announced to the world.

"Chris, in the second paragraph of section two, could you take out the reference to North Korea and the United States living in 'peaceful coexistence.' Several of us don't like it. It's an old Cold War term."

Dreading the prospect of reopening the text with only minutes to go, I asked what the problem was substantively.

"It's a Cold War line. The Soviets used to use it all the time in our agreements. We need to take it out."

"Um, Madam Secretary, that line has been there in the text for weeks now. Uh, I'm standing here looking over at the main room, where television cameras are being set up right now. Do you have any thoughts on what we could put in its place?"

"Doesn't matter. You just need to take it out." I suspected someone was pushing her on this and decided not to be my usual pain-in-the-neck self.

"Well," I said, thinking about the meaning of the phrase—hideous Cold War relic that it may be, "instead of peaceful coexistence, could I change it to 'exist peacefully together'?"

"Sure."

"Okay, Got it. Gotta go." I turned off my phone to make sure I didn't get any more incoming calls and rushed to get the change in the text, explaining to Wu that it would be clearer English. He started reaching for another pack of cigarettes and it was only 10 A.M. After all, I said cheerfully, this "peaceful coexistence" line is very Cold War–like. We're moving on . . .

"You tell me you are trying to change the text at this point?!"

"Really, 'exist peacefully together' is much better English. Ambassador Randt, don't you think so?"

"Absolutely." (Memo to self: buy that man a beer.)

Wu accepted the change, noting that in his official view it was a translation fix, and we were done.

Minutes later we were in the large conference room with the plastic tulips, and for the first time I was able to look at my closing statement as written for me in Washington. The substance of the statement was fine, although the tone didn't quite achieve the near-euphoric atmosphere in the room. The statement helpfully included a definition of the "appropriate time" when the North Koreans could expect the parties to "discuss, at an appropriate time," the subject of the provision of a light water reactor. The definition of appropriate time was based on North Korean action in fulfilling its denuclearization obligations, hardly something the North Koreans could object to. But another line in the statement caught many people's attention: ". . . the United States will take concrete actions necessary to protect ourselves and our allies (whether they ask for it or not) against any illicit and proliferation activities. . . ."

The effort to attack the North Koreans for illicit activities had been ongoing through the summer months. North Korea had long played by its own rules, most famously using its diplomatic pouch to smuggle cigarettes and other tax-free items to its embassies in several northern European countries for the purpose of financing their operations. As several investigative journalistic pieces had revealed over the years, the North Koreans operated a wide range of bank accounts whose primary function appeared to be the financing of the family fortunes of the Kim dynasty, as well as the importation of luxury items into North Korea to satisfy the demands of the elites and, more generally, to finance foreign trade.

Even while we were furiously negotiating the Joint Statement in mid-September, the U.S. Treasury announced the designation of Banco Delta Asia as a primary money-laundering concern. Banco Delta Asia was an obscure bank operating in Macao, a former Portuguese colony known for its casinos. I was not surprised about the designation, but the decision to announce in the middle of negotiations seemed to confirm the suspicions of many—including some on my team—that the purpose was not to give me added negotiating leverage (something I would have welcomed), but rather to sidetrack the negotiations entirely.

I had absolutely no doubt that North Korea was engaged in illicit activity, nor did I have any doubt that the sleepy and sleazy gambling mecca of Macao, could well be the hotbed of it. Over the months, teams from the FBI and Secret Service that had found their investigations often running through Macao had briefed me thoroughly on the issues as they related to law enforcement. But I also found these teams of professionals very skeptical and not amused about some of the efforts of media-savvy nonprofessional, political appointees in the Treasury and State Departments to publicize North Korean activities rather than use them, as law enforcement professionals would do, to trace more such activities, work with local authorities in whose jurisdiction the activities taking place, and get them shut down.

In addition to being impressed by the obvious professionalism, calmness, and just-the-facts approach of the FBI and Secret Service agents who would gather in my EAP office, all wearing their trademark dark suits and white shirts, I believed that they could be a valuable complement to our negotiations. I had on many occasions told the North Koreans what I had also said publicly, that when a country pursues weapons of mass destruction, has the world's worst human rights record, and counterfeits foreign currencies, it should not expect these sorts of activities to fly below the radar screen. And as intrigued as I had been by the efforts of State and Treasury, I became far more interested in professional law enforcement efforts that would make the North Koreans understand where their activities had put them. Most important, by simply following normal law enforcement efforts and not specially set-up structures in the State Department, the North Koreans would start to notice that the noose was tightening. At the same time, they would have little to complain about because there was nothing publicly being said about it.

However, Stuart Levy of the Treasury Department, a highly politicized protégé of John Bolton who had been part of the Florida recount battle in the 2000 presidential election, kept good relations with the media and briefed them frequently, often overselling his product. My predecessor at EAP, Jim Kelly, had hired David Asher, a young, very bright, but ideologically minded political appointee, as if to say "EAP can be crazy, too." Asher, also an overseller of financial measures, saw to it that many developments came to light with the press.

Thus when the Banco Delta Asia announcement came, it infuriated almost all our Six Party colleagues—especially China, South Korea, and Russia—and was widely seen as a challenge to the entire negotiating process, not to speak of a return to unilateralism. For the Chinese, it was an example of something they had seen during the course of recent centuries: extraterritorialism.

"What are you doing?" Wu asked me.

"It is law enforcement," I answered wanly.

"That is not how law enforcement officials behave," he responded without a trace of his usual good cheer.

Wu was right. The designation of the bank as a primary money-laundering concern had been made according to a domestic U.S. law, the PATRIOT Act, which had been passed in the wake of 9/11. But by 2005, the notion that the extraterritorial provisions of the law were necessary to "protect" America did not hold water in places like Beijing. Instead, it was seen as a vehicle for the United States to impose its will in any jurisdiction where it saw fit to do so.

FBI and Secret Service agents would privately complain to me that the Treasury Department's antiterrorism finance office and the State Department's Illicit Activities Initiative, in their ongoing talkative relationships with think tanks and journalists, were not helpful to long-standing criminal investigations.

I agreed with them and others that the public treatment of the issues might be undermining professional investigations, and I also believed that the publicizing of our efforts was undermining the negotiation track. And what's more, they seemed intended to do just that.

Moreover, these efforts were completely oversold within the U.S. government as something that could supplant the negotiations by inducing the North Koreans to declare *no mas* and give up their nuclear ambitions (not likely), or could somehow lead to North Korea's collapse (even less likely). There was no question that these steps had brought little Banco Delta Asia in far-off Macao to its knees (indeed, much to the glee of U.S. government sanctioneers, depositors big and small were lined up around the block in Macao to withdraw their deposits), but the $22–25 million worth of North Korean accounts frozen by Banco Delta Asia authorities in September 2005 was hardly going to have any macro effect on North Korea's economy. No serious analyst of North Korea's behavior believed that their response would be to give in at the Six Party Talks, or to collapse altogether. Indeed, the only effect of the steps against the bank was to derail the prospect of negotiation for some eighteen months and, of course, to make the North Koreans more careful about moving their funds around.

I repeatedly told the North Koreans that this was the world they had chosen, that banks all over the world would be increasingly unlikely to take their funds out of concern that they would face the kind of existential issues currently facing Banco Delta Asia. I explained to Kim that the United States, like any country, had the right to take action to protect itself against illicit activities of the kind that the bank was complicit in. Kim was not entirely convinced that the United States was truly living in mortal fear over what bad governance at the Macao bank could do to the U.S. economy. Even before the ink was dry on September 19, 2005, I knew this was not going to be easy.

On that day when we reached agreement on the Joint Statement, I settled into my seat on the United Airlines flight for the long journey home. An American flight attendant approached me.

"I have a question," she said.

"Oh, I am sorry," I said as I started fumbling in the seat jacket for the menu, to see if I was going to choose the beef or the chicken.

"No, not that," she said. "I want to know why we can have nuclear weapons and the North Koreans can't."

16

HEART OF DARKNESS

By the time I had reached Chicago, North Korea had issued a statement. They would insist on a light water reactor (LWR) in the context of denuclearization. An LWR, relatively more difficult to use to produce bomb-making material than a graphite-moderated reactor, had been envisioned during the Clinton era "Agreed Framework," but the Bush administration was having none of it. I did not disagree with keeping the LWR off the table, especially for a country that had lied in its previous commitments, but I thought the best way to manage the issue was to put it off. Later on, I thought, if that were the only issue separating us from a blockbuster deal, we should take a look at it. But that kick-the-can-down-the-road approach was not the stuff some in the Bush administration were made of. Why say no when *hell no* seemed the more honest approach?

The statement that day suggested to some that the North Koreans were not going to live up to their obligations to denuclearize unless they received a light water reactor. In fact, the statement was simply an attempt to define North Korea's interpretation of the provisions of the agreement that dealt with their assertion of a right to a civil nuclear program. Washington was polarized on the agreement, pitting those who oversold it as peace in our time (Neville Chamberlain at Munich, 1938) against those who saw it as not worth the paper it was printed on. Some argued that the North Koreans had only agreed when they saw the oncoming freight train of sanctions in the Banco Delta Asia case.

When I staggered into work the next morning, the sense of pride in the Bureau of East Asian and Pacific Affairs was palpable; it was at the center of the action. Kathleen Stephens, who had been running the bureau while I was in Beijing, briefed me on what had gone on in my absence. I wasn't in much of a mood for high-fives, partly because I didn't have the energy to raise my arm that high, but mostly because I knew that the work had really only begun. Moreover, as Kathy remarked to me, the opposition efforts were formidable.

The Six Party agreement had a positive, electrifying effect on the mood in Seoul. The dividend was a much-improved view of the United States and a belief that the U.S.–South Korean alliance was back on track. In China, too, there was a positive buzz, especially among those who saw cooperation with the United States in their country's future.

The bank scandal, however, would bedevil the Six Party Talks for the next eighteen months, during which time there would be almost no negotiation. The next round of talks, which took place in Beijing on November 9, 2005, made no progress amid a deteriorating atmosphere in the Six Parties.

The North Koreans, as if to demonstrate they would not be intimidated (and to show they may also have a sense of irony), fired off a cocktail of short-, medium-, and long-range missiles on July 4, 2006. They launched seven in all, including its longest-range missile, the Taepodong-2. The other six tests included Scud-C and Nodong ballistic missiles, all launched from the new Kittaeryong test site. The United States issued a statement describing the launches as "a provocative act," pointing out that they violated the voluntary moratorium on longer-range flight testing, but in the absence of any negotiating process, we could not have really expected such a moratorium to hold.

In July 2006, after the missile launches, the UN Security Council adopted Resolution 1695, condemning North Korea's missile launches and calling for a return to the Six Party Talks. The resolution was as strong a resolution ever taken against North Korea. And most importantly, China and Russia supported us, something that probably would not have happened had we failed to engage in the talks. It even included provisions for banning luxury items to North Korea. In October 2006, North Korea exploded an underground nuclear device. It was probably a fizzle, that is, a failure to create the nuclear chain reaction necessary to explode a weapon, but no one doubted that they were planning to try and try again until they succeeded. In the wake of the October underground nuclear test, Secretary Rice thought we needed to get back to the talks and she began an intensive but quiet round of telephone calls with the Chinese foreign minister.

The North Koreans signaled, and later confirmed to us, that they had no intention of engaging in further negotiation unless the actions taken in the Banco Delta Asia case were reversed and the North Korean accounts restored to them. Estimates of the amount of those accounts varied from $22 million to $25 million. Wu and many others in his delegation had worked hard to reach the Joint Statement of September, but he did not see where we could go with the process, now halted over a sum of $25 million.

I told Secretary Rice that it didn't look like any progress was going to be made. I told her I was all in favor of pressuring the North Koreans, that no one disliked that regime more than I did, but that there is a time to make one's point and a time to move on, and $25 million was not enough of a haul to scuttle the Six Party process.

Rice and Hadley agreed, but when it came time to reverse the action, it was clear that it was a one-way trip down sanction way.

The problem had to do with the legal designation. Once a bank is designated a primary money-laundering concern, there can be certain steps undertaken in internal controls and other management issues to undesignate it, but the North Korean accounts had been in the bank at the time, and as part of the basis of suspicion against the bank could not easily be returned to the customer. Moreover, simple solutions like Banco Delta Asia wiring the money to another bank were not easy because that other bank would be reluctant to take tainted money and risk being designated for money laundering, too. Indeed, in the case of receiving North Korean funds and then passing them back to the North Koreans, any bank's legal department would have good reason to advise against it.

Leverage, I always thought, was something one could use or not, as needed in the circumstances. We threatened Milosevic with air action, we suspended the air action, and we resumed the air action. But Banco Delta Asia had become a kind of sanctions doomsday machine that could not be turned back off, at least not to the satisfaction of the holder of the bank accounts, North Korea.

Once, while Secretary Rice was en route in the back of a SUV to a meeting at the White House Situation Room, she asked Undersecretary Joseph about how to reverse the sanctions. Joseph, quiet and well-mannered, viewed talking to North Koreans about as enthusiastically as talking to the devil.

"It is complicated," he condescendingly replied, not answering her straightforward question, "very, very difficult and probably cannot be done." I couldn't imagine giving an answer like that to my boss, but such were the ideological wars within the Bush administration.

I had been on a trip that took me from Tokyo to Hong Kong to Fiji for a Pacific Island forum, then on to Vanuatu, where I planned a day-and-a-half visit to that tiny country where the U.S. official presence consisted of eighty Peace Corps volunteers.

I arrived at the airport on a late-night flight from Fiji, with a cold and chills. There was a driving rain as I walked down the stairs onto the dark tarmac, to be greeted by an official welcome of Vanuatu "warriors" who met me with a traditional "island greeting," ceremonially threatening me with their spears; then, according to the script, upon closer inspection, seeing that I was not hostile, they escorted me to the VIP room of the three-room airport.

Peace Corps country director Kevin George briefed Steve McGann (the EAP office director for the Pacific states) and me on the program in Vanuatu as we drove our way to a spartan hotel with a great view of the ocean. At the check-in desk I was handed a message to call the State Department Operations Center. I marveled how they had tracked me down in Vanuatu, and after about thirty minutes of dialing for an outside line (there was no cell phone service), I reached the Op Center and received word that Secretary Rice wanted to speak with me. I stood by as the operations officer connected me, and when she did, I found I was talking with Philip Zelikow.

Phil was Secretary Rice's counselor, a senior position for which there is no job description apart from what the secretary wants the counselor to do. Once upon a time Phil had been a Foreign Service officer, a stint on which he relied heavily when dispensing advice from his position as counselor, often starting with "When I was an FSO . . ." He was probably too intellectual to be an FSO, too much the academic. He had a brilliant, integrated mind, and if one could get over the fact that someone from Texas should not have an Oxford accent, he had many useful thoughts to offer. For the most part Phil had moderate and sensible views on issues, even if they were offered in somewhat baroque terms.

Phil (or Philip, as he preferred) was spread rather thin in the State Department, dropping in on what seemed like random issues, then dropping out when the secretary would call him to do something else. I could discern during senior staff meetings, while I was waiting my turn to discuss North Korea, that he was one of the first to understand the Sunni Awakening in Iraq's Anbar Province, and its significance for overcoming the early de-Baathification mistake which had so harmed our efforts in that country I would later serve in. I was impressed listening in on these discussions. He understood things that many others had not.

But working alongside Phil was not for the faint of heart. Operationally, that is connecting people or pushing an issue forward so that it could be implemented and be of use as part of a foreign policy, he was like a human computer virus who would infect and destroy the simplest of tasks. Why was I being connected to him? I wondered as he came on the phone.

"Chris, can you get to a secure phone there?"

"Uh, not easy, Philip, what with my being here in Vanuatu."

"Okay, well I'll just have to talk around it." What a disappointment, I thought. For the Vanuatu intelligence service this was probably the most interesting telephone call on the island since the invasion of Guadalcanal was launched from there in 1942.

"Um, okay, go ahead, Phil."

"The secretary has had some in-depth discussions with her counterpart in the biggest Six Party country." ("Biggest . . ." Oh, I get it. He's talking about China. Boy, those poor Vanuatan eavesdroppers must be scratching their heads over that one.) "They agreed that you should go there very quietly and meet your little friends. Can you get there by Monday?" "Little friends?" I repeated to myself, the rain still beating on the hotel's tin roof. I have lots of little friends. Oh, I got it . . .

"She wants me to meet those guys?" I said, referring to the North Koreans. "And with the Chi—, I mean, the biggest country present, I assume." I didn't want to go through another such episode.

"She expects the big guys to start the meeting, then you will talk with your little friends bilaterally."

"Okay, I'll be in Sydney thirty-six hours from now. If I could get some more details of how to handle these talks sent through our consulate there, I'll figure out how to get to Beijing and what the logistics are."

The next morning I met the president and the prime minister of Vanuatu, then spent the rest of the day visiting Peace Corps volunteers in their villages. In one place, the chief and two volunteers working on public health turned out the entire village for my visit. I wondered whom the villagers thought they were meeting, since assistant secretary is not a title that necessarily means a lot to a Vanuatan villager.

One of the volunteers explained: "We told them you were important and had once been a volunteer like us."

"Perfect," I replied, wishing I were back in Cameroon on my Suzuki 125 dirt bike.

I gave a short speech about how the Pacific Ocean, which was lapping up against the edge of the village, joins my country to this village, and that the same waters flow between us. As someone afflicted with a fever and chills I was relieved I had come up with lines like that on the spur of the moment. I was channeling my Peace Corps days. (Once I had told an audience near Tiko, Cameroon, "Ask not what your credit union can do for you; ask what you can do for your credit union.")

The chief of the Vanuatan village told an inspiring story about the fact that during "the war" American soldiers (marines) had left a large pile of no-longer-needed equipment in the village, and how honored everyone was that the Americans chose their village for that.

I shook hands with a long line of people, and when after about forty-five minutes I could feel my hand beginning to throb, I realized that people were shaking my hand and then getting back in line to do it again. I asked the Peace Corps volunteer about it, and he answered: "Happens here a lot with visitors. There otherwise isn't much going on here."

I arrived in Beijing Monday night, slipped down the stairs from the plane to a waiting embassy car, and headed off to the apartment belonging to Deputy Chief of Mission David Sedney, where I spent the night. The next morning I began discussions with the North Koreans out at the Diaoyutai, and this time the Chinese showed up.

What the Chinese had delivered was a willingness of the North Koreans to attend the next session of the Six Party Talks. What they had not delivered was any flexibility on the part of the North Koreans to engage in actual negotiations. Essentially, the Chinese delivered North Koreans who would attend but not engage.

I explained to Kim Gye Gwan what I had explained to him the previous November: that there was nothing I could do about the sanctions situation, and that the matter was in the banking world. Wu didn't try to suggest otherwise, perhaps already knowing that the fix was in and the North Koreans were prepared to return to the talks, even if just to sit there.

In December 2006 we had the next session, three days and out by the twenty-second, just in time to get us all back to our families by Christmas. I presented a phased denuclearization plan, but the North Koreans would not comment, though they did agree to take it back for study.

The Chinese issued a "Chairman's Statement," a weaker formulation than a Joint Statement like the one issued in September 2005. The statement fecklessly reaffirmed that the parties all continued to be committed to the September 2005 Joint Statement, noted the fact that candid discussions were conducted in bilateral channels, and declared the Fifth Round to be in recess pending consultations in capitals. In short, the talks had not moved an inch since September 2005. During the December round, there were side discussions between the Treasury Department representatives and the North Koreans on the subject of the sanctions against Banco Delta Asia. These too got nowhere, although I was glad to let the Treasury representatives, led by a very reasonable and knowledgable deputy assistant secretary, Danny Glaser, have the pleasure of dealing with the North Koreans on this issue.

On the evening of December 22, Victor Cha, the NSC director for Northeast Asia, accompanied by Korea office director Sung Kim, visited the North Korean embassy and discussed next steps with Li Gun and Choi Sun Ai, the North Korean deputy (Victor's counterpart) and the "interpreter" (who at times behaved like the head of the North Korean delegation).

To Victor's and Sung's surprise, Li and Choi suggested a quiet meeting somewhere in Europe where we might be able to make progress on the denuclearization issues, with the proviso that the Banco Delta Asia sanctions eventually be reversed before anything could be actually agreed and implemented. I immediately informed Secretary Rice, who was intrigued by the possibility but suggested I get home and that we take up the matter after Christmas.

I met with her immediately after New Year's. She had already communicated the possibility to the president, who was prepared to explore it further. After considerable discussion, the decision was made to go ahead with Berlin, a traditional venue for East-West interaction. Condi and the president wanted to limit the publicity and told me to find an excuse for why I was in Berlin. I called Holbrooke, who, long out of government, was, among his other activities, chairman of the American Academy of Berlin. We worked out that I would speak at the Academy. He agreed to be in Berlin, saying so in a tone that convinced me that he would not want to be anywhere else in the world. Holbrooke loved this stuff. It would be like old times, I thought, except he would be my wingman.

We arrived in Berlin on January 15, 2007, for two days of talks with the North Koreans, starting the first session early the next morning in our embassy. We sat across a table in a sparsely decorated U.S. Embassy conference room. Box lunches were brought in and we ate separately in rooms reserved for the two delegations. Following a set of talking points that had been approved by the president, Hadley, and Rice (and not too many other people), I told Kim that we could commit to a process leading to the unfreezing of North Korean assets, but that we had to identify a means to unfreeze the North Korean accounts at Banco Delta Asia, and that wasn't turning out to be easy.

In addition to offering heavy fuel oil to North Korea, I also proposed to open embassy-like "interest sections" in each other's capital. The Chinese were very enthused about this idea, since it had been the basis for developing U.S.-China relations in the aftermath of the 1972 Shanghai Accords. Washington was less enthusiastic, as many believed this was too big a plum for the North Koreans. The issue became moot when Kim Gye Gwan told me his government was not interested in pursuing interest sections at all. I was not entirely surprised. What the North Koreans would get out of such an arrangement would be access in Washington, but they would not appreciate an active U.S. mission in Pyongyang, its officers fanning out to make contact with North Korean society.

It was clear from the discussions that the North Koreans needed fuel oil (how much would need to be negotiated at the next round) and would be prepared to disable their nuclear facilities (with details to be negotiated at the next round of talks).

A major problem remained. The North Koreans were not prepared to discuss our well-founded suspicions about their uranium enrichment program (UEP). We knew that they had made purchases consistent with a UEP, but in the absence of any proven facility, and dogged by the Iraq experience, in which allegations resulting in a war had proven to be inaccurate, we were reluctant to hold up negotiation to eliminate a known site—the Yongbyon plutonium site—for the sake of suspicions but little proof. Our formulation with the North Koreans continued to be that this was an "outstanding question" that needed to be answered to everyone's satisfaction.

My hope throughout the process, a hope shared by Rice and others, was that the more we could get on the ground in North Korea, the more we could assess the status of the uranium program, whether it was real or something the North Koreans had tried and failed at. Stanford University scholars Siegfried "Sig" Hecker and John Lewis, both of whom had known Secretary Rice for years, made an impassioned case to her for getting on with shutting down the plutonium-producing reactor as the clear and present danger, and keeping the door open to finding out more about the highly enriched uranium (HEU) program. I believed that was good advice, as long as we never dropped the HEU issue.

Berlin marked an important step forward. By logistical happenstance, Rice came through Berlin while returning from a trip to the

Middle East. Taking my entire five-member team with me, I briefed her in her sparsely appointed suite, whose décor was pretty much limited to a reproduction of a large oil portrait of a frightening Frederick the Great. Yuri Kim leaned over to me and said, "Can we cover him up? He's scaring me." Condi, oblivious to Frederick's glare, was intrigued by the idea that we could get some disablement of facilities, put international inspectors on the ground, and share the fuel oil costs with the other partners. A key item on the price tag, however, was to reverse the Banco Delta Asia sanctions, something nobody had yet figured out how to do.

The next morning I spoke before the American Academy in Berlin, at the Adlon, a proud, historic hotel that unfortunately had become known around the world as the place where Michael Jackson dangled his baby outside a fourth-story window for no apparent reason other than to pose before the crowd below. "No, guys," I told my team. "We are not going to look at where Michael Jackson held the baby."

I met Holbrooke in the café and walked with him to the ballroom where I would be giving the talk. He was lamenting the lack of notice and what he feared would be too small a crowd. He had clearly forgotten the habits of the East Asian press. Swarms of them, including a couple of Japanese television crews, met us at the elevator and followed us to the ballroom. Trying to get a better shot of me, one hit the back of Holbrooke's head with a camera. Holbrooke turned to the diminutive journalist and threw him to the floor before he had a chance to apologize. I was so upset by the incident, the wounding of Holbrooke's pride more so than the bump on his head or his smackdown of the journalist, that I began the remarks with lengthy odes to Dick and his accomplishments. The bump on his bruised head seemed to go away.

At lunch, Dick and John Kornblum took my team and me to a Chinese restaurant on the top floor. Dick asked me if I would mind if he addressed the team, and I said of course not, walking away to have a side conversation with John and let my old boss perform. I knew he missed it badly. For ten minutes, he told them to relish being part of a team working on negotiations of real consequence. At best, we might bring to bear our collective diplomatic skills to hammer out a deal with the North Koreans. At the very least, we would have learned lessons that can only come through experience. Either way, he told them, they would come out stronger, better diplomats. And one more thing, he concluded: enjoy the moment, because "you may never have another like it." His tone was impassioned and deeply personal, one generation imparting wisdom to another. Not that any of this team needed a pep talk, but it moved them all deeply. As I spoke with John I could see Yuri, Victor Cha, Tom Gibbons, and Sung Kim sitting there spellbound, listening to every word.

On February 8, 2007, we arrived in Beijing for what we hoped would be real progress after almost eighteen months of virtually none. The talks were tough as the North Koreans pressed for more fuel oil in compensation, and often the discussions ran deep into the night. We knew that to get anything agreed, we would have to reverse the sanctions at Banco Delta Asia, and that no one had yet figured out how to do that. But it was clear that we were going to get some disablement of facilities in return for a supply of heavy fuel oil for the North Koreans, whose cost would be shared among the participants, giving them all a stake in the game.

In one of my telephone updates to Secretary Rice, I told her we had agreement to bring back international inspectors to Yongbyon, and agreement on some disablement steps, but that the North Koreans were holding out for too much fuel oil. I told her I was sure we would get them down to 40,000 tons rather than 50,000.

"Chris, don't be too hard-line on this. Keep in mind that others are sharing the burden, and really, ten thousand tons of fuel oil is not very much, is it?"

"Okay," I told her, enjoying the thought that I was the hard-liner here.

On February 13, Wu Dawei announced a new joint statement, the first since September 2005. The key elements were that the North

Koreans had agreed to shut down the plant, take disabling measures, and invite back international inspectors. The statement represented considerable elaboration on the September 2005 one, including the creation of working groups (or, as the Russian interpreter called them: "the groups that work, that is to say, the WGs") with representatives from all six parties to discuss the creation of a Northeast Asian Peace and Security Mechanism. The "groups that work" began meeting soon after the February Joint Statement, but it was clear the North Koreans were simply not able to gear up on all these fronts and little progress was made.

Meanwhile, back in the trenches of Washington, D.C., renewed fighting broke out over the commitment we had given the North Koreans to restore their Banco Delta Asia accounts. The problem was still that no bank was prepared to take tainted money, for fear that they would become a target. Efforts by Secretary of the Treasury Hank Paulson to support Secretary Rice earned him a nasty, tendentious story in the *Financial Times,* evidently leaked by subordinates who had no interest in implementing the commitment to reverse the measures.

The impasse continued for months, as Paulson and colleagues from the U.S. Federal Reserve Bank worked out an arrangement with the Russian central bank to transfer the funds out of Banco Delta Asia, in effect laundering the $25 million through these two central banks. In June 2007, Russia announced that it had agreed to take the frozen accounts from Macao and transfer them to the Russian Far Eastern Bank, where North Korea held several accounts. On July 14, after receiving a fuel aid shipment from South Korea, North Korea announced its part of the bargain: it would shut down Yongbyon and upon confirmation of the funds would invite the international inspectors to verify.

The announcement had been long hoped for, but by June I was beginning to think it would never happen. I was on three-day trip to Mongolia to visit our embassy and call on senior officials in that windswept, sparsely populated country. I went on a weekend trip north from Ulan Bator to get a sense of the vast Mongolian steppe and, as I always tried to do in visits to countries throughout the region, to meet Peace Corps volunteers. Being a Peace Corps volunteer, as I always told them, was the best foreign service assignment I ever had.

We spent the night in a tourist hotel in the middle of nowhere that offered as a side treat the opportunity to sleep in a Mongolian yurt, or *ger*, a traditional round hut with a wood-burning stove in the center. The weather was freezing at night and there was a hard driving rain, a rarity, I was told. Some seven Japanese journalists, who, having been taken by surprise in the "Berlin shock," were under strict orders by their editors to shadow my every move since January, followed me to the remote hotel.

One of the journalists informed me that the North Koreans had actually announced the shutdown of the plant and had called for international inspectors. Tom Gibbons, the East Asian and Pacific Affairs Bureau's special assistant, managed to find a telephone that worked to try to confirm the news. I said very little to the press except that we had a long way to go in the process. Getting inspectors on-site was just the beginning.

I retired to my room in the hotel, my Mongolian *ger* having been flooded out by the pounding rain. I pondered how long it had taken to get this far, and if I really had the stomach to stay with this much longer. It was not just the physical toll, but also the beating I was taking within the administration at the hands of its neoconservatives, who continued to regard any negotiation with North Korea as an exercise in appeasement, for which anyone directly engaged needed to be punished. Anytime there was progress, it was attributed to such measures as the freeze on the Banco Delta Asia accounts. I felt I was far too visible a spokesperson on the issue, and that any approbation I earned for our country in East Asia was more than offset by the berating I was getting.

There was no question that the secretary and the president were supporting me, but there seemed to be little effort to rein in those inside the administration who were trying to scuttle the talks. Condi responded to my every word about such people by telling me to ignore them and understand that the president fully supported me, which I deeply appreciated. Having the support of the president should have been the gold standard, but Washington had become a sort of free-fire zone and it was not at all clear to me that the president could protect an expendable Foreign Service officer.

At one point, the Undersecretary of State for Political Affairs Nick Burns called and told me that the new United Nations secretary-general, the former Korean foreign minister and a close acquaintance of mine, Ban Ki-moon, had asked Rice if I could join him in the UN. Before I could even weigh what I thought was an offer, Nick explained that she had told Ban that she needed me where I was, and that Ban had agreed. Nick said he just wanted me to know, and concluded cheerfully that it is always good to be wanted. Wanted, I thought, was a pretty accurate description of my predicament with some of these critics.

As I headed to the airport in Ulan Bator, I received word from our embassy in Beijing that Kim Gye Gwan had asked me to make an urgent trip to Pyongyang. We were still a couple of weeks ahead of the actual shutdown, and I had no intention of visiting the Yongbyon nuclear facility to watch them process material for weapons of mass destruction. But in talking it over with Rice, we agreed there might be some value in making the trip to Pyongyang to ensure that all was on track.

For reasons I never fully understood, there had been persistent reports in the press, attributed to unnamed sources, that for months I had sought to go to North Korea but had been blocked by Vice President Cheney. I had never made any such request, because I never saw the value in going. A trip to North Korea needs to pay off to overcome the added hostility back in Washington. Years after Secretary of State Albright had visited and met with Kim Jong Il, she was still being subjected to criticism, as if she hadn't known how to handle an encounter with a dictator.

In one meeting in the White House Situation Room, Rumsfeld raised the possibility of sending someone on a visit to Pyongyang, especially as no official American had been there since Albright's visit in October 2000. Back in the fall of 2005, Rumsfeld, who often raised "out-of-the-box" ideas—and in so doing, demonstrated why the box was there in the first place—elaborated on his suggestion, saying, as I sat three feet away from him, "if we do send someone we need to send someone with a higher status than Hill." Vice President Cheney, not particularly known for empathy, looked over at me and motioned that I shouldn't take it personally.

On June 21, I arrived in Pyongyang in a driving rainstorm, accompanied by a very small team that included Sung Kim, Tom Gibbons, Henry Haggard from our embassy in Seoul, and Jeesoo Jung, a Korean-American interpreter also from our embassy in Seoul. We had started the day checking out from our hotel in downtown Tokyo, slipping out the hotel entrance past the journalist stakeout, and then heading in a minivan over to an air base. From there we flew a U.S. military plane to Osan Air Base in Korea, an hour south of Seoul. There we picked up another U.S. military plane for the forty-five-minute journey up the North Korean coast and on to Pyongyang. Green, wooded hills in South Korea gave way to the brown and barren landscape of North Korea, and like a movie that goes from color to black-and-white we knew we would soon be landing in North Korea.

After our small jet came to a halt on the bumpy cement runway, a vehicle came to guide us closer in to the cinder-block airport building. When we got to the arrival area several camera crews greeted us, along with officials from the Foreign Ministry, including Li Gun and Choi Sun Ai. I knew that shaking hands was inevitable but also recalled the effort that Holbrooke and I would always make in meetings with Milosevic never to smile when cameras were present. On the other hand, I also remembered the advice of our science attaché in martial law Poland: don't look angry, because it could be mistaken for fear. I allowed a smile.

We stayed at the presidential guesthouse, the lap of luxury for North Korea and the most honored place we could have been housed. The rooms were enormous, as if size of rooms was that year's central plan indicator. The decorator seemed to favor pinks, reds, and lime green, and my bed's headboard, made of white enameled wood, had motifs featuring naked cupids and other sparsely clothed figures. My television, an older Japanese model, had a remote that could not be operated from the bed, the distance being too far. From about ten feet I was able to make it work, only to find out that there was but one channel anyway. As head of delegation I had an adjoining library, whose shelves were completely filled with Kim Il Sung's life works, as well as various books about communist worker movements in such places as Romania. I looked at such titles as the life of (East Germany's last leader) Erich Honecker and reflected on the sense the North Koreans must have of being the last communist country still standing, like someone who has outlived all contemporaries.

The food was traditional Korean and featured a small, unfilleted fish, a delicacy in Korea that at lunch was served longitudinally on the plate, and at dinner, for no apparent reason, latitudinally, the only difference in the evening menu from that of lunch. Kim Gye Gwan accompanied us everywhere, including a nighttime drive through Pyongyang presumably for the purpose of showing us that many buildings did in fact have electricity in the form of single, naked lightbulbs hanging from the ceiling of apartments, most of which seemed to be without curtains.

The discussions at the Foreign Ministry, a 1970s decorated building, no worse than many I have sat in throughout the world, was unremarkable, other than the conference room's attractive dark wood paneling. It was clear that Kim Gye Gwan was interested in making sure his bosses saw that he had been able to summon the Americans. I politely declined offers to see tourist sights, especially as nothing had yet been actually accomplished in the talks, and I did not want to be seen visiting such places as the Self-Reliance (Juche, more or less translated) Tower, or worse yet, Kim Il Sung's plasticized remains under glass.

On June 25, three days after I left Pyongyang, the well-traveled $22 million came into the North Korean bank accounts and the North Koreans announced that they would begin shutting down the nuclear facilities.

The international inspectors began boarding the flights into North Korea, to arrive the next day, June 26, 2007. It was the first time since 2001 that the reactor had been shut down for anything other than maintenance, and therefore the first day that North Korea hadn't, in effect, been making more bomb material.

17

SHOWING UP

When I wasn't working in North Korea and the surrounding countries in Northeast Asia, I was in Southeast Asia. It is a very different feel from the countries of Northeast Asia. First of all, the weather is hot and humid, and unlike the Koreans or the Japanese or the Chinese, nobody is in any particular hurry. That is not to say there are no problems there, the political turmoil in Indonesia or Thailand over the years being notable examples, but compared to the issue of North Korea's nuclear aspirations, Southeast Asia was a bit of a respite.

I visited China and Korea and Japan some thirty-five times, while visits to Southeast Asian countries amounted to a small fraction of that. Still, six trips to Thailand, five to Indonesia, two to far-off (and almost forgotten) East Timor, five to the Philippines, and several out to the Pacific Island states, all added up.

Once a year, the countries of Southeast Asia hold an annual summit meeting, after which a broader group is invited, including the United States. If a secretary of state has not visited Southeast Asia at all during the year, she or he can clean the slate by showing up at the ASEAN Regional Forum (ARF), usually held in a resort hotel in a beautiful place. (ASEAN is the Association of Southeast Asian Nations.)

Usually, nothing is decided at an ARF. There is a communiqué that member states argue about in the weeks leading to the event, but that gets taken care of at some point and is often quickly forgotten within days.

The secretary of state is expected to go to the forum to represent a "partner nation," participate in various soporific meetings and conferences, and take part in one other event: a skit. Given what little secretaries of state have to do through the rest of the year in Southeast Asia, it is not a lot to expect them to attend. But if they don't, they will never hear the end of it.

Condi Rice, one of the most peripatetic secretaries of state in history, failed to show up at the first ARF, and it was discussed for years. She sent her deputy secretary Bob Zoellick, a consequential official well known throughout the world. But Bob wasn't the secretary. Condi's point in not attending was that she had other, very consequential things to do—Middle East peace, Iraq, to name a couple of them. The ARF is not a place where people actually do things. It is a place where people simply show up. If, as the old aphorism goes, 80 percent of life is just showing up, at the ARF it is almost 100.

The Cambodia of 2006 bore little relationship to the country that Americans knew from the Vietnam War, and certainly from the Khmer Rouge period, which started in the mid-1970s and drenched the country in the blood of three million victims. The killing fields had long ago returned to rice cultivation and Cambodia had become a developing country, struggling to improve its economy, manage weak institutions that often produced more corruption than services, and endure a political system that concentrated power in the hands of one leader, a former guerrilla commander named Hun Sen.

I went there in January 2006 to take part in the opening of the brand-new American embassy in Phnom Penh, an extraordinary building for Phnom Penh. It followed the basic architectural design of U.S. embassies around the world, featuring a large atrium in the center and balconies from the offices above. Newlyweds in the Cambodian capital began to pose in front of the embassy in the weeks before it opened. It was the best-looking building in the city.

But in addition to taking part in the embassy opening, my mission had another purpose. Hun Sen had just arrested several of the leading figures in the Cambodian human rights movement, including Kem Sokha, the director of the Cambodian Center for Human Rights. Our very courageous and energetic ambassador there, Joe Mussomeli, had taken on Hun Sen in the media and seemed destined to come out a distant second.

I asked the ambassador what kind of person Hun Sen was.

"He plays golf well," Joe said helpfully.

"I don't," I replied less helpfully.

I looked carefully at the bio and noticed he was born in the same year and the same month as I.

"What is the Cambodian word for older brother?"

"Bong," Joe answered.

Bong. I thought I could remember that.

I walked into Hun Sen's office. Rather than the rows of chairs laid out Chinese-style in a semicircle, he preferred sitting across a narrow table from his visitor. He looked younger than his years, thin and hungry, and tough. He had seen a lot during his lifetime. I found myself looking directly at him, partly to see if I could figure out which eye was the glass eye that replaced one lost during the war. It was hard to tell. What I could clearly see, however, was that he didn't seem to be looking forward to the meeting.

"Mr. Prime Minister. I am pleased to have this opportunity to meet you. With your permission I would like to raise something at the beginning—"

"If this is about the four persons recently arrested, there is nothing I can do about them. Our country has an independent judiciary. They are in the judiciary process. There is nothing I or anyone else can do to change that process. Cambodia is very proud of our independent judiciary system."

"Mr. Prime Minister, actually I wanted to ask you something quite different. I noticed you were born in August 1952 and I wanted to know what day."

"Why?" he asked, beginning to show some traces of humanity.

"Because I was born on the tenth and I need to know whether I must call you my 'Bong.'"

First Hun Sen started to laugh, and then his entourage did.

"The twenty-second," he replied, still laughing. "You are the Bong here today."

"Okay," I said, enjoying my newfound status. "Let me turn to another subject. Mr. Prime Minister, I know very little about Cambodia, even less about your independent judicial system (and for good reason). But I do know something about Washington. And this situation here is not understood there. I am worried that if this continues, Cambodia is going to have a reputation like Burma's. And what that will mean is that the relationship will become very complicated. Mr. Prime Minister, I like to keep things simple."

Hun Sen leaned over for an animated talk with his advisors. I kept looking over to the embassy interpreter to see if he was able to pick up any of it. Finally, Hun Sen turned back to me.

"What if I release them by two o'clock today?"

"Two o'clock? Um, that will work. Kamala, is two o'clock okay?" I thought if Hun Sen was consulting with advisors, I should turn to the East Asia Pacific special assistant, Kamala Lakhdhir.

"Um sure," Kamala replied, not sure what I wanted her to say.

"But you didn't pressure me," Hun Sen continued.

"No, never. I would never do that, Mr. Prime Minister."

"It is my gift to you on the occasion of the opening of your new embassy."

"Right, your gift to me and our embassy. A gift. A present. Thank you."

"It will happen at two P.M., but do not tell anyone."

"Nobody," I replied. "My lips are sealed."

My next meeting was with several senior members of the human rights community. They wanted to know how my meeting with the prime minister had gone. I told them that he had asked that the judiciary system be given a chance to function (an answer that didn't earn me any points), but I promised that I would remain active on the issue until they were released. I glanced at my watch and realized that was not much of a commitment. It was already noon.

After lunch with the ambassador and several of his team, followed by a tour of the new embassy, we went to the grand opening. The atrium was packed with foreign diplomats, Cambodian officials, and members of the business community. A hard monsoon rain was falling outside in the steamy city. I was chatting with the Polish military attaché when Kamala came up to me and whispered, "They are out."

"Where are they now?" I asked, almost shaking with anticipation.

"You'll meet them soon enough. They are coming here to join the party."

Some forty-five minutes later, Kem Sokha, Pa Nguon Teang, Mam Sonando, and Rong Chhun, all sporting new beards, arrived at the embassy along with a large group of supporters who had greeted them at the prison and escorted them here. I greeted them, but tried to keep my role quiet since I didn't know whether Hun Sen was the sort to change his mind.

"Kamala, what time is our flight tonight?"

"We're leaving at eight P.M."

"Good. I wouldn't want it to be much later."

When most people think about New Zealand, very pleasant images emerge—a far-off Pacific island country with snowcapped mountains and green valleys and pastures dotted with healthy sheep ready to supply the world with wool. Its people seem warm and relaxed, moderately minded, and have a sense of humor that seems to have been issued at birth. When in 1942, British commander Lord Mountbatten reviewed Kiwi troops following the epic North African turning point in El Alamein, he is said to have commented to the New Zealand commander that his troops did not seem to know how to salute very expertly. The commander, General Bernard Freyberg, replied, "No, but if you wave at them, they will surely wave back in a very friendly manner."

For the United States government, New Zealand had become a kind of pariah state over a decision taken in 1987 to make itself one of the world's nuclear-free zones, in effect banning the U.S. nuclear navy.

New Zealand's move began in 1984 and culminated with legislation in 1987 that reflected the worldwide debate on the subject (many U.S. college towns had symbolically done the same), but in New Zealand's case there was a regional issue. France had used its French Polynesian atolls to test some two hundred nuclear explosions in the atmosphere before finally halting the program in 1974. These tests had helped build a large antinuclear movement in New Zealand that did not fade away with the ending of atmospheric tests. In 1987, the Labor Party government of David Lange succeeded in passing the Nuclear Free Act of 1987, which banned not only nuclear weapons, but also vehicles of nuclear propulsion.

The United States, having watched with growing concern nuclear-freeze movements around the world, but especially in Japan and Europe, decided to make an example of New Zealand by abrogating the alliance with New Zealand and banning military cooperation.

New Zealanders, in addition to their cheerful disposition, are also known for a certain streak of independence, and the decision by the Reagan administration reinforced the sense of national pride in having achieved the world's only successful nuclear-free zone enshrined by legislation.

Since that time, the United States had maintained correct relations with New Zealand, but not much more. There were visits by U.S. members of Congress and occasional visits by senior officials, and by President Clinton when he attended an Asia-Pacific Economic Cooperation meeting in 1999. Apart from the occasional economic or environmental government visitor, most of these were in connection with international conferences taking place in New Zealand, rather than official bilateral visits. While New Zealanders often deployed alongside U.S. forces (notably in Afghanistan), U.S. forces could not train alongside the Kiwis because the U.S. had broken off military-to-military agreements in the wake of the Kiwi's nuclear declaration. Occasionally the New Zealanders hosted visits by senior U.S. military visitors, but even as late as 2005, Secretary Rumsfeld issued guidance forbidding any more such visits. Nuclear-free zones were long since past, yet the U.S. relationship with New Zealand had remained minimal since the mid-1980s.

That state of affairs was about to change.

In November 2005, John McKinnon walked into my office in Washington. John was the New Zealand deputy secretary of foreign affairs responsible for international politics and security. He seemed to reflect the stereotypes of New Zealanders: pleasant, well-mannered, very smart, and direct. We talked a little about the regional situation, especially China and North Korea, but he soon turned to the purpose of his visit, the U.S.–New Zealand bilateral relationship. The New Zealand government had gotten wind of the possibility that the United States was prepared to take a second look at a long-standing policy.

"We heard there might be some new thinking in Washington about the relationship with us."

"Not that I am aware of," I responded, "but it is funny because we had heard that there might be some new thinking about the nuclear issue in Wellington." I had in mind a series of telegrams our departing ambassador to New Zealand had sent hinting (against any evidence I was aware of) that New Zealand was rethinking the ban on nuclear ships.

"Not that I am aware of," McKinnon answered, as if to mimic my reply to him.

We talked about New Zealand's nuclear ban, its durability, how it came to pass in the first place, why it continued to enjoy support from both the Labor and Conservative parties, a kind of "identity issue" for the Kiwis.

"Well," I began, worrying that John had come a long way for this short conversation, "perhaps we can talk about how things are going in the Pacific."

There are fourteen Pacific Island states, all tiny states with big problems, and all ones that New Zealand was carefully tracking. John explained New Zealand's efforts to counter human trafficking, build up capacity in police forces around the region, provide humanitarian assistance as well as economic and other technical aid, and support regional integration. The list went on. As he continued, I realized there were many things we should be doing with New Zealand. We should not permit a Cold War–era, frozen disagreement from the 1980s to divide us.

John concluded by asking if I could visit Wellington whenever my schedule permitted it. With his briefing on New Zealand's regional activities very much on my mind, I asked if I could meet with some of the people performing these tasks in the ministry. "Frankly, I would like to go and discuss everything under the sun—except the nuclear problem," I told him.

I had found the perfect antidote to North Korea and its nuclear ambitions: a country with quite the opposite instincts in every respect. I told Secretary Rice that I thought we could do something more with the New Zealand relationship, especially given their work in the Pacific Island states. I told her we ought to "park" the nuclear disagreement, a kind of relic of the Cold War, and agree to disagree.

East Asian and Pacific Affairs Bureau Special Assistant Kamala Lakhdhir and I arrived in Wellington in March 2006 on a visit to follow up on some of the discussions McKinnon and I had in Washington. Wellington is a quiet sort of capital. As one Kiwi explained, it would be like Bethesda, Maryland, without Washington, D.C., next to it. As promised, the New Zealanders kept us busy through the two days, meeting parliamentarians, politicians, foreign ministry officials, and Prime Minister Helen Clark, who discussed bilateral issues with me while working through her in-box, an impressive display of multitasking, I thought, as I watched her scrawl notes on the corners of memos while simultaneously asking me questions about North Korea. During the visit we discussed everything, except for the elephant-in-the-room nuclear issue.

At the concluding press conference, the always feisty New Zealand journalists pressed me to talk about the nuclear issue to see if the U.S. position had changed (big news for them!), or if New Zealand's position had changed (even bigger news!). I kept my remarks to an expression of appreciation for New Zealand's Provincial Reconstruction Team in Afghanistan, and for New Zealand's work on police training in the Pacific Island states. The discussion on the nuclear issue went something like this:

"Has Washington changed its position on the nuclear issue?"

"No, our position has not changed."

"What is the U.S. position on the nuclear issue."

"Our position on the New Zealand nuclear-freeze zone is well-known."

"Can you restate it here."

"You can look it up on our website."

I left Wellington without publicly mentioning the New Zealand nuclear issue, convinced that if we could just move on there was a lot we could cooperate on.

I returned to Washington and asked Secretary Rice to invite Foreign Minister Winston Peters to Washington to discuss regional issues and what we could do to improve the bilateral relationship, understanding that neither side was going to change its views on the nuclear-free zone.

Peters arrived in Washington having taken an unusual route through Las Vegas, where he had stopped to see a boxing match. Though not a boxing fan (to my knowledge), Condi was one of the most enthusiastic sports fans I had ever met, so the explanation that the New Zealand foreign minister was on his way to Washington via Las Vegas was a good prelude to the meeting. A few months later, Secretary Rice saw Foreign Minister Peters at an international meeting talking about the North Koreans.

"He's really great," she whispered, as Peters excoriated the North Koreans with the kind of dripping sarcasm that went over many heads in the room, but which Condi and I were getting a kick out of.

"The New Zealanders are pretty intense on nuclear stuff. They really don't like nukes," I deadpanned.

Nine months later, Prime Minister Clark, who had made no friend of the White House given her strong criticism of President Bush in the aftermath of the Iraq invasion, was welcomed by President Bush in March 2007 in a sign that relations between the United States and New Zealand were much improved. (The visit was in part facilitated by Australian prime minister John Howard, who had told President Bush a few months earlier that he and Clark worked well together despite their political differences.) By the time Condi Rice arrived in Auckland in July 2008, she pronounced that differences over the nuclear-free zone would no longer hold the relationship back. "We have moved on," she said. With Prime Minister Clark standing at her side Secretary Rice described New Zealand as a "friend and ally."

18

BREAKFAST WITH CHENEY

In July 2007, Secretary Rice asked me to join her in the Oval Office to brief the president and vice president on the North Korean process. The president was energized by the fact that the Six Party Talks, the multilateral framework that he and then Chinese president Jiang Zemin had worked through at the president's ranch in Crawford, Texas, some from years before, was finally making some progress. I did all I could to lower expectations, explaining that we had taken a long time to get to this point of shutting down the plutonium plant. It would probably take another long period of time before we could expect the North Koreans to turn over plutonium already produced.

As I explained the state of affairs to the president, who was seated to the right of the fireplace while the vice president sat in the wing chair to the left, I noticed out of the corner of my eye that the vice president, quiet throughout, had fallen asleep. As I enumerated my first two points with my right hand, starting with my thumb, I turned slightly to the left to the sleeping veep for the last two, "Thirdly, we are going to need to work closely with the South Koreans . . . and fourthly . . ." He remained sound asleep.

As Condi and I walked to the black SUV, waiting on West Executive Drive outside the West Wing side entrance, she commented, "I think you noticed the vice president. That happens a lot these days." She didn't elaborate on what "that" was and I didn't ask her to since it was pretty clear. A day later, it was reported that the vice president had entered George Washington University Hospital to have a procedure to replace the pacemaker on his heart. I felt some guilt at having made fun of someone with a bad heart. I also reflected on a vice president who, having been laughably (not to speak of tragically) wrong about rose-petal-covered streets in Baghdad, seemed to continue to conduct his own foreign policy, regardless of the president's views, and seemed, especially in the second term, so out of sync with his boss. Of course, it wasn't just the president's views he ignored. Cheney didn't seem to care what anyone thought.

In a Situation Room discussion presided over by the president and attended by several cabinet-level members, Cheney began a lengthy, but completely faulty, retelling of a report he had obviously not read particularly carefully that morning, concerning North Korean cooperation with Iran. It fell to Condi, as the president looked on, to speak up and say, "Mr. Vice President, with all respect I read that report and that is not what it said." I watched anxiously from my backbench position behind Condi to see what Cheney would say. There was no rejoinder from the vice president.

I was in Sydney, Australia, in early September 2007 with President Bush when he learned that the Israelis had attacked a Syrian nuclear facility under construction by what we understood to be North Korean crews, and had completely destroyed it. (Interestingly, the Syrians finished the job by plowing the rubble under the desert sand, as if to say it had never existed in the first place.) The president shook his head at the thought that the same people we were trying to engage in a dialogue were engaged in building a nuclear reactor in one of the most troubled regions on earth. Bush asked what impact it would have on the negotiations with

North Korea, and I responded that these events really helped me explain to the North Koreans that as long as they engaged in this type of behavior, either we or someone else would come after them. They would never have a day of rest. The president liked that. Some two weeks later the CIA allowed me to show certain photos to the North Korean nuclear delegation of their countrymen visiting with Syrian nuclear experts.

"Mr. Kim [Gye Gwan], can you help me understand these photos? It looks to me that your countrymen have been in Syria helping the Syrians build a reactor. Look, Mr. Kim, isn't that the head of operations at Yongbyon? Do you know him?"

Kim tried pathetically to talk about Photoshopping, an explanation I brushed off. As for the head of the Yongbyon complex he was never seen again.

The neoconservatives, aided by a vice president's office with deep suspicions of the Foreign Service, seem to believe that the State Department negotiated with the North Koreans because we enjoyed it. Our effort to explain to these critics that this process was for the time being the best way to make progress fell on deaf ears. Nor was there the slightest acknowledgment that these same individuals who worked behind the president's back to thwart his interest in cooperating with the Chinese and others on North Korea—Vice President Cheney, John Bolton, Bob Joseph, Eric Edelman (the list is long)—were completely wrong about Iraq's having had weapons of mass destruction, did not have the good manners or common decency to admit their mistake, and preferred to blame the intelligence agencies whose information they had shamelessly cherry-picked, and in Cheney's case with his trips up to CIA headquarters, tried to shape. But with Iraq in the midst of a completely predictable catastrophic civil war, these undaunted neocons continued to roam the waterfront looking for other outlets for their aggressiveness.

At a meeting in the White House Situation Room in early 2008, a former colleague of mine, a Foreign Service officer who had worked extensively for Vice President Cheney and was now in the Office of the

Secretary of Defense, informed us that the U.S. Navy had been following a suspicious-looking North Korean ship en route to Burma.

The navy wanted to board the vessel to see what was on it, but the FSO was concerned that such an action could "hurt Chris's negotiation." His comments, dripping with ill will, implied that I would really want us to look the other way while North Koreans shipped missiles or other weapons to customers such as the Burmese junta. I told the meeting, "Please go ahead. As far as I'm concerned the navy should sink it. From the negotiation point of view, it reinforces the point I try to make to them every single time I meet with them: their proliferation and nuclear policies have put them in a world of hurt." The navy never got near the ship. It was just a hoped-for opportunity to make the State Department appear as the appeaser.

In October 2007, the president invited Condi and me to a breakfast with the vice president, who seemed more chipper with his newly installed pacemaker. National Security Advisor Steve Hadley and White House Chief of Staff Josh Bolten were also invited.

We met in the small dining room off the Oval Office. I walked in with Condi from the hall entrance. The others soon joined us as President Bush entered from the door off the Oval Office.

The breakfast was one of the president's opportunities to hear directly from someone in the field, and so I expected he would turn to Condi and me for a briefing. He sat on the end of the table set for six. The vice president was on his left and Condi on his right. I sat to Condi's right, across from Bolten, and Hadley sat on the other end of the table from the president. There was a fruit cocktail pre-positioned at each place setting with some yogurt and orange juice. Food was the last thing on my mind as I got ready for the stress-inducing briefing of the president of the United States. A White House steward took orders for more, but all waved him off, satisfied with the fruit cup, juice, and coffee. Everybody, that is, except the vice president, who ordered fried eggs and bacon.

The president started with some baseball trash talk with me, knowing

I was a Red Sox fan and saying that he didn't think the Sox could get past the Angels and their ace pitcher John Lackey in the first round of the playoffs. I told him he had to be kidding (as Condi looked worriedly in my direction), because the Red Sox had never had a problem with Lackey, etc. We continued on for almost a minute discussing the superior Red Sox starting pitching.

Back on the North Korean nuclear issue, Condi took the lead, providing for the president a thoughtful, detailed, structured, and, most important for me, sober account of where we could expect to go from here. She was riveting, and I marveled at her capacity to integrate every aspect of the Six Party Talks, from the precise plutonium amounts already produced to our efforts to create a Northeast Asia security mechanism. The president interrupted frequently with specific questions that conveyed that he was well informed on the issues, and occasionally I chimed in with further explanations. The president was very hopeful that we might be able to put the plutonium already produced under some kind of international supervision or monitoring, before eventually getting it out of the country. I could not be optimistic that we were at that point, but said it was a goal we should strive for in the current phase of the process. Hadley and Bolten listened attentively, while the vice president seemed more attentive to wolfing down his remaining eggs and starting in on his heavily buttered toast.

The president turned to the vice president and said, "Dick, do you have any questions for Condi and Chris?"

Cheney looked up from his breakfast and responded, "Well, I'm not as enthusiastic about this as some people."

Condi didn't seem to want to take that one on, so I did. "Mr. Vice President, I'm not enthusiastic, either. I'm doing the job I have been asked to do and trying to get home at night."

The president seemed to sense the tension in my voice. "It's okay, Chris," he said. "The vice president was simply expressing some concern about what the verification regime will look like."

Condi gestured to me that she would take it from there. She explained, very presciently (because the lack of an adequate verification regime ultimately was the issue that ended the process), that if we are unable to arrive at a satisfactory verification regime, we would obviously not continue. Cheney grunted and returned to his breakfast.

1960. The Hill family, aboard the SS *America* en route back to my dad's assignment in Yugoslavia. Traveling by ship for Foreign Service families soon became a relic of the past.

1975. Cameroon, Africa. As a Peace Corps volunteer visiting the credit union in a palm oil plantation.

3

July 1991. Tirana, Albania. With Mother Teresa and the pilot of a C-141 carrying aid supplies. Mother Teresa expressed concern that the aircraft was "too big to fly."

October 1991. U.S. Embassy Tirana, Albania. Raising the flag with Mrs. Agani. Her husband had worked for the U.S. Embassy in 1946 and was later shot by the communist authorities after U.S. diplomats departed.

August 1995. President Clinton conducting a meeting in the chapel at Fort Myers (Arlington, Virginia) immediately after a memorial service for Bob Frasure, Joe Kruzel, and Nelson Drew, our three colleagues killed on Mount Igman Road near Sarajevo. (*I am at left in front of the bookcase.*)

September 1995. With Ambassador Dick Holbrooke en route to the Balkans on the peace shuttle. A mentor and a tormentor.

November 12, 1995. Wright-Patterson Air Force Base, Ohio. Visiting with Slobodan Milosevic in his suite in the Visiting Officers Quarters.

November 20, 1995. Wright-Patterson Air Force Base, Ohio. Discussing the map of Bosnia. *From left*: myself, Dick Holbrooke, Secretary of State Warren Christopher, President Izetbegovic, and Slobodan Milosevic.

1997. Macedonia. Up along Macedonia's border with Serbia visiting U.S. troops who were patrolling under a UN command.

March 25, 1999. Skopje. Embassy Skopje attacked by thousands of demonstrators on the first day of the Kosovo War. They never got through the door despite using our flagpole as a battering ram.

11   April 1999. Skopje. With Deputy Secretary of State Strobe Talbott (*at right*) visiting President Gligorov (*shaking my hand*) and Macedonian defense minister Handziski (*in profile at rear of photo*). The smiles belied tough discussions about Macedonia's willingness to take in a quarter million Kosovo refugees.

12

May 1999. Skopje. First Lady Hillary Clinton conducting an NGO meeting in the residence living room. That day in the dining room she signaled to Christiane Amanpour that she was interested in running for the Senate. She later returned with her husband and announced more economic assistance for Macedonia.

June 1999. Skopje. Greeting refugees in Stenkovac camp two days after riots in the camp had almost caused the death of a Roma family.

June 1999. Skopje. At the airport with Secretary of State Madeleine Albright and British General Sir Michael Jackson (*back to camera, gesturing with his hand*).

June 1999. Skopje. Waiting with President Clinton while the First Lady talks to U.S. troops at the airport.

facing page: May 2001. Warsaw University library. President George W. Bush greeting attendees at his speech, in which he signals his support for continued enlargement of NATO.

August 2000. Warsaw, Poland. Presenting credentials to Polish President Aleksander Kwasniewski, who served as Poland's president from 1995 to 2005 and helped to achieve Poland's entry into NATO and the European Union.

17

18

May 2003. Taking a walk with Secretary of State Colin Powell at midnight in Krakow's central square.

19

August 2004. Seoul, South Korea. With Foreign Minister of South Korea Ban Ki-Moon. Ban would go on to become the Secretary General of the United Nations.

February 2007. Beijing, China. The U.S. negotiating team.

July 2007. Pyongyang, North Korea. The first of three trips to the heart of darkness.

July 2007. En route to Beijing from Seoul with South Korean counterpart Chun Yung-woo.

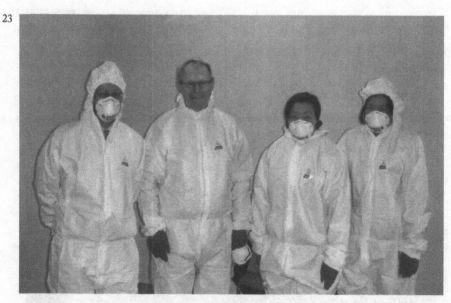

December 2007. Second trip to North Korea. This time a visit to the nuclear reactor now shut down per our negotiation. I'm flanked by Special Assistant Chris Klein and Yuri Kim and our South Korean interpreter on the end. No one was looking forward to the visit.

24

July 2008. Singapore. With Secretary of State Condoleezza Rice attending a meeting on North Korea on the fringes of the ASEAN Regional Forum.

October 2008. Third and last visit to North Korea. This time I walked across the Demilitarized Zone in the "Truce Village" of Panmunjom, leaving behind North Koreans and being welcomed by U.S. personnel and South Koreans.

25

26

January 2009. Washington. Vice President Joe Biden saw me at a State Department event and talked me into one more Foreign Service adventure. The next day I learned from Secretary of State Clinton that the adventure in mind was Iraq.

April 2009. Baghdad. Meeting President Talabani late on my first night in Iraq, having arrived that same evening at 7:00 P.M.

April 2009. Baghdad Airport. Greeting Secretary Clinton on my second day in Iraq. Chairman of the Joint Chiefs Admiral Mullen had been visiting and also came to the airport to greet her.

July 2009. Washington. The end of a meeting on Iraq in the White House Situation Room with General David Petraeus, General Ray Odierno, and President Obama.

August 2009. Erbil, Kurdistan. A formal meeting with Kurdish Regional Government President Massoud Barzani.

November 2009. Kurdistan. Taking a walk in the mountains of Kurdistan, well protected by Kurdish Peshmerga forces.

November 2009. Meeting with Ayad al-Samarrai, the Speaker of the Council of Representatives, to discuss the election law. Samarrai's calm manner helped in the law's final passage, thus clearing the way for March 2010 elections.

May 2010. Baghdad. With Ammar al-Hakim, leader of Islamic Supreme Council of Iraq (ISCI). Hakim would withhold support for Prime Minister Maliki for months, prompting many to believe he would instead support the Iraq National Party with its Sunni base. He eventually came around to Maliki.

19

"THAT'S VERIFIABLE"

As we looked ahead to what would transpire in the next few months, reaching agreement with the North Koreans on a verification protocol that would give us the necessary latitude to inspect and verify their declaration of nuclear programs was fast becoming the main issue. Those of us close to the process knew it could be the ultimate deal breaker.

By the fall of 2007, international inspectors were working in Yongbyon monitoring the closed nuclear plant. After a five-day meeting of the Six Parties that ended on October 3, we agreed on a Joint Statement that called on North Korea to provide a "complete and correct declaration of all its nuclear programs—including clarification regarding the uranium issue." Pyongyang also agreed to disable its facilities and, repeating a previous pledge, not to transfer nuclear material, technology, or know-how.

Experts worked through the October talks to agree on eleven steps that would disable the plant. Some of the measures were easier to reverse than others, but the totality of the disablement was aimed at taking Yongbyon off-line permanently, or at least ensuring that the repair bill would be exorbitant. These steps had never been accomplished in previous negotiations with the North Koreans. We worried about the unexplained indications of a uranium program, but the plutonium reactor was there for all concerned and the world to see, and had already produced enough for some six nuclear weapons.

In November, at a bilateral meeting in the North Korean embassy in Beijing, Kim Gye Gwan informed me that the specialized aluminum we believed had been purchased in connection with an enrichment program had actually been purchased for a shipboard gun system. I took that explanation back to our technical agencies in Washington, and the answer came back: "Highly doubtful." When I next met with Kim, I told him that we wanted to see the facility where these so-called rustproof guns were produced. He took the proposal back, and soon Sung Kim and NSC staff representative Paul Haenle, who had replaced Victor Cha on the team, were on their way to visit the factory where the weapons were allegedly being produced. I asked Sung to make sure he was able to bring back samples of the aluminum, and to our mutual surprise, he was allowed to carry out a couple of small pieces in his briefcase.

Sung turned over the aluminum to a specialized U.S. government agency, and to our astonishment, the results came back that the aluminum contained traces of highly enriched uranium. The tests were inconclusive, especially on the issue of how uranium could have been on the aluminum chunks, but its presence suggested that our insistence on clarification of the uranium issue was justified.

When the story was leaked to Glenn Kessler of the *Washington Post* in December 2007, it was fodder for those dedicated to the effort to scuttle the talks. Those talks, of course, in the first place, were what had gained us access to the aluminum, yet the article suggested that the discovery would "force" U.S. negotiators to demand a detailed explanation, as if we would have preferred to sweep the matter under the rug. After all, it came months after the news that North Korea was building a reactor in Syria, the smoking-gun piece of evidence that our proliferation concerns about the North Koreans were real. What the article did not touch on was the obvious fact of how we had made progress on uranium enrichment. The progress was due entirely to an overall negotiating process that gave us access to facilities that we otherwise would have only guessed about from satellites. The problem with the newspaper leak was that it could signal the North Koreans the extent of our technological capabilities and cause them to refuse to give us further such samples.

Secretary Rice took on the issue in a press conference in Canada. She explained that our goal had been and continued to be to receive a "complete and accurate" declaration from the North Koreans on their nuclear programs. This is what was called for in the October Six Party Talks. We knew that an incomplete and inaccurate declaration was not acceptable, but we did not believe that even a supposedly complete and correct declaration was acceptable. We needed the means to verify the declaration. At the same time, we were also intent on making progress on disabling the plutonium program in Yongbyon and did not want newspaper leaks to scuttle the effort to shut down the plutonium operation where the bomb material was actually coming from. For this reason, we continued to accept more vague formulations about uranium than about plutonium. Our intention was to buy more time while we installed teams of technicians in Yongbyon to disable and, we hoped, eventually dismantle the plutonium program.

Later in November 2007, I went back to Pyongyang and Yongbyon to view the now-shut-down reactor and meet with our technicians, who were living in a guesthouse next to Yongbyon. It took about two hours to make it out to the site in our convoy of vintage North Korean official Mercedes. After about an hour and a half, we turned off the main two-lane road onto a dirt track through a village that had four-story apartment buildings with plastic sheets in the window frames. It was classic communist architecture, with that "instant aging" feature I remembered so well from living and traveling in Eastern Europe in the 1980s.

After a mile or two more, the convoy halted. There were agitated voices on the two-way radio sets, followed by an equally agitated meeting of drivers and security agents shouting at each other. We made our way back through the village with the four-story apartment buildings and back onto the main road. Ten minutes later, we made the correct turnoff (in fairness to our handlers, there were no signs to guide us to the nuclear facility) and after another thirty-minute ride through similarly depressed-looking villages, we arrived.

We met some of the international inspectors and our own "disablers" in their guesthouse, where we had a spartan lunch of rice and something in an unidentifiable room-temperature sauce. On a piece of paper I took down the names of our people with a promise to try to call their families back home in the States. I so admired what these highly skilled technicians were doing for our country. I knew too that they would not have been there were it not for our negotiation efforts, an obvious point that completed eluded many of our hard-line critics in Washington.

We visited all the sites where our engineers were assisting the North Koreans to disable the facility. We donned white gowns and hoods as we got ready to enter the ramshackle reactor. Our North Korean unit chief Yuri Kim and the bureau's special assistant Chris Klein both looked at me as if for reassurance this was all going to be okay. I deadpanned, "Milosevic may have been a war criminal, but he never made us do something like this." The dark corridors, stairways, and work areas in the reactor had the look of an aged manufacturing facility. Nothing had been painted in years. We inspected the disabling measures now under way. Some were more dramatic than others—for example, sawing off ten-foot-long sections of twelve-inch-diameter pipes and leaving them to rust on the ground. None of these measures assured irreversible disablement, but as we looked around at the barren landscape and the humble 1960s-like construction, it was clear that reversing matters would not be easy. I saw that what our disablers had done in the interior structures of the large cooling tower had rendered it useless. What remained was a large cone-like structure made of ugly preformed cement, like what a nuclear plant looks like from a distance. I wondered what would be involved in just having the whole thing blown up to make the entire process far more understandable.

I had arrived in North Korea bearing a letter from President Bush to Kim Jong Il. It was essentially the same one he sent to all the members of the Six Party process, but in this instance I thought there might be an opportunity to deliver it directly.

In Pyongyang I told our handlers, "My instructions are to convey this letter from our president to your chairman, and if I am unable to do so, I am to bring the letter back with me." The latter part was not quite in my instructions, but I didn't believe there was any harm in trying. I was hoping that a letter from President Bush would be of interest. The North Koreans were unimpressed.

"Our leader is not in Pyongyang today."

"No problem. I will wait."

"He won't be in Pyongyang tomorrow, either."

"No problem, I will wait longer."

"He is visiting other places far away from Pyongyang."

"No problem. I can go to where he is."

I went nowhere, got nowhere, and with the hours of the visit dwindling, I huddled up with Paul and Sung and decided that we really had to deliver the mail. In an effort to save face, I informed our hosts that I had received "new instructions" and was permitted to deliver the letter to the foreign minister.

In the apparent absence of a working elevator, we were directed to trudge six floors up a narrow unheated stairway (indeed the entire building was unheated), until we arrived at the foreign minister's outer office. It was a lot warmer than the rest of the building, with space heaters doing their best to deal with the cold. The warmish office was some consolation for our vertical trip. I went into the foreign minister's modest office. I always enjoy having a quick look at the bric-a-brac. In this case it consisted of gifts from various human-rights-challenged dictatorships primarily from Africa. The foreign minister, clearly pleased with himself, took the envelope with both hands to indicate some respect for the sender, if not the deliverer.

Two hours later, as the wheels of our plane lifted off the runway, our entire six-person team broke into spontaneous applause at the thought of soon being in that flower garden of relative freedom—Beijing.

On March 13–14, 2008, my team and I met with Kim Gye Gwan and his team in Geneva for talks on the elusive North Korean declaration that had been due on December 31. I was intent that the leaked report of enriched uranium traces not scuttle the progress we made in shutting down the Yongbyon facility, but I did make use of the leak to remind Kim that the issue could not be ignored in any declaration.

We looked for ways to move forward on the declaration, while Kim only acknowledged our concerns on uranium enrichment, never admitting to an actual program. I was struck by how he never said he didn't know, simply that it had never existed and was a figment of our imaginations. "Is it possible," I asked, "that there was a program, but that it was discontinued?" I thought that might be the reason he had been categorical in denying its existence. He stuck with his story. In contrast, his deputy, Ri Gun, had remarked that the issue "is complicated." If it never existed, it could never be complicated. I had enough negotiating experience in the Balkans to know that sometimes people just flat out lie, and in this case I suspected that Kim, and perhaps not Ri, was doing just that. I had always remembered Milosevic telling me, in his singular English-language syntax, "I will never lie you." He just did it again, I thought at the time.

A month later we were in the U.S. Embassy in Singapore working with Kim Gye Gwan on a declaration that would be complete on plutonium and hold open the door to explore the enrichment riddle. While we would not sweep the uranium issue under the carpet, Condi, in Washington, was working to give us running room. I was trying to keep the process going until we could be assured that we knew all there was to know about the plutonium program. Some in the administration wanted all the negotiations shut down, as if to guarantee that there would never be another negotiating process. But even the detractors, several of whom had taken to expressing their views through like-minded columnists and editorial writers, had to acknowledge that we were getting an important look at North Korean programs.

As a result of the Singapore meeting, Sung Kim and Paul Haenle were given permission to return to North Korea and cart back through the demilitarized zone on the 38th parallel between North and South Korea some eighteen thousand pages of documents, consisting largely of logs dating back to 1986 on the operation of the facilities at Yongbyon.

When the specialized agencies were able to analyze the documents, they also analyzed what was on the actual paper—and as with the aluminum, traces of enriched uranium were discovered. Could there be a uranium enrichment facility in Yongbyon that we had not yet detected? The possibility was increasingly likely, but to get further we needed to make a tough decision.

It was, as too few people noted, a success at diplomacy. We had succeeded in gaining access to information that no one had obtained before. But the criticism against diplomacy ran far deeper than an analysis of its pros and cons. Negotiation threatened the theory that nothing could be achieved by talking with dictators. Any and all achievements, such as obtaining the operating records of the Yongbyon nuclear plant going back to 1986, not to mention the pixie dust of uranium that covered the reams of paper (and Sung Kim's Ferragamo loafers), were dismissed as unimportant.

For this degree of North Korean cooperation, we had to make concessions of our own. In addition to providing North Korea with our share of fifty thousand tons of heavy fuel oil, we had agreed at the Berlin meeting to remove the North Koreans from the Trading with the Enemy Act, as well as from the list of state sponsors of terrorism.

Technically, the removal from the list of state sponsors of terrorism was fairly straightforward. The purpose of the statute is to prevent an administration, any administration, from selling military equipment to a country on the list or supporting positive votes in international financial institutions to provide funds to any listed country. We were obviously not going to sell North Korea weapons, nor, since they are not members of the World Bank, could we support a positive vote even if we wanted to. An interagency team looked at the issue for the purpose of determining whether North Korea had engaged with terrorist groups in the "past six months." I spoke with Dell Daily, the state department's counterterrorism coordinator, to stress that any decision to remove North Korea from the list was ultimately President Bush's to make. We simply wanted to know whether from the point of view of the statute they could be removed. After several weeks, the committee returned a verdict that there was no evidence that North Korea had assisted any terrorist groups and thus, for the purposes of the statute, they were eligible to be removed.

It was not so simple. North Korea had participated in many terrorist acts over the decades, including the infamous bombing and murder of the twenty-one members of the South Korean cabinet accompanying President Chun Doo Hwan on a state visit to Burma in October 9, 1983. Chun, the target, had narrowly missed being killed when his car was delayed at the ceremony. Two of the bombers were captured, and one confessed to being a North Korean assassin.

But the issue that made our concession so difficult was the abduction and kidnapping program the North Koreans had engaged in during the late 1970s and early 1980s against Japanese nationals. The issue had flared up in 2002 when the North Koreans released several abductees, a stunning admission that did more to inflame public opinion than to calm it, especially as the North Koreans had backdated and in effect falsified death certificates of others who had not returned. Deputy Secretary Richard Armitage, who had numerous ties to Japan from his many years holding the East Asian account at the Pentagon and later as a business consultant, declared in a speech in Tokyo in April 2004 that the United States would include the abduction issue in the annual report on global terrorism. Within days, Armitage was accused of having promised that

North Korea would not be removed from the terrorism list unless the abduction issue was resolved. Whether that was a logical inference of his statement or not, the fact remained that he never said it. It would have been beyond his ability to make such a promise.

President Bush agonized over the issue for months. He understood the payoff in drilling deeper on North Korea's nuclear program and disabling the plutonium, but he also understood the Japanese issue. He once commented to Condi and me in the Oval Office that if there were a "bad guy list" (or more colorful words to that effect), it would make more sense for the North Koreans to be on that one.

On June 26, Pyongyang delivered its long-awaited nuclear declaration to the Chinese delegation of the Six Party Talks. It contained important elements, such as the precise amount of plutonium it had used in its nuclear tests. The president, to the enduring dismay of his vice president, who continued to try to run a separate foreign policy in channels both public and private, followed up with the announcement that in response to the declaration the United States would rescind the application of the Trading with the Enemy Act with respect to North Korea, and would provide forty-five days' notice of intention to remove North Korea from the list of state sponsors of terrorism. The declaration was incomplete and incorrect, but we were well on our way to what we considered the far more important phase, the verification protocol.

I asked Sung Kim to deliver a U.S.-drafted protocol that we intended to use as a guide for verifying their declaration of nuclear programs. The key element of our draft was to verify the nonexistence of their uranium program.

"How did it go?" I asked Sung, who had already commenced a rueful shaking of his head. "Never mind," I told him. "This will probably mean at some point one more trip back there."

On June 27, the day after the delivery of the nuclear declaration, North Korea fulfilled its part of this phase by blowing up the Yongbyon cooling tower. Television cameras from all over the world, including CNN, recorded the event. Sung Kim was there, as was Paul Haenle. President Bush watched it from the Oval Office and told aides gathered there, "Now that's verifiable." Sung, in a memorable quote (for which he has taken good-natured ribbing from his colleagues ever since) made to Christiane Amanpour on CNN, said, "As you can see, the tower is no longer."

I watched the collapse while in Kyoto, Japan, at a foreign ministers' meeting for the G-8 nations. I had hoped to go, but Condi, who was increasingly worried about the hard-right backlash against the Six Party Talks and against me personally, told me to stay behind with her in Kyoto. We watched the event on Japanese television.

I had first raised the idea of blowing up the tower with Kim Gye Gwan, pointing out that the event would be watched around the world and would help us overcome any doubts that our journey—at least on the plutonium production—was real. He was interested, but cautious. In Beijing I told Wu Dawei we needed a gesture that would give meaning to all the sawing of exhaust pipes and other disabling steps. As I spoke I was rolling my notes into the shape of a cylinder and stood them on end. When Wu asked what I had in mind I told him, "We should collapse the cooling tower like this," slamming the spindled notes with the palm of my hand. Eyeing my crushed notes on the table, he said, "We'll convince them."

The cooling tower collapse would prove to be the last accomplishment that year of the Six Party Talks. The entire core group of our team—Sung Kim, Paul Haenle, Yuri Kim, and Chris Klein— agreed that the real endgame was not the North Korean declaration, which we knew would be incomplete. The real issue, we all understood, was to have a workable verification protocol that would give us the needed freedom of movement to find what we already knew existed in some stage or another, namely a uranium enrichment program.

Having turned in an incomplete and inaccurate nuclear declaration, the North Koreans dug in their heels on any further moves, waiting to see if they would be removed from the terrorism list. As the forty-five-day clock ticked down on removal from the list, they did take some steps with the Japanese to agree on procedures for addressing the abduction issue, but nothing came of it. At the end of the forty-five days President Bush removed North Korea from the list of state sponsors of terrorism, a move that upset many Japanese as well as those who were using the abduction issue as a way to block any progress in the talks.

Sung and Paul worked hard to continue the negotiation on a verification protocol. One of the North Koreans, committed to the process, suggested we agree to something, and simply get people on the ground to start the process, expanding out from there. If we had been dealing with a country unlike North Korea, this might have been an acceptable way to start. But with North Korea it was not a proposal I could sell to anyone back in Washington and so I rejected it on the spot.

With time running down on the verification protocol, I made one more trip to Pyongyang in October 2008, accompanied by Sung, Paul, and Yuri. This time the North Koreans made a point that our delegation was not going to be treated to any special privileges. We were not permitted to bring a U.S. military plane, as we had done on the two previous trips, nor were we offered the presidential guesthouse. Instead the North Koreans made reservations for us at a Japanese-run commercial hotel (where, unlike anywhere else in North Korean, we had access to CNN). We had dinner with a very somber Kim Gye Gwan, and I could tell that North Korean interest in the give-and-take of negotiation was coming to an end.

Paul and Sung worked through the day with Ri Gun and his team, while Kim Gye Gwan and I stayed away from the actual negotiation, a practice we had employed in the past by which Kim and I would take up in the evening the issues unresolved from the day. This time, there were too many of those.

We returned from Pyongyang through the demilitarized zone, where, comically, there was a large group of Chinese tourists who asked us to pose for photos, our team having become quite the celebrities in China. We crossed the DMZ by foot, empty-handed, with little to show for our efforts. A few weeks later, in November, the Six Parties met once more, but it was over. The North Koreans were not serious about the verification protocol, and we could not go forward with what we had in hand from them, a verification protocol that only included the facilities that we were already completely familiar with in the first place. I called Secretary Rice, pulled her off her elliptical machine one last time, and told her we had to break it off. She understood. "Come home," she said. "That's a wise decision. You've done all you can do."

I had worked on the North Korean nuclear issue since February 2005, through almost four years and some forty trips to China, South Korea, and Japan. The U.S. reputation in Asia had been transformed due to our willingness to engage as a partner in a process, and the onus of blame was put where it belonged, with the North Koreans. It was step-by-step, "action for action," meaning that our concessions never got out ahead of what we gained and we never gave up something for nothing. We had also led that process, and in so doing had built on the relationship with China by working cooperatively on something that mattered to both of us. The gaps we had with the South Koreans that were threatening the quality of our alliance had been closed. Indeed, when the South Koreans held a presidential election in 2007, the U.S. relationship was not an issue and no candidate employed anti-Americanism.

President Barack Obama had been elected in the meantime, and his administration was expected to take up the negotiations quickly. But as the months and years rolled by without any resumption, it was clear to everyone that the North Koreans were at fault. Unlike in the past, nobody blamed the United States.

20

GLOBAL SERVICE

"The secretary wants to see you at five thirty," my assistant, Evelyn Polidoro, called into my office at 4 P.M. One of the many odd things about election transitions is the seamless way the career Foreign Service reacts to the fact that the title of "Secretary" after January 20 now refers to an entirely different person. Evelyn was referring to Secretary Hillary Clinton, who had begun her duties days before. I didn't think much of the request to see me, assuming as I did that Secretary Clinton wanted to talk with me yet again about North Korea and what it would take to get the denuclearization talks restarted.

Since camping out in a first-floor State Department office with her incoming staff in December, Secretary Clinton had been interested in my views about the talks and whether they could be restarted after collapsing in the fall of 2008 over the North Korean refusal to agree to an adequate verification regime. She was most interested in exploring the idea that the North Koreans had essentially broken off the talks in anticipation of working with a new administration in Washington, which, if true, suggested a willingness on their part to get them moving again without too much loss of time.

Theories abounded on this point, though I was of the view that the North Korean resistance to go further in the fall of 2008 had more to do with an internal decision that we could surmise had been complicated by Kim Jong Il's stroke and his incapacitation that summer. I couldn't rule out, however, that fresh faces in Washington could help the situation. Many North Korean watchers had viewed with dismay, during the 2001 presidential transition, incoming President Bush's unwillingness to pursue the Clinton administration's "Agreed Framework" in which the U.S. side held direct talks with the North Koreans on a set of agreements whose essence was to provide North Korea with two light water reactors in return for dismantling their existing nuclear program. The incoming Bush administration officials were especially concerned about mounting evidence that the North Koreans had continued to engage in clandestine purchases of equipment for a uranium program. The result was that the talks went into hiatus while the nuclear program accelerated.

This time, that danger still existed, but it was the North Koreans who had stopped the talks, not us. Moreover, it was not clear what we could do to continue them, since the issues had come down to the essential one of agreeing on a verification regime. Without an agreement on, for example, allowing inspectors the right to inspect a site previously not on the declaration, we could not begin to verify the North Korean nuclear declaration, a document we already knew to be incomplete in its absence of any references to a uranium enrichment program, past or present. The disagreement was a serious one: we were not prepared to accept a verification regime limited to known plutonium sites, and insisted on the right to inspect undeclared sites, especially ones that we might in the future develop information about. The North Koreans had dug in their heels in a way that even for them was unusually stubborn. It invited different theories within the analytical community as to whether they were waiting for a new administration or for Kim Jong Il's health status to be clarified.

The nuclear talks had consumed me as nothing I had ever been involved with, but with the North Korean nuclear reactor shut down and no longer producing the spent fuel rods for plutonium, and with the U.S.–South Korean relationship now in good shape, unlike before the Six Party Talks, when many South Koreans believed the impediment to progress was the bellicose United States rather than the truculent North Koreans, I felt the negotiations were at a good moment to pause; it was a propitious time to pass it on to a new administration that had shown a strong interest in continuing them and avoiding the kinds of problems with the South Koreans that had occurred in the first term of the Bush administration when it hit the pause button. So much of what one does in government is to pass on problems to the next generation with the understanding that they should be passed on in better shape than when one found them. I felt we had come to such a moment with North Korea.

I was also, after some thirty-two years, ready to move on from the Foreign Service to take a lecturing and writing position at Yale University. I had had three ambassadorships, in Macedonia, Poland, and South Korea, had been special envoy to Kosovo, a member of Ambassador Holbrooke's team in ending the Bosnian War, and was finishing up as assistant secretary of state for East Asia, which had come with another hat as chief of the North Korean negotiations.

My involvement in the North Korean negotiations had the life cycle of a typical Washington story. The press, looking for signs of a new approach to diplomacy at the start of the second Bush term, settled on the talks as the poster child. At first, I was heralded in press profiles, and in one *New York Times* editorial had received the death sentence when it suggested to Secretary Rice that in dealing with Iran she should ask: "What would Chris Hill have done?" (I skipped the senior staff meeting that day.) Later, as talks stalled, they became known as "failed talks."

At about 5 P.M., I reviewed the latest information about the Six Party Talks, checking to see if there was anything new in the intelligence that day that would have prompted the secretary to call for me. At 5:25 P.M. I went up to her office suite and was waved in by her assistant Claire. Clinton met me at the door of her outer office and motioned me to one of the two wing chairs that sat on either side of the large fireplace. I noticed that some furniture rearranging had taken place in the past couple of days.

But before I could think about whether it was good feng shui for the room or not, I was a little startled to see that in three hard-backed chairs sat incoming Deputy Secretary Jim Steinberg, Chief of Staff Cheryl Mills, and a worried-looking undersecretary for political affairs and the most senior career Foreign Service officer, Bill Burns. I thought: North Korea policy is getting upgraded.

Secretary Clinton opened the discussion by saying some very nice things about my service, especially my handling of the North Korean negotiations. I sat back in my wing chair thinking how pleasant can this be, a last scene in a feel-good movie, as if I were a sort of Foreign Service Bilbo Baggins at the conclusion of my adventures. I glanced over at Bill Burns, who continued to have a troubled look on his face. I thought perhaps he had eaten one of the specials in the State Department cafeteria that day.

And then the secretary said, "And, so I would like to ask just one more thing of you."

(Oh dear, I thought, another memo on our next steps with the "Norks"—I was on a *Lord of the Rings* riff in my head, rhyming the acronym for the North Koreans with Tolkien's "Orcs.")

"... I would like to ask you to replace Ryan Crocker in Baghdad."

My mind raced forward. Oh my God, Iraq, the real fire of Mordor, wait! I thought dealing with North Korea was the fire of Mordor!?

I snapped out of it and said, "I'm very honored you would ask. I know the importance of this, but I am going to have to think about it."

"Of course, of course," she replied with a graciousness that was a pleasure to hear. She explained that she would back me up, including through the Senate confirmation process, which was increasingly looking more like a gauntlet than a process. I knew, and she knew as well, that there were several senators who did not support the negotiations with the North Koreans and held me personally responsible, as if I were merrily conducting my own foreign policy without any instructions from above.

Secretary Clinton knew (and I knew as well) that the negotiating process with the North Koreans had become an emotion-laden exercise, with the opponents regarding it as a dangerous violation of the theory of the case that "bad guys" (and who on earth fits the description better than the North Koreans?) are people one should never talk to. My instructions for my Six Party negotiating sessions in Beijing forbidding me to join in any toasts in the presence of the North Koreans had become a source of amusement around the department.

Clinton went on to explain that this would be a critical year for the United States in Iraq. It would represent a moment when the United States would be "civilianizing" its mission. She said the situation required a strong presence, someone who could in effect wrest control from the military and explain to the media and the public what we were doing. She noted that Ryan Crocker would be leaving in a matter of days and that I would have to be prepared to move quickly. I told her I understood but nonetheless would need to sleep on it.

I staggered back to my office, and Evelyn, joined by the bureau's special assistant, Yuri Kim, asked me what it had been about. Evelyn had never believed it was about North Korea.

"If you go, I'll go," Evelyn said.

"Hey, me too," Yuri chimed in. Actually, Yuri was already set to go out to a Provincial Reconstruction Team in Anbar Province in western Iraq, but I knew that if I went to Baghdad she was going to work there in a senior position in the political section. I told them I really needed to think about all this. I had never thought about going to Iraq, but I knew that tonight I would be doing just that.

That night, I thought long and hard. Service in Iraq was not popular in the State Department. The war had started on a very wrong note, with the sidelining of the State Department's role in favor of a civilian mission that was inspired and directed by the Pentagon. The Foreign Service was vilified for not "stepping up," even though the role it was asked to play was a very subservient one, that of civilian avatars for the military. The embassy I knew was the largest in the world, but it had a reputation for being supersized out of a misplaced need to keep pace with the military personnel system whose appetite for sending more people seemed endless. Story after story came back from Iraq of people having little to do, of sitting around in endless meetings and writing telegrams that no one wanted to read. Most of the Near Eastern Bureau's Arabists had gone for their service there, come back having checked the box, and vowed not to go again.

The people who served repeated tours in Iraq, as opposed to those who simply wanted to check that box, were often seen as those who could not get jobs elsewhere, or who viewed Iraq as a place to go to line up a next assignment to a cozy job in Europe. The State Department's personnel system had been skewed as a result of Iraq, with those who had returned being offered jobs ahead of everyone else. I had dealt with some of the distortions in our own personnel exercises in the East Asian Bureau when we were told that we had to accept a person for a position in Bangkok solely for the reason that he or she had served in Iraq. Iraq, it was said, had also become a kind of French Foreign Legion, where after a particularly unsuccessful assignment somewhere, a person could wipe the slate clean and start afresh.

I later learned how complex the picture was. Some of the criticism was well deserved, but much was not. No doubt a very few of those assigned to Iraq and especially to some of its Provincial Reconstruction Teams—our presence in the provinces, sort of proto-consulates—were unfit for other assignments, but others were doing their best in the worst of circumstances, where venturing outside the barbed wire was a difficult and courageous effort.

The nadir of this dismal dynamic had come earlier in 2008 when the Foreign Service's director general, the person responsible for assignments, had hosted a "town hall" meeting in the State Department at noontime to discuss assignments in Iraq (and Afghanistan) and why all Foreign Service officers should expect to serve a tour there. The meeting was, for reasons no one can now recall or understand, caught on video by CNN as employee after employee posed hostile and provocative questions to the embattled director general. A Foreign Service officer who gave the appearance of never having served east of the Rhine River posed the one melodramatic question that was played over and over again on CNN. "If we must go, who will take care of our children?"

At precisely the time the director general was answering those questions, eight floors above, Secretary of State Rice was bidding farewell to her undersecretary for public affairs, Karen Hughes, who was returning to Texas. The highlight of that gentle affair was the secretary telling the polite audience that Karen made a great sacrifice in coming to Washington all the way from Texas and disrupting her children's lives. It was a kind of upstairs, downstairs story.

I shuddered as I remembered those meetings, and how the press covered the downstairs meeting as a sample of the Foreign Service's lack of dedication, while on the eighth floor the self-congratulatory talk of sacrifice and service in Washington was celebrated. Global service was something every Foreign Service officer agreed to on entering the service, and essentially, I was now being asked to fulfill that obligation.

21

TAKING THE FIFTH

When I woke up, early, I had decided I was going to Iraq. I arrived early at the office and found that my executive assistant, Evelyn Polidoro, had talked to her husband and was prepared to go. Yuri Kim, the bureau's special assistant, was also ready, as was Deputy Assistant Secretary Patricia Haslach. Chris Klein, our bureau chief of staff and member of the North Korean team the previous summer, called from his new post at the Paris embassy to say he had heard I had been offered the job and that he wanted to join the team as well. Cameron Munter, who had served as the deputy chief of mission in Warsaw with me seven years before, called in from Belgrade, where he was ambassador, to ask if what he had heard was true, because he was ready to come, too. Glyn Davies, the bureau's principal deputy assistant secretary and one of the best FSOs I ever worked with, told me, "You gotta do this. I wish I could join you."

My office was filling up with people at that point as front office personnel came in for our "morning huddle" staff meeting, to review events that day and anything overnight from the region. From the morning huddle I would go straight to the secretary's large staff meeting, attended by my counterparts from other functional and geographic bureaus. My morning huddle was important because I did not want to have someone in the secretary's meeting raise an issue related to East Asia that I was not aware of. If there was a big story in the U.S. morning papers about, say, a new trade problem with Japan, I wanted to make sure I was familiar with the latest developments on the issue and, more important, what we were doing to address it.

Early in the morning my own office looks like a train station at rush hour. Desk officers try to catch their front-office bosses to clear press guidance that they anticipate will be requested by the press office. Every morning the press office prepares the spokesperson to brief on the State Department's reaction to events overnight. The spokesperson gives the briefing based on guidance received from the bureaus, usually written early in the morning by the desk officers who know their areas best and can anticipate what the spokesperson might be asked. More often than not there are far more pieces of guidance than are used (no matter what happened in Papua New Guinea overnight, the spokesperson is not going to get a question about a Pacific Island state), but an overprepared spokesperson is better than the alternative, and part of our mission was to make sure the spokesperson had the answers and didn't have to promise to get back to the reporter later, or worse yet, have to wing it.

Even though people had different pieces of paper in their hands, they had all figured out what was going on with me. Okay, I thought, I'd better tell the secretary that I am going before one of these guys does.

I had a few minutes to detour to Dick Holbrooke's office to track him down and tell him of my decision to go. Back in government with the return of the Democrats, Dick was on his way to another meeting (catching Holbrooke in a sitting position was pretty much impossible), but we talked in the corridor outside his office for a few minutes as streams of State Department employees walked past us with early morning coffee.

Dick had not tried to encourage or discourage me, but emphasized that the secretary really needed to know that it was a top priority to fill the position and to begin a transition from the military to a civilian lead. He had expressed on many occasions his concern about a "militarized" foreign policy and said putting it back in the hands of the State Department would not be easy. "But that is what she wants you to do." He hesitated, and added, "Chris, you understand how ugly the issue of Iraq is in our country. For some people, nothing this administration will do in Iraq will ever receive credit. Anything good that happens will be credited to your predecessors, and anything bad to you."

"Dick, it's not that stark."

"You're right," he responded, in what seemed like more of an effort to convince himself than me.

In late morning Bill Burns called to apologize for not having warned me about the agenda of the secretary's meeting. I told him not to worry, that I could see from the look on his face that he was as surprised as I was. He then mentioned a new development. Clinton had asked him whether he thought I would take the job and whether a call from the president would help me decide affirmatively. He said he tried to discourage it, and I assured him that such a call was not going to be necessary. Being asked by the secretary of state was enough for me. I told him about the recruitments going on in my office that morning. Bill, a career FSO, was pleased to hear it.

I wasn't able to get an appointment with Secretary Clinton until 4:30 P.M. I told her my decision, but also made clear (as I had done with all the day's volunteers for Iraq) that I could commit for only a year. I had accepted an academic position and could put that off for a year, but I did not want to do so for any longer. She said that was fair and repeated her promise to be personally supportive through the Senate confirmation process. I had gone through Senate confirmations four times (three ambassadorships and one assistant secretary position), but in the current state of political acrimony I knew that an easy confirmation even for a career FSO could not be taken for granted. "This is the fifth time," I told her. "Don't worry," she repeated. "We will back you."

The meeting with the secretary was brief, but for me, poignant. Just a few days on the job, Secretary Clinton was booked with back-to-back meetings, so I took just a few minutes of her valuable time to talk to her in a less used corner of her outer office. I sat perched on a chair near the window on the other side of the room from the fireplace and wing chairs where we had been the day before, while she sat on the end of a couch under the window. Over her right shoulder I could see Arlington National Cemetery in the twilight and I could not help but reflect on the Iraq War as we spoke about its legacy for our generation. Emotional moments like that are rare in the pace of the State Department. Four thirty in the afternoon is almost midday given how the building grinds on until late in the evening. Often one has to be home in bed before even realizing the importance of a conversation conducted during the hustle of the day. She seemed relieved I had taken the job. I could almost see her mentally crossing off the item from her to-do list. ("Find someone to replace Crocker. Done.")

As I walked out of her office, I ran into Holbrooke. He was heading to the secretary's office for her next set of meetings on his portfolio of Afghanistan and Pakistan. He asked if I had told her I was going to take the job and I told him yes. He put his hand gently on my shoulder and said we would talk later. My eyes watered a bit, a combination of a delayed reaction to the sight of Arlington out the secretary's window, but also to my legacy with Dick. We had worked together in the 1990s, had been friends since, and now, even though he was not dealing directly with Iraq, we would be working together again. I felt a deep sense of satisfaction at that thought as he rushed to her office and I headed downstairs.

I exited onto the sixth floor and turned in the opposite direction from my office along the long corridor that parallels C Street below. The State Department building plan consists of even- and odd-numbered corridors that form a grid. The "first corridor" on the sixth floor stretches from the

EAP front office at one end with its view of C and Twenty-Third Streets, down past the front office of the Africa Bureau, on to the Near East Bureau (NEA), located much closer to C and Twenty-First Streets. For the first time that I could ever recall I walked into the NEA front office. I thought momentarily of the fact that I had never even had an assignment in NEA, but was immediately seized by the usual FSO competitiveness as I checked out the furnishings to make sure they had nothing on us in EAP. The office was adorned with numerous photos of the Middle East peace process. Pictures of various NEA officials and ambassadors shaking hands with robed Persian Gulf sheiks were a reminder that NEA was more than just about the Israeli-Palestinian issues. I did not immediately see anything from Iraq. I began to reflect on the criticism of NEA that it was inadequately seized with the problem of Iraq, that NEA somehow had collectively determined that Iraq was the military's problem. But just as I spotted some photos of Iraq, Deputy Assistant Secretary Rick Schmierer came out of his small office.

I had never met Rick. I told him I was looking for reading material to get myself going on the assignment. He hadn't heard I was going to be the nominee, but he didn't miss a beat in welcoming me to the club. Foreign Service officers specializing in different parts of the world often have a reputation for being very clubby and dismissive of anyone not from that club, and NEA, due in part from the need to spend years studying Arabic, had that reputation. Arabists were often accused in the popular media of not being sufficiently seized with Israel's plight, and for being excessively solicitous of the Sunni Arab perspective throughout a region that others had exploited for their natural resources. But typical of such stereotypes, it did not hold up at the first person I met. I explained to Rick that I had read all the recent books on the war, including two excellent books by Tom Ricks: *Fiasco,* in which the military could do nothing right, and *The Gamble,* where some of the same generals could do nothing wrong. There were also an extraordinary four books by Bob Woodward; George Packer's brilliant *Assassin's Gate,* which weaves the two realities of Washington and

Baghdad; Rajiv Chandrasekaran's horrific *Imperial Life in the Emerald City;* and others that were more from a Washington perspective. I asked Rick for suggestions that could help me with the history. I deadpanned that I needed something on the six thousand years that preceded the 2003 invasion. Rick laughed. "I can help you with that too," as he went to his bookshelves for more.

As we talked I realized that without any prompting from anyone I was doing exactly what every other FSO does on receiving an assignment: head to the library and start reading until your eyes fall out. Rick immediately did what every self-respecting FSO who has written a book does first: he handed me a brand-new copy of it. Then he turned to a truly impressive collection of Iraq books on the shelf beyond his desk and for each gave a review worthy of the *New York Review of Books*. It was clear he had read them all.

It was a day when I was so proud to be an FSO. First, I did the right thing. Then my colleagues did the right thing. And finally, I had just met someone on the other end of the sixth floor whom I had never laid eyes on before, but who opened up his heart and his bookshelf to make sure I was going to get off to a good start.

I had read a great deal of Balkan history, but to learn about the other end of the Ottoman Empire was instructive as I found familiar patterns. I was particularly struck by the sectarian divide in Iraq, and by the short shrift that it received in the U.S. media. The Kurdish question was well understood in the United States, mainly because it offered the promise of the creation of a new state. But the Shia-Sunni divide was now exacerbated by the U.S. invasion, which had taken a Sunni-run Arab-majority state and turned it into the first Shia-led state in the Middle East, with the farcical notion that a divide which spanned centuries could be repaired in a matter of months. "Ancient hatreds" had been overblown in the Balkans, an intellectual shortcut to understanding ethnic enmity there. I was certainly prepared to believe that sectarianism in Iraq was also exaggerated.

In the Balkans the tasks of conciliation fell to the participants. Iraq was an example of the "Pottery Barn rule," famously attributed to Colin Powell. *If you break it, you own it*. I watched a clip of General Petraeus's and Ambassador Crocker's testimony to Congress, a tour de force in handling a skeptical Congress by providing a plethora of facts and figures, and ground truth, the totality of which suggested to the audience that we were on top of everything in every village. It was clear from the testimony that nothing happened there without our guiding hand, and that achieving our goals of democratizing this most undemocratic of states was very possible as long as we stayed the course, and, of course, believed in the secret sauce of counterinsurgency, the surge. I thought momentarily about Holbrooke's comment that all the credit for Iraq has already been handed out, and that the successors would have a difficult time.

On Monday I started filling out forms for the Senate confirmation process—my fifth. The paperwork is a little like trying to get admitted to a hospital. Many of the questions are posed over and over again in different formats. Could the State Department after thirty-one years really not know my Social Security number or my date of birth? There is also a background report that needs to be submitted by the State Department's Diplomatic Security (DS) Bureau, the gist of which is filled in by a DS agent, who among other duties visits one's neighborhood and asks neighbors whether the person "who is being considered for a senior-level post in the U.S. government" has shown any signs of unexplained wealth or has behaved oddly in any way, and could be recommended for a "position of trust" in the government.

Contrary to an undeserved reputation, the State Department takes security very seriously. Security officers in the department and U.S. marine guards at overseas embassies rummage through offices at night looking for unlocked safes, or for classified papers that might have been left out on the desk, or inadvertently thrown in a trash can along with a potato chip wrapper or a soda can. Computer-based records ensure that "security violations" or their less serious cousins, "security incidents," stick to one's file like flypaper for years. Three violations and one can expect to be suspended without pay for a few days. I was proud not to have had a security violation in decades. How did you manage that? a junior officer once asked me, upset over a violation in the form of a pink slip left on his desk by the marine security guard overnight. I told him, "If you were on my desk at the end of the day, I would have locked you in the safe as well."

After the FBI and IRS reports are in, after the nominee has returned all the forms to the presidential appointments office, and after the DS security background check has been completed, the nominee is invited for an interview with a paralegal in the presidential appointments office, the purpose of which is to find out whether there are any other issues. These may be ones the nominee has honestly forgotten, or is simply too embarrassed to want to tell anyone about. The purpose of this interview is to protect the nominee and the president's staff from being blindsided during the Senate hearing. If known ahead of time, the issue can be managed with Senate staff. If not, last-minute problems can be fatal.

I sat down with a young woman who had gone to Wellesley College at about the same time as my daughter Amelia. The opening went something like this:

"Ambassador Hill, it is such a pleasure to meet you. I have completely reviewed your file and I am so impressed by all the things you have done for our country. You have served in so many difficult places and have been a three-time ambassador. It is such an honor for me to meet someone like you.

"So if you don't mind I just have a few questions on this questionnaire that we ask all our prospective appointees. The first is: Have you ever been arrested for public drunkenness?"

By February the nomination was ready to go to the Senate for confirmation, and the president was ready to announce it in the course of a speech about Iraq policy. The problem was that a key step had not yet been taken: *agrément*.

Agrément, French for "agreement," refers to the process by which the government to which the ambassador is to be accredited has the opportunity to search its own police files and make sure that the nominee has not broken any of its laws. Agrément is very rarely withheld, and when it is refused the reason is often political factors (for example, a nominee, perhaps an academic, has a written record of criticism toward the receiving country, or perhaps insulted the king of the accrediting state), something that normally would have come out at some earlier point in the course of the vetting process. Therefore, with no expectation of any problems, and with a speech to be given in Camp Lejeune only hours away, President Obama telephoned Prime Minister Nouri al-Maliki and received the Iraqi government's agrément for my appointment.

With my nomination now in the public domain, the pace of preparations accelerated. I met with General Petraeus, then the new head of U.S. Central Command, who told me about the enormous strides Iraq had made, more optimistic in his tone than in the recent hearings. Totally engaging and thoroughly likable despite the excessive use of the vertical pronoun "I" to describe his role in all the good things going on in Iraq, he told me about efforts to beautify the road in from the airport and how nice it looked these days with flowers compared to before. A few days later General Ray Odierno, who had replaced Petraeus in Iraq and was in Washington for a few meetings, stopped by to tell me about his concerns about the difficulties ahead.

Ray, a giant of a man with a shaven head, who looked every bit like the football lineman he once was, didn't much care whether or not any flowers had been planted on the airport road. He was more concerned about the political calendar that needed to unfold in order to keep the U.S. troop withdrawals on schedule. Ray listed the issues ruefully, starting with an election law that would need to be passed by the summer if the Iraqis were to hold parliamentary elections by the end of the year or the start of 2010. And he confirmed what Colin Powell had pointed out to me four years before, that the airport road, flowers or no, was still unsafe.

I had known Ray from the time he was Secretary Rice's military liaison. He is a man whose passion for achieving success in Iraq was even more imposing than his size. I also met with Ryan Crocker, who had just left Iraq. Unlike Petraeus, Crocker painted a grim view of the situation on the ground ("we've been very lucky") and was not optimistic about the future or about the embassy's capacity to deal with it. Given the annual turnover at the embassy, he expressed concern about whether there was anyone left who had useful contacts with the Iraqis (in other words, you're not very lucky). His body language seemed that of a severe critic of the war, in contrast to public statements in which he called for more investment of resources. I asked how much he had engaged in Iraq's internal politics and he surprised me by saying that he stayed away from it except on the candidacy of the justice minister, who he felt would be inclined to open up the detention centers.

Crocker left no opportunity for personal banter and never smiled. He deflected questions about the new embassy, explaining that he had hardly been there, since it had just opened weeks before. I asked whether he thought we had ever met before. He said only if I had been stationed in the Middle East. After about ten minutes, he said, "Okay?" suggesting that he was ready to leave. I thanked him for his time and never saw him again.

I moved a small box of personal things from my sixth-floor office in EAP, which would remain empty until the new assistant secretary would arrive some six months later, down to the Iraq section of NEA. Unlike my EAP office with its view of the Potomac River, the Iraq desk was located in a windowless office suite on the second floor of the State Department. It was grim surroundings, but I was struck by how dedicated the desk officers were.

In the State Department, every country, large or small, has a desk. Some desks have two officers, some even more. The Korea and China offices in the EAP Bureau had some twenty-five officers and staff. The Iraq desk sprawled out through the northwest end of the second floor in hastily designed office space. Everyone was packed into tiny cubicles, working ten-to-twelve-hour days. Most were Foreign Service officers, some were regular civil service employees, but others were one-year contract employees brought in to handle the surge of work.

I also started to get acquainted with NSC staff engaged with Iraq. National Security Council staffs serve the president and are relatively small, especially at the start of an administration, when the president has made a pledge (which will soon be broken) to keep the NSC staff to bare bones and rely instead on the State Department and other national security departments.

Whereas the State Department might have twenty persons working on a given geographical or function issue, the NSC staff would have only a handful and therefore have to outsource memos to the State Department. When the president is meeting a foreign leader, the NSC directorate will ask the State Department for a memo, which becomes grist for an NSC paper.

NSC staff have a well-deserved reputation for being bright, in many cases the best and the brightest. Many come from other USG agencies and do not have political profiles. But they also have a reputation for being quick and instinctive about where power resides. These traits are especially on display in the hand-off from one administration to the next, when a staff person for the previous administration hoping to stay on will want to demonstrate competence and a capacity to transfer loyalty. Ideally, the NSC staff works well with the State Department's bureaucracy, especially the geographic bureau, but this is not always the case. The State Department's layered look involves numerous clearances that frequently slow down a decision.

In a highly charged place on an issue like Iraq, the pace is relentless, nerves are frayed, and bad-mouthing of other agencies abounds. The State Department comes in for more than its share of this because of the lingering sense that it is an elite organization whose officers often seem more interested in admiring problems than in solving them.

But often the State Department doesn't deserve the skepticism. One fairly junior-level NSC director, originally from the CIA, when briefing me on the situation in Iraq kept referring to so-and-so as a "typical Foreign Service officer." The third time I stopped her and asked how long she had been in the government. When she said six years I said that I was not sure she had earned the right to criticize people on that basis, that she was free to criticize individuals, but that I too was an FSO and I didn't appreciate it. I am sure that from that day I got added to the ranks of "typical FSO."

In February 2009 I was returning from a quick overnight trip to Jacksonville, Florida, where I had addressed the World Affairs Council. (The subject was North Korea, not Iraq, since nominees must be very careful to hold their comments until after confirmation by the Senate. Nominees are strongly advised to say nothing about their future assignment until they have testified to the relevant Senate committee, which in the case of ambassadors is the Senate Foreign Relations Committee.) I found on my BlackBerry that there was a story in various news outlets that morning to the effect that the administration had offered the Iraq ambassadorship to a former CENTCOM commander, retired four-star general Anthony Zinni, but had pulled back and given it to me instead. Worse yet, the on-the-record source of the stories was a very upset General Zinni, who explained that he had been promised the job and had started the process of divesting himself of any activities that could have been interpreted as a conflict of interest, only to be told he wasn't getting it. Zinni made no secret of the fact that he was hopping mad and provided details of the alleged failure of senior officials, including his soon-to-be best ex-friend of thirty years, National Security Advisor Jim Jones, explaining that the administration had decided to go with a career Foreign Service officer. According to Zinni, Jones went on to offer Zinni something else, possibly the ambassadorship to Saudi Arabia, which Zinni promptly dismissed.

An ambassadorial nominee can find bad news in a winning lottery ticket, so I started enumerating what could go wrong and braced myself for the nomination headaches that were sure to come. The first problem was the mere existence of a "controversy" even though it had nothing to do with me. I talked to Bill Burns, who had figured in Zinni's account as one of the officials who had failed to call him back. Bill has the world's most impeccable phone manners (we used to joke he would return the call of a telemarketer). He expressed skepticism that Zinni had been offered the position, but I could sense there was probably more to the story than just a preliminary sounding out of interest.

I didn't want to appear too interested, but I checked with a few friends at the Pentagon and the NSC staff and, sure enough, the version of events was pretty much as Zinni had described them, but with a definite twist: this was not a military versus FSO issue. Rather, when some senior army generals heard that a retired CENTCOM commander—a marine, no less—was slated to be the ambassador to Iraq, they quickly went into action to protect their own four-star on the scene, General Ray Odierno.

Secretary of Defense Bob Gates shared the concern that eight stars in Bagdad might be excessive, and made the case with Clinton that at a time when the United States was seeking to civilianize the Iraq mission, we should not send a former senior military officer there as ambassador. She had supported her old friend Zinni, one of many military leaders she had cultivated during her time as a member of the Senate Armed Services Committee, but quickly understood Gates's message and went to work to find a Foreign Service officer. The search hadn't gone well. Former European assistant secretary Beth Jones, an officer with considerable Middle East and South Asian experience, including as a deputy assistant secretary for NEA, was willing and highly regarded, but she ran into vetting problems due to her work with a consulting firm.

From my point of view, however, the damage was done. Dick Holbrooke's name got dragged in as someone who was trying to install one of his protégés and therefore extend his own empire of activities in Afghanistan and Pakistan. Meanwhile, some of Zinni's friends rallied to his cause saying that he was a victim of the Foreign Service. Blogs sympathetic to him and suspicious of the new administration's commitment to the Iraq mission and to me, given my North Korea experience, implied that I had schemed my way into this "plum" assignment.

Two days later, Senator John McCain (R-AZ), a close friend of

Zinni, and Senator Lindsey Graham (R-SC) issued a news release questioning my qualifications for the post. McCain would later say to the full Senate that "we have a choice here, between Hill and Zinni," as if it were to be a run-off competition. The McCain-Graham press release referred to my "controversial" role in the North Korean negotiations. Suddenly my nomination, according to an Associated Press story, was in doubt and "embattled."

Not to be outdone, Senator Sam Brownback (R-KS) issued a statement announcing that I had "lied to the Senate" in my North Korean negotiations and that he would have no choice but to place a hold on the nomination.

My "lie" was the following: Senator Brownback strongly opposed the Six Party nuclear negotiations with North Korea, and in the summer of 2008 had held the ambassadorial nominee to the Republic of Korea, Kathleen Stephens, for four months while he figured out what he wanted in return. With the intervention of Senator John Warner (R-VA), who fully understood the madness of not sending an ambassador to one of our most important partners in the world, Brownback agreed to lift his hold, provided I would say in testimony that if we got to the stage with the North Koreans of negotiating normalization of relations with them, I would agree to open a separate track to discuss North Korea's abysmal human rights record. I told Senator Brownback in testimony that I would invite our North Korean human rights envoy, Jay Lefkowitz, to any and all Six Party meetings, which I did though he never had the time to make it out to Beijing.

The sad truth was that nobody in the Six Party Talks had the slightest interest in inviting the U.S. North Korean human rights envoy to the meetings. As my Russian colleague asked, "What is problem? You don't think getting DPRK [North Korea] to give up nuclear weapons is hard enough?!" In fact, were we to get to normalization talks it would have been entirely appropriate and essential to include human rights in the negotiations, just as we have done in many other such talks with in-from-the-cold dictatorships. Of course, we never got to the stage with North Korea that we would normalize, nor, frankly, did I think we ever would. But the request to raise human rights in that context was entirely reasonable, and in any event I was committed to making it a separate track if the normalization talks had ever proceeded.

There was another issue. Congress had worked hard to get the Bush administration to name a human rights envoy. The decision to name Lefkowitz, a close confidant of Brownback with an impressive background in forging the Bush administration's position on the stem cell issue, was controversial because he had a full-time job in New York as a litigator. It was not clear to many of his critics that he would have the time to devote to unpaid chores as a human rights envoy for North Korea, a subject with which he had zero familiarity. Some congressmen and senators, concerned about whether the envoy would have enough time to devote to the duties, wrote into the legislation that the person must not be "double hatted," that is, cannot also hold another job in the State Department, but should be paid and considered a full-time Department of State employee.

Since he was sometimes reported to be critical of the bureaucracy for not implementing his approach to North Korea, I made sure that my entire North Korea team understood that they were to support him and never try to edit his op-eds. In the interagency meetings I went out of my way to support him on ideas that had come to him from various Korean groups in the United States to beam propaganda to North Korea via radio or, my favorite, leaflets carried inside giant helium-filled balloons that had the shape of huge condoms.

In mid-February I went up to my family's farmhouse in Rhode Island for a weekend alone. After picking up the newspapers on Sunday morning in the general store I went home to sit down with coffee in my favorite mug and watch CNN's *Late Edition*. Dick Cheney was John King's guest. I watched with growing surprise at the degree to which the former vice president, only weeks out of office, was willing to take direct swipes at the new president. Cheney's approach to the new administration was in stark contrast to the gracious way President Bush had conducted himself in departing office. As I studied the *Boston Globe* sports section to see how some of the Red Sox pitching prospects looked on the eve of the first spring training games, King asked the former veep: So what do you think of the president's choice of Chris Hill to be ambassador to Iraq? I looked up to see the former vice president respond, "There are a lot of better candidates than that."

I sat in my late mother's recliner, motionless, one hand clasped around my Joshua L. Chamberlain Museum coffee cup, the other keeping my jaw from dropping to the floor. I shook my head slowly and asked no one in particular what it takes for a former vice president, who for a period of eight (very) long years was only a heartbeat away from the most powerful position in the universe, to stoop to a cheap shot like that on national television against a nominee for service in Iraq.

As I was preparing for my confirmation, the *New York Times* ran a front-page story about a new insurgency tactic. The insurgents were making handkerchief-sized parachutes so that the explosive device, upon being hurled in the air, would come down slowly on the less protected roofs of U.S. vehicles. I read that story and thought, maybe Brownback likes me after all.

The nomination process is never quite as bad as it seems at the time, and indeed many senators from both sides of the aisle came forward in support. Importantly, I met with Lindsey Graham, who told me that he had talked to a number of U.S. generals who had worked with me over the years and strongly supported my nomination. General Petraeus and General Odierno signaled their support, as did all the former U.S. ambassadors to Iraq. "If you are good enough for them, you are good enough for me," Senator Graham told me (he was to visit twice while I was in Baghdad). I asked him for advice on Brownback. "I can't help you with Brownback," suggesting they were not the closest of friends.

On a domestic airplane trip I had sat next to Senator John Barrasso (R-WY), who subsequently supported me. On the Senator Foreign Relations Committee both Senator Richard Lugar (R-IN) and Senator John Kerry (D-MA) promised strong support, as did most of the other members. I reached out to as many senators as would see me, and was honored that one of my own senators from Rhode Island, Jack Reed, a Vietnam veteran and an expert on Iraq, agreed to introduce me at the hearing.

Senator McCain issued a stinging press announcement questioning my competence, seizing on the fact that I did not speak Arabic and raising Zinni again. As a prominent Republican explained to me, McCain had "nothing personal" against me; he opposed the nomination on principle because of Obama's refusal during the campaign to give credit to the "surge" of U.S. troops into Iraq in 2007.

Before the Senate vote I went to McCain's office to meet him for the first time. He was armed with talking points full of distorted comments attributed to me in connection with the North Korean negotiations. Months before, a *Washington Post* reporter asked me during an evening reception at the nonprofit organization Search for Common Ground's annual awards what I thought of North Korea's human rights record. I replied that every country, including our own, needs to work on its human rights record, but that North Korea had the most work to do because it had just about the worst human rights record on the planet. The article suggested the possibility that I had come to the conclusion that the U.S. and North Korean human rights record were somehow equivalent. McCain read from that story in a disgusted tone.

I was dumbfounded, but the confirmation process being what it is, I sat before the senator taking it all in, trying to occasionally draw his attention to my thirty-one-year record of service and my qualifications for the job. He was not interested. Instead he undertook an impassioned soliloquy on the surge and Obama's perfidy in failing to acknowledge its role in winning the war.

I tried to suggest this was all rather over my pay grade. I told the senator that if confirmed I would look forward to working with him on the best policies for U.S. interests in Iraq. He continued to express his outrage over President Obama. He seemed so consumed by his anger that when the interview was over, he was uninterested even in shaking my hand, instead sitting in his chair, continuing his inner dialogue with himself about the president's failure to endorse the surge. I contrasted what seemed like deep-seated, pent-up anger that was so out of proportion with anything I or the president for that matter had done, with his public persona, that look of earnest but rueful sorrow and seriousness, and playful sense of humor that he regularly displays on Sunday morning talk shows. "Great job!" his embarrassed staffer told me.

The committee hearing went fine, but Senator Brownback maintained his hold on the nomination, in effect demanding a floor debate and delaying my departure at least another three weeks due to the Easter break. Once floor action was scheduled it was a foregone conclusion that the Senate would approve the nomination, at which point one does begin to question the motivation of a person like Brownback, who had shown no interest in the Iraq War one way or the other, to hold up the departure of the ambassador.

A staff member on the Senate Foreign Relations Committee suggested privately that Brownback was perhaps fund-raising, that is, holding the nomination at the behest of special interest groups. I got on the Internet to look at Brownback's donor list. It was a motley crew whose only common denominator seemed to be that many had nothing to do with Kansas, par for the course in modern political fund-raising. I was not able to find any group that would have been exercised about me or about sending an ambassador to Iraq, not surprising given that Brownback's own views on Iraq seemed to be a blank slate. I concluded his opposition to me must have been based on the great line from the *Star Wars* bar scene when someone says to one of the protagonists: "He doesn't like you!"

As I prepared for what turned out to be a desultory meeting with Brownback, some of my colleagues in EAP did some research to explore whether there was anything Brownback and I had in common. (Who knows, one of them said: "Maybe he likes the Red Sox.") They reported that Brownback has a tremendous interest in Mother Teresa. Perhaps I could talk about my work with her. Since the time I worked with her in Albania, I had kept a few pictures in a frame in my office, including a note from her: "To Chris Hill, God love you for all the help you have given our poor. My gift is my prayer for you."

I said, "Mother Teresa might be a way to break the ice with him." Then my colleague added, "You should also know that every year around Easter, Senator Brownback washes the feet of his staffers." I looked back at him and said nothing.

"Don't even think about it," he said.

I said on the record in my hearing that I would leave immediately for Iraq as soon as I was confirmed. I made the commitment for a couple of reasons. The first was that I was troubled by Ambassador Crocker's comments that everyone who knew anything in the embassy had left, and second, my commitment to get on a plane immediately added to the sense of urgency of getting the nomination through.

My concern about an ambassadorless embassy was heightened when I received a call from NEA, asking me to call a contractor in the embassy's political section and suggest he not submit for publication in the *New York Times* an impassioned plea to the Senate to confirm me. I asked why I should call, and was told that the State Department and Embassy Baghdad leadership both felt the op-ed could be counterproductive in the sense that some senators might be offended that the State Department was encroaching on their prerogatives. I asked in that case why didn't the chargé (interim ambassador) or the employee's immediate supervisor tell him not to publish it. After all, he was in Baghdad as a U.S. government employee, paid for by the U.S. government and not there to run his own foreign policy. He won't listen, I was told. I realized I was dealing with a different kind of embassy. My thoughts turned to how quickly Eagleburger would have handled that situation in Embassy Belgrade.

When the Senate floor debate finally came on April 20, it was essentially Kerry versus Brownback. Senator Kerry was energetic and generous in his support. I kept thinking about how I wished my parents were alive to hear him.

On the other hand, I was glad my parents were not around to hear Brownback's half of the debate. He opened by reminding the Senate that this was Holocaust Remembrance Week. I asked Glyn Davies, who was standing in my office with me watching the debate on C-SPAN, "Where's he going with this?"

"Maybe he thinks you're Hitler."

It soon became apparent that the connection to the Holocaust was that some FSOs in Switzerland in the late 1930s had refused visas to Jews, dooming them to return to Nazi Germany and certain death. In Brownback's world, I was the living prodigy of that. As he droned on I was running a grainy slide show in my head of things I had done in the course of my government career. Peace Corps, the Solidarity movement in Poland, reporting on democracy demonstrations in South Korea in the spring of 1987, meeting in remote prison work camps with the families of political prisoners in Albania in 1991, gaining access to mass graves in Bosnia in 1995, meeting with displaced persons in central Kosovo and helping to provide them with food and shelter in the summer of 1998, a midnight visit to the Stenkovac refugee camp to protect Roma under attack from angry gangs of Kosovo refugees, working (quietly and effectively) with Chinese officials to allow North Korean refugees to get out of the diplomatic compound in Shenyang on to new homes in South Korea, convincing Cambodian prime minister Hun Sen to release immediately Kem Sokha and other arrested members of the human rights movement . . . I sat slumped in my chair watching the closing statement as the Senate readied a vote. McCain stood to denounce me, employing that mournful, concerned voice he uses in public.

The vote was 73–23. "If you had been a treaty" (that requires a two-thirds majority) Strobe Talbott cheerfully told me, "you would have been confirmed with votes to spare." Several senators from both sides of the aisle called me later that night to apologize for the three-week delay and promised to visit me in Baghdad. Many of them did visit, including McCain, who was always gracious to my team and me during both of his trips. At one point during the second trip, after my security detail and I had snuck him out beyond the Green Zone to an Iraqi pastry shop, McCain draped his arm over my shoulder, thanked me, and apologized for supposedly "hurting" my "feelings" during the nomination process. I called a few other Senators to pass on my thanks to them, and, more for my own therapy than his, I put in a call to Brownback to express the hope that he would come out to Baghdad. He never returned the call or visited Baghdad. (The rather "unexpeditionary" Brownback also never visited Korea.)

I headed for my newest outpost within thirty-six hours of the vote. My son, Nathaniel, had returned just days before the vote from a six-month tour of duty at Camp Slayer in Baghdad, dashing my hopes to overlap with him in Iraq. I asked him for some advice.

"Keep your head down and bring a good pair of sunglasses," he told me.

22

THE LONGEST DAY

It was April 24, 2009, the start of the seventh year of the Iraq War, when I arrived in a C-35, a small Lear-type military jet, at Baghdad International Airport. I was exhausted but relieved to touch down after a three-part trip that consisted of a twelve-hour commercial flight to Kuwait International Airport, a drive through various U.S.-manned checkpoints over to the military side of the Kuwait airport, and finally a ninety-minute flight over the dark desert below to my new home in the "cradle of civilization."

After making a "tactical landing," a stomach-churning dive with all aircraft interior and exterior lights shut off to thwart the aim of any would-be attacker, I emerged from the plane a little woozy. Patricia Butenis, the deputy chief of mission who had been holding down the fort since Ryan Crocker had departed in February, met me at the bottom of the short flight of stairs. Pat, a superb officer who had served with me in Warsaw ten years before as head of the consular section, apologized repeatedly for the ongoing sandstorm, as if it were somehow her fault. It was 7:30 P.M. and pitch-dark except for the sand in the air that was illuminated by the headlights of the several armored black SUVs that had come to take me to the embassy.

I had been thinking about what I would draw on from my past in this assignment. As past posts flickered through my mind—Belgrade, Warsaw, Seoul, Albania, Skopje, even Buea in the Peace Corps—each was very different and offered its own lessons. I knew I would now need to draw on a lifetime of experiences to get through this one.

I knew, and not just because of my prior work in places like Albania, about the necessity of success. But the stakes in Iraq were so much higher. And the feel-good aura of opening up new post–Cold War states in Europe would not make an appearance in the nerve-racking and meat-grinding world of Iraq.

I also knew that the expectations for the embassy in Iraq were enormous and out of proportion to what could be done well and in a realistic time frame, and were not necessarily geared to the withdrawal dates for our troops. Moreover, I knew that people who might have had little idea about the situation on the ground, or even of what an embassy or any embassy anywhere can actually do, were setting these expectations. The overall capacity of Iraqis to absorb the Marshall Plan–worthy load of advice that was being poured on them by our fire hoses was far more limited than Iraq's social index of literacy and other educational achievements might otherwise suggest. Development economics literature often cites "the absorption capacity" as a factor in determining whether a country can make use of foreign funds, technical assistance, and other forms of assistance. Most often what determines a country's absorption capacity may have to do more with embedded sociological and even psychological factors. Sociology can be changed over time but cannot be trumped by politics or economics, conveyed in a kind of American secular Bible school. And of course there was the additional burden that whatever the actual transcript of the Petraeus/Crocker testimony read, the music of it was that the war had been won.

In 1989, when Poland threw off its communist system, its prime minister, Tadeusz Mazowiecki, addressed the Polish parliament on the day his government replaced the last government of the communist era. Mazowiecki's bent frame and deeply lined face seemed a perfect living metaphor to describe not only the system his government was to replace, but also his tasks ahead.

The clear-headed Polish intellectual captured the issue brilliantly: "We in Poland do not want a Polish way, a third way, because we know what works in the world and we know what doesn't work and we want what works."

Mazowiecki set a course of a kind that no Iraqi leader had thus far articulated. Poland, he was suggesting, should not be a world leader in producing new ideas and tailor-made concepts for social and economic development. Poland embraces what works in the world and wants it, and, most importantly, by its own internal reforms would prepare to receive and make the best use of it.

The fact that Iraq is not Poland was hardly the only factor at work. U.S. goals in Iraq, increasingly economic ones, were often set by senior U.S. officials, including senior military generals, who had neither the expertise nor the patience to slog through the no-man's-land of economic development projects and capacity-building. The military had become the largest dispenser of foreign aid in Iraq for programs whose primary and more sober purpose was to convince the Iraqis not to shoot at our soldiers.

In occasional unguarded moments, senior generals would admit to their civilian counterparts the profound difficulties they had in understanding the place. As General Odierno, late at night over cigars, once said to me, "You know, when we came here [Iraq] we had absolutely no idea what we were doing or what we were facing." But these moments were few and far between. What came between these rare moments were exhortations to "dominate the battle space," identify the "drivers of instability," as the PowerPoint slides obligingly did, and move on to the next development machine-gun nest. Thus, if the problem of declining date palm production in Diyala Province found its way onto a slide as a "driver of instability" (young people otherwise employed as date palm harvesters might turn to the insurgency for their livelihoods), this problem became the subject of follow-up meetings and briefings aimed at a solution through a "mitigation strategy." And because, after all, senior officers had identified the problem as important, unsustainable money transfusions were thrown at it. In today's army, money is indeed a weapon of war.

If the opinion of local Iraqis was sought, the favorite question was "What do you need?" And if the answer, as it often turned out to be, was "money," the response was "We can work with you."

The sheer size of the Commander's Emergency Response Program (CERP) funds and even the smaller civilian funds, which had long since peaked before 2009, meant that senior officials in Washington working the issues of Iraq became familiar with local place-names, which often gave them a false sense that they understood the issues. Their poor understanding of the issues was compounded by being thousands of miles away, or worse, by the fact that a past eighteen-hour trip to Iraq empowered them to speak with certainty in the windowless confines of the White House Situation Room, where the interagency squabbles dragged on and played out. And when things don't go well, especially for a new administration anxious to demonstrate that it could handle Iraq, out come the micromanaging tinkerers and the proverbial 8,000-mile-long screwdrivers.

During my preparation time in Washington, I tried to arrange to arrive at the civilian side of the Baghdad airport. I thought entering through the civilian terminal would be a powerful symbol of the changing mission in Iraq, that this would be an era of transition from the military to the civilians, and that, just maybe, we were entering a period of increasing "normalcy," a state that the Iraqis desperately wanted.

In some previous posts I had looked for a gesture, a symbolic step to convey that the new ambassador would represent change. Successful ambassadors increasingly tend to be those who understand that they are not just accredited to the foreign ministry or the government, but rather to the broader public. Such a symbol in Iraq was not so apparent. The Iraqis I talked to before my departure told me over and over that what their families in Baghdad wanted was a "normal" life; they were desperately seeking signs that things could get better. Thus I thought I could start that by coming through the civilian terminal.

The embassy and the military insisted I come the same way every one of my predecessors had come and gone, slipping in through the darkness on the military end of the runway. Security concerns were appropriately paramount, and no security officer in a war zone is particularly interested in symbolic gestures, but I felt the lack of enthusiasm for change or transition was deeper than just the nervousness of the security office.

Baghdad was having another one of its infamous sandstorms. Sandstorms at their worst are a kind of London fog, with a brown tint rather than blue, and are as old as the Bible. But in Baghdad in 2009, everything was laid at the doorstep of the U.S. presence. Many people in Iraq made the case that it was entirely Americans' fault, that U.S. tactical vehicles in the deserts in Anbar and Ninewah were stirring up sandstorms!

Pat explained we would have to drive in a convoy to the embassy instead of taking the usual UH-64 Black Hawk helicopter ride. That was fine with me. I had taken enough Black Hawks in the Balkans to last a lifetime. The chief of my security detail, Derek Dela-Cruz, gave me my Kevlar helmet and "PPE" (personal protective equipment), a bulletproof vest. I climbed into the armored Chevy Suburban and off we went into the darkness, with Derek riding shotgun next to the driver and me in the backseat with Pat.

That was the first of many times I would ride with Derek, then later his successor, Ian Pavis. For an ambassador overseas, a close relationship with a security detail is crucial. Often compromises needed to be found between the ambassador's wish to be out in the field and the security detail's fervent desire that the ambassador stay locked up in the embassy. Conversations often ran along these lines, "Sir, we can support your idea for a three-day visit to place X, but it would involve Y and Z resources. Could you consider an early morning departure and return that night?" I always agreed. Sometimes the security detail would come into possession of a tactical piece of information that would require some adjustment in the route or schedule. "Huh?" I responded once to Derek when he pulled me back from getting into the car. "Sir, please humor me." And I did because he had a job to do.

As he drove into Baghdad, I spent the twenty-minute drive staring out the three-inch-thick ballistic window at the scenery, such as it was. I was struck by the fact that even though I was riding in a six-vehicle convoy of armored-up vehicles and anticipating the thousands of embassy employees awaiting my stewardship of the U.S. mission, I felt as alone as I had some thirty-five years ago arriving in Douala, Cameroon, for my Peace Corps service.

The fine sand, besides finding a way into every human pore, turned every building and road sign into varying shades of brown, and the view of "Route Irish" (all major highways in Baghdad, like many war zones before, were given very clear Western cultural names—another one for example being Route Tampa—to facilitate memorization by our soldiers) was not much of a view at all. I kept looking for signs of flowers and landscaping, which General Petraeus in his Chamber of Commerce speech to me weeks before had mentioned. "Where have all the flowers gone?" I muttered to myself. We entered the Green Zone, a place so nicknamed for its level of supposed personal safety than for any particular commitment to the environment. Minutes later our vehicles arrived at the main gate of the vast embassy compound, where a very professional Peruvian contract guard in a khaki uniform and floppy hat waved the vehicles through the gate.

U.S. Embassy Baghdad is a 104-acre facility that has cost American taxpayers some half a billion dollars. A company called First Kuwaiti General Trading and Contracting built it, and often bore the brunt of numerous employee complaints when things didn't work well. First

Kuwaiti, along with numerous other subcontractors, employed construction workers from all over the globe—except Iraqis, who were deemed a security threat, and in some cases probably for very good reasons. Media descriptions of the property depicted it as a luxury facility on the banks of the Tigris River, with a food court and other amenities that would remind its happy thousand or so full-time inhabitants of home. In reality, there was nothing luxurious about the compound, and it definitely did not remind anyone of home. All the buildings had windows that could withstand blasts from 107mm rockets, and all the roofs were built to a bombproof standard, at least in the event they were hit by the type of rocketry that was regularly fired at the Green Zone from Sadr City and other "points of origin," or "POOs," as the military described them in this acronym-rich environment. We drove past the so-called food court. It consisted of a veranda where sullen-looking people—mostly in military uniforms—lounged on plastic chairs smoking and using the Wi-Fi.

I stared out the SUV window at what was unfolding in front of my eyes. I have seen embassies all over the world. Served in many. This one lived up to its reputation as a colossus. Bright white lights along the barbed-wire-tipped, ten-foot-high cement wall gave it a look more appropriate to a corrections facility. The chancery building, where the ambassador's office is housed, was also lit up by security lights. The building was a familiar design to anyone who has seen one of the many new U.S. embassies that have cropped up in the unfertile soils of newly independent countries since 1989: brown, utilitarian buildings, which looked like giant cardboard boxes with air holes and housed the thousand-plus employees, were bathed in white light. The starkness of the flat-roofed housing buildings, the lack of even the slightest sign of landscaping save for a giant, forlorn lawn in front of the chancery building, gave it the look of a Mars colony.

The convoy stopped every hundred feet to manage the metal speed bumps. Peruvian contract guards in brown uniforms and floppy desert hats walking in pairs, their M-16 rifles loosely slung over their shoulders, waved and saluted as we went by. We went past an enormous brown open space that could presumably have furnished all the necessary sand and dust for a countrywide sandstorm. Finally we turned into a metal, grilled front gate and entered the small front yard of the residence of the ambassador. My new home. I took off the body armor and helmet in the car (I had felt foolish wearing it, even though I understood why the regulations required it) and got out to meet the staff of the residence. It was about 8 P.M.

The residence was shaped vaguely like a giant shoe box. It too was painted brown. Windows were long and narrow and appeared to be designed more as someone's concept of a shooting position than as a source of light. Like every other window on the compound, the glass was several inches thick and could not be opened, even with direct rocket fire. A porch on the upstairs seemed at first glance to offer some respite from this dreary look, but it too was retrofitted with thick Plexiglas to guard against the possibility that someone might aim a weapon at it.

Inside, however, furnished with the State Department's limitless supply of Drexel furniture and by an equally endless supply of industrial-strength Oriental carpets, the residence was rather pleasant. I looked at the artwork that adorned the walls. The theme, by and large, was the American flag, and many of the pieces featured numerous patriotic scenes of America that the State Department's office of interior designs and furnishings had chosen.

Pat explained what had been planned that evening. The foreign minister was waiting for us at his office, where at 9:30 P.M. I would present to him copies of my "letters of credence and credentials," a 350-year-old diplomatic practice by which an arriving ambassador presents letters from his head of state to the effect that the person was in fact the real ambassador and not some imposter. Copies were presented to the Foreign Ministry because in most countries an appointment with the receiving head of state could take weeks or months, and meanwhile the ambassador would need to get to work. In Baghdad, however, my appointment with President Jalal Talabani to present the letters was scheduled for 10:30 P.M., an hour later.

Our six-car convoy lumbered up to the Foreign Ministry, which stood all too close to a busy intersection, with a small army of security guards, some of whom had already been deployed to the site in anticipation of the visit and were there to join the protocol officers greeting us on arrival. I made my way into the building and, accompanied by the protocol official, went up the elevator. Foreign Minister Hoshyar Zebari, a former Kurdish Peshmerga guerrilla fighter who was a confidant of Kurdish president Massoud Barzani, was a gregarious, roundish-featured Kurd wearing a double-breasted blue suit, with a friendly smile, an optimistic outlook, and excellent English. In his Baghdad home he prominently displayed a picture of himself and President Barzani, in younger years, both in their brown Peshmerga uniforms wearing red and white turbans, sitting cross-legged on top of a snow-peaked mountain far up in the wilds of Kurdistan. The always fit President Barzani would later comment to me with his dry and ironic sense of humor that he was not entirely sure that Hoshyar could make it back up to that mountaintop for another such photo.

Hoshyar (as he was called by all) welcomed me warmly in his fourth-floor outer office, introduced me one by one to his senior team, and took the outsized envelope containing copies of my papers. I tried my best to introduce my team, but having arrived in the embassy just an hour before I didn't know who half of them were. We sat in two chairs at the end of a long, ornate room, decorated with display cases of bric-a-brac from various diplomatic visitors. Our embassy staffs and foreign ministry sat in two long rows, forming both sides of a U, his to his left, mine to my right, with coffee tables end to end placed between the two rows. It was a scene I had participated in numerous times throughout my career whether in Ban Ki-moon's office in Korea, or Kiro Gligorov's in Skopje. The only difference was that for this meeting I had a small army of security standing guard outside the office door, inside the door, at the elevator, at other elevator stops on other floors, at the back stairs, on the ground floor at the elevator and the stairs, at the building entrance, at the back entrance, inside the vehicles, and in a small helicopter circling overhead. That, I thought, was something new.

Hoshyar confirmed that we were scheduled to meet President Talabani in about an hour and we chatted for a few minutes in a friendly style, one that Hoshyar never departed from over my entire time in Iraq, no matter the pressure of the moment. He was proud of the ministry that he had run for five years, and was especially pleased that just twelve hours later he would be hosting Secretary Clinton in his office.

I had almost—but certainly not completely—forgotten that I had a visit from the secretary at nine o'clock the next morning. How late, I wondered, would the 10:30 P.M. meeting with President Talabani go? Normally, visits by a secretary of state are a logistical nightmare for an embassy. As François Truffaut once said of making films: they start as an effort to create a masterpiece, and end as something you just want to get over with. Such is the case with a secretary's visit. Everyone in the embassy is mobilized for such a visit. "Site officers" are assigned to each meeting location. Senior delegation members also have control officers available for every wish, whether to fetch a bottle of water or to arrange a meeting with a lesser official while the secretary is having "downtime" (unscheduled time, usually used for something like a phone call back to Washington or to some other place where there is another crisis going on).

But Embassy Baghdad was the visitor capital of the world. It had an entire visits unit staffed with former military personnel, more political and economic officers for note-taking than any embassy I had ever seen in the world, and logistical strengths in terms of a motor pool that were second to none. Managing the highly choreographed visit of a secretary would pose no strain on the embassy, so much so that Hoshyar was the first to mention it that night. I decided not to worry. After all, I was sure Clinton would be coming every few months.

Before the secretary was to arrive at nine the next morning, I had a breakfast scheduled with the CIA director Leon Panetta at 7:30 A.M., followed by a brief airport meeting at 8:30 A.M. with the chairman of the Joint Chiefs of Staff, Admiral Mike Mullen, who was due back to Baghdad from northern Iraq and would also be at planeside to meet Secretary Clinton. I hoped that the meeting with President Talabani would be brief, just to present my credentials.

I walked into President Talabani's home just outside the Green Zone at 10:30 P.M. Foreign Minister Zebari, having somehow taken a shortcut to be there ahead of me, stood in the receiving line. The president greeted me in a friendly, avuncular style that belied eight years of war in Iraq, not to mention his own heroic history of fighting in the mountains against Saddam Hussein's forces. Like Zebari, President Talabani had put on a few pounds since his days in the mountains, but at seventy-eight years of age, and in chronic ill health, he showed no sign that he would rather be in any other place in the world than welcoming me to his home, and invited me into his dining room for a full-blown Kurdish feast. It was 11 P.M. when I entered the dining room and saw the piles of rice pilaf, eggplant, salads, lamb, and turkey. "Which part of Turkey do you like the most?" he asked, using an English language play on words that in the scores of dinners and lunches that were to follow he seemingly would never tire of. The food that was displayed in various platters along the middle of the table reminded me of what the Kurdish mountains look like—steep and high, with valleys in between then still more mountains steep and high.

Talabani did not eat much during the dinner but took great care to make sure his guests were well fed. He continually surveyed the table of some twenty people from his seat in the middle for signs that someone's plate was not at least 90 percent full. His watchful eyes would come to rest on a plate that fit that description, and with a mock sense of urgency he would quickly motion the waiter or an Iraqi dinner guest nearby to attend to the potentially starving American.

We talked Iraqi politics and U.S. relations. Over the course of my career I had met leaders like Talabani before. He was first and foremost a reconciler of conflicting views, a mediator who relished the possibility, however long the odds, of taking two people who did not like each other and finding ways they could get along. That is a skill in any country, but in Iraq it was rare and something that we needed a lot more of.

He was also very good at it, far better than some of his foreign interlocutors, especially jet-lagged, get-to-the-point American visitors. His sense of humor was disarming, but it often had a deeper purpose. Some of those who listened to his jokes through to the often-flubbed punch line completely misunderstood what he might be probing for or sizing up, or how he might be stalling for time for some reason the visitor had no idea about. Talabani enjoyed telling one story about how he told a senior visitor from Iran that his ambassador, sitting next to him, had agreed with the U.S. ambassador at the time on something, and after glancing mischievously out the corner of his eye for the look of panic to emerge in the Iranian ambassador would say, "They both think my kebabs are the best in Baghdad."

Talabani often tried to hint about the need for U.S.-Iranian dialogue. He also, to the great consternation of many Americans, kept some excessively close Iran relationships, which were indeed troubling. Kurds and Iranians are not known to have a history of close relationships. But all history is local. Months later, I was to visit Talabani's hometown of Sulemaniyah and the nearby village of Halabja, where Saddam Hussein had used poison gas and killed hundreds in their homes. That day, Iran had opened its border crossings and taken in many refugees, including children who had just become orphans. Many people are alive in Halabja because of what the Iranians did that day.

Talabani was also a creature of Baghdad and its relative cosmopolitan and secular feel. But this comfort level in the big city meant that he was losing touch with the growing problems in his region of the eastern part of Kurdistan, in Sulemaniyah. Later during my time in Iraq he was to spend an increasing amount of his work time dealing with local issues in Sulemaniyah as political opposition grew to challenge the hold of his Patriotic Union of Kurdistan. His political problems prompted Washington analysts to conclude he was somehow a spent force, but to analyze his position in Baghdad in terms of his base in Sulemaniyah was to misunderstand his role.

Over the course of my time—and his meals—in Baghdad, I would come to respect Talabani's judgments about other politicians and in particular about Prime Minister Nouri al-Maliki. "There is a good Maliki, and a bad Maliki. We need to encourage one, and discourage the other," he liked to say. In Iraq, the powers of the president were very weak, but Talabani's capacity to talk to all sides meant that he could if possible punch above his already considerable weight. In the take-no-prisoners world of Iraqi politics, there were very few politicians with such skills.

My convoy lumbered back to the embassy, the speed bumps seeming to hit with added force on my exhausted body. At 1 A.M. I staggered up to where I remembered my bedroom was located to lie down, and just as I did that night in Cameroon, thirty-five years ago, asking myself as I went to sleep what I had gotten myself into. I slept through until the morning.

After the breakfast with CIA director Panetta, I took a helicopter out to the airport to await the arrival of Secretary Clinton. While waiting I spoke briefly with chairman of the Joint Chiefs, Admiral Mullen. I thought about the attention being paid Iraq: CIA director, chairman of the Joint Chiefs, secretary of state. Who's coming tomorrow? I asked myself.

Secretary Clinton put herself through a grueling day: meetings with Zebari, Prime Minister Maliki, President Talabani, and women who had lost their husbands to war and violence (alas, sometimes at the hands of our forces). Also, a kind of holdover from her days on the campaign trail: the proverbial town meeting with all sorts of people, young, old, women, men, muftis, seculars in gray suits, sheiks in flowing robes and keffiyehs, women in black chadors and checkered *shemaghs*, just about everybody.

The secretary batted every question thrown her way effortlessly, a tour de force. She posed for numerous photos and worked lines of people. I stood on the side in this embassy "common room," wondering what the Iraqis were thinking of her and the whole event. Sometimes events that are culturally specific, such as a New England town meeting, make more sense in a place like New Hampshire than in Baghdad. They don't necessarily make the leap over the cultural divide, and I was not sure this town meeting had done so. But I also wasn't sure it hadn't. I didn't know what to think. There was such a campaign feel to it I wanted to clap my hands and cheer for her, but she was secretary of state, I kept having to remind myself.

Finally, at the end of the long day there was the meeting with the U.S. Embassy staff in the large embassy atrium. The advance team had ensured that the crowd was in place when Secretary Clinton emerged on the second-floor balcony after a small meeting in my office with the United Nations representative Staffan de Mistura and his senior staff. As she walked slowly down the main staircase, waving each step of the way, the crowd, two-thirds of which was affiliated with the military in some way or another, surged with enthusiasm. She got up on the platform specially constructed on the instructions of her advance team. The deep-blue velvet drape and piping backdrop had a professional look to it. I thought about how the embassy in Tirana had hosted senior visitors, including Secretary Eagleburger, or how Embassy Skopje had hosted Secretary Albright without any stage or bunting or drape and piping. I thought back to how in Tirana we had asked Secretary Eagleburger to stand on a wooden crate turned on its end ("Hill, if I fall and kill myself, I'll have you fired!").

Secretary Clinton, seeming to make eye contact with every person in the room, spoke eloquently and passionately, and with a sincerity that brought tears to some eyes. She said how important Iraq was to her, a top-tier issue, and how much she valued the staff at this embassy. She kindly introduced me as the ambassador she would leave behind, and said she would look forward to working with this embassy in the years ahead.

To thunderous applause she walked the rope line, connecting, it seemed, with everyone she shook hands with or simply touched. She took photos effortlessly with people, waited patiently as employees turned amateur photographers fumbled to find the flash switch on their cell phone cameras. She finally made her exit out of the embassy to the waiting car, her nervous security detail beginning to breathe a sigh of relieve that it was all coming to an end soon. I said good-bye in the car on the edge of the helicopter landing pad, and she made clear that I should call her whenever I needed her help—and I would really need help, she said in mock seriousness. Exhilarated and grateful, I stood on the edge of the landing zone in a line with a few other embassy personnel, all of us waving farewell to our secretary with the expectation she would be back soon.

Three months later, Vice President Joe Biden took the lead on Iraq policy and she never returned.

Embassy Baghdad was the biggest embassy the world had ever seen, the joke being that like the Great Wall of China it was visible from outer space. But to the military it was no larger than many of the "forward operating bases" (FOBs) that dot the Green Zone, and small compared to the giant military bases that housed the major army formations. Even though it was a diplomatic establishment, there were legions of uniformed military working on the "new embassy compound," or NEC, as it was known to the military. To many it was indeed another FOB in Baghdad, like Camp Liberty and Camp Union.

In the middle of the NEC stood the chancery building. With its large atrium, the chancery was something out of the central drawings of the generic embassy. But in addition to the chancery, there was an Annex One, where the consular section and many of the administrative operations were located. There was also an Annex Two, where many of the foreign assistance implementers were housed. And of course, there was also a large recreation building that housed a "food court," with an off-brand coffee shop, a Pizza Hut, a Subway sandwich shop, and a small commissary for buying primarily soft drinks, frozen foods, some limited clothing, a few electronic goods, and DVDs whose selections were clearly geared to a young age group. There was also a post office and a unisex barbershop where for four dollars one could get a haircut that could turn the most shaggy-haired political section wonk into a marine recruit look-alike. It paid to pay attention to what the barber was up to.

There was also a bar called "Baghdaddy's," which was open two nights a week and otherwise would be used for community events including church services. Next to the bar stood an indoor basketball court, the back half converted to a gym whose weight and cardio machines seemed to be in full use morning, noon, and night. Outside the food court there was a large cement terrace that Chris Klein dubbed the "corniche," where groups of people barbecued hamburgers and hot dogs and sometimes brought in an Iraqi caterer to grill shawarma on a huge spit.

The NEC was built to last, a contrast to the U.S. military bases with their temporary structures, usually a down-on-its-luck Saddam-era palace or Republican Guard cement building complex with such kitsch décor as a plastic chandelier, surrounded by Containerized Housing Units, or "CHUs" (pronounced "chews"), erected by one of the many U.S. contractor firms that accompany the U.S. military to war in this age. The NEC also had a few CHUs, but by and large buildings and even the beginnings of some actual landscaping suggested a different kind of overall facility than the American presence elsewhere. Buildings on the NEC also had "overhead cover," a deluxe option, not found on military bases, that protected the buildings from 107mm rocket fire. We looked like we planned to stay.

I thought the latter point was an important one, and felt that it was my best means to show the Iraqis that we desired a "normal" relationship (albeit, with overhead rocket-proof protection of our buildings), and that the scale of the embassy, its bricks and mortar, would help suggest our commitment to a long-term relationship.

The staff of this "expeditionary" embassy was an extraordinary mishmash of people, only a minority of whom were Foreign Service officers. Many were active-duty military, or often reservists, working in the "Joint Directorate for Strategic Effects" (better known as J9) of the USF-I Command. The J9's mission was to engage and influence Iraq's political leadership, government officials, and civilian society in general—it was essentially a parallel embassy run entirely by a major general, with some 250 people attached. The embassy also employed legions of support staff: gardeners, cafeteria workers, auto mechanics, housing engineers, most of whom were on loan from other U.S. embassies around the world. Beyond that there were technical assistance contractors providing services to the Iraq government through such U.S. government agencies as the Agency for International Development (AID) or the Treasury Department. Throughout the embassy, in order to fill out sections such as Economic or Commercial, there were one-year contractors, known as 3161s, a number that refers to the civil service code that permitted the temporary hiring of persons with needed skills.

And then, of course, there were the security force contractors. Normally, an embassy's outer fences are protected by host country security services, usually simply police. For obvious reasons, Embassy Baghdad could not rely on the Iraqi government to provide such protection, hence the engagement of contracting companies that in turn would hire guards from other countries, such as Peru and Uganda. There were also mobile security teams that would protect diplomats and others on their visits to Iraqi government facilities.

For this tower of Babel to be an embassy of the future, or a model for something, would be to commit our country to further such massive deployments of troops and their camp followers—and a few professional diplomats. In taking my first walk around, the size of the workforce of the embassy was by any measure totally unsustainable.

Why so big? Because the military wanted it that way.

Both Secretaries of State Rice and Clinton were consistently challenged by military counterparts to demonstrate that the State

Department was in fact committed to the mission. And the metric for that commitment was size—the bigger, the better. As the level of violence began to recede in 2007, due primarily to internal Iraqi reasons, the military expressed doubts about whether the State Department would gear up. General Petraeus's rueful questions posed to Secretaries Rice and Clinton in interagency meetings in the Situation Room, "Where are the civilians? Where's the State Department? Where is the civilian surge?" were typical of the expectations that the military had for the State Department as a follow-on force, the continuation of war by other means.

Petreaus's "wingman" Ambassador Crocker (Petraeus also conferred that honorific on Dick Holbrooke, much to the latter's amusement) had long broken the code in dealing with the military and understood the need for staff, which would soon cause Embassy Baghdad to dwarf any other U.S. embassy in the world. Crocker became a frequent critic of the State Department's sluggishness in matters of personnel, and called for directed (forced) multiple tours in Iraq, demands that came as a delight to the military, whose members were being deployed on multiple tours and viewed the State Department as challenged to "step up."

But the task of finding people for all these new positions (let alone the challenge of finding meaningful work for those filling jobs whose creation was simply to reassure our military of our spiritual commitment to the Iraq operations) fell to the beleaguered State Department Human Resources Bureau.

Thus the Foreign Service began to send both its best, and sometimes its not so best, to Iraq.

I was soon to meet in our embassy some of the most gifted Americans one will ever meet in or out of uniform. AID officers under the direction of Chris Crowley, for example, would come to my office to show what they had accomplished in terms of numbers of trained officials and how some of the ministries were now led by people we had trained. It was impressive. The Treasury Department program, which always had absolutely top-notch leadership, too, demonstrated it had come to Iraq to make a difference. Similarly, the embassy's political and economic section, made up of Foreign Service officers, came in a mood to make a difference in what was truly one of the most complex problems facing the United States and the Arab world. After all, our invasion had made Iraq the only Shia-led Arab majority country in the Middle East, and the new Iraq was not particularly welcomed in the neighborhood.

But there was also a mood in some quarters of the embassy, especially among those back for repeat tours, that they wanted their Iraq experience to remain the same. Whether it was a variant of the Stockholm syndrome to have grown fond of the circumstances, bad as they were, or a basic human need for familiarity, I was soon to see that making changes would encounter resistance.

As any organization, the Foreign Service is driven at the top by a highly motivated class of officers who didn't need to be encouraged to go, who were eager not to miss an assignment in a post that would be a subject of discussion for decades to come. There were the Middle East specialists, who were naturally drawn to both the duty and the opportunity to bring their skills to bear. But there are only seven thousand or so FSOs to staff more than 194 diplomatic posts around the world. There were not enough qualified, high-caliber volunteers to fill the hundreds of slots for FSOs in Embassy Baghdad and its subsidiary posts, the Provincial Reconstruction Teams (PRTs). And so there were people who were simply told by their personnel officers in Human Resources that they were going to Iraq. Everybody had to go, and the best thing to do was to go soon and get the requirement over with.

There were those who saw Iraq as a ticket punch, a place to go for an assignment on the understanding that the next assignment would be to a cushy place in Europe. There were those who went for the money. Danger pay and hardship pay could double one's salary, and so some parts of Embassy Baghdad often looked like a near retirement home, with people who were soon to retire from the Foreign Service adding to their nest eggs.

There were also some who did not have the experience of other posts to draw on (as seasoned Foreign Service officers did) and considered Baghdad the baseline of what should be done and how one should behave in a foreign country. Often visitors from Washington who had served previously in Embassy Baghdad came back out gushing with a sense of nostalgia from tours of duty there, cheerfully relating tales of sacrifice and woes as if these were the best moments of their lives. A comment as innocent as "it's hot today" (what with the temperature approaching 120 degrees) would be greeted by derisive laughter and the all-too-familiar "That's nothing. You should have been here in August of '07 when . . ."

One visitor serving as a special advisor in the State Department, and who considered her Iraq service as if it had been her time at a college sorority, cheerfully told a group in my living room before dinner about the time seven Turkish air-conditioning workers repairing duct work in the old embassy (the Republican Guard Palace) had all gotten lost in the maze of metal and had died, in effect cooked to death in an aluminum oven. Horrified, I leaned over and whispered to a person next to me who had previous experience in Iraq, "Oh my God, did that really happen?" He answered, "Well, who knows, but she just loved her Iraq experience."

Despite the enormous numbers of State Department personnel, I was surprised to learn that the political section, the heart and soul of most embassies, and in Iraq one of the absolute largest, was often bypassed in managing the embassy's relations with Iraqis and in its reporting back to Washington in favor of contractors who had come to Iraq as a one-off opportunity, rather than as part of a foreign service career. Often this small number of temporary contract appointees based in the front office and under the direct supervision of the ambassador and/or the commanding general were the key people to maintain contacts with the Iraqis.

Based on what I heard during my preparations in Washington, I felt that the political section had been sometimes poorly led in the past, its expert officers relegated to attending endless internal meetings or escorting Washington visitors around to secondary officials in the Green Zone.

I thought the Foreign Service hadn't stood up for itself in Baghdad, had allowed its normal structures to be undermined in favor of improvised solutions, with a dubious justification based on the catch-all, argument-ending point that "we're at war" and therefore nothing can be done according to normal procedures. When I looked at the breadth and quality of the Foreign Service officers in the political section in late spring of 2009, I was determined to change that.

Whether it was the luck of the draw that year or something else, the 2009 recruitment class of political officers was among the best I had ever seen in the Foreign Service. The head of it all was Gary Grappo, a twenty-year Foreign Service veteran who had most recently served as U.S. ambassador to Oman. An Air Force Academy graduate, Gary spoke fluent Arabic, as did many of the political officers, and he had a broad context for the region, having served in Saudi Arabia as the number two officer. He was a born leader. Others in the political section included Bill Roebuck, another Arabic speaker with tremendous Middle East experience and a gift for telegram writing, and Eric Carlson, also a brilliant writer and an Arabic speaker. John Godfrey was a rising star in the service with fluent Arabic and broad experience, including in Libya when the U.S. reopened the embassy in Tripoli. Steve Bondy had special responsibilities to liaise with some of the Sunni extremist groups and was another class act, as was Evyenia Sidereas, who had probably the best Arabic skills of anyone and had served in Egypt. Derek Hoffman, one of the most junior members of the section, had learned Arabic as a child and followed some of the Shia political parties—and was wise beyond his years.

We also had the services of Mustafa Popal, another rising star who had the added skill of speaking Dari and whom we were able to use in contacts with the ayatollahs based in Najaf, once sending him there with a hidden beacon in an unmarked car, a courageous act by a courageous young officer. His telegram about his conversations with the ayatollahs was read by Vice President Biden, who sought him out on his next visit (Biden was to visit four times during my sixteen months in Iraq).

Finally, I had the ace of the whole operation, the former East Asia special assistant Yuri Kim, who had signed up earlier for Iraq to work in a Provincial Reconstruction Team in Anbar. When I realized I was going to Iraq, I broke her assignment and brought her to the embassy. She knew me well, and understood what I was trying to achieve. As I explained to Gary, who had not yet met Yuri because she had spent most of her career in East Asia, she is really just about the best the Foreign Service has, and "we will all someday work for Yuri," I explained. And though, unlike the others, she did not have Middle East experience or the language, I knew that if she were assigned to the planet Jupiter she would learn the local language and figure the place out.

I met with her and with Gary first, and then with all of the officers, and told them that there would be no more so-called special assistants running around the embassy and around town pretending to be professional political officers. The political section officers were what we had, they were among the best I had ever seen, and I was going to sink or swim with them. One of the first moves I made was to have Yuri and Gary and Chris Klein, who were always around the action, work with their military counterparts to begin embedding the military's "embassy," the J9, into the political section. Major General Dave Perkins, with whom I had worked in Macedonia some thirteen years before, was key to the merger. So too was General Odierno, who understood that it was time to begin civilizing and professionalizing the mission, hard as that was for some. It was an important step, with many challenges ahead.

Occasionally, I was able to have visitors come out from the States to help on a short-term basis in working with host country officials. One of these was Robert Sweet, a senior judge from the Southern District of New York, who some eighteen years earlier had visited Albania when I was there to provide technical assistance to that country's fledgling judiciary system. Bob was eighty-seven years old when he touched down at Baghdad's airport after an overnight flight from New York via Amman, Jordan. He had a youthfulness of body, mind, and spirit that had his Iraqi and American interlocutors in awe. ("Just good genes," he would explain to those who wanted to know his secret formula.) On the day of his arrival in Baghdad, I arranged to have DJ, one of our best security officers, meet and escort him to the embassy. DJ found Judge Sweet at the passport control area and gave him the requisite Kevlar helmet and flak jacket. He told me later that day that he explained to Sweet, "Judge, if there are any problems I want you to stay close to me." I chuckled in anticipation of what the World War II veteran's response probably was to that. "So what did the judge say?" I asked.

"Sir, he just said to me, 'No, kid. If there are any problems I want you to run like hell. I'll be fine.'"

23

WINDING DOWN
THE WAR

It was clear the Obama administration had two objectives in Iraq: first, demonstrate to the American public that it had taken over from the previous administration without squandering any of the fragile gains of recent years; and, two, wind down the war and bring our troops home. These were spelled out in detail when President Obama delivered his February 29, 2009, speech to a war-weary military audience of marines at Camp Lejeune, a speech I watched with great interest in my office in the East Asian and Pacific Affairs Bureau as I prepared for the assignment. Achieving these goals was not going to be easy. Proponents of the first saw it in conflict with the second. Senator McCain, who initially expressed cautious optimism about the speech, had run his presidential campaign largely on the basis of support for President Bush's "doubling down" on the Iraq War, the decision to increase the number of U.S. troops by thirty thousand in what became known as the "surge."

Candidate Obama had never acknowledged the surge as a driver of supposed success in Iraq, a description that would have given credit to another chapter of his opponent's narrative as the courageous but sometimes lonely figure willing to do the right thing for the country even if it did not pay him political dividends. Throughout the campaign McCain helped to transform the surge into something much broader than the technical issue of adjusting troop-to-task ratios in Iraq. It became in his mind a proxy for leadership and courage. He had no intention of allowing Obama a free ride on his leadership express.

To those who supported the idea of sending more troops to Iraq when everybody else was advocating pulling out, the surge was a signature moment, a kind of validation of one's own courage and boldness. While many were calling for troop withdrawals, supporters of the surge instead called for more troops. Like Horatio at the bridge, or John Paul Jones's "I have not yet begun to fight," it was a moment when the protagonist fought on rather than retreat, with a moral foundation that would instill confidence in the inevitable triumph.

Because it was widely viewed as a success, the surge had many fathers eager to see their names in the history books of this lost cause now turned into supposed triumph. Ray Odierno, who always gave credit for the surge where it belonged, with President Bush, told me a story at the end of a long and difficult day in Baghdad. Petraeus and he had been briefing a congressional staff delegation when Ray explained to the staff members that he had ordered additional troops for the Kirkuk area, in effect additional troops who would in the counterinsurgency (COIN) jargon have a mission to seize, hold (that is, protect the local population), build (that is, give the population jobs and opportunities), and transfer (to Iraqis, the exit strategy). Ray's order had come at a time when Petraeus was still in Fort Leavenworth supposedly etching the tablets of the army's new COIN doctrine and surge strategy. After the congressional staffers had left, Petraeus, according to Odierno, asked him to remain for a minute. Petraeus then sternly told Odierno, "Ray, don't ever make that mistake again. The surge was my idea!"

So it may have been, but what it wasn't was a cure-all, nor was ordering more U.S. troops the only reason, not even the primary reason why violence had started to subside. Sunni sheiks in Anbar province, increasingly disgusted by the bloody tactics employed by Islamist insurgents, began to turn their militias against them. Meanwhile, U.S. marines in Anbar and U.S. soldiers elsewhere, often young lieutenants and squad leaders at a tactical level, began to do what marines and soldiers have done for centuries: they adapted to the battlefield. In the Iraq case, it meant embracing a complex set of skills based on developing relationships and incentives for local leaders to turn against extremists. They worked one sheik at a time, convincing them, sometimes with argumentation, sometimes with money, to consider their futures. One army lieutenant from upstate New York told me of having built a fence to help keep the sheik's cattle accounted for, provided, of course, the sheik improved security. The lieutenant described to me another incident in which he had worked with the trainer of a military explosive detection dog so that in front of a line of suspected insurgents the dog barked specifically at those whom the lieutenant suspected ahead of time of lying; it was a "lie detector dog," as he told the frightened suspects. "You learn any of that in a COIN manual?" I asked him. "You kidding?" he laughed. Stephen Ambrose once wrote a book about citizen soldiers who improvised their way from Normandy to the liberation of Germany. When the history of the Iraq War is finally told, it will be about a similar journey undertaken by brave and resourceful young Americans, ably led by their generals to be sure, but also by their own battlefield resourcefulness.

As for the generals, I never subscribed to the view of some correspondents that our military's leadership was incompetent. Many of these writers, however fascinated by the military, based their strong opinions on unnamed sources who often had axes to grind and email addresses to provide. Iraq was a tough mission and lessons often had to be learned on the fly. No one had to learn these lessons faster and harder than General Ricardo Sanchez, a newly appointed commanding general who was the first in and who confronted an Iraq that was completely different from the one he and his troops had trained and prepared for.

The generals I knew while I served in Iraq—Odierno, Huntzinger, Jacoby, Anderson, Perkins, Helmick, Petraeus: the list is long—were all men whose dedication to their duty I had the highest respect for.

Among the very best was General George Casey, who replaced Sanchez and was to serve the longest as the commanding general, from June 2004 until February 2007. We had first met during the Kosovo crisis and I had watched with great satisfaction his meteoric rise in the ranks to four-star general. Casey, who never failed to give credit to others, was the leader who developed much of the COIN tactics for the war. He created a COIN academy in Baghdad for all incoming commanders, in essence a retraining school. When Casey and the army leadership agreed on General Petraeus as the next commanding general, Casey urged that Petraeus be sent to Fort Leavenworth and along with teachers from the academy rewrite the army's doctrine on counterinsurgency.

Petraeus, whom I first met when he was a colonel accompanying the chairman of the Joint Chiefs Hugh Shelton on trips to the Balkans during the Kosovo war, was well prepared to be Casey's replacement and to implement his tactics, operations, and strategy. He had served as a divisional commander of the 101st Airborne, which had fought its way along with the rest of the invasion force up through Iraq and who moved in and occupied Mosul after army special forces with Kurdish guerrillas had liberated it. Later, he took command of the training mission in Iraq, a courageous but thankless assignment that was absolutely essential to readying the Iraqi army to take over for U.S. forces. Petraeus approached that difficult job with the same level of thoroughness, dedication, and enthusiasm he put to use in all his assignments. His production of weekly statistics demonstrating progress in the training of Iraqis was essential to planning for the U.S. drawdown.

Seldom did Secretary Rumsfeld hold a press conference in Washington without referring to the progress Petraeus was making to ready the new Iraqi forces. Unfortunately, sometimes the metric of trained Iraqis played the same kind of role that "body count" did during the Vietnam War: numbers that were somewhat misleading and had little to do with the reality of who was winning the war. The number of training certificates issued does not determine the readiness of an army to fight, and certainly Petraeus—and probably even Rumsfeld—knew that.

Not everything that happened in Iraq had to do with what the Americans were up to. On the Shia side of Iraqi's sectarian divide, Prime Minister Maliki employed another approach from those advocating a protect-the-civilians COIN strategy. Against the advice of the U.S. military, he sent his army to crush Shia militia groups in Basra, the southernmost city in Iraq, and which like Mosul in the north had never been cleaned out of its militias. Maliki's troops soon got in trouble, and as the U.S. military could not resist backgrounding the press, ultimately required augmentation in prevailing over the militias in Basra. His decision to use force against fellow Shia cemented his reputation as a tough leader, but it also created huge political problems for him during the government formation period in 2010, especially with the Sadrists, who had numerous links to the militia groups. But most importantly for the future of his country, Maliki's message that the militias must disarm had been sent and received.

While anyone in country was aware of the Sunni-Shia divide and the fact that the name of the game in Iraq was politics, in Washington the issue orbited around counterinsurgency and its immediate tactical cousin, the surge.

As the COIN strategy took hold in Iraq, it became an even higher-stakes game in Washington. Counterinsurgency efforts had been given credit for the fact that the killing had been much diminished (credit it only partially deserved), and for that, people whose faith in the Iraq War had wavered were very grateful to the doctrine and its disciples. But for others, especially those whose faith never had wavered, COIN offered the vast prospect for a renewed dedication to the task of the forced perfecting of the rest of the world to the benefit of U.S. interest. COIN not only "won" the Iraq War; it would, in this worldview, soon win the Afghan War and any other war we chose to engage in. Counterinsurgency and the surge became the watchwords of the ever faithful, tools to realize a very ideological (and frankly warlike) agenda as to how America can always get its way in the world.

With Iraq defined as a security situation, rather than a political problem involving local players who did not cooperate well together, politics became reduced to another element of COIN. Diplomacy, the set of deployed skills necessary to get people to do things they didn't otherwise want to do, also became a subfield of COIN. In the fine print of COIN there was the calculation that U.S. forces in any particular conflict would need years to complete the mission, probably more years than the American people, or frankly any people, had the patience to endure. The fine print got smudged and came to be interpreted to the effect that long-term follow-on force would not be more soldiers, but rather more diplomats. Thus the diplomatic effort became an essential part of the "whole of government" approach so often ballyhooed in Washington: the total war effort, the marshaling of all instruments of power behind the tip of the military's spear. Proponents of the war now looked to diplomacy to address the "nonkinetic space" (to use a particularly irksome military term), where they understood the war could be won or lost.

Coming out of the pressure cooker of North Korean negotiations, where half the Bush administration opposed the negotiating process, I had thought that those working on the gut-wrenching issues of Iraq, however stressed, were united in their cause. In fact, nerves were frayed on a daily basis and blame-game politics seldom took much of a break. The military had its internal issues, but so did the State Department in trying to run an embassy that had outgrown any conceivable economies of scale, out of proportion with everything else the department was doing in the rest of our 194 posts around the world (with the exception of Kabul, which was also fast ramping up), as the inevitability of the military's departure became clear. Much of what I saw on my arrival in April 2009 was the effort by the military to set up the State Department as the successor organization in charge of Iraq.

But letting go is hard to do, and the military was clearly uncertain whether the State Department, much less Embassy Baghdad, was ready for the responsibility. The military and its civilian camp followers were used to running everything in Iraq. Iraqi national security meetings held on Sunday nights included U.S. military officials as well as (for civilian sensitivities) the U.S. and British ambassadors, even though the British had pulled their troops out and could not even agree with the Iraqis on a residual maritime patrolling mission. I was appalled by the idea that anyone but Iraqis should be in attendance at an Iraqi national security meeting, but was told to avoid thinking that anything in Iraq should be what is considered normal elsewhere.

I soon learned that the word *normal*, which I always thought was on balance a good thing, was taken as a sign that the person did not really understand Iraq, a bellwether of that person's naïve state of mind. To suggest that our goal should be a normal place was a failure to understand what had gone on there, and what would probably continue to go on there for some time. "We have stayed more than a half century in Germany," was the supposed barn burner of an argument, whose reference to Iraq was in fact not particularly persuasive.

All this yielded a peculiar form of political correctness. In a talk on Iraq I gave at the Brookings Institution in Washington in the summer of 2009, I explained Iraq's oil bidding process to a group of think tank researchers from around Washington and laid out the challenge of the coming parliamentary elections. I spoke of the progress being achieved, the jockeying for political advantage, the fact that the sullen Sunnis were clearly in a mood this time to try to unite and take part in the political process, albeit with the understanding that Iraq would continue to be run by a Shia, and of the growing sense of achieving normal politics, even though for the foreseeable future parties would tend to build their platforms along the sectarian divide. The organizer of the event, Brookings scholar Kenneth Pollack, a liberal interventionist of the 1990s and a strong advocate for the Iraq intervention, rushed up to me after the talk and warned, "Be careful. Don't use the word *normal* around these people."

Even embassy briefings for visitors were not what I would consider normal. I have taken part in numerous embassy staff meetings and briefings over the course of my thirty years, from discussions of who to invite to the Fourth of July reception, to deciding whether to evacuate Embassy Skopje in the wake of the assault by an angry mob. In Sarajevo, I sat with Ambassador Menzies to discuss ongoing embassy operations during a bloody part of the siege of the city by Serb heavy weapons. In Warsaw during General Jaruzelski's martial law, we discussed how to deal with the pressure that was mounting on the embassy to cease its outreach to the Polish public. But nothing in my experience prepared me for my first briefing at Embassy Baghdad.

In a session for several U.S. governors whose national guards were on duty in Iraq, I walked down to the embassy's Conference Room. I noticed that on my side of the table I was in the center, with General Odierno immediately on my right. To his right, the remaining five seats, as well as to my left the remaining four seats, were all reserved for senior military, who would explain to the five governors ongoing military operations, and deployment and withdrawal schedules.

I took my seat next to Ray, looked behind me, and saw that all the backbenchers were in military uniform. I followed the line of uniformed aides behind me going to my left, and finally, after the end of the conference table, still on a back bench, I saw a solitary political officer flipping through what looked like a stack of Arabic press clips. Glad he was busy, I thought. Looking on the bright side, I thought perhaps he was confident of my ability to master my part of the briefing without receiving any whispered factoids. Given how far away he was seated, he would have practically needed a telephone to tell me anything. I glanced across the conference table and noticed that all the coffee cups at the place settings for the governors were emblazoned with the letters MNF-I (Multinational Forces—Iraq). Each governor also had in front of him a pad of paper and a U.S. military pen, as well as a large coin, the size of a drink coaster, with General Odierno's signature and the seal of MNF-I, a lamassu (a human-headed winged bull) from Nimrud, the capital of ancient Assyria.

I looked at the lamassu at my own place setting and wondered whether the embassy conference room setup quite embodied the spirit of civilianizing the Iraq mission. To our right was an enormous screen on which would soon be shown the slides of the briefing. I realized why my political officer was half a mile away. He already knew that so-called joint embassy/MNF-I briefings had little input from the embassy. General Odierno briefed on the first sixteen slides. When slide seventeen flashed up on the screen it mentioned "Embassy" and the "Strategic Framework Agreement."

"Mr. Ambassador," General Odierno asked, using my honorific for the benefit of the visitors, "would you like to say a few words about the SFA?"

At the close of the briefing I bid farewell to the governors who were lining up to have their photos taken with the marine security guard, and called a quick embassy staff meeting. I asked whether this was how briefings had always been conducted, with the commanding general handling 95 percent of it while the ambassador sat like a bobblehead doll, nodding his approval. I asked whether during the so-called heyday of civilian-military cooperation, the Petraeus-Crocker period, this was how briefings were conducted. Petraeus, I was told, was in the lead, but he encouraged his "wingman" to jump in when he chose to do so. I told the staff that henceforth embassy briefings for VIPs should reflect, both in substance and style, the partnership between the civilian and military missions in Iraq. For starters, and I told them I would convey this to Odierno, that would mean there should be just as many suits at the table as uniforms, and following long-standing protocol, the ambassador, who is after all the president's representative, would lead the briefing. If there were going to be trinkets at each place setting, they needed to include something from the embassy.

"Don't we have a coffee cup with an embassy seal, or maybe an embassy baseball hat?" I asked. "Yes, sir, but who's going to pay for them?" came the lame answer. Our intrepid chief of staff, Chris Klein, leapt in before I could answer and said, "I will figure it out."

Odierno would soon come to my office to report that some of my staff had offended some of their military counterparts on these new procedures. I assured him that I would correct any problem immediately, but I wanted to make sure that he understood that no ambassador could sit in his own embassy and play a subservient role in a briefing for American elected leaders. I told him it was a first symbolic step in fulfilling the mandate President Obama had given me, had indeed given both of us, to begin civilianizing the U.S. presence in Iraq. He said he understood completely, and supported this effort, even if some of his staff, never having seen an embassy in operation before Iraq, did not. Ray related how his staff, including his British national political advisor, had to take the lead in organizing for President Obama's visit in March, including having his British political advisor contact Prime Minister Maliki and deliver him to the airport for his meeting with President Obama. "What was the embassy doing?" I asked, incredulously. "I don't know, but I am sure glad that that will change." I appreciated his collegiality, which never wavered during our time together in Iraq.

Within a couple of weeks, however, some journalists in the United States were reporting that Odierno and Hill were in conflict. Odierno told me repeatedly that he never, ever implied such a thing with anyone, let alone a journalist, and that he didn't know where in the world it was coming from. I never had a reason not to believe him. Ray and I spent many evenings together in each other's quarters, sometimes one-on-one, sometimes with close-in staff. We smoked cigars, talked lots of football and baseball, and, of course, discussed our common mission and why we must succeed. We met senior Iraqis together, and traveled together. Despite all the pressures on us in Iraq, never once were we ever short with each other.

However well Ray and I worked with each other, the command system in Iraq was problematic because of the dual system that existed between the ambassador, as the president's representative in-country, and the commanding general, who reports directly through his own chain of command in Washington (namely the secretary of defense). From the military's point of view, the notion of dual control in the "battle space" could never sit well with any commander, especially when the "battle space" overlapped as it did in Iraq with the role of civilians. Odierno limited integration of immediate staff with the embassy, preferring to retain his own structures and his own separate political advisor.

Political advisors, or "polads," are almost always drawn from the ranks of the Foreign Service on detail to the military. They normally have two main tasks: to help the commander interpret political developments on the ground, and to be a liaison with the embassy and to help the commander interpret embassy views. In the case of Iraq, Odierno employed on a personal services contract a very capable but independently minded British national. Prior to Iraq, she had never visited the United States, nor had she ever worked with a U.S. embassy before. She did, however, have an extensive background with British assistance programs in the Middle East, especially in the Palestine-controlled areas of the West Bank. Moreover, she impressively and courageously had been in Iraq almost the entire time since the allied invasion of 2003, certainly more time than any of the embassy political officers with whom she had challenging relations given their relative short time in country and her almost resident status. Unlike her embassy counterparts, she also was frequently featured in the international press with the dominant narrative, especially in the UK press, being that she had vociferously opposed the war but was now working with the U.S. military to help it right the mistakes of that intervention. She became a vigorous advocate of COIN, referring at one point to an alleged prior indifference to civilian casualties (what is sometimes called "collateral damage") as "mass murder." As she told the *New York Times* in one of her frequent on-the-record interviews, "When you drop a bomb from the air and it lands on a village and kills all those people and you turn around and say 'oh, we didn't meant to kill the civilians,' well, who do you think was living in the village?" Such comments did not always endear her to Americans. Neither did her on-the-record endorsement of the U.S. military as an institution somehow better than the United States itself: "America doesn't deserve its military."

Indeed, managing these civil-military relationships in times of war is the stuff of lengthy books, and for good reason. In the case of Iraq, the perception that the State Department somehow came late to the action never really went away. As big as the embassy was, it was a tiny part of vast Camp Victory. The main chancery with its large atrium was a small outbuilding compared to the main palace at El Faw, which housed the offices of General Odierno and his many senior flag officers. I would often joke to Odierno, "Welcome to FOB [Forward Operating Base] Embassy."

Ambassadors sometimes have an imperious reputation, but at most posts that simply isn't the case. In the mornings I would walk by myself, certainly no aides in tow, from the house to the embassy, greeting the Indonesian cook, the Bulgarian gardeners, and Peruvian guards along the way. As I entered the embassy building carrying a briefcase and unread newspapers, I would salute the marine on duty on my way to the office, managing to open every door on my own without any assistance. When General Odierno came to the embassy for a meeting or to his large office suite near mine, fifteen to twenty aides accompanied him, a surrounding sea of green. Posted ahead of him and his entourage would be enlisted men at each door, sometimes waiting ten minutes to hold the door while the general and his aides passed through. In addition, a security team would have pre-positioned themselves for his trip through our atrium, blocking anyone from walking across it in anticipation of the "move-ment" of the commanding general, procedures that were not particularly welcomed by embassy employees. General Odierno was the last person to insist on such attention, and I am sure would have discontinued the practice if someone had brought it to his attention. But Ray probably inherited the system from his predecessor, who inherited it from his, and so on.

Joint meetings in the embassy were another teachable moment. Embassy political and economic officers would discuss economic assistance matters, and whether we would be able to get a congressional committee to approve our assistance budget in time. General Odierno and his staff would shake their heads in disbelief at the paltry sums involved, well to the right of the decimal point for the numbers that he dealt with on a daily basis. "Twelve million dollars?" he exploded. "The future of the police training program hangs on whether we can get twelve million dollars?" He offered to fund it from an account that was the equivalent of petty cash.

To some extent, the State Department's budget problems engendered sympathy from our colleagues in uniform, but they also fostered a sense that the State Department is so small and incompetent it cannot even raise $12 million for one of its most pressing needs.

The military also was careful to make sure it had allies back in Washington, and plenty of them. Visiting journalists, academics, and think tankers were invited, often at taxpayers' expense, to spend several days embedded with units to see operations from the ground level while soldiers and officers were encouraged to speak freely about the day-to-day challenges, and share their emails for future contacts. The overall effect was to create an atmosphere in which the visitor was convinced that any and all problems were being fully aired and addressed by the military, not to speak of the opportunity to develop terrific sources in the field.

The definition of Iraq as a security problem now on a fast track to being solved—thanks to the surge!—of course missed the main point of what the country's challenges were. Sitting on the fault line of the Shia and

Sunni world, Iraq had security problems that were a symptom of deeper political problems that no one who understood the situation could believe would go away any time soon. Iraq's Shia community, so long oppressed by the Sunni minority, had no intention of returning power to the Sunnis. Many foreign visitors, especially those who view the 1,300-year-old Sunni-Shia divide as just another challenge in the security environment, saw sectarianism as a by-product of weak governance and poor economic performance, a passing inconvenience rather than a main driver of the crisis. After all, sectarian killing had been reduced because of the surge. Soon, the thinking went, it would be eliminated with a stronger economy and the emergence of "issues-based" politics. The surge was the wonder drug for all that ailed Iraq, even centuries of sectarian political conflict.

In fact, during the several elections that had taken place since 2004, rarely did Sunnis vote for Shia or vice versa. The sectarian conflict that broke out so horribly in 2006–2007 represented not just frustrations in the Sunni community about the "de-Baathification campaign" so clumsily and inopportunely launched that to this day no one in the Bush administration acknowledges who made that decision to begin it. The Sunni insurrection represented a deeper frustration that they (along with their cousins in Syria) were the only Sunnis in the Arab world being forced to live under the indignity of Shia rule. The State Department Arabists, trained in previous assignments throughout the (Sunni) Arab world, were an ideal choice to try to work with the Sunni community in Iraq, but Sunnis in Iraq could not put to rest the fact that the United States had turned a Sunni Arab country into a Shia Arab country, a potential gift to Shia-led Iran. They could not understand why the Americans had done this, and neither could some of our own Arabists who believed the 2003 invasion was a mistake for that reason alone.

Nor could the Shia, who believed that sooner or later the Sunnis would expect to return to power. With Americans drawing down in 2010, and the election process gearing up, the Sunnis expected that moment to come very soon.

But as essential as the Sunni-Shia fault line was to understanding Iraq's politics, many Iraqis themselves, especially educated classes, preferred to downplay its significance in conversations with foreigners, as if sectarianism were a family secret that to acknowledge would be to suggest that the country's politics were divided along embarrassingly primitive lines. Thus, the leadership of the Iraq National Party, "Iraqiyya," never spoke about its Sunni origins. Nor did the leadership of "State of Law," Maliki's election coalition, admit to foreigners that it was a Shia party. Each accused the other of sectarianism.

At 7 A.M. on May 25, 2009, most of the embassy employees and I stood outside the chancery while a bugler played a moving, even haunting version of taps. I gave a short speech on the meaning of Memorial Day, explaining why those who lost their lives in Iraq did not do so in vain, but rather to ensure a new beginning in Iraq and to do their duty to our country. We must, I paraphrased from the Gettysburg Address, take renewed devotion from their sacrifice and complete the unfinished business.

A few yards away, a convoy of Chevy Suburbans stood ready for the end of the ceremony and a trip to Anbar Province to inspect a water treatment facility under construction near Fallujah. Standing outside his vehicle ready to jump in was Terry Barnich, a three-year Embassy Baghdad veteran, the deputy director of U.S. reconstruction projects. Just a couple of weeks before, Terry and I had been throwing a lacrosse ball around, and Terry, the ultimate team player, had then ordered a dozen lacrosse sticks to help form a small club. "We need some exercise around here," Terry explained.

That Memorial Day, at around 3:30 P.M. near Fallujah, Terry together with Navy Commander Duane Wolfe and a civilian contractor, Dr. Maged Hussin, were killed when their Chevy Suburban triggered an improvised explosive device (IED). Their remains were brought back to the embassy that night. Terry's lacrosse sticks arrived in the mail the next day, now part of his estate. The deaths of our colleagues affected the entire embassy. Barnich was very popular, his water projects so obviously helpful to the Iraqis, and yet he died in a senseless attack. I thought about what

Katharina Frasure had said to me on going out to the Balkans soon after Bob's death, "How can you do this to your family?"

Soon after I arrived in Iraq, I was asked to produce a weekly memo for the president to update him on what was going on in Iraq. This request turned into a monthlong tug of war between the NSC staff and the State Department, because if I was to write a regular memo, surely it should be addressed to the secretary first. Finally, in a decision worthy of King Solomon, it was decided that the memo would go to both the president and the secretary, but it would first make its way to the State Department, addressed "Madam Secretary," so that the secretary could read and reflect on it, then forward it on to the president with her own cover note.

On May 27, 2009, I began the series of memos that gave further details about the loss of our three colleagues two days before, discussed the Iraqi efforts to invite international oil companies for tenders and addressed some of the Iraqi challenges in normalizing relations with neighboring Kuwait (Saddam Hussein had invaded Kuwait almost twenty years before, and yet sanctions on contemporary Iraq were still in place). I also weighed in on discussions with the interagency committee on what kind of Iraq election law we should support (whether closed-list candidates or open list, though I thought this was a subject more appropriately discussed in Iraq by Iraqis, rather than among well-meaning micro-managers in Washington), explained the state-of-play on developing a mechanism for dealing with the Kurdish-Arab internal boundary disputes, and concluded with some thoughts about the upcoming visit to Washington of Prime Minister Maliki.

The State Department had put up a ferocious fight to make sure these memos did not go directly to the White House, but in fifteen months of writing them, I never received a single comment from anyone in the State Department. President Obama was the only person I ever heard from on the weekly memo. During a briefing Odierno and I gave to him in the Oval Office, he noticed the content of the briefing overlapped with that week's memo. "You covered that in last week's memo," he said. I was impressed by the fact that at least someone reads back there.

It was increasingly clear that Iraq remained the military's problem, not the State Department's. It is not to say that Iraq was not on people's minds in Washington. But it was increasingly a legacy issue, a matter of keeping faith with our troops rather than seeing Iraq as a strategic issue in the region.

Shia-led Iraq did not fit into any broader theme that the administration was trying to accomplish in the Middle East. The launching of former Senate majority leader George Mitchell's mission as the Middle East envoy had been grounded almost immediately by the decision to press the Israelis for a settlement freeze as a precondition to the resumption of talks. In June 2009, Mitchell's team began to consider options for how to approach President Bashar al Assad in Damascus to explore whether there might be flexibility on the issue of the Golan Heights. CENTCOM commander Petraeus had taken the view that the Syrians had in fact been helpful on the increasingly peaceful border with Iraq, and that this level of cooperation should be rewarded with a senior U.S. trip to Damascus and discussions with Assad about broader issues. A senior-level trip to Damascus on Middle East peace would be controversial enough, so a cover story was concocted in which the discussion would involve border stability with Iraq. The department asked me to inform Maliki of our intentions to talk with Assad, and to reassure him that the discussions were very preliminary, and that if they went anywhere they would surely not involve any requests made of the Iraqis.

I had already met with Maliki on several occasions in my first few weeks at post. He was intelligent and thoughtful, tending to get down to business faster than the average Iraqi politician. He had a dry sense of humor, and some irony that also eluded many of his contemporaries, not to speak of Washington visitors often frustrated at the lack of any English language capacity. Apart from saying "very good" excessively to visitors, Maliki appeared to offer very little. Extremely thin-skinned, he devoted much of his interpersonal skills to detecting any slights, real or imagined. Fortunately, this extreme sensitivity did not appear to extend to the casual clothing sometimes chosen by Washington visitors to the war zone. Maliki wore dark suits and dark neckties seemingly every day of the year.

He listened to the reassurances I offered on Syria, and thanked me for the heads-up. Then, at first politely, and later not so, he got to the point, "You Americans have no idea what you are dealing with in that regime," he said. "Everything for those people is a negotiation, like buying fruit in a market." He gestured at the luncheon table. "If you even mention us [Iraq], Assad will see it as something you are concerned about losing and will make you pay in the negotiation for it. Please do not even say the word *Iraq* to him. Just keep it on your Middle East negotiations. That is your business, not mine." Okay, I thought. That became a typical meeting with Maliki. Not a lot of fun, but at least I know where he stood.

So much, I thought, for the idea that Maliki had some kind of special relations with the Assad regime. I sent the telegram in to the department. Within a few days I learned from the embassy's political-military counselor, Michael Corbin, who was soon to become the Iran-Iraq deputy assistant secretary and briefly visiting Washington in preparation for that assignment, that the proverbial road to Damascus had been closed for permanent repair. Not that I had thought it a particularly good idea to go there in the first place, but I asked Michael why the idea had been shelved, and whether Maliki's skepticism had played any role. "No idea," he told me, reflecting the chaotic information flow in Washington. "But I'm sure it had nothing to do with what anyone in Iraq said about it."

As the Obama administration spent its first six months sorting out who was going to do what, it was increasingly unclear in fact just who was doing what. An embassy, especially a large player like Embassy Baghdad, needs someone in D.C. to watch its back. I had had high hopes that Undersecretary Bill Burns would play that role, but he seemed to have been asked to do everything not Iraq, including taking on the task of ensuring that Iran policy would not be taken over by the White House with the creation of a special envoy position. Although special envoy Dennis Ross, a former Middle East envoy and an internationally respected expert on the region, was to sit at the department, the ease with which he enjoyed relationships in the White House (indeed, all across Washington) made it understandable why the secretary had wanted a crafty operator like Bill to shadow that issue.

The decision to pull Bill away from Iraq meant that our backstop would be Deputy Secretary James Steinberg. Although a political appointee, Jim had had vast experience in the State Department and the White House during the Clinton administration and could be counted on as a steady presence in the interagency process, often a microwave cookbook of bad, half-baked ideas (such as micro-managing what kind of candidate lists to have in the Iraqi election law). Jim had an appetite for facts and figures, and a talent for taking any idea, good or bad, and analyzing the perils of it in such a way that soon everyone would want to wheel it back into the garage for further work. Jim saved people from themselves on a daily basis.

But within months, there were rumors that Jim was unhappy with his role at State. Jim was above all a foreign policy realist, especially on China, where he had delivered a thoughtful speech on the need to overcome "strategic mistrust" (during the first term of the Obama administration the word *strategic* was often married with another word, for example *patience*, to convey thoughtfulness in foreign policy), but his reflections on China were not necessarily what the administration was looking for at the time. He seemed increasingly unhappy with the more strident tone the Obama administration was taking on China and other issues. I knew he could not be counted on for long to carry water for us back in Washington.

The Near Eastern Bureau leadership was often criticized for being inadequately seized with Israel's agenda. Many of NEA's leaders had already done their Iraq time and had no intention of doing any more if they could avoid it. Iraq, so the thinking went, was someone else's problem—especially the military's, and rarely did Shia-led Iraq help on any regional issues that NEA was concerned about. Assistant Secretary Jeff Feltman, a veteran Arabist who had had a career in the region in small but important posts, culminating as ambassador in war-torn Lebanon, seemed particularly distressed by Iraq, insofar as it caused him problems with the rest of the region and with the Pentagon suspicions that the State Department lacked commitment. Iraq got the bureaucratic reputation as a loser, something to stay away from. No question, Shia-led Iraq was the black sheep of the region, with no natural allies anywhere.

Meanwhile, NEA was far more concerned that George Mitchell's Middle East peace efforts be integrated with its own. The bureau was always focused on the elusive peace in the Middle East, but it also was the traditional sounding board for ambassadors from the Gulf Arab states and peninsular Arab states to come into the State Department and complain about their neighbors—in this case about Shia Iraq. The Saudis were the most vociferous of these—repeatedly accusing Maliki of "lying to the king," without offering any details of what the alleged prevarication was. In turn, I would receive messages from the department to go in and tell Maliki he had a problem with the Saudis and needed to solve it. I never got very far with him.

In June 2009, President Obama announced that Vice President Biden would take on special responsibilities for Iraq. I welcomed the vice president's involvement, especially since no one else seemed to have our back in Washington. There was the usual Washington silliness that followed the announcement. First, that the president was fobbing the issue off (in fact, the vice president is a pretty senior person). Then, that Secretary Clinton wasn't interested (her plate was rather full trying to deal with the rest of the world). After that passed, Biden jumped in, and soon I would receive telephone calls that often started with "Hey Chris, this is Joe." The vice president (I never called him Joe, nor did anyone else that I could see) visited Iraq on the Fourth of July, and his interest never wavered. He brought with him a talented staff, including Tony Blinken and Herro Mustafa.

On June 30, 2009, Prime Minister Maliki gave a speech to announce a major development in the U.S.-Iraqi Security Agreement. The occasion was the anniversary of the 2003 assassination of the Iraqi Shia leader Ayatollah Mohammed Baqir al-Hakim. After a few words in memory of the fallen ayatollah, Maliki shifted gears to describe the moment that U.S. forces would withdraw from populated areas as a great victory for the Iraqi people, which did not sit well with those who had backed the war effort. After all, Maliki was suggesting that what had happened was the U.S. forces had in effect been ordered to retreat. But as he talked more about the sacrifice that must attend such a great victory, I began to understand better what he was saying. In essence, Maliki was acknowledging that the Iraqi forces that would soon take over checkpoints and mobile patrols would have their problems doing so. He was bracing people for more casualties to follow.

I understood what he was saying, but it sure didn't win him any friends in Washington. Ray Odierno spoke with him soon thereafter to tell him he needed to make a gesture, suggesting that during his upcoming visit to Washington he visit Arlington National Cemetery and lay a wreath. He did so, but it was too little, too late. Maliki's reputation never recovered in Washington, and complaints about him, whether in matters of human rights or relations with Sunni neighbors, or his attitudes toward Americans, or political alliances within Iraq, all seemed to reinforce each other with the conclusion that Iraq would be better off with a new prime minister, perhaps one who did not seem systematically to upset every conceivable constituent group. Nonetheless, Maliki was a formidable player who could outwork and often outthink his rivals. For years, U.S. officials had looked for a strong Iraqi leader, and having found one they objected to the fact that he didn't do what he was told. As Bob Frasure had once said about a certain Balkan leader, "We wanted a junkyard dog like this for a long time. Why would people expect him to start sitting in our lap?"

The Washington-based concerns about Maliki, reinforced by the complaints from other Arab countries, gave rise to the view that somehow we needed to replace him, as if this were our responsibility let alone within our capability. Foreign ambassadors in Baghdad, having heard the discontent reported by their colleagues in Washington, came to my embassy to ask me, "So, how are you going to get rid of him?" as if I had instructions to do so. My sense was that these foreign ambassadors were hearing typical Washington grousing and were then pole-vaulting to the conclusion that we were hatching a plan. Obviously that was not the case, but I could tell that the talk was reaching the ever paranoid Maliki and not helping our relationship with him. I could see that a similar process was unwinding in Afghanistan. Even if the United States were a latter-day Roman Empire as some neocon pundits seemed to want, we still have to work with local leaders like Maliki and Afghanistan president Hamid Karzai. Our ability to cooperate with them is not facilitated by reports that we are trying to get rid of them.

But even if we wanted to topple Maliki, you can't beat something with nothing, and the Iraqi political landscape was not exactly blooming with new political prospects. As sparse as that landscape looked to me, I never lacked for advice coming from Washington, where some seemed to think that choosing Iraqi leaders was akin to forming a fantasy football team. People who had served in Iraq, and for whom time froze when they left, increasingly manned Iraq policy. Thus I was treated to suggestions, often in the form of admonishments, as to why I hadn't recently visited such-and-such a politician, who, I was to glean, had been some kind of hot prospect back in 2004 and 2005.

The months wore on, through the hot summer and then the fall of 2009, punctuated by an enormous truck bomb that had devastated the Foreign Ministry building and killed several hundred people. I was visiting Kirkuk that day, but people in the embassy, miles from the ministry, reported they could feel the blast in their offices.

I visited the victims who had been taken to the U.S. hospital for emergency help in attempting to remove shards of glass that were dangerously lodged near vital organs and in their eyes. Victims lay on hospital cots, bloody gauze everywhere. Some moaned, but most stayed quiet in their misery as family members gathered around each bed. Whether it was because they were dazed or whether because they were Iraqis, nobody complained. Later in the day I went to the Foreign Ministry, where I saw the extent of the damage, the façade ripped off to reveal what had been normally functioning offices just seconds before. There was an enormous crater where the tractor-trailer truck had been parked in front of the building on the near lane of a four-lane road. Nearby automobiles, including a lime-green taxi, had been hurled into the air and had somehow landed on the other side of the road; bloodstains were easily visible on the doors and windows of the taxi.

Foreign Minister Zebari met me in a makeshift ground-floor office, smiling and otherwise indicating that there had been but a minor disturbance, rather like a leak in a water main or an interruption in the electricity. He clearly had emerged from the horror determined not to allow it to defeat him, drawing on an inner toughness that his years in the mountains of Kurdistan had given him. He took me on a tour of the ground floor and introduced me to the structural engineer, who pronounced the building sound and ready for reconstruction as soon as the cleanup, already fast under way, was finished. Nobody seemed interested in the American forensic investigators' advice to leave things as they happened to allow "evidence" to be collected. Everyone wanted to clean it up and try to forget it happened. "How long will it take to rebuild it?" I asked the engineer.

"Oh," he said, looking at the chaos around us, "maybe about twelve months, not longer." Zebari added, "Less, if we have Kurdish companies do the work."

On May 18, 2010, some eight months later, a consortium of Kurdish companies finished their work and the ministry was open for business. The front lobby, which had been totally destroyed yet miraculously had held up the building above it, was transformed and beautifully decorated, a newly installed plaque on the side listing the names of the dead. The ceremony included goose-stepping soldiers wearing white tunics and white pith helmets of the kind that would have looked more familiar in the kaiser's army, who laid wreaths during a ceremony presided over by Prime Minister Maliki and Foreign Minister Zebari.

The soldiers stomped on the polished marble floor with a determination that seemed to symbolize the moment. Junior officers stood at their office desks on all floors, explaining to visitors like me where they had been at the bombing but much more interested in describing their current duties: "I handle Iraq's relations with Southeast Asia. . . . I manage relations with South America. My Spanish is good, but I am also learning English." I so admired them and what they did, and felt as never before in Iraq a sense of brotherhood and common cause. I concluded my memo to the secretary and president that week with a description of the reopening, and closed with the thought that one got the sense from every Iraqi minister, goose-stepping soldier, and junior diplomat that if it happened again, they would rebuild everything, and go on from there.

The fall of 2009 was a daily grind in Iraq's political corridors as we lobbied the parties for the passage of an election law, on the basis of which there could be an election in early 2010. I met with the speaker of the parliament, a slow-talking, gentlemanly Sunni Islamist named Iyad Samarrai, repeatedly in early October to press for the progress that Washington was demanding. Samarrai's laconic pace was in sharp contrast to the impatience in Washington for progress. The embassy's political section, under Gary Grappo, spent far more time in the Council of Representatives (Iraq's parliament) than in the embassy (and, frankly, more time than some Iraqi parliamentarians), and at night drew up the reporting cables for Washington. The Iraqis understood they needed to agree on an election law, but they would do so on their timetable, not ours. Hurrying them, as was Washington's instinct to do, seemed to reinforce in the Iraqi minds that what we really wanted was to get an election, a new government, and pull our troops out. In diplomacy, being in a hurry never makes things easier or even faster. I repeated on several occasions to the press corps and others that working on Iraq offers no refuge to those in need of instant gratification.

On November 8, the Iraqi Council of Representatives overwhelmingly approved an election law, a vote several of us watched later that Sunday night in my office. It was the culmination of weeks of effort and gallons of tea and coffee, served in windowless rooms in the basement of the parliament during discussions with small caucuses of politicians, most of whom were heavy smokers. A day later President Obama called to thank me for the embassy's efforts to get the law passed. His tone was weary and perhaps a little wary about the news, as he knew from our reporting how precarious things had been. I tried to sound optimistic that progress was being made, and assured him we would stay engaged for the election cycle.

But on November 19, Vice President Tariq al-Hashimi, the Sunni representative to the collective presidency, which also consisted of the Kurdish president Talabani and the Shia vice president Adel Abd al-Mahdi, used the power vested as a member of the presidency to veto the law. I received the news while I was visiting a displaced persons registration office on the outskirts of Baghdad outside the Green Zone. It was a scene I knew all too well from my Balkan days, which combines hollow-faced despair with third world bureaucracy and red tape. Amid crowds of desperate Iraqis who had been thrown out of their homes during the worst of the sectarian violence, all seeking compensation allotments to survive another period of internal exile, in a narrow, poorly lit corridor I pressed up against the whitewashed wall to take the call from Gary Grappo on my cell phone. I listened to the bad news as I looked at the scene. "We'll have to start all over again, but we'll get it done," Gary concluded. I was still taking in the human misery at the registration center. "That's right, Gary. Pull the team together and see what can be done and get the cable off to Washington. I'd rather they get the bad news from us."

Hashimi was a former military officer, an English speaker who fell out early on with his fellow Sunni Saddam Hussein, and had political ambitions of his own, if only the Americans would come to understand that secular order in the country needed to be restored once they stopped supporting the Shia, almost all of whom, in Hashimi's view, were sectarian. The fluent-English-speaking Hashimi was articulate and well-spoken, and cut a reasonably impressive figure in his Western suits. He had been an early hope of the U.S. occupation to bring the Sunni community along in embracing the new Iraq. Those hopes had long faded and my visits to the frustrated Hashimi became more akin to a painful visit to the dentist. Like many senior Iraqis, Hashimi's home and office was an elegantly appointed palace in the Green Zone, where he held court with political operatives and with foreigners. He treated us to such downbeat assessments of Iraq's future that one went away thoroughly depressed despite his kitchen's unusually good fruit nectars.

Hashimi's main line of concern with me was the perfidy of the Shia (and Kurds), and with Odierno he spent the lion's share of his time seeking the immediate release of nefarious persons inexplicably, in his view, picked up by U.S. forces and held in detention centers. Ray always politely accepted to look into the matter, and would send back his political advisor to Hashimi with the bad news that the individuals in question could not be released at this time. The British-trained Hashimi would take advantage of Ray's British political advisor to give a further spin on how bad things were—and how they were getting worse—due, of course, to the Americans. He then would give her still more lists of persons in detention who in his view had done nothing wrong.

Hashimi vetoed the election law based on an issue that was very much a Sunni concern, but which had not played a major role during the parliamentary discussion of the law—the right of out-of-country Iraqis (read: Sunni refugees) to vote. Although the Council of Representatives (COR) could have easily overruled Hashimi, more Sunnis would have supported this "Sunni position," and the result would have been a sectarian divide in the COR, not something we wanted to see as an outcome. The narrative at the time was that somehow back in 2007 the U.S. had faced down the insurgency and in so doing singlehandedly put a thousand years of sectarianism in the rearview mirror (in some ten months of work), and we certainly didn't want to see its ugly head again. Of course, endemic centuries-old sectarianism could hardly have disappeared in a matter of a few months. Iraq's future would tell whether politics became more "issues based" rather than sectarian based, but for now, Sunnis supported Sunnis and Shia supported Shia, and the Kurds generally found ways to support the Shia against the Sunnis, whom they had mountains of reasons to distrust over the centuries.

Within weeks, a compromise was worked out on out-of-country (Sunni) voters. Gary Grappo and the rest of the political section convened direct talks between the Shia and Sunni caucus with our own deputy political counselor, Yuri Kim, sitting in the middle of lengthy discussions that went late into the night. I worried, as did Gary Grappo and the rest of the embassy's political section, that in reopening the text, now the Kurdish delegation to the COR would use the opportunity to gerrymander some districts in Kirkuk to make sure they would become Kurdish districts, and encroach on the dialogue about the status of the Kirkuk area, a subject of UN mediation. In turn, this move pitted some of the smaller minorities in the area, including the often put-upon Turkomans, with whom I had personally spent hours in a basement room of the COR. Vice President Biden, Washington's point man on Iraq, and President Obama were pressed into service making telephone calls to senior officials, including offering a Washington visit for Kurdish president Barzani.

I was pleased that Barzani was being offered a visit to Washington, but the motivation—to urge him to support the election law—was misplaced. Barzani was always working with us. "We want to be part of the solution, not part of the problem," he often told Ray and me. His problem, in Iraq's fractious political scene, was that he did not have absolute power over the Kurdish delegation in the COR, and like the rest of us could only cajole and try to convince this most stubborn of COR caucuses. The fact that even immediate postconflict societies have intense politics seemed lost on many people in Washington (and, alas, sometimes on our military), who believed that the issue was all about simply imploring people to do what we told them to do.

I welcomed Obama's and Biden's direct interest, but I knew that these senior-level phone calls were adding to the perception that the United States was desperate for an election law so that U.S. troops could be withdrawn. By signaling our interest in withdrawal, we began to lose more influence on the ground.

The high-level calls had another unhelpful impact on our efforts on the ground. They became part of the toolbox of our efforts, meaning that whenever there was an impasse on the ground, the idea of ginning up a telephone call quickly emerged on the to-do list. Senior phone calls also had still another negative impact on our efforts: Washington bureaucrats went operational. Thus we began to receive missives offering such nuggets of advice as "Never ignore Hashimi!" Of course, we had been in regular contact with him, but he wasn't the great hope that some of these veterans of the early years had thought. Some of the Washington micromanagement extended to offering me advice as to whom from the embassy I should bring along for meetings with Maliki and others. It all added up to an impression that Washington wanted out of Iraq.

The parliamentary election on March 7, 2010, was a peaceful day. U.S. troops, working with Iraqi counterparts, ensured security throughout the country, and the number of incidents was remarkably low. I barnstormed through the country on March 6 to meet with our Provincial Reconstruction Teams, from Mosul in the north down to Basra in the south. All had impressive plans for monitoring the vote the next day. Whether the Iraqis were ready or not, I knew that the embassy and our twenty-two reconstruction teams scattered around the country were prepared to do all we could. The rest would be up to the Iraqis.

And of course, as in the Balkans and elsewhere, we also had visiting American delegations to help monitor the elections. One group, the

National Foundation for Women Legislators, had monitored elections all over the world, and, thanks to the military, were to be taken around in heavily armored vehicles to monitor a few polling stations in Baghdad. I hosted a reception in my home two nights before and found myself in a pleasant conversation with one of the members from Texas, who, perhaps reflecting some of the concerns of her constituents, asked me, "Do the Iraqis have a plan for repaying us for introducing democracy to their country?"

Unfortunately for him, Foreign Minister Zebari stood nearby, and I pulled him over and repeated the question for him to respond to. I moved over to another part of the room before I could hear the answer.

The election results took weeks to tabulate, and when they finally came in they were very close. Ayad Allawi's Iraq National Party, or Iraqiyya, a party that was disproportionately Sunni, won 91 seats, while Maliki's State of Law coalition had 89 seats. A total of 163 seats would be needed to gain a majority of the 325-seat Council of Representatives, and it meant that the two top coalitions would be off to the races.

The difference between Maliki's and Allawi's approaches was striking. Maliki went to work, while Allawi went to CNN. Anytime I visited the prime minister's office I would have to pass a row of tribal chiefs waiting their turn to be wooed with some political favor in return for their willingness to support Maliki. Allawi thought it was enough to get on CNN to accuse Maliki of becoming the "new Saddam." Allawi also thought that what became known as the government formation period was a good occasion to fly around the Middle East and complain about Maliki. According to a Kurdish leader with good connections to the Egyptian government, Allawi had gone to Cairo to complain to President Hosni Mubarak about Maliki, prompting the Egyptian strongman to respond: "Why are you telling me this? I don't vote in Iraq. In fact, if the situation is as you describe, what are you even doing here?"

In a perfect parliamentary world, the party or coalition that garners the most seats is given the opportunity to form the government. If Iraq were part of that world, Ayad Allawi should have been given the right to form the government, having come through the elections with two more seats than Maliki. But the reality of the situation was that with both main coalitions in a statistical dead heat, neither was going to step aside for the other. We knew it would be a long, hot summer.

In addition to working harder on the ground for additional seats, Maliki also outpaced Allawi in aggressively challenging the vote count, a decision that opened him to the charge of being a sore loser, and a possible cheater. His recount demands also exposed him to the charge that he was ultimately not going to respect the results of the voting and might, as Ray Odierno suggested in a teleconference with Washington, try to stage a "rolling coup d'état." Ray surprised everybody with that comment. It was nothing he had ever said to me in private, nor had he taken that tone in any conversation with Maliki. I always tried to make sure we spoke with one voice on the teleconferences with Washington, but I fell silent when he expressed that opinion, especially as he hadn't warned me. The effect of his comment on Washington was to heighten concerns about Maliki's intentions.

Ray's staff often worried about the influence his British political advisor had over him, especially as she was known for harboring very strong opinions generally, and especially on the subject of Maliki. Indeed, Maliki's tough-minded behavior, his own bitter disappointment at not coming out ahead of Allawi, and his increasing feistiness on every issue were making him a thoroughly unlikable and unlikely candidate to replace himself. The foreign press corps was completely against him. Most foreign diplomats were against him, including the U.S. Embassy's own political section.

I noticed too that a pattern I had seen many times in the Balkans was playing out in Iraq: Iraqis would tell foreigners things that were different from what they would tell each other. Time and time again, a politician would say things like "never will I support Maliki," but two weeks later he would be in Maliki's office cutting a deal of some kind. Thus a foreign observer—especially a visitor—could come away with a very wrong-headed assessment of Maliki's relative support.

Maliki was far from my ideal candidate, but I had real doubts whether someone else was going to be able to unseat him. "Can't beat someone with no one," I kept repeating to Gary, Yuri, and other members of the political section, who always seemed to fall silent when I asked the question, "If not Maliki, then if you were king who do you suggest for prime minister?" as if it were our choice to make. As the crucial postelection weeks of April and May 2010 rolled by, Allawi spent more of his time traveling abroad, using a jet provided him by the Gulf states, and never building any additional political support beyond the ninety-one seats he already had. I also noticed that regardless of Maliki's volatile and at times ugly behavior, there seemed to be no swing from the other Shia blocs toward Allawi, despite kind words that people had for Allawi in discussions with foreigners.

The process suggested to me that much of what we were seeing from the other Shia was just bluster and an effort to give Maliki a well-deserved hard time, but that whenever Maliki was prepared to show some real respect and humility toward them, he could also gain their support. Maliki's Shia detractors had plenty of kind words for Allawi, but I could not see that any of them were truly prepared to support Allawi's Iraqiyya. Listening to the Kurds in Erbil, many describe Iraqiyya as a crypto-Baathist party. I became skeptical that Allawi's party would ever be allowed by the Shia and Kurds to become the governing party. He seemed to have no chance of increasing the number of seats through coalition building beyond the ninety-one he had won in the actual election.

Allawi was a Shia, but he was not a Shia leader. Those foreigners, and especially those foreigners who had not seen these political patterns in other countries, who believed that a Shia without Shia constituents could become prime minister in Iraq's current circumstances didn't understand the game being played. During my time in the Balkans, every leader I ever met had members of the other ethnicities at his side to claim that he had broader support than just his own people. But the fact that Milosevic had an Albanian or two in his delegation, or Tudjman had a Serb, or Izetbegovic had a Croat really did not change the basic political calculation.

The fact that the Sunni community had Allawi, a "secular Shia," as its leader did not have an impact on how the Shia voted. During the hard-fought campaign, Allawi never ventured into southern Iraq, where most of the Shia lived. In short, he did not make the slightest effort to gain Shia votes. I concluded that the government formation period was not going to be even close, but I hedged my comments to Washington, not wanting to seem pro-Maliki or anti-Allawi. I concluded we needed to focus on a better Maliki than he had been in his first four-year term, rather than engage in a quixotic effort to try to oust him.

By the end of April I was reporting to Secretary Clinton and President Obama that Allawi could not win, but that Maliki "remains a force to be reckoned with," however unpopular he was in some circles. I concluded in my note that "we need to be mindful that at the end of this messy process, Maliki could still wind up on top."

The thought that Maliki could ultimately win was not welcomed by many Iraq watchers, especially those for whom experience had taught them the bitter lesson to be very attentive to Sunni sensitivities. For these veterans of those painful times, a victory by the "secular" Iraqiyya seemed to be what the doctor ordered. But as secular as it looked to foreigners, within Iraq, especially among the Shia, Iraqiyya looked a lot like an all-in Sunni party. During the election campaign, Shia leaders, including the neoconservative hero Ahmed Chalabi, had waged what was an unspoken anti-Sunni campaign using the old de-Baathification boogeyman. Chalabi had been a consistent voice in Washington for the invasion, and was expected by many to assume a place in the Iraq senior leadership. As with many people who have been away from their country for decades, he wasn't as well-known in Baghdad as he was in Washington.

I spent numerous sessions over the months convincing Maliki to distance himself from this smear tactic, but Maliki understood the successful politics of it and was not going to completely disassociate himself. (Indeed, my efforts with him earned me a public rebuke from Maliki's spokesman for interfering in Iraq's politics.) Sectarianism was on the rise through the campaign, and the government formation period offered the prospect of things getting even worse.

After one of our daily, morning joint leadership meetings, in which Ray Odierno gave a glass-half-empty monologue for some ten minutes, complaining about Maliki's shortcomings, I half-jokingly told him and the others that "worrying is not a policy," nor is "pique a substitute for policy," Eagleburger's old line. If we thought it would be in our interest to steer things one direction or the other, we would certainly need support from Washington, but my reading was that the major concern was not who became prime minister, but rather the fact that the weeks were going by and there was no prime minister. I suggested we ought to support a "grand coalition" government and bring Maliki and Allawi together. Ray agreed, our staffs agreed, and even Washington agencies agreed that this would be our approach.

Encouraging Allawi and Maliki to work together was far-fetched stuff, but I had seen stranger bedfellows before (Izetbegovic and Tudjman, to name one such odd couple). Besides, the drift in Iraq politics during that spring was that Maliki was being forced to reach out to the other Shia parties, something that appeared attainable provided he was willing to eat a hefty portion of humble pie; but if he succeeded, it would exacerbate the Sunni-Shia rift. As much as the Sunnis tried to suggest (especially to uninformed foreigners) that Maliki was a sectarian/Iranian agent, in fact, State of Law under Maliki was one of the most secular of the Shia political structures. Enlisting to the Shia coalition the viscerally anti-American and populist Sadrists would not be a step forward toward more secular rule.

As I often did for an in-country sanity check, I went up to Kurdistan to meet with President Barzani. This time Barzani had a special treat in mind, hiking around the mountains of eastern Kurdistan. Certainly,

Barzani has his critics, but for me he was what I wished for in all the Iraqi politicians—sensible, intelligent, moderate, pragmatic, and with a sense of history (he and his father had lived it) and timing. He understood Iraqi Arab politics better than the Iraqi Arabs did. And while he, like most Kurds, wanted an independent homeland, he also understood that the best route to that destination lay through a positive and enduring relationship with the United States. We walked along the mountain ridges, looking out and up at rock-strewn and sharply pointed mountaintops, a wild and forbidding landscape in one of the world's most remote regions. Barzani, wearing his trademark Peshmerga khaki uniform with billowing trousers, a more traditional military shirt, and red and white checkered tribal turban, assured me, as he always did, "Don't worry. When the time is right, we will be part of the solution."

I was indeed worried. Our efforts to get Maliki and Allawi to work together were really going nowhere, and meanwhile there were growing signs that the Shia were beginning to tighten up their own internal lines of communication and perhaps even bring the Sadrists into the coalition to help Maliki increase his total of 89 seats to the 163 he needed to control the Council of Representatives. My team had arranged a meeting between Maliki and Allawi, down to furnishing each the cell phone number of the other so they could be in direct communication, but it seemed to have no carry-over effect, and I was left to believe that perhaps both leaders had agreed to meet to get us off their backs rather than for each other, much less for Iraq.

I suspected that Allawi knew what I also knew, that he did not have any chance of running the country. Allawi had a special problem, however. Many of the Sunni Arab states, especially in the Gulf, who had backed him—indeed bankrolled him—as head of Iraqiyya had also believed his promise that he could pull off the political miracle: essentially returning Iraq to a Sunni- or quasi-Sunni-based government. I tried to encourage NEA to spend less time listening to Sunni Arab states' complaints about Maliki and more time convincing them that Maliki was not an Iranian agent but wanted to play a role with the Arab states, provided they could get over the fact that he was a Shia leader. In fairness to NEA, their Gulf Arab interlocutors were not going to listen to a pitch about Shias in Iraq and change their minds, but I thought we needed to show more support and confidence in what we had essentially created in Iraq, that is, majority rule, which in the current context of political identity meant Shia-led rule.

I told President Obama and Secretary Clinton in my April 20 note to them that the risk of Iraq becoming an Iranian client state was "negligible" because there was far too much nationalism in the country for that to happen (nationalism that made foreign interference in the government formation process risky). The real problem, I pointed out to the president, was for Shia-led Iraq to become "an Arab outcast, isolated from and resentful of its neighbors."

In late April, I spent a day in Qatar visiting Al Jazeera studios, followed by another day in Oman, where I met for a couple of hours with the sultan. In Qatar, I sensed the depth of mistrust toward the Shia Iraqis, the fervent hope that Allawi's Iraqiyya would ultimately prevail and somehow restore the order of Iraq. But with the wise and deliberate sultan of Oman, I received a different message: that Americans needed to stop, in effect, jamming square pegs into round holes. "Your country is welcomed in this part of the world, but be respectful of what you encounter on the ground, what the forces are, and that sometimes change can come in the air, and when it does it can be difficult to analyze just in terms of politics."

The sultan talked about Maliki in historical terms, not just in terms of the politics of the moment. He sat in his armchair, in his flowing robes, a large embroidered sash around his small waist, with a ceremonial dagger, its precious stones and brilliant colors reflecting in the light, tucked in the front. The conversation concluded after about ninety minutes, but I could have listened to him all night. Iraq was different from other countries, with two rivers and a unique history that flow through it, he explained.

My goodness, I thought as I slowly walked out of his palace, still pondering his wisdom. How I wished the sultan could address the interagency meetings back in Washington.

On May 10, in my note to the president and secretary I emphasized again that in consultations across the political spectrum of Iraq (except for the Sadrists, whose vitriolic views of the American presence meant that we had only minimal contacts over the years) "none" of them could see Allawi's way to the prime minister position. I met on several occasions with Ammar al-Hakim, the leader of the Supreme Council of Iraq (ISCI), another major Shia party. Hakim's party had not fared well in the elections, but because he was a frequent critic of Maliki and Maliki's Dawa party, I looked for clues whether Hakim's often kind words for Allawi might eventually become outright support. It never happened. Instead it was a useful reminder that what Iraqi politicians tell foreigners should not be confused with what goes on inside Arab councils.

In the meantime, Bill Roebuck and Eric Carlson, two members of our very strong and active political section, worked with President Talabani's staff to draft an Iraqi presidential statement, effectively ending the notorious "Accountability and Justice Commission," aka the de-Baathification Committee, which Chalabi and his henchmen had used to try to ban Sunni politicians from taking their seats in the new Council of Representatives.

While the political stalemate continued, on May 28 I took a day trip along with General Vince Brooks, the enormously gifted commander of our forces in the south of Iraq, and senior British Petroleum officials down to the Rumaila oil field to see Weatherford International, an American drilling company based in Houston, Texas, and working for BP, as they struck oil.

May 2010 was an unusual time to be extolling the virtues of BP. Just a month before in the Gulf of Mexico, on April 20, a BP offshore well had blown out, killing eleven workers and spilling 200 million gallons of crude oil, endangering the wetlands and beaches along much of the Gulf

Coast of the United States. But in Iraq, BP's investment and start-up operations represented a crucial and hopeful moment for the future.

Iraq had not seen a foreign oil producer search for oil on its territory in more than forty years, due to a combination of Iraq's own nationalistic policies and international sanctions. The consequence was that oil was in the hands of various Iraqi state oil companies whose own technology levels, not to speak of their environmental record, had much to be desired. Flying over Iraq would reveal pools of oil sitting in the desert, and at night flares of gas illuminating the desert.

Given the role that oil had played in the international debate about the war in the first place, populist nationalistic sentiments in Iraq against foreign oil companies continued to persist despite Iraq's desperate need for foreign investment. These sentiments, which were strongest among Iraq's oil worker unions, combined with a political deadlock over the sharing of power and wealth between the provinces and the central authorities. Both acted to thwart progress in passing the hydrocarbon legislation in Iraq's fractious legislative body. Proposed legislation had sat in the Council of Deputies since early 2007 with little prospect for approval.

The embassy's interest in Iraqi oil was never to safeguard the oil for American companies, but rather to ensure that whatever process the Iraqis agreed on, it would be fair and transparent to all the oil companies. As much as oil was publicly discussed as a motivation for the war, it was never really considered in those terms. Rather, from the president on down, oil was described as a huge revenue source for the Iraqis, and as a potential means to help keep the Kurds within the Iraqi state, the three provinces of Iraq that made up the Kurdish Regional Government.

When Secretary Clinton arrived for her whirlwind, six-hour visit back in April 2009, Iraqi deputy prime minister Barham Salah informed her of a very tentative plan to move ahead with technical service contracts even in the absence of the hydrocarbon legislation. The Iraqis, under Oil Minister Hussain al-Shahristani, had launched this process in 2008 along with a prequalification review, only to drop the proposal later that year in the face of political and labor opposition. This time, according to Salah, they seemed ready to move to approve long-term contracts in the absence of the elusive hydrocarbon law. The Iraqi concept was to retain ownership of the fields and pay for the production activity with oil. He asked for technical assistance in the form of an American advisor.

The embassy's economic section immediately got to work. By coincidence we had an oil expert, an academic, coming to Iraq anyway. After two weeks of working with the Oil Ministry he endorsed the Iraqi plan as feasible even in the absence of the much-anticipated hydrocarbon legislation.

Back on June 30, 2009, the first bid round opened in a ballroom in the al-Rashid Hotel with television lights and cameras turned on as representatives of major oil companies made their way to the stage to deposit their bids in a large Plexiglas urn. I watched the show on live television, suspecting that the oil companies, as their representatives had told me, were not going to be aggressive in trying to meet the Iraqi demands. The embassy's economic section, led by John Desrocher and his deputy, John Carwile, and our oil expert, Patrick Dunn, were present for the bid. There was a buzz in the room as the bidding got under way, but when Oil Minister Shahristani announced there would be no sharing of profits, but rather a fixed price paid for each barrel, there was a stunned silence, and some laughter when he announced the figure two dollars above the benchmark. As it turned out, only BP and a Chinese partner (the China National Petroleum Corporation, CNPC) won their bid for one of the major blocks, the Rumaila field, with estimated reserves in excess of 17 billion barrels. The international press pronounced the event a complete failure. After all, the Iraqis had put up some of the largest oil fields in the world and had failed to reach their minimal demands.

The international press had a field day with the apparent failure of the bidding process, while other Middle East countries, which had been somewhat worried about Iraq's potential as a rival, breathed a sigh of relief.

I invited Oil Minister Shahristani to my home to talk about the situation, and to my surprise he told me that in fact he was very pleased with what had happened. Importantly for him, there were some Iraqi oil worker protests of the BP bid, but overall his concerns about mounting antiforeign sentiment never materialized. BP, he pointed out, was not exactly an insignificant player, and had jumped in on Iraqi terms to take the largest field. By the end of July 2009, the BP contract was approved, and Shahrastani was fast putting together plans for a next round of bids.

I briefed Vice President Biden, who visited a few days after the bidding round, during the Fourth of July holiday, and told him that the situation had gone better than many believed and that Shahrastani had plans for another round. I told him that there might be another benefit to how the Iraqis were handling their oil. If other major companies follow BP's lead, that might start to convince the Kurds that their interests are served by staying in Iraq and getting their share of the giant amounts of oil that will be produced in southern Iraq.

"You mean oil can actually become the glue that eventually holds Iraq together?" he asked. As I listened I thought how I wished I could occasionally think of big, gushing metaphors like that. "You're absolutely right, Mr. Vice President," I responded still, trying to gauge how badly a line like that would go down in a State Department cable, even though he had grasped something that most of our experts in the State Department had not.

In November 2009, oil company executives again converged on the al-Rashid Hotel and one by one approached the Plexiglas urn with envelopes containing their bids in hand. This time thirty-two firms were involved in the bid, and several of the largest came away with a field: The Brits and Dutch (Shell), the French (Total), the Russians (Lukoil), the Italians (ENI), the South Koreans (Kogas), and the Americans with Exxon Mobil and Occidental. Several of these bids were ultimately changed as some oil companies sold them and others wanted in. As a Total executive said, "It is difficult for any major oil company not to be in Iraq."

The desert was flat, and the dirt and sand packed hard. Looking out over the vast landscape on that day with General Brooks in May 2010, I could see nothing growing, not even a shrub. It looked like the surface of the moon.

We toured the facility and saw the housing being erected for international workers. There was also a set of CHUs to house the Chinese workers. Chris Klein, cupping his hand against the side of his mouth, whispered to me, "Those are the Fu Man CHUs."

We congregated in a boardroom, located in one of the prefab structures that now sat defiantly on the inhospitable desert, the air-conditioning struggling mightily to counter the sweltering 130-degree heat outside. There were BP officials and local Iraqis representing local government and the Basra Chamber of Commerce. The mood was festive as we raised our glasses to toast BP. I leaned over to Chris Klein: "I must be the only American ambassador in the world toasting the accomplishments of BP this month."

I spoke to several of the newly employed Iraqi engineers, all wearing bright orange overalls, about their new careers working for an American oil drilling company. They were proud of the affiliation with Weatherford and obviously pleased to be employed, and their mood was buoyant. I told them I was making a visit to Baghdad University and meeting students the next day. What should I tell them?

"Tell them to learn English," one engineer instantly answered. "Tell them to study math and chemistry and computers, but above all tell them to study English. That is the language of engineering, and of democracy."

On May 18, 2010, I wrote to the president and secretary that Maliki is "in the driver's seat." I added a note of caution about how it was not in our interest to be seen running around forming the government. We needed to show some patience toward the Iraqi process, such as it is.

But patience is a hard thing to find in Washington, as I knew from Korea and the Balkans. Soon we were getting offers of assistance. The assistant secretary of NEA came out to post together with a member of the National Security Council staff for the first of several visits to "help."

"Did you say, help?" Gary Grappo asked me. Gary, like the rest of his team, was working all day and half the night meeting with difficult Iraqi counterparts in their offices and homes, trying to forge consensus on points that could pave the way for a winning bloc that could cobble together the 163 seats necessary for a majority in the 325-seat parliament. He didn't want to pull fully employed political officers off to become babysitters for Washington visitors.

Petraeus was the first to offer reinforcements starting with his two Arab-American interpreters, who over the course of his time in Iraq had morphed into his political advisors. A few months before, one of them arrived in Baghdad unannounced to say that Petraeus had sent him to help with the election law. I told Ray: "He's all yours. I don't need him." Ray didn't need him either and put him on the next flight out. When the request came again (this time at least in advance), the political section did some due diligence and told me they wanted nothing to do with these people. I got the same reaction from Iraqis, including, amusingly, Maliki and Allawi and one of Barzani's aides. "Finally, Maliki and Allawi agree on something!" I told Gary. When I learned that Petraeus had flown the then-retired Ryan Crocker up from Texas in a military plane to accompany him as a kind of civilian avatar for consultations in Washington on what we were doing wrong in Iraq (and Afghanistan), I looked up at the calendar on my wall to see how much more of this I needed to endure before my planned August 2010 departure. I had promised Secretary Clinton one year and now I was in extra time. I had seen a lot of micromanaging from Washington over the course of my career, but I had never seen a four-star general take an interest in staffing up junior positions in an embassy's political section. "What do these people have on him?" was the usual question people had. Crocker was a class act about what he obviously understood were rather poor manners in second-guessing two embassies in the field (offering free advice to our colleagues in Kabul was also fast becoming a cottage industry in Washington). I sent an email to Crocker to ask for his version of what had transpired in the meetings in Washington. He responded that he had limited his own comments to his view that the State Department needed to do a better job of recruiting FSOs to multiple tours in the war zones, a point he had made before to many audiences in and out of government.

Within a few weeks, Petraeus was on his way to Afghanistan to take over for General Stanley McChrystal.

"That was an interesting move," I said to Vice President Biden about Petraeus's assignment to Kabul when Biden visited in early July 2010. As he got into the backseat of a Chevy Suburban with me I asked, "Whose was it?" He tapped his own chest with his thumb and had a look on his face that told me all I needed to know.

With Biden again in town the "rocketeers" in the Sadr City section of Baghdad, four miles away, soon greeted him. One rocket screamed over the head of the vice president as he prepared to get out of his Chevy Suburban.

The type and amount of fuel packed into the 107mm modified Russian weapon (which came into the hands of the Shia militia groups via Iran) varied considerably. Some rockets (like the one that flew over the vice president's head) landed harmlessly in the river beyond. Other rockets landed on the way to the American Embassy, sometimes short, on the nearby compound belonging to the Korean embassy, which was in the line of fire from Sadr City. The Korean ambassador, Ha Tae Yun, a career diplomat, had earlier invited me over to see his modestly sized facility (he slept in the back half of his small office) and hosted me in his dining room to some of the best Korean cuisine I had ever had outside of Seoul. I turned to Chris Klein, who was sitting beside me, and commented, "Isn't it great to be back with Koreans having great food but not having to talk about North Korea's nuclear program?"

The visits of the vice president were often an eventful time for the Koreans. During a briefing of foreign ambassadors a day after Biden's visit, Ambassador Ha said, earnestly but with a Korean sense of humor that sometimes goes over the head of westerners not expecting Korean irony, "We understand that for security reasons you cannot tell us ahead of time that you have a senior official visiting, but if you could just give us just a few minutes' warning so we have time to get into our underground shelter it would be very appreciated."

The vice president was indeed a frequent visitor. He had come just a few weeks before I arrived and a couple of weeks after I left in August 2010, six visits in a space of not much more than twenty months. Biden is known as someone who likes to talk, but I admired the fact that when he came to Iraq he did an awful lot of listening. We discussed the way forward, the fact that unless we wanted to create a political crisis in the summer of 2010, we were going to have a difficult time encouraging the unseating of Maliki, if that was really what people wanted. I told him that the other idea, circulating around Washington at the time among so-called Iraq experts, was that somehow President Talabani could be coaxed out of the presidency and replaced by Allawi.

I told Vice President Biden that I could understand the logic, but that kind of radical political surgery undertaken on Iraq now, in the year 2010, made little sense. The United States continued to have much influence in this country, I told him, but picking and choosing winners (and losers) was way beyond anything we could do by then. Perhaps back in 2004 or 2005, but in 2010 Iraq was its own country with its own political system, which we would interfere with at our peril.

Talabani remained popular in Iraq, with broad appeal that crossed sectarian lines. His ability to speak with all sides of the political equation was as unusual as it was valuable. He often kept Maliki in check when no one else would or could. He no doubt had his flaws, but for the United States to get down into the mud of Iraqi politics and force him out of the ring left me speechless. After seven years in the country we apparently had learned nothing, and forgotten nothing.

Part of the implied justification for pushing Talabani out (apart from the expediency of making Iraqiyya happier) was that he had a friendship with the Iranian Quds Force commander, the murderous Qasim Sulaimani. It was a reminder that in Iraq, politics can be very local, as well as very personal. As mentioned earlier, when Saddam Hussein's forces used chemical weapons in the village of Halabja, near Talabani's home in Sulemaniyah, the Iranians had kept the border open to give refugee to the survivors of the massacre. When I visited Halabja, I never heard a negative word about Iran.

I told the vice president that my team and I had one other idea that we had been working on for a couple of weeks, but that it too could be just another dive into another empty swimming pool (a metaphor Bob Frasure had often used while we struggled to find governance solutions in Bosnia). It was to create a new position for Allawi as the head of a powerful national security council. I told the vice president that I had asked one of our embassy lawyers, the young, imaginative, and practically minded Ben Metz, to see what could be created, with the understanding that we could not try to change the constitution. Ben looked carefully at the constitution and told Gary and me and the rest of the political section that it could be possible to create such a position that did not undermine the roles already established for the prime minister, the presidency, and the speaker of the parliament.

We worked on it for several weeks over the course of June and July 2010. Allawi and Iraqiyya seemed interested. Maliki agreed to consider it, although I suspected he was only being cooperative from being certain in the knowledge that Allawi would not take it as long as the prime minister remained the key position (as the constitution intended). There was no getting around that situation. I increasingly believed that Maliki would eventually prevail as the next prime minister, but it was a conclusion not so much based on any groundswell of support for him, as it was on the complete lack of viable alternatives. Outside of his own State of Law coalition, he seemed to have little support among the Shia, the Kurds, and of course the Sunni for a second term. But as I told the president and the secretary in a June note, no one else seemed to have any better prospects. A few names were being floated: Adel Abd al-Mahdi (every Washington visitor's favorite Shia leader because he spoke perfect English and for the good reason that he was educated and practical); Oil Minister Shahristani, because he seemed to have clerical support as well as being an English-speaking technocrat; Ali al-Adeeb, because he was a powerful parliamentarian; and/or Ibrahim al-Jaafari, because he had been prime minister before.

Yet none of these putative candidates seemed to have a remote chance of competing with Maliki for the position. For the United States in the summer of 2010 to be seen blackballing a leading candidate, the sitting prime minister at that, in favor of putting forward one of our dark-horse favorites, would have been completely out of step with Iraq's growing sense of sovereignty. And yet that kind of paternalism was what a few Iraqi watchers, for whom time had frozen sometime early in the occupation, were suggesting in Washington, D.C., and at CENTCOM headquarters in Tampa, Florida.

As the summer wore on, Maliki, who unlike Allawi rarely left the country or even, it seemed, his office, started making progress with the other Shia and some small Sunni parties. While no one was overtly committing to him, it was clear that he was building the momentum to expand well beyond the 89 seats he already controlled. Allawi, still stuck at 91 seats, at one point met with the Shia cleric Muqtada al-Sadr in Damascus, a bizarre meeting evidently arranged for Allawi by Syrian president Bashar Assad, who (probably) had tired of Maliki and his public allegations against the Syrians for terrorist attacks in Iraq. Allawi's meeting with Sadr didn't lead to anything.

In the meantime, Barzani began to soften his line with Maliki, and to say that Maliki might be an acceptable choice after all. Barzani had no interest in a Kurdish-Shia alliance that would isolate the Sunnis, but he had realized, just as I had, that there were no good alternatives to Maliki.

In early August Barzani invited me to his hometown of Barzan, up in Kurdistan, but this time instead of hiking, the outdoor activity would be to go swimming and jet-skiing in the ice-cold Zab River. Barzani had done this once before with Zalmay Khalilzad, the Afghan-American who had served as U.S. ambassador before Ambassador Crocker. Never having been on a jet-ski before, I listened to Barzani's instructions carefully as I got on behind him and held on for dear life. We raced up river for ten minutes, dodging menacing rocks in the water, before disembarking to float leisurely wearing our life preservers back to the starting point. The mountain water was cold and refreshing, a contrast to the summer air mercilessly heated in the midday sun.

After four round trips, we had a feast by the side of the river. We talked nonstop about the political deadlock and about Barzani's welcome decision to invite Maliki to his palace in Sulehaddin, above the Kurdish capital of Erbil the next day. By prearrangement, at 4 P.M. my cell phone rang and a voice, identified as "Joe," was on the other end of the line, as in Vice President Biden. I gave the phone to Barzani, who sat down on a folding chair cupping his other ear to reduce the roar of the river. He and "Joe" had a good discussion about the importance of the next day. We knew that the upcoming meeting with Maliki would make or break the government formation.

I said farewell to Barzani that evening outside the guesthouse. I knew it was my last visit to Kurdistan, and given that I was leaving Iraq a few days later, and my career in the Foreign Service a few days after that, I knew it was my last chance at diplomatic deal making. The odds are often stacked against these deals working out, and when they do they are sometimes short-lived, but the sense that one has done everything possible is a very good one. And better yet was the appreciation for someone like Barzani, who, unlike a visiting diplomat, has to live with the consequences that any political deal would involve. We performed our awkward hugs and kisses before I headed to the helicopter for the trip back to Baghdad.

I met Maliki in the morning and told him I thought the road was open to a rapprochement with Barzani, provided he was willing to address Kurdish concerns about their oil contracts and previous understandings about disputed territory with Arab Iraq. Much later that day, word came from Erbil that the meeting between Maliki and Barzani had gone well. They had met over a late lunch and then gone out in front of the cameras. They pledged to work together for "inclusive" government— i.e., there would be a Sunni component as well. Now a new government seemed only a matter of time, a comforting thought, as I got ready for my departure.

Three days later, I climbed in my last Black Hawk helicopter, strapped myself into the seat next to the window, and rose up from the embassy landing pad. We crossed out over Baghdad, its bright city lights shining in the gathering dusk. At the airport I said farewell to my security detail, now led by Ian Pavis, who had replaced Derek Dela-Cruz a couple of months before, and got onto a small plane en route to Kuwait. I slept the entire distance.

In Washington a day later, Secretary Hillary Clinton asked to see me in between appointments. She was busy that day, and even though it was my last day in the State Department as a Foreign Service officer, I knew she had other things going. I quickly briefed her on the embassy operations, and said how pleased I was that a very good successor, the U.S. ambassador to Turkey, Jim Jeffrey, had been named to follow me and would be arriving in another day. I told her about my next career as dean of the Korbel School of International Studies at the University of Denver, and thanked her for her support in allowing me to leave Baghdad and visit there in May to interview for the position. She warmly said good-bye and thanked me for my thirty-three years of service, a long time, I acknowledged. And then she asked me a question as I started walking through the outer door of her office.

"Who could have ever thought Maliki should have a second term?"

"Beats me," I answered.

A couple of months later I was in Washington again, and this time would have the opportunity to see Dick Holbrooke, who had always seemed to be on the road when I occasionally visited Washington from Iraq. I realized I hadn't actually seen him since early 2009, though we had talked occasionally on the phone when I was in Baghdad. I called him from a cab at the airport.

"You're not going to a hotel, Chris. Forget it. You're staying with me. Kati and I have a little place in Georgetown. We can have dinner at La Chaumière—you remember, my favorite French restaurant—and walk to our townhouse from there."

"Okay, okay, that's what we'll do. See you at the restaurant when, seven, seven thirty?"

"Would eight forty-five or nine work for you?"

"Um, eight forty-five? Sure, Dick, whatever. See you then."

He walked into the restaurant at nine fifteen, smiling and claiming that he had been waiting at the bar for ten minutes.

"I thought we were going to meet at the bar."

"No, Dick, we never said anything about the bar. Besides, you hardly drink."

"I'm going to have a glass of white wine," he announced, changing the subject.

"Dick, where have you been today? You look a little tired."

"I got in from Pakistan this morning at around four thirty A.M. It was a long trip. Then I had lots of meetings at the White House. I just came from a speech at Brookings. Strobe says "hi." (Strobe Talbott had by this time taken the helm of the Brookings Institution.)

He did look exhausted, perhaps from his travels that day, but he also looked a lot older than when I had last seen him before heading out to Iraq. He had clearly thrown himself into his work as the coordinator for Afghanistan-Pakistan, but the toll on him seemed enormous, albeit magnified by the fact he had just flown in from Pakistan that day and obviously needed some sleep.

We caught up in no time, and soon realized it was midnight; Dick had actually had almost two glasses of white wine before switching to his usual green tea. I had heard that he had some health problems, including a fainting episode, but he brushed off the subject when I asked and went back to comparing notes on Iraq and Afghanistan, and on dealing with the military, his favorite subject that evening.

"What was that weird little story about you and Odierno not getting along?" he asked. I told him it was a nasty place. Press leaks, even outright press fabrications, were the least of it. In these places, I riffed on, foreigners sometimes take on the habits of the war zone. These places often seem to bring out the worst in everybody, I explained. As for the specific story, I had no idea; I was always proud of my relationship with Odierno, and told Holbrooke about the good times Ray and I had smoking cigars, hitting golf balls into the lake, and talking sports, and of course discussing the mission—the 24/7 experience of Iraq.

"You'd like him. He's a Yankee fan," I said, recalling the time Holbrooke had called me up at 4:30 A.M. in Warsaw in 2003 to tell me the Yankees had just beaten the Red Sox and were going on to the World Series.

"You did the same the next year," he noted.

We walked up to the townhouse, stopping at a drugstore to buy replacement razor blades. He had no idea what he needed and I found myself holding various packages of blades in my hand. "Do you remember the name? Maybe Gillette? Schick? Track II, or perhaps Track III?"

We entered the darkened house. Apart from his suitcase, which had been put inside the front door at some point during the day, the place hardly looked like anyone lived there. "Sorry, I don't have anything in the refrigerator; no coffee, either. There might be some tea somewhere." Looking around the townhouse, I could see he had no life in that house apart from what he did at the State Department, no reading material, no apparent favorite chair. We walked up the narrow wooden staircase, where he showed me the guest room just opposite his. He couldn't sleep and I stood at the door to his room while he lay on his bed in his clothes, talking and talking about what he was trying to do in Afghanistan. He steered clear of any Washington politics, and I didn't want to probe about stories I had heard that he was having problems with people in the White House. After about forty-five minutes I told him I had to get some sleep, because I had to get myself off to the airport for a 7 A.M. flight. I saw a blanket over on the chair and asked if he'd like me to put it over him. "No, I'm okay," he said,

I got up at 4:30 A.M. and tried to slip out of my room down the stairs without waking him.

"Chris, you leaving now?" he called out from his room. "When are you back in D.C.? We need to have a good talk. Let me know."

"Of course. We'll talk. We'll talk not just about Afghanistan and Iraq, but let's talk about other stuff, too. I miss that. How are the Knicks going to do this year? And by the way, you need to start taking better care of yourself. Get some sleep now."

I walked out of the townhouse, descending the half dozen steps to the brick sidewalk, streetlights still on in the pre-dawn. The walk was covered with soggy leaves from the overnight rain. It was a chilly late October morning, and I pulled my light coat up against a cold breeze. As I waited momentarily for the taxi, I reflected on how I should have been in closer contact with him while I was in Iraq. He needed me, I realized now, and I needed him, I had to admit to myself. I was determined this time to stay in better touch. Maybe we could work on something. Or maybe just go to a baseball game together.

He died in December, before I could ever see him again.

EPILOGUE

A week before Richard Holbrooke died in December 2010, Steve Solarz, the congressman I worked with after my first Korean assignment, passed away as well. Steve was an energetic representative from Brooklyn who never saw a problem in the world he didn't want to jump on and solve. A few months later in 2011, Larry Eagleburger, my first mentor, died. At his memorial service I listened to the eulogy by his mentor, Henry Kissinger. In this grim harvest of my own mentors, it was not to say that diplomacy died, but replacements for these pragmatic problem solvers were slow in coming.

I spent thirty-three years in America's foreign service. My dad spent three decades in it as he and my mother took their five children around the world. In all these years, what has not changed is that the world still looks to the United States to lead by example; what has changed is how we are responding to these expectations. We live in a time when ideology is hotly debated and where there is a diminished consensus, and a collapsing middle ground about who we are and what our values are and how we pursue them. One of the casualties is our willingness to talk to all sides. One might think that the logic of the old adage that one does not need to make peace with one's friends would be enough. But having had to defend my role in talking with Milosevic in the midst of the Yugoslav wars, or in negotiating with the North Koreans, that seems not so.

Finding practical answers to tough problems seems to take a backseat to ideology. Nowhere is this issue more pronounced than in weighing the rapid imposition of democracy against more evolving change. We must always be clear about human rights. These rights are a set of international values embraced by the United Nations Charter and many of the founding documents of our era. But human rights are not identical with democracy, which is a system of governance, certainly the best to protect those values. Our diplomats must be clear about human rights, but in a country's choice of governance, we would do well to lower our voices and offer our help when asked. Pragmatism offers no refuge for those in need of instant gratification, but its track record in implementing those values is better than armed intervention. Diplomacy is more complex than three-dimensional chess in that time, the fourth dimension, is also a crucial factor.

We might also focus on whether everything we know has to be shouted from the rooftops via social media. The use of new media may be a worthy effort to address the complexity of a globalized world, where states are no longer the only actors, but Facebook pages and Twitter accounts are not necessarily geared to solving problems or building trust. "Mentions," or being "liked," or "going viral" are really not enough in this line of work.

Diplomacy has often had to work with the military, and that task has become increasingly complex as the military is called on to perform tasks that are more diplomatic than military in nature. In the wake of 9/11, the military has had to fight wars whose uncertain objectives make some seem endless, stretching beyond the patience of the American people, whose support is essential.

There is an overlap, therefore, in the world of the military and the diplomat, but diplomacy is not a continuation of war by other means. Nor do our generals need to become diplomats, or our State Department and Foreign Service officers to become soldiers. The State Department and the Pentagon need to respect each other and learn from each other. Diplomats will be increasingly deployed (assigned, that is) to war zones. The State Department will find itself in the mix of interservice rivalries. This meshing of military and State Department cultures will take time and tact. In the end, we all work for our country, and ultimately for each other, a band of brothers and sisters.

No diplomatic period of history, neither my father's nor my own, has looked like a triumphant march to inevitable victory. I negotiated for several years in Bosnia, culminating at the Dayton Peace Accords, and then in Kosovo. Neither was a sure bet. For four years I negotiated in the Six Party Talks with North Korea, only to see those talks founder in the first term of the Obama administration, and subsequently be crowded out. After some five years of being shut down, the North Koreans started up the bomb-making reactor we had so laboriously worked to disable. Diplomacy failed to shut down North Korea's nuclear ambitions.

Diplomacy doesn't work everywhere or in every circumstance, but in the case of North Korea it was hard then and is just as hard now to understand what the alternative is. The neoconservatives fought any deal with North Korea as illusory. They did not produce a policy alternative that could accomplish anything, apart from infuriating many South Koreans and leaving the entire region wondering what the United States was thinking.

In February 2012, I visited Shanghai to give the keynote address at a conference on the occasion of the fortieth anniversary of one of America's greatest diplomatic achievements, the breakup of the China-Soviet axis and the inauguration of better ties with the United States. The Shanghai Accords are one of the signature moments of American diplomatic history.

I was twenty years old at that time. If my dad's diplomatic career hadn't convinced me to be a diplomat, Kissinger and his team slipping into China from Pakistan sealed the deal. In addition to ushering a new age of China-U.S. relations, those same accords ushered out the China-Soviet relationship and meant the beginning of the end of the Soviet Union.

The celebratory mood was dampened, however, when that same day in 2012, China joined Russia in casting a veto on Syria. Many U.S. commentators, both left and right, were satisfied that the veto exposed China and Russia for supporting a hideous regime. But for those of us who believe in the importance of the Sino-U.S. relationship, it was an unhappy reminder of the unfinished work ahead, the fact that a relationship too big to fail cannot find a balance. Similarly, our relations with Russia will remain fraught and burdened by a long and bitter history whose patterns will be difficult to break.

Iraq, bloody Iraq, remains what it has been for centuries, the badlands, the borderlands of Shia and Sunni, of Arabs and Kurds, of Arabs and Persians. That was true before our occupation and will continue to be so after our departure. Whatever political configuration Iraq eventually becomes, it will remain this dangerous conjunction of political, ethnic, and sectarian identities, whose national identity is unlikely ever to be summarized by that phrase *e pluribus unum.*

Four months after I departed Baghdad, Nouri al-Maliki was confirmed on December 22, 2010, for a second term. Pressed by our successors at the embassy, his cabinet was indeed "inclusive," to use what has become a tiresome American expression to describe the need for political balance. His twenty-eight-member cabinet included nine Sunni Arabs, including a deputy prime minister, and another six members from the Kurdish list that also included a deputy prime minister. It was about the same proportion as in Maliki's first cabinet.

Oil production was on the rise, security was improving, and there were good reasons to expect Iraq to continue stumbling forward. But in

2011 and 2012 things began to fall apart. Maliki never appointed new ministers of defense and interior as he had promised to do. Instead he kept those most important of ministries for himself and his office cronies to run. The Sunnis, who had expected to have one or the other of these complained bitterly, and dialogue within the cabinet deteriorated. Maliki failed to follow through on assurances made to Kurdistan President Barzani. When I saw President Barzani in November 2011, just a year and three months after our swim in the Zab River, he was adamant in his opposition to Maliki, saying that he had not fulfilled promises made during the government formation period. Maliki went after his critics, especially the Sunni Vice President Tariq al-Hashimi and later deputy Prime Minister Rafi al-Issawi. He drove Hashimi into exile and Issawi out of the government in 2013. Whatever the transgressions of those two Sunni leaders, Maliki, bereft of allies in the region, showed little wisdom or restraint in attacking Sunni leaders. Meanwhile, President Jalal Talabani's fragile health deteriorated until a stroke in late 2012 incapacitated him. He no longer played the role of encouraging the "good" Maliki, or of reassuring the Sunnis, whose distaste for Shia-led government never waned. Maliki turned increasingly inward, ever less interested in "inclusive" government.

In Syria, a democracy movement sparked by the Arab Spring quickly degenerated into a sectarian knife fight, the intensity of which has yet to abate. Sunni extremists there began crossing the border into Iraq to "liberate" more "Sunni lands" from the apostate Shia. They found a mostly receptive Sunni audience, chafing under Shia rule. Those who were not so receptive were eliminated, often by execution and assassination. In 2012 and 2013 Sunni extremists launched a wave of bombing attacks against Iraq's Shia population in an effort to discredit their Shia leaders and draw them into a sectarian battle. As if to cover up for a lack of concerted policy in Syria, from where these blood-soaked fighters came, international leaders blamed the attacks on Maliki's political failures at Sunni outreach.

Responsibility for Iraq's descent into a sectarian abyss is often laid entirely at Maliki's feet. While he surely deserves his share of the blame, the Sunnis in Iraq have done little to reconcile themselves to living under the majority rule of the Shia, whether the prime minister is Maliki or some other Shia. One-thousand-year-old enmities die hard.

Whether Iraq eventually succeeds as a single state ever again will depend on the Iraqis themselves. It always does. The Obama administration has been wise to tread carefully, but its slowness to grasp the complexities of the region, the seeming confusion within its foreign policy team between of wars of democracy and sectarian enmity, has created a sense that Iraq and the Middle East more broadly are beyond its capacities to manage.

The Obama administration's difficulties in dealing with the Middle East crises and its wariness about any high-stakes engagement there has given the unrepentant neoconservatives a chance to rise from their crypt and claim they were right all along about the need for endless American war in the Middle East. But the fact remains that they never understood sectarianism either, and never understood that a majority-ruled Iraq which necessarily involves Shia leadership is unlikely, putting it mildly, to become an inspiration to the Sunni-dominated Arab Middle East.

The failure of neoconservatives and their fellow travelers to explain what they were trying to accomplish in Iraq remains one of the most disgraceful performances by a foreign policy class in America. It has been a failure to acknowledge mistakes, and a shameful effort to shift the blame, in the case of Iraq, to nameless intelligence analysts, as if they were responsible for the full-court pressure on President Bush to convince him to go to war. They quickly attacked Obama; and like architects who blame the builder, they never tire of offering bad advice then attack the implementers for not following their plans to the letter. Despite the intellectual origins of many of their devotees, they bear much responsibility for reducing America's own discourse on foreign policy to little more than a barroom brawl. They have much to answer for. Perhaps, for starters, they could observe a period of silence while the rest of us try to deal with the practical realities of a difficult global structure.

In 2011 and later in 2013 my wife, Julie, and I visited Kosovo, a place that years ago had fit Secretary Christopher's description of the Balkans as a problem from hell. We went to the small village of Malishevo, where a dozen years before I saw its population driven into the hills, its houses and mosque burned to the ground. It had taken Tina Kaidanow, Phil Reeker, and me hours to get there over narrow roads. Now we sped down an interstate highway built by the American engineering firm Bechtel.

"Where's Malishevo?" I asked the driver, eager to see this town that I knew so well, and confused by the changed scenery and the fast pace of driving on an interstate highway. He pointed to a blue highway sign: MALISHEVO: EXIT 6: 2 KILOMETERS. We turned off the highway and drove into the town. The houses were all rebuilt. There was a pleasant restaurant and café nearby, and the mosque that had been hit by a tank round was also rebuilt. Children played in a swimming pool in the center of town. I learned from the village elders who gathered around me that the old man who had thanked me for returning him to his home after spending weeks in a mountain forest had died peacefully in his sleep, in his home, some months before.

Kosovo is on its way to a better future, as are Macedonia, Bosnia, Croatia, and even Serbia. But the memories of those difficult days seem to stay fresh. In 2011, my wife and I were driven to Macedonia from Pristina, the capital of Kosovo, where I had met with the prime minister, now in a gray pinstripe suit that fit him better than the military fatigues of twelve years before. The car sped down through the canyon whose every turn in the road I knew so well, and to the border for the last thirty minutes to Skopje. I showed Julie where the Stenkovac camp had once stood, packed with thousands of refugees who had streamed down this same canyon road, clutching what they had been able to grab of their belongings. In the restfulness of a brilliant mid-September day, I had a hard time recalling or even imagining the dark mood of weeks when nothing was clear about the future. I paused for a second to look out on the now-peaceful rolling hills and the small farms, the grain harvest under way, and Stenkovac, an unmarked place along the road.

The driver said, "Mr. Ambassador, sorry to interrupt, but I was in that camp for two months. My family and I had waited at the border for days. We thought we might all die those days. The Americans saved my life. They saved all our lives. My sister. My brother. My parents. All of us. We are all well today, all well because you saved our lives. I just want to say thank you now because I will never get a better chance. Sorry to interrupt you."

In the fall of 2013, I met a student who had just enrolled at the University of Denver's Korbel School of International Studies, where I had become dean. I noticed his accent was from the Balkans, and I guessed correctly he was from Bosnia. He was now an American citizen, born to a Serb father and a Bosnian Muslim mother, hailing from a small town in eastern Bosnia that would never be the same again, since the war had torn it apart. His parents had taken him to the United States, where he learned English in elementary school and had become a football and baseball fan. He wanted to study international relations. I asked what he wanted to do once he gets his master's degree.

"I want to become an American diplomat," he answered.

I looked at him. "Maybe I can help you with that."

Acknowledgments

After a career in government, where two-page memos are the norm, writing an entire book is a challenge. It took more than a village to accomplish the research, the editing, and the marketing.

This book is largely about representing our country overseas. It afforded me an opportunity to revisit moments in history, to make better sense of them in the fullness of time, and to reconnect with colleagues who lived those moments with me. I am especially grateful to those secretaries of state—Warren Christopher, Madeleine Albright, Condoleezza Rice, and Hillary Clinton—who proposed me to presidents Clinton, Bush, and Obama for nominations to five Senate-confirmed positions, a privilege and an honor.

Everybody has a story to tell, but not everybody has people who provide the encouragement to tell that story. I had many supporters who suggested I write a book, and wouldn't take no for an answer. I'm especially grateful to Strobe Talbott, president of the Brookings Institution. He offered insights on early manuscripts and gave much needed advice and assistance. So did a dear friend, Wanda Rapaczynski, who was a key advisor in reading and commenting on the manuscript. Bob and Adele Sweet were also early on the bandwagon of support as were Bob and Kathy Owen.

I want to thank the University of Denver and its Korbel School of International Studies for supporting me, in particular Provost Gregg Kvistad, and the staff, including executive assistant Janet Roll. I want to thank my agent, David Halpern, of the Robbins Office, for embracing this project, walking me through the book proposal, and ultimately connecting me with Simon & Schuster. Of course, I could not have found David without my good friend and former colleague Chris Klein. I also want to thank the Academy of Korean Studies for its support of this project and in particular Victor Cha of CSIS.

So many people helped with comments and editing. I'd like to thank Cliff Martin, our work/study at Korbel, for being the first to help turn my State Department prose into something people might want to read. Strobe, Wanda, and Chris Klein helped here too, but there were others. Colleagues and friends Carol and Ken Adelman, John Burley, Mitko Burcevski, General George Casey, Lynn Cassel, Glyn Davies, Charlie Firestone, New Zealand Ambassador Roy Ferguson, Tom Gibbons, Phil Goldberg, Pat Haslach, Walter Isaacson, Eric John, Paul Jones, Edgard Kagan, Yuri Kim, Sung Kim, Andy Koss, Kamala Lakhdhir, Cameron Munter, Brett McGurk, Andy Nagorski, Jim O'Brien, Evelyn Polidoro, Jeff Prichard, Phil Reeker, Laura Rosenberger, Kathleen Stephens, Charlie Stonecipher, and Pam Traas jogged my memory and provided advice and editing. David Brody, a friend and author in Denver, volunteered to edit, bringing an important perspective of someone not steeped in foreign service lore.

I am lucky to have the world's finest publishing team in Simon & Schuster. Jonathan Karp encouraged me from the start and especially in reading and commenting on the manuscript. My editor, Alice Mayhew, kept me on track with detailed notes and rigorous edits that ensured the flow of the manuscript. She was directly involved in all phases of production, and I join many other authors in saying she is simply the best. Assistant editor Jonathan Cox kept the production going, ensuring deadlines were met, and reassuring me throughout. Kate Gales and Julia Prosser are brilliantly managing the publicity, while Stephen Bedford is wonderful at the online marketing of the book. Elisa Rivlin, from the legal office, protected me from myself with her careful review. Ruth Lee-Mui provided an excellent interior design, and Jackie Seow a superb cover. Production editor Mara Lurie was an oasis of calm in handling last-minute edits and keeping the manuscript on schedule.

My wonderful children, who shared my life in the foreign service—Nat, Amy, and Clara—encouraged me throughout, as did my siblings Prudence, Elizabeth, Jonny, and Nick. I also want to thank my stepdaughter, Mary, for her support.

Finally, my wife, Julie, provided all the love and encouragement that an author could ever ask for. She read every word of every chapter, provided research, helped select and organize the photographs, and balanced sharp criticism with high praise. Her good cheer and optimism sustained me throughout. Without her, I could not have done it.

Notes

Prologue

2 *U.S. forces had liberated Nasiriya:* William Branigan, "A Brief Bitter War for Iraq's Military Officers," *Washington Post,* April 27, 2003, p. A25, retrieved 13 October 2009.

3 *"Strategic Framework Agreement":* http://georgewbush-whitehouse .archives.gov/news/releases/2008/11/20081127-2.html.

4 *Security Agreement:* http://www.cfr.org/iraq/us-security-agreements-iraq /p16448.

4 *Status of Forces Agreement:* www.atimes.com/atimes/Middle_East /JL02AkO1.html.

4 *the framework agreement:* http://iraq.usembassy.gov/american-iraqi.html.

6 *that money can be a weapon of war:* Commander's Guide to Money as a Weapons System, Handbook No. 09-27, April 2009.

6 *Commander's Emergency Resource Program ("CERP"):*

6 *U.S. Army field manual:* "How Petraeus Changed the U.S. Military," CNN.com/2012/11/10/opinion/Bergen-petraeus-legacy/index.html.

7 *L. Paul Bremer:* Peter D. McManmon Jr., "L. Paul Bremer, III: Managing the Iraq Reconstruction Effort," http://www.thepresidency.org/storage /documents/Calkins/McManmon.pdf.

9 *Fifteen minutes into the ride:* "Bomb explodes near U.S. Ambassador's convoy in Iraq," *USA Today,* July 13, 2009.

Chapter 1: Early Diplomatic Lessons

15 *Congolese leftist leader Patrice Lumumba had been killed:* Alan Riding, "Belgium Confronts Its Heart of Darkness," *New York Times*, September 21, 2002.

17 *Duvalier had just declared himself president for life: Encyclopaedia Britannica*, s.v. "Duvalier, François."

Chapter 2: Peace Corps

19 *to a University of Michigan crowd of five thousand:* "Remarks of Senator John F. Kennedy," http://www.peacecorps.gov/about/history/speech.

Chapter 3: First Mentor

32 *Hollywood's view of the Foreign Service:* See, among many others, *Missing* (Universal Pictures, 1982).

Chapter 4: A Force of Nature

43 *"'We the People'":* "Walesa Makes Historic Speech to Congress," *Harvard Crimson*, November 16, 1989.

58 *calling on Gorbachev to tear down the Berlin Wall:* "Berlin Wall" speech, posted by Reagan Foundation, http://www.youtube.com /watch?v=5MDFX-dNtsM.

Chapter 5: Frasure

69 *UNPROFOR:* The United Nations Protection Force was created by UN Security Council Resolution 743 in 1992.

73 *taking of UN hostages:* See http://en.wikipedia.org/wiki/Operation _Deliberate_Force.

81 *Mount Igman:* See http://en.wikipedia.org/wiki/Igman.

Chapter 6: A Peace Shuttle

89 *NATO bombing of Serb positions was front-page news:* NATO bombing of Yugoslavia—Wikipedia, the free encyclopedia.

Chapter 7: Unfinished Business

101 *As Dick made the announcement:* nytimes.com: COLLECTIONS, GREECE.

Chapter 8: On to Geneva

108 *"sniper alley":* See http://en.wikipedia.org/wiki/Sniper_alley.

109 *The story of the Dayton Peace Accords:* Richard Holbrooke, *To End a War* (New York: Random House, 1998).

Chapter 9: "Your Beautiful Country"

115 *the first ambassador to Macedonia:* www.gpo.gov/fdsy/pkg/CREC-1996 -06-28-pt1-pgs7336-3htm.

118 *question from a Greek journalist:* "U.S. use of Macedonia instead of FROYM," macedoniaonline.eu/content/category/1/13/45/50/5095.

Chapter 10: Kosovo: "Where It Began and Where It Will End"

120 *the Battle of Kosovo:* http://www.balkanhistory.com/kosovo_1389.htm.

122 *Kosovo Liberation Army:* http://www.pbs.org/newshour/bb/Europe/july -dec98/kla_7-15.html.

124 *included former smugglers:* There are many references to this allegation. Start with http://en.wikipedia.org/wiki/Kosovo_Liberation_Army.

130 *"hyperpower":* http://www.nytimes.com/1999/02/05/news/05iht-france.t _0.html.

132 *a KLA fighter looking like Che Guevara:* He turned out to be a KLA member visiting from his home in Denmark. Much to the consternations of the Danes, there were many connections of the KLA to Scandinavian countries. See, for example, http://thebloodyellowhouse.wordpress.com /albanian-mafia/.

Chapter 11: Unfinished Peace

135 *"the most dangerous place in Europe":* Galen Guengerich, "The Most Dangerous Place in the World," September 27, 1998. www.allsoulsnyc2.org /publications/sermons/fcsermons/most-dangerous-place-world.html.

145 *"the Hill Plan":* http://www.washingtonpost.com/wp-srv/inatl/longterm /balkans/who.htm.

149 *intercepts of his cell phone calls:* http://en.wikipedia.org/wiki/Ra%C4%8Dak _massacre.

157 *On March 24 the bombing began:* www.pbs.org/wgbh/pages/frontline /shows/kosovo/etc/cron.html.

Chapter 12: The Safe Room

160 *I ordered all hands down to the vault:* For a good account see www
.washingtonpost.com/wp-srv/inatl/daily/march99/macedonia26.htm.

167 *slowdown at the border:* www.cnn.com/WORLD/europe/9904/07/kosovo
.refugees.03/.

170 *bombs struck the Chinese embassy:* There continue to be those who believe
the attack on the Chinese embassy was deliberate. In fact, it greatly complicated the NATO effort. See http://news.bbc.co.uk/2/hi/340280.stm.

173 *the main Stenkovac camp:* http://www.afsa.org/pdf/inside_us_embassy
-tales_from_the_field.pdf.

Chapter 13: Patterns of Cooperation

185 *George W. Bush arrived in Warsaw:* http://georgewbush-whitehouse
.archives.gov › President.

192 *"No U.S. ambassador had ever visited the cemetery:* english.chosun.com/site
/data/html_dir/2004/09/. . ./2004091761035.html.

201 *his February 2003 speech:* http://www.foxnews.com/story/2003/02/05
/raw-data-text-powell-un-speech-part-ii/.

203 *openly criticized the Roh government:* John Bolton, *Surrender Is Not an Option* (New York: Threshold Editions, 2007), p..

Chapter 14: Calling an Audible

216 *"They are coming now":* For a description of my first meeting with the
North Koreans, see Mike Chinoy, *Meltdown* (New York: St. Martin's
Press, 2008), p.

Chapter 15: Plastic Tulips

220 *went out to meet the press:* www.foxnews.com/story/2005/07/10/rice-says
-n-korea-talks-just-start/.

221 *the resumption of talks was "only a start":* www.foxnews.com/story/2005
/03/20/rice-warns-europe-on-weapons-to-china.

233 *Washington's press cycle:* http://www.donaldgross.net/2005/10/breakthrough
-at-the-six-party-talks/.

241 the *Joint Statement:* www.atomicarchive.com › Special Reports › Nuclear
Crisis: North Korea.

241 *designation of Banco Delta Asia:* http://www.treasury.gov/press-center
/press-releases/Pages/js2720.aspx.

242 *developments came to light with the press:* Donald Greenlees and David Lague, "The Money Trail That Linked North Korea to Macao," *New York Times,* April 11, 2007.

Chapter 16: Heart of Darkness

247 *adopted Resolution 1695:* www.armscontrol.org › Arms Control Today › September 2006.

256 *announced a new joint statement:* www.washingtonpost.com › World › Special Reports › North Korea.

257 *tendentious story:* "North Korea Sanctions," *Financial Times.* www.ft.com › World › Asia-Pacific.

260 *On June 21, I arrived in Pyongyang:* "U.S. Nuclear Envoy Arrives in Pyongyang," http://english.cri.cn/2947/2007/06/21/1321@240822.htm.

Chapter 17: Showing Up

265 *Hun Sen had just arrested:* www.hrw.org/news/2006/01/03/cambodia-hun-sen-systematically-silences-critics.

Chapter 18: Breakfast with Cheney

274 *had entered George Washington University Hospital:* usatoday30.usatoday.com/news/2007-07-28-cheney-surgery_N.htm.

Chapter 19: "That's Verifiable"

280 *wanted to see the facility:* New Doubts on Nuclear Efforts by North Korea: www.washingtonpost.com › World › Special Reports › North Korea.

287 *including CNN, recorded the event:* edition.cnn.com/2008/WORLD/asiapcf/06/27/amanpour.yongbyon/.

Chapter 20: Global Service

293 *impediment to progress:* There have been numerous studies to demonstrate that attitudes toward the United States in 2003–2004 had worsened, due in part to differences on engaging with North Korea. See "RAND Study Warns That South Koreans' Long-Term Support for Alliance with U.S. Threatened by Differences over North Korea," http://www.rand.org/news/press/2004/03/12.html.

297 *a "town hall" meeting:* "Rice tries to quell staff dissent over forced duty in Iraq," http://edition.cnn.com/2007/POLITICS/11/02/state.iraq/.

Chapter 21: Taking the Fifth

302 *looking for reading material:* Thomas Ricks, *Fiasco: The American Military Adventure in Iraq* (New York: Penguin Press, 2006).

304 *General Petraeus's and Ambassador Crocker's testimony to the Congress:* articles.washingtonpost.com › Collections › Iraqi Government.

309 *a very upset General Zinni:* "Zinni Gets Undiplomatic Treatment from Obama Team," http://thecable.foreignpolicy.com/posts/2009/02/04/zinni_unloads.

310 *Dick Holbrooke's name got dragged in:* Al Kamen, "The Not-Quite-Man Act," *Washington Post,* February 25, 2009, http://www.washingtonpost .com/wp-dyn/content/article/2009/02/24/AR2009022403543.html.

311 *issued a news release questioning my qualifications:* http://www.lgraham .senate.gov/public/index.cfm?FuseAction=PressRoom.PressReleases &ContentRecord_id=fcc1fcc3-802a-23ad-4420-7c7e728928fb.

311 *"lied to the Senate":* https://votesmart.org/public-statement/412493/ brownback-disappointed-by-nomination-of-chris-hill-to-serve-as -ambassador-to-iraq#.Uky__r-E7ww.

312 *Dick Cheney was John King's guest:* CNN *Late Edition,* http://transcripts .cnn.com/TRANSCRIPTS/0903/15/sotu.01.html.

316 *an impassioned plea to the Senate to confirm me:* http://thecable .foreignpolicy.com/posts/2009/03/18/top_brass_disturbed_by_gop _stalling_of_iraq_ambassador.

317 *Senator Kerry was energetic and generous in his support:* http://votesmart .org/public-statement/419169/nomination-of-christopher-r-hill-to-be- ambassador-to-iraq-continued#.UkzNPr-E7ww.

Chapter 22: The Longest Day

324 *A company called First Kuwaiti:* First Kuwait was the prime contractor of a project that became fodder for much that was wrong in Iraq. http://www .mcclatchydc.com/2007/10/18/20676/criminal-probe-into-us-embassy .html.

325 *Peruvian contract guards in brown uniforms:* Most worked as subcontractors for a company called Triple Canopy, one of several private military contractors, the best known of which was Blackwater. For a general discussion on the phenomenon see http://en.wikipedia.org/wiki/Private _military_company.

331 *the arrival of Secretary Clinton:* http://www.nydailynews.com/news/world /hillary-clinton-visit-iraq-secretary-state-iraq-track-article-1.359990.

Clinton never returned to Baghdad. Part of the reason she did not return was that soon thereafter, President Obama asked Vice President Biden to oversee efforts in Iraq. Nonetheless, many argued that as holder of the State Department's largest post, she should have made an appearance there.

Chapter 23: Winding Down the War

342 *audience of marines at Camp Lejeune*: President Barack Obama, "Responsibility for Ending the War," Camp Lejeune, North Carolina, February 27, 2009.

343 *"The surge was my idea"*: The success of the surge had many fathers, Petraeus among them. Wikipedia has a good summary of it. http://en.wikipedia.org/wiki/Iraq_War_troop_surge_of_2007.

353 *"America doesn't deserve its military"*: Alissa J. Rubin, "In Iraq, a Blunt Civilian Is a Fixture by the General's Side," *New York Times*, November 20, 2009.

356 *Terry Barnich:* "U.S. officials: Roadside bomb kills3 in Fallujah," http://USAToday30.usatoday.com/news/world/Iraq/2009-05-26-iraq-bomb_N.htm.

361 *announced that Vice President Biden would take on*: http://abcnews.go.com/blogs/politics/2009/06/obama-gives-biden-iraq-assignment/.

363 *bomb that had devastated the Foreign Ministry building:* http://www.csmonitor.com/World/Middle-East/2009/0824/p06s01-wome.html.

366 *approved an election law:* http://www.nytimes.com/2009/12/07/world/middleeast/07iraq.html?_r=0.

378 *"It is difficult for any major oil company not to be in Iraq"*: A French oil executive quoted in "U.S. Companies Shut Out as Iraq Auctions Its Oil Fields," *Time*, December 19, 2009.

Index

About the Author

CHRISTOPHER R. HILL is the dean of the Josef Korbel School of International Studies at the University of Denver. As a career diplomat, Hill was a four-time ambassador nominated by three presidents. He served as Ambassador to Iraq, the Republic of Korea, Poland, and the Republic of Macedonia and as President Bush's Assistant Secretary of East Asian and Pacific Affairs.